SUBJECT TO IDENTITY

Knowledge, Sexuality, and Academic Practices in Higher Education

SUSAN TALBURT

State University
of New York
Press

Published by
State University of New York Press, Albany

© 2000 State University of New York

Production by Susan Geraghty
Marketing by Dana Yanulavich

Printed in the United States of America

For information, address State University of New York
Press, State University Plaza, Albany, N.Y., 12246

Library of Congress Cataloging-in-Publication Data

Talburt, Susan.
    Subject to identity : knowledge, sexuality, and academic practices
in higher education / Susan Talburt.
        p.   cm. — (SUNY series, identities in the classroom)
    Includes bibliographical references (p.   ) and index.
    ISBN 0-7914-4571-2 (hard : alk. paper). — ISBN 0-7914-4572-0
(pbk. : alk. paper)
        1. Lesbian college teachers—United States—Social conditions Case
studies. 2. Lesbians—United States—Identity Case studies.
I. Title. II. Series.
LB2332.32.T24 2000
378.1'2'086643—dc21   99-38823
                                                                         CIP

10 9 8 7 6 5 4 3 2 1

SUBJECT TO
IDENTITY

Themes

① voice/silence (connection to
knowledge/ignorance)

② disembodiment/reimbodiment

③ gender, sexuality, & religion

④ performativity, what does it mean
to perform lesbian

⑤ gender and race

SUNY series, Identities in the Classroom
Deborah P. Britzman, editor

CONTENTS

ACKNOWLEDGMENTS

During the process of writing this book, which ponders, among other things, the haunting of the present by the past, I have become acutely aware of the persistent presence and intermingling of past and present in my own life and work. The voices with which I speak and write are not fully my own, but have been created and made possible through my relations with others. There are numerous individuals to thank for various reasons. I name here a few, but not the only, persons who have contributed in their ways to making this project possible: Melissa Stewart, Diane Lee, Marcy Singer Gabella, Valerie Traub, Paula Salvio, Deborah Britzman, Meredith Lester, Toni Marcovecchio, and my mother and father, Tommy and Holly Talburt.

Several earlier versions of work that appears in this book have been published elsewhere. I thank the following publishers for permission to revise and reprint this work. Portions of chapters 3, 4, and 5 pertaining to Olivia are a revised version of "On Not Coming Out: Or, Reimagining Limits," forthcoming in *Lesbian and Gay Studies and the Teaching of English: Positions, Pedagogies, and Cultural Politics*, edited by William J. Spurlin (Urbana, Ill.: NCTE), Copyright 2000 by the National Council of Teachers of English, reprinted with permission. A portion of chapter 2 is a revised version of my chapter "Identity Politics, Institutional Response, and Cultural Negotiation: Meanings of a Gay and Lesbian Office on Campus," forthcoming in *Thinking Queer: Sexuality, Culture, and Education*, edited by Susan Talburt and Shirley R. Steinberg (New York: Peter Lang). A portion of chapter 3 pertaining to Julie's pedagogy is a revised version of my "Open Secrets and Problems of Queer Ethnography: Readings from a Religious Studies Classroom," published in the *International Journal of Qualitative Studies in Education* 12(5), 1999.

CHAPTER 1

Haunted Questions,
Inhabited Spaces

Something seems to make many people uneasy when they hear the words "lesbian" and "academic" in the same sentence. Individually, each word may carry meanings that are fixed or fluid, alien or familiar, positive or negative, but rarely neutral. Putting together the two words to say "lesbian and academic," "academic and lesbian," or "lesbian academic" can bring about a sort of disequilibrium, a questioning. What does one have to do with the other? For some, it may connote a political agenda at the expense of an intellectual one. For others, it may connote privilege and a neglect of urgent political and material matters. And for yet others, there may be a response of "so what?" There is no clear "so what," for it can never be definitively said what one term has to do with the other. There are times that the meanings of "lesbian" and "academic" may be intertwined and times that they may be discontinuous, unrelated.

One of the perplexing things about speaking of lesbian academics is that *lesbian* is often understood as a private term, referring to who one is or what one does in one's private life. *Lesbian* invokes the body, sexual practices, carnal knowledge rather than public knowledge. *Academic*, on the other hand, is often understood as a public term, referring to who one is or what one does in public life. Although *academic* invokes the mind, often understood as private, it also invokes the communication of ideas, or knowledge brought into the public sphere. To bring the terms *lesbian* and *academic* together is to disturb conceptions of what is private and what is public, to ask what their intersections might be, and in what ways they might be mutually implicated.

My purpose in this book is precisely that: to disturb habits of thinking about the points of intersection of *lesbian* and *academic* as these terms have been constructed in the late twentieth century in the United States. Through ethnographic case studies of three women who are faculty members at a public research institution, I explore what it might or might not mean to dwell in these two categories. My focus is on social and institutional discourses, personal conversations, and the lives and actions of specific individuals within and beyond a university. I seek to rethink constructions of identity and knowledge in an academic setting by looking closely at the ways three women are defined by and (re)define *lesbian* and *academic* and their relations. I explore the women's ideals of research, teaching, and service, and their enactment within a university setting. At the same time, I investigate the university itself, including how knowledge and professional roles are constructed and legitimated within the intersections of institution, department, and discipline, as well as official and unofficial recognition and representations of lesbians' presence. Thus, my inquiry into the construction of academic practice includes "levels" of society, university, department, discipline, classroom, and individual. To speak of "levels," as Adrienne Rich says, is to speak both of a person's "positioning in society" as well as her "*level* of responsiveness, of responsibility, to what lies around [her]."[1] Levels are never discrete, but interact to constitute the ways humans respond to each other and to circumstances. Richard Terdiman has offered, "To respond is to be engaged with someone *else*; simultaneously it is to remain different or diverse. . . . To respond is to pursue further and yet to cross, to mesh but not to fuse, to be inside the interlocutor's discourse and outside it at the same time. . . . To respond is thus to be and to sustain one's status as an *other*. . . . Conversely to be responded to is to know . . . that someone else is there."[2] Response invites a questioning of how we live within and beyond the given.

To speak of responses to social and institutional formations is a complex task that can never be complete. The questions that can be asked and the theories that can be considered, as well as the complexities of three persons' professional lives, render such a project inherently partial, in multiple senses of the word. Inquiry into the academic practices of lesbian faculty is situated not only within discourses of higher education. It resides in the nexus of shifting conceptions of self and identity, the relations of multiple communities, and the effects of social and institutional cultures and ideologies. As a starting point in this chapter, I outline the ways *lesbian* and *academic* have been configured together in the contexts of oppositional social and intellectual movements over the past three decades. By questioning understandings of *lesbian*, *academic*, and *intellectual* practice, I suggest a more contextualized understanding of their relations than has been set forth in the identity-based discourses that continue to structure conversations about lesbian academics.

In the post-Stonewall era, an epoch of proliferating social, political, and intellectual activism by gay men and lesbians, the joining together of the terms *lesbian* and *academic* has produced two primary constructs: (1) an authentic (essential) lesbian who, consonant with identity politics, should be empowered to speak and be seen as lesbian, and (2) a postmodern lesbian intellectual who eschews the essentialism of identity categories and who, through her work, may or may not speak *as lesbian*. Each of these standpoints informs this text, either as their assumptions inform my thinking, as they find resonance in the women's thoughts and actions, or as they structure the possibilities and limitations of empirical inquiry. As I shall argue, a helpful formulation for inquiry neither relies on identity nor disavows its salience in social and institutional discourse, but focuses on practice within and across contexts.

As I originally conceptualized an ethnographic study of three lesbians' academic work at a research institution in the United States, I wished to bring together two areas of interest: how lesbians make their lives in a society that denies, even as it attaches meanings to, their existence, and how institutions of higher education function as sites for the production of knowledge through teaching and research. I wished to examine how lesbians have constructed their roles as faculty members in order to problematize social, institutional, and personal dilemmas created by their presences and actions. How do institutional and social structures participate in shaping the work of lesbian academics? How do they reciprocally participate in shaping the structures of which they are a part? I hoped to offer both lesbian- and non-lesbian-identified readers narrative and analysis that would expand understandings of the intertwinings of social and institutional discourses of identity and knowledge, and prompt a rethinking of assumptions (whatever they may be) regarding lesbians' academic work. In short, I came to the study with a belief that inquiry into the experiences of lesbian academics, whose voices often do not have a place in the canonized knowledge of their disciplines and whose pedagogical relations remain largely unexplored, could offer new perspectives on the constraints and possibilities of higher education.

The assumptions and purposes I brought to my work were clearly embedded in a humanist project that, although reticently, constructs sexuality as a meaningful category of identity and looks to enlightenment through narratives of resistance. Implicit in my thinking were beliefs that there may be something "different" in the work of lesbian-identified academics, that their "voices" are not canonized, and that they may have identifiably different relations to students or knowledges *because they are lesbian*. I took *lesbian* to be a site of causation. Despite my skepticism of simple understandings of the constitution of agency, the subject, experience, and knowledge, my awareness of the potential dangers of producing locatable, or disciplined subjects, and my distrust of attaching meanings to the category *lesbian*, I began with *lesbian* at the center of my inquiry. To invoke the category locates me, I suspect, as a person who has benefited from participation in social, political, and intellectual projects undertaken by lesbians, despite my ambivalences. The tension of calling on a category whose meanings and constructions I wish to interrogate appears throughout the project, as the humanism implicit in my purposes and ethnographic processes conflicts with the posthumanist interpretive frameworks I engage.

In order to contextualize the theoretical, epistemological, and ontological tensions of which my project partakes and which it seeks to interrogate, I turn to social, political, and intellectual work in the post-Stonewall epoch, which finds a principle point of origin in identity politics. For some, identity functions as a tactic to secure rights within a liberal political system; for others, identity forecloses fundamental conversations about relations of power and the transformation of society. Of interest are the meanings identity takes on in university contexts, in which knowledge production is a central purpose. Throughout this text, identity and knowledge will enter into tricky, sometimes theoretically unresolvable, relationships. I begin with a moment in the early 1970s when activists and scholars began to investigate systematically the roles of gay and lesbian university faculty. Initially, identity and community activism defined the possibilities and purposes of much gay and lesbian oppositional intellectual work. Over time, ongoing work undertaken by gays and lesbians has transformed social, institutional, and disciplinary configurations that would define these possibilities and purposes. Multiple frameworks mediate gay and lesbian academic practices such that their meanings cannot be located in identity per se. I argue that identity collapses as a useful rubric for understanding lesbians' academic work and turn to theories of practice as an alternative that engages the complexities of living in institutions of higher education.

SEEKING TO FOUND A LOCATION: THE GAY ACADEMIC UNION

Gay and lesbian work in academia did not coalesce in significant, organized forms until after the Stonewall uprisings of 1969. On the heels of social and political activism by "gay liberationist" groups, gay and lesbian academics began to question their places as scholars in institutions of higher education. Although isolated courses pertaining to "gay issues" had been taught in universities as early as 1972, the first organizational work was the formation of the Gay Academic Union (GAU) in New York in the fall of 1973.[3] The GAU's statement of purpose, published in a monograph of its first conference proceedings, "assert[ed] the interconnection between personal liberation and social change" and outlined five organizational goals: "(1) to oppose all forms of discrimination against all women within academia, (2) to oppose all forms of discrimination against gay people within academia, (3) to support individual academics in the process of coming out, (4) to promote new approaches to the study of the gay experience, and (5) to encourage the teaching of gay studies throughout the American educational system."[4] While startlingly prescient of the stated aims of many gay and lesbian disciplinary caucuses in academia today, the goals must be understood in their historical context, as they were shaped by activism outside the university and the search for legitimation inside academia.[5]

The GAU's statement of purpose embraced liberal tactics, including principles of nondiscrimination, assumptions of the interrelations of personal and political dimensions of visibility politics, and a belief that a body of knowledge about the "gay experience" could be created. The first point, that the GAU should oppose all forms of discrimination against women in academia, brought together work that links gender oppression to gay and lesbian oppression, and was hotly contested from the beginning. Disagreements over feminist analysis quickly led to the formation of separate men's and women's caucuses within the organization. The second point, to protect gays and lesbians in academia against discrimination, was consonant with civil rights models of organizing and took on a distinctly educational mission as GAU members endeavored to educate the "general public" to bring about attitudinal change and decreased discrimination. Consonant with this logic was the group's third purpose, to support individuals in the process of coming out so that they could work toward personal integration and social change. Individuals would educate by providing positive examples of gay men and lesbians while also constituting a group in need of rights. The fourth and fifth points, to promote new approaches to the study of "the gay experience" and the teaching of gay studies throughout the educational system, were the first organizational commitments to gay and lesbian scholarship and teaching.

The work of GAU members was instrumental in legitimating a field of study that rejected then-dominant models of social, medical, and psychological deviance in the study of gay and lesbian lives. What George Chauncey, Martin Duberman, and Martha Vicinus have called the pioneering work outside of academic institutions initiated new scholarship by offering evidence that there were historical documents to be interpreted, such as the publication of GAU member Jonathan Katz's *Gay American History* in 1976, or the inauguration of grassroots archives, such as the Lesbian Herstory Archives, founded by GAU members Joan Nestle and Deb Edel in 1973.[6] This push to legitimate the presence of gay and lesbian persons and studies in universities set a context for gay and lesbian-affirmative talk and action in the academy. Identity models of activism—the constitution of a group with a history, literature, and culture—were used to validate areas of study, while academics constituted themselves as a group with specific concerns and goals. Toward these ends, during its some ten years of existence, the GAU held conferences and published newsletters, a bulletin, and briefly a journal. In its early years, GAU annual conferences included a nearly even split of scholarly panels and workshops devoted to such topics as coming out, gay and lesbian therapy, combating bias in the media, and ending discrimination in academia.[7]

Converging in the period from 1976 to 1978 were several trends that led to the GAU's demise. First, since its formation, the GAU had been beset by two principle problems, each reflecting conflicts in gay and lesbian social movements. Membership was split between an assimilationist perspective and beliefs that incorporated Marxist and Freudian concepts to argue for the complete transformation of social relations. Bound up with this split were the GAU's predominantly male numbers and outlook. Frustrated by many of the men's inabilities to understand the links between sexism and heterosexism and to address issues specific to lesbians, the women's caucus withdrew from the GAU in 1976. Second, as GAU members had success in facilitating the formation of caucuses within disciplinary professional organizations, scholarly activity shifted to academic disciplines as a primary site for defining and validating gay and lesbian work and the GAU increasingly focused on extra-academic issues.[8] Issues of outsider status in the gay/lesbian movement and of disciplinary legitimation in the academy, then, shaped much initial lesbian academic work, but were not unique to the domain of "gay studies."

At the same time that lesbians worked within and at the edges of the gay movement, their networking and scholarship were enabled and shaped by the feminist movement and the gradual institutionalization of women's studies programs. However, despite lesbians' participation in inaugurating many academic programs and political organizations, the problematic nature of their relationships to both should be kept in mind. Homophobia in the women's movement, as evidenced by Betty Friedan's notorious 1970 commentary on the "lavender menace" in the National Organization for Women (NOW), was equally endemic in Women's Studies, particularly in its early struggles for legitimacy. NOW added lesbian issues to its platform in the mid-1970s; however, it was not until the mid-1980s that academic feminism, largely in response to critiques by women of color and lesbians, actively sought to include those it had previously excluded.[9]

Marginalized in both the early gay/lesbian and feminist movements, lesbians intensified their efforts to legitimate their identities, traditions, and concerns. Gay and feminist work in the academy developed around identity politics and collective experiences—a strategy that has excluded lesbians at the same time that lesbians have appropriated it in order to define and validate their own specificities. Initial work in gay and lesbian history focused on biography and creating histories of oppression and resistance; in literature, it centered on identifying gay and lesbian authors and themes. Early feminist scholarship involved recovering "lost" works and history and challenging the literary canon.[10] Such work was appropriated in lesbian projects, first in the quest for visibility and then in definitional anxieties around the lesbian and an area of study. Essays such as Caroll Smith-Rosenberg's historicization of nineteenth-century "female friendships," Barbara Smith's reading of *Sula* as a lesbian novel, Adrienne Rich's naming the "lesbian continuum," and Bonnie Zimmerman's overview of lesbian feminist criticism contributed to and reflected the canonization of defining lesbianism as key to lesbian scholarship.[11] Definitional strategies forged a common lesbian identity and made possible the construction of historical narrative accounts of lesbian lives. Much lesbian scholarship thus came to conflate definition and identity, a move that paralleled the work of its feminist and gay partners as it produced lesbian icons and role models for those sharing in the common definition and identity.

From the late 1970s to the early 1980s, there were shifts in the political and academic spheres: women of color and lesbians challenged white middle class heterosexual feminism and decentered universal womanhood as a rubric for organizing at the same time that so-called "sex radicals" challenged cultural lesbian feminists' identity models of lesbian sexuality and politics.[12] These breaks with monolithic understandings of women and lesbians were enabled by the rise of social constructionism, a theoretical trend that argued for the social, historical, and discursive formation of identities rather than the existence of fixed, timeless identities. This perspective was strengthened by poststructuralism and embraced in much gay scholarship influenced by the work of Michel Foucault, particularly his *History of Sexuality*. In the 1980s, then, social constructionism rose in academia, never entirely displacing essentialist models of identity, yet superseding them and in many disciplines, particularly in the humanities, gaining theoretical respect and credibility.[13] The shift in thinking has not been without controversy; poststructuralist accounts were critiqued for being devoid of praxis and essentialist accounts critiqued for relying on exclusionary accounts of identity in order to organize for change.[14] An effect of poststructuralism and social constructionism has been to displace the stable lesbian identity and history constructed through activism and scholarship with a focus on ideology and the cultural construction of identity categories,[15] thus placing poststructural thought in tension with identity-based political activism.

I offer this brief overview of the Gay Academic Union and related developments in gay, lesbian, and feminist scholarship and activism to illustrate how the tensions that play out in academic gay and lesbian work have come to be imbued with problems of individual and collective identity. Although not all gay or lesbian academics choose to "come out" or to work in gay and lesbian studies, their intellectual and institutional locations are frequently understood through the logic of identity politics. Identity politics' creation of gay and lesbian academic voice and visibility has effected institutional, disciplinary, and social changes that bear both on academics' choices for action and on the ways their practices can be understood. In fact, the imbrication of voice and visibility in the construction of identity and knowledge surfaces throughout my representation of the three women's academic work.

LESBIAN IDENTITY POLITICS: THE LIMITATIONS OF FULL DISCLOSURE

> What or who is it that is "out," made manifest and fully disclosed, when and if I reveal myself as lesbian?
> —Judith Butler, "Imitation and Gender Insubordination"

Borrowed from the tactics of social movements, the definitional anxieties over lesbian identity underlying scholarly legitimation are predicated on voicing and making visible group identity and experience. Identity politics deploys identity representationally to bring persons together under a rubric of shared positions and experiences of "otherness" that are immanent to categories of race, gender, or sexuality. For example, in her discussion of pedagogy, bell hooks valorizes the voicing of identity and experience for empowerment: "Identity politics emerges out of the struggles of oppressed or exploited groups to have a standpoint on which to critique dominant structures, a position that gives purpose and meaning to struggle. Critical pedagogies of liberation respond to these concerns and necessarily embrace experience, confessions and testimony as relevant ways of knowing, as important, vital dimensions of any learning process."[16] Identity serves as a foundation for social recognition, inclusion, and equality; experience, constructed as coextensive with identity, offers a place from which to speak and a privileged means of representation.[17] Identity highlights the common to suggest a representable *set* of differences or similarities that are stable and whole.

A provocative critique of the uses of identity has been formulated by

Judith Butler, whose theory of gender performativity, as elaborated in *Gender Trouble*, calls into question the liberatory nature of representations of identity and experience. She describes "identity" as produced by "regulatory practices [such as compulsory heterosexuality] that generate coherent identities through the matrix of coherent gender norms" (17). Because identity is an effect produced by relations of power, she argues, invoking identity as an originary substance is complicit in naturalizing the structures that operate to create and maintain it. Thus, representation of identity as foundational conceals the formation of that identity by the very "assertion of that foundation" (6). Butler poses a key challenge to identity's usefulness in representing subjects, for she points out that identity demands adherence to a norm that cannot represent what it purports to represent. In other words, because identities are organized around a central difference and indicate continuous links in a chain of binary oppositions, such as sex-gender-desire, they exclude differences that do not flow from this center as incoherent, thus dictating who or what becomes intelligible as an identity in a political economy predicated on visibility. If what the lesbian "is" continues to be knowable through a system of compulsory heterosexuality and its attendant gender norms, the value of definitional strategies is undermined, for these definitions depend on and reinscribe an imposed coherence. As Judith Roof has said, "The lesbian's configuration of unrepresentability is a product of a heterosexual weltanschauung. Its exceptional quality relies entirely upon the heterosexual categories it appears to challenge. Naming and defining it makes sense of the lesbian position as both an exception to and mimetic of a heterosexual rule."[18] Not only is *lesbian* unrepresentable but also a socially, psychically, and historically contingent category, as Valerie Traub has described:

> To ask, "What is a 'lesbian'?" is generally to elicit a direct, descriptive response: "A lesbian is such and such." But the very simplicity of this question is, in fact, disarming, for part of the theoretical and existential problem of defining the "lesbian" is the variability of the category to which "she" belongs. To answer the question is to fix that which is fundamentally unstable, to immobilize what is in fact a shifting field of only temporarily meaningful significations. Whatever a "lesbian" "is" is constantly negotiated—a matter of conflicting and contradictory investments and agendas, desires and wills. Although "love" and "desire" for other women is a historical constant within a consistent minority of the population, how that love and desire are experienced and expressed—individually and culturally—are historically changing phenomena.[19]

Despite the unknowability and instability of lesbian, voice and visibility have become defining tropes[20] of identity politics in order to validate individual and collective identities.

As illustrated in the GAU's political work, the logic of speaking and making visible one's identity assumes that "coming out" is personally transformative for individuals and necessary for gays and lesbians to be an identifiable group in seeking civil rights. Bonnie Zimmerman, for example, has argued, "Speaking, especially naming one's self 'lesbian,' is an act of empowerment. Power, which traditionally is the essence of politics, is connected with the ability to name, to speak, to come out of silence."[21] The assumption that speech (voice) leads to visibility, which leads to personal and collective "empowerment," has been commonplace in lesbian writing. Adrienne Rich has described the imposition of invisibility as "not just a matter of being told to keep your private life private; it's the attempt to fragment you, to prevent you from integrating love and work and feelings and ideas, with the empowerment that that can bring."[22] But if lesbian voice and visibility must draw on social norms to be intelligible, what are their effects within existing structures? By asking such a question, I do not wish to deny the personal integrity and wholeness individuals have experienced or the political gains won by groups through "naming." However, I do wish to question whether such actions *inherently* challenge existing power relations. As suggested by poststructural critiques of identity politics, visibility may serve to reinscribe the givenness of preexisting identities rather than interrogating their production through relational differences or structures of power. In other words, when a person speaks to become visible, "what is made manifest and fully disclosed," as Judith Butler asks, depends precisely on the configurations of power in which a lesbian becomes visible. Because identities are "seen" through certain matrices, or norms, they may never be "seen" at all—except as they can be understood within a discursive system. The notion that voice leads to visibility must be rethought as a reciprocal relation in which visibility also structures one's voice and what can be heard. Underlying tropes of voice and visibility is a belief that each produces knowledge. Yet that knowledge is already partly written by the context of speech.

A key challenge to the positive effects assumed to come from speaking lies in Michel Foucault's *The History of Sexuality*, in which he suggests that the proliferation of discourses on sex have not repressed, but on the contrary, have "produced and determined the sexual mosaic" (47). Arguing that power and knowledge have become linked to produce a belief in sexuality as revealing identity, or the "truth of sex" (77), he demonstrates that from the seventeenth century on, instead of silence, there has been a proliferation of discourse of sex, "an institutional incitement to speak about it" (18) as the human sciences have appropriated the church's techniques of confession to analyze and classify persons' pleasures. Knowledge-power has focused increasingly on determining what the subject "is" via sex: "Causality in the subject, the unconscious of the subject, the truth of the subject in the other who knows, the knowledge he holds unbeknown to him, all this found an opportunity to deploy itself in the discourse of sex" (70). Identity politics' reliance on *testimonies* of experience to present reality and self carries traces of Foucault's formulation of confession as producing the belief that people can tell the truth of themselves and ignores the personal and historical conditions under which lived experiences are recounted.[23] As Foucault makes clear, communication invariably takes place in relations of power, making impossible communication devoid of the constraints of the structures within which it takes place. To understand voicing identity and experience as "an exercise in recognition"[24] that is inherently transformative is to believe that persons can speak who they are, that others can hear and understand them, and that such recognition necessarily enables dialogue and action. Unquestioned are the relations of self to experience, social-discursive formations, and audience. What if voiced experience and identity are comprised of shifting identifications and interpretations? What if what is heard and seen is unevenly received by spectators and listeners? I am concerned that identity politics takes identity to be a self-evident category from which knowledge and experience flow and elides the ways knowledge and experience are discursively and historically mediated.[25] Identity seeks recognition, yet depends on social relations and social knowledges to be recognized. As Lacanian arguments point out, recognition is never "full" or complete; it "is not conferred upon a subject, but forms that subject."[26] This mutually constitutive relation of identity and recognition belies the possibility of "authentic" knowing, for both are predicated on existing discourses.

Queer theorists' formulations of coming out or being closeted as performative speech acts highlight the role of others in the creation of one's voice and visibility. Eve Sedgwick has described the dynamics of secrecy and disclosure, or "the epistemology of the closet," thus:

> Every encounter with a new classful of students, to say nothing of a new boss, social worker, loan officer, landlord, doctor, erects new closets whose fraught and characteristic laws of optics and physics exact from at least gay people new surveys, new calculations, new draughts and requisitions of secrecy or disclosure. Even an out gay person deals daily with interlocutors about whom she doesn't know whether they know or not; it is equally difficult to guess for any given interlocutor whether, if they did know, the knowledge would seem very important.[27]

Transactive knowledges and the perpetual (re)negotiation of information are constitutive of lesbian voice and visibility. The ignorance or

[handwritten marginal note:] but this is not true

knowledge of others—and the significance they are perceived as attaching to knowledge—may construct one's use of voice/silence in becoming visible or maintaining invisibility. Preceding Sedgwick, Erving Goffman's theorization of strategies of "stigmatized" persons for negotiating social relations points to the context-bound, unstable nature of "knowledge." Goffman does not place visibility and voice as sources of knowledge; instead, others' knowledge constructs visibility and voice as persons manage their identities (managing what others see and hear) through "passing" to avoid revelation or "covering" in order to reduce tension by diverting others' attention from the stigma, or, for those who have achieved a degree of eminence, acting as "professional representatives" of their category.[28] Voice/silence and visibility/invisibility, then, are not origins of knowledge/ignorance, but both consequences and elements of it. In other words, voice does not lead to visibility that in turn leads to knowledge. Knowledge may set the terms for the use and reception of voice and visibility. For example, in the case of the GAU, existing social knowledges and ignorances were productive of the ways gay and lesbian academics constituted themselves as a group seeking positive (re)definition through the construction of individual and collective identities and histories. Theirs was a project of rewriting knowledges that limited the visible by constituting an affirming visibility that nonetheless was legible through the very knowledges of the moment. Thus, there is a complex interplay among voice, visibility, and knowledge—and gradations of their opposites—in which they are in mutually constitutive relationships dependent on context. Causality is lost to instability.

Contrary to a formulation of coming out as signifying movement from secrecy to disclosure, theorists such as Sedgwick argue that incoherences surrounding gay definition prohibit "authentic" disclosure of self. Because gay definition is unstable, voice and visibility do not create knowledge. Persons may never know when or how disclosure occurs or what meanings it takes on: "no one person can take control over all the multiple, often contradictory codes by which information about sexual identity and activity can seem to be conveyed" (79). Conversely, as Butler suggests, disclosure may conceal more than it reveals:

> In the act which would disclose the true and full content of that "I," a certain radical *concealment* is thereby produced. For it is always finally unclear what is meant by invoking the lesbian-signifier, since its signification is always to some degree out of one's control, but also because its *specificity* can only be demarcated by exclusions that return to disrupt its claim to coherence. . . . If I claim to be a lesbian, I "come out" only to produce a new and different "closet." The "you" to whom I come out now has access to a different region of opacity.[29]

Butler points to the lack of control one has over signification and stresses the illusion of knowledge produced in speech due to the false coherence of lesbian. Because "lesbian" cannot be known yet is presumed to be knowable as "such and such," lesbian takes on different meanings according to context. The limitations of representation suggest that rather than merely hearing or seeing the voiceless and invisible, it may be more efficacious to learn of the meanings and relations of voice and visibility, silence and invisibility in specific contexts. What knowledges are implicated in their workings? The shift I propose from the representation of identity to an inquiry into knowledges in practice requires a comment on the theoretical frameworks I draw from, as well as their difficulties.

Shift from definitions of identity to the question of how we come to know,
(learn more about ideas which contribute to identity)

IDENTITY INTO PRACTICE

Critiques of identity politics and the effects of knowledge/ignorance, voice/silence, visibility/invisibility have been evolving over the past several decades, primarily in literary and cultural studies. In the social sciences, there has been little scholarship that goes beyond "giving voice" and "making visible," possibly for good reason. The social sciences' reliance on empirical-perceptual data (datum: that which is given) leaves little room for interpretive approaches that seek to go beyond the given, particularly when the given is an unrepresentable and unstable identity. A difficulty of this inquiry is that of bringing epistemologies that rely on sensory modalities of seeing and hearing into conversation with epistemologies that question what is seen and heard, related to a topic whose epistemology may be that there is no seeing, hearing, or knowing. My inquiry is characterized by several tensions as I draw from the social sciences, the humanities, humanism, and poststructuralism. Instead of placing the individual as origin, I am interested in subjectivity and agency as they are formed through discourses and actions. In considering identity and experience as constructed rather than given, my questions turn not to "what are the women's experiences?" but to "how are their experiences produced in the sociocultural and institutional discourses in which they live and work?" and "how do they challenge or adapt to these discourses as they enact their scholarship, pedagogy, and departmental relations?" I am less interested in representing "selves" than in asking how "selves" are articulations of specific dilemmas found at the intersections of institutional space and time. Yet my ethnographic approach assumes identity and experience as starting points and does not easily allow such interpretive leaps. Thus, a number of contradictions structure this work: What does it mean to conduct an empirical study of lesbian academics if *lesbian* does not carry stable meanings? Does ethnography enable the interrogation of the construction of identity and knowledge by looking at and listening to their manifestations? If processes of construction are beyond ethnographic reach, are there other formulations that, taking construction for granted, may help to understand the intertwinings of *lesbian* and *academic*? I have found that although discourses may be identifiable through fieldwork, connecting them to the *construction* of academic practice has not always been possible. Instead, in order to understand how three women enact their relationships to *lesbian* and *academic*, it has been helpful to identify their practices within specific domains, which I analyze as sites of agency. By agency, I mean the possibilities persons have for effecting change and for pursuing projects they find meaningful.

Humanist understandings of agency have been contested by those who embrace postmodern understandings of the subject, as described by Butler: "In the one view, agency is an attribute of persons, presupposed as prior to power and language, inferred from the structure of the self; in the second, agency is the effect of discursive conditions which do not for that reason control its use; it is not a transcendental category, but a contingent and fragile possibility opened up in the midst of constituting relations."[30] This second view of agency, from which I draw, is consonant with Butler's understanding of identity as existing not prior to discourse and action, but as constituted "within practices of *signification*."[31] These practices are *"not a founding act, but rather a regulated process of repetition"* (145). It is precisely repetition that allows for "the possibility of a variation" (145), which leads to Butler's argument that agency lies not in the doer but in the deed. This open-ended construction of the subject—through actions within discursive formations—is what makes possible "subversive repetition" (147): *doing,* rather than *being,* allows for new iterations of regulatory norms. In her example of gender as performative, performances of gender (thought to be a *being,* but actually a *doing*) are imperfect copies of the norm and thus "swerv[e] from their original purposes" (29) to expand what is culturally intelligible. Although the performance of discontinuous gender identities may demonstrate the arbitrariness of categories of compulsory heterosexuality, I do not share Butler's optimism that it will in and of itself create within the "matrix of intelligibility rival and subversive matrices of gender disorder" (17). Attention to historical and contemporaneous contexts may enable an understanding of how such a *doing* can lead to new possibilities.

Butler's recent work, *Excitable Speech,* signals more nuanced attention to temporality and context. In it, she points to the historical traces in all speech, figuring it "as repetition, not as origination" (39). Drawing on Austin, she explains that the "subject speaks *conventionally*, that is, it speaks in a voice that is never fully singular" (25). Time is confused, for conventions are informed by the past, yet speech takes place in a present and presumes a future: "Who speaks when convention speaks? In what time does convention speak? In some sense, it is an inherited set of voices, an echo of others who speak as the 'I'" (25). Historicity, or the sedimentation of uses of language, lends contemporary speech its meanings. In this, Butler borrows Derrida's formulation of citationality to argue that a speech act "*accumulates the force of authority through the repetition or citation of a prior and authoritative set of practices*" (51). With the opening of this temporal dimension, the space in which one speaks or acts may also be opened: "Not only defined by social context, such speech is also marked by its capacity to break with context. Thus, performativity has its own social temporality in which it remains enabled precisely by the contexts from which it breaks" (40). Speech acts are performed in contexts beyond those for which they are intended. These breaks with ordinary usage are key to the possibility of "contest[ing] what has become sedimented in and as the ordinary" (145). To suggest that one draws on norms, yet never reproduces these norms faithfully or in faithful contexts, offers the beginnings of a theory of appropriation. However, a question of what enables practices to arise in new contexts remains.

Several theorists have suggested that performance and the performative have links to Michel de Certeau's theory of practice.[32] De Certeau situates his theory of practice as breaking with more deterministic social theories, such as Bourdieu's socially reproduced habitus and Foucault's sometimes seemingly inescapable disciplinary grid. Practice is a theory of usages loosely informed by Saussure's distinction of langue (a system of language) and parole (an act of speaking) that focuses on "situating the act in relation to its circumstances, 'contexts of use'" (33). De Certeau's interest in the practices of "consumers"—the reader of a text or the pedestrian in a city—blurs the dichotomy of producers-as-active and consumers-as-passive. Practices of everyday life are "'ways of operating' or doing things" (xi), "modes of operation or schemata of action" (xi), an "ensemble of *procedures*" (43) within social relations. Practices may either be strategies, which are used by institutions and those in power, or tactics, the use or appropriation of existing systems and institutions by the "other."[33] Strategies, which pertain to the *propre*, "a spatial or institutional localization" (xix), are circumscribed spatially, "and thus serve as the basis for generating relations with an exterior distinct from it" (xix). These spaces seek "a certain independence with respect to the variability of circumstances. It is a mastery of time through the foundation of an autonomous place" (36). Tactics, on the other hand, are temporal; they have no spatial location but are created improvisationally within space, and have the effect of redistributing space: "A tactic insinuates itself into the other's place, fragmentarily, without taking it over in its entirety" (xix). The indeterminacy of tactics makes them a potential source of resistance, for their intuitive, unspoken (tacit) nature disrupts the predictability, order, and visibility space would impose: "The order of things is precisely what 'popular' tactics turn to their own ends, without any illusion that it will change any time soon. . . . Into the institution to be served are thus insinuated styles of social exchange, technical invention, and moral resistance" (26). Tactical practices must be understood as appropriations of space, responses to networks of relations.

While space would erase the variability introduced by time, the improvisations of tactics complicate the coherence space would impose, for they are "composed of many moments and many heterogeneous elements. It [a tactic] has no general and abstract formulation, no proper place. It is a memory" (82). As de Certeau explains, "Like those birds that lay their eggs only in other species' nests, memory produces in a place that does not belong to it. . . . [M]emory derives its interventionary force from its very capacity to be altered—unmoored, mobile, lacking any fixed position" (86). Memory, or the intersecting historicities of spaces, acts, and individuals is "mobilized relative to what happens" (80) and brings new responses to what it finds. Practice may be thought of as the creative use of what is available, "conditioned by places, rules, and givens; it is a proliferation of inventions in limited spaces."[34] Thus, as de Certeau points out, the visible locations that panoptic disciplining would produce are disrupted, for "[t]here is no place that is not haunted by many different spirits hidden there in silence, spirits one can 'invoice' or not. Haunted places are the only ones people can live in."[35] Other times are constitutive—in unpredictable ways—of spaces and present practices, just as spaces create the conditions for tactics' possibilities and effects, as Cindy Patton has explained:

[What] de Certeau calls tactics, but which may as easily be called performance, involves deployment of signs which have already attained meaning and/or standard usage within the legitimated discourse and crystallized practices of a "social," understood as a place of contestation. . . . Performance operates through timing and repartee, and is not recognizable except as defacement within the space-oriented domain of the proper.[36]

This understanding of the social as a multiply contemporary, historical, and spatial dimension in which knowledges are put into practice in new contexts shares assumptions with William Sewell's theory of the "transposability of schemas."[37] In his reworking of Bourdieu's theory of fields and habitus and Giddens' structuration theory,[38] Sewell argues that actors' schemas (akin to procedures for practice) draw on existing resources to create new resources for action. Structure and agency presuppose each other (as space and tactics presuppose each other, and as langue makes possible parole), yet actors' schema and practices are not isomorphic with one structure but are derived through movement across structures. This movement through multiple domains, cultures, and locations forms actors' strategies for action, which they bring to new locations. Relocated and recombined in new contexts, these actions constitute the possibility of agency to rearrange spaces by appropriating aspects of them for new uses and meanings.[39]

Practice underscores the mutability of *lesbian* and suggests that identity might be reconceptualized as but one tactic, or form of practice. Certain discursive spaces encourage certain articulations of the self: voices and practices are created within the conventions and knowledges contexts allow and offer. In the same way, *intellectual* and *academic* are not fixed categories but forms of practice, ways of responding to circumstances. Although at times I seem to use the terms "academic" and "intellectual" interchangeably, I intend a distinction. "Intellectual" suggests a relation to knowledge and society, whereas "academic" highlights the mediation of that relationship by the space of universities. Consonant with the temporal nature of practice, Bruce Robbins has urged historical attention to "what social changes may have occurred *around* intellectuals so as to shift their value, function, and potential for resistance."[40] Equally important, and germane to location in academia, are institutional changes that affect the work of lesbian faculty. In understanding academic practices as responses, I draw on Bill Readings' theorization of the "post-historical" university, or the university constituted by multiple spaces and times.

INTELLECTUAL PRACTICE AMONG THE RUINS

In *The University in Ruins*, Readings traces the development of the modern university from the emergence of a Kantian university guided by reason, to a Humboldtian project of culture-building through research and teaching, to a recent technobureaucratic emphasis on "excellence." The modern university was an institution centered by "an idea that functions as its referent, as the end and meaning of its activities."[41] The Kantian University of Reason had as its central purpose to create progress by developing autonomous reasoning subjects and rational communities in the "perpetual conflict between established tradition and rational inquiry" (57). Slowly displacing the centering of reason was the Humboldtian University of Culture (the model for U.S. research universities), which developed a unified culture for the nation-state and merged the cultivation of the individual and the nation (or the subject's relation to the nation-state): "On the one hand, culture names an *identity*. It is the unity of all knowledges that are the object of study. . . . On the other hand, culture names a process of *development*, of the cultivation of character—*Bildung*" (64). The projects of culture and reason are not a simple chronology, but contemporaneous. For example, these two discourses join in the American preoccupation with the literary canon, a definition of heritage and culture that is partly handed down, but also chosen "in a free exercise of rational will" (85). The now-classic call for giving students the "discipline and furniture of the mind"[42] figures academic subjects as having intrinsic value for their cultural content and their ability to develop habits of reasoning. The study of "the best that has been thought and written," particularly in the humanities, "would train the moral intelligence, working to produce a community with shared values, and would provide foundations for thought and action."[43]

A contemporary manifestation of the nexus of culture-reason lies in the idealized conceptualization of the university as populated by universal intellectuals engaged in the disinterested pursuit of knowledge to impart to future generations.[44] The "crisis of the humanities" begun in the mid-1980s calls for a return to canonical authors and core Western knowledge. The teaching of high culture as a "common culture" to be transmitted inducts citizens into "our national heritage" and teaches skills to reason.[45] Such formulations appeal to liberal democratic principles of equality of opportunity and freedom from indoctrination despite their elision of relations of power, the inherently interested and contextual nature of knowledge, and the value-laden nature of selecting traditions to be taught. The teaching of culture becomes largely monumental and leaves little room for social criticism; figured as naturalized heritage, culture "serves as a trope to decouple knowledge from power."[46] Reacting to changes in university curricula effected by protest movements of the 1960s,[47] neoconservatives argue that those who teach from openly committed positions pose a threat to the university's autonomy. In the context of the "culture wars," much oppositional intellectual work that has sought to dispel the universal intellectual has been based in individual and collective identity, as in the work of the GAU. These efforts continue to be tied to culture and reason—with the added twist of identities that seek location. Representation and recognition of identities—rather than the differences that produce identities—become the terms of the debates in the culture wars through the appropriation of culture and reason.

With the decline of the nation-state as the primary unit of economic production, the lessening importance of culture to the global economy, and increasing acknowledgment of a lack of a unified culture, culture-building and the development of rational communities have lost their status as the unifying ideas of the university. Displaced as fixed referents, culture and reason become contested centers. What Readings calls the "post-historical" university, or "the University without an idea" (118), is an institution that "has outlived itself, is now a survivor of the era in which it defined itself in terms of the project of the historical development, affirmation, and inculcation of national culture" (6). In their stead has arisen the University of Excellence, in which, he argues, "The need for excellence is what we all agree on. And we all agree on it because it is not an ideology, in the sense that it has no external referent or internal content" (23). Because Excellence has no meaning, cultural and political questions of value are not at the center, but economic criteria of "performativity in an expanded market" (38). Research comes to be gauged by its exchange-value in the market rather its use-value for the nation-state (175). Pedagogy becomes part of the apparatus of transnational exchange and no longer serves citizens but "contemporary students [who] are consumers rather than national subjects" (53). The Excellent university is a space that carries traces (ruins) of the past, in which the purposes of intellectual work, of teaching and research, become uncertain. Faculty can neither restore nor ignore "traditions" that have historically defined the university but instead must sort through its ruins to give them contemporary meaning. Dwelling in the ruins of the university requires "attention to the present complexity of its space, undertaking an endless work of détournement of the spaces willed to us by a history whose temporality we no longer inhabit" (129). Echoing de Certeau's idea that "Haunted places are the only ones people can live in,"[48] Readings says of the university in ruins, "the past is not erased but haunts the present" (170). Memory intrudes to make the space of the university multiple.

This confused temporality maps onto de Certeau's distinction between place and space to offer a means of conceptualizing the implications of the ruins for academic practice. Place represents an order of distributed relationships, location, and fixity, such as a given culture to be transmitted, an interpretation to be learned, or defined skills and methods of reasoning to be acquired. Space, on the other hand, is a "*practiced place*" that is "composed of intersections of mobile elements" (117). The intrusion of memory diverts disciplined places that would be fixed to create spaces that are emergent, incomplete, and unpredictable. The ruins of the university become spaces that are multiple, for if space is a place in use, it is made ambiguous because it is "dependent upon many different conventions" (117). In this context, intellectual practice is not a prescripted performance, but an interpretation of the resources found among the ruins. Intellectuals respond to the discontinuities and uncertainties of their and others' circumstances, aware of the impossibility of final knowledge or understanding. Knowledge ceases to be independent, transcendental, or transmittable, information and skills cannot be dispensed, and students are no longer autonomous subjects to be developed. In short, the indeterminacy of excellence creates a renewed ethical imperative to conceptualize intellectual practice as networks of obligations to self, society, and students. A decentering, or indeterminacy, is not a state to bemoan, but a site of possibility for the tactical use of the space of the university. With the loss of fixity, either in the university's purposes or the role of intellectuals, intellectual practice is emergent, contingent on circumstances, open to interpretation.

Foucault's specific intellectual, who has been said to break with the "totalizing ambition of the universal intellectual,"[49] offers an example of intellectual practice as implication, as contextual response. Foucault has described intellectual practice as "not to shape others' political will; it is, through the analyses that he carries out in his own field, to question over and over again what is postulated as self-evident, to disturb people's mental habits, the way they do and think things, to dissipate what is familiar and accepted."[50] Located in institutional and social spaces, intellectuals' role is less to shape will or reveal false consciousness than it is to play a part in questioning and shifting the discourses in which they are implicated. Discursive formations rather than identity per se are constitutive of intellectual practice.[51] A useful extension of Foucault's formulation can be found in Andrew Ross' description of "new intellectuals," who are historically and personally positioned and who intervene not only in specific locations, as Foucault describes, but also in a "broader" public sphere. The "new intellectual" is not bound by a singular identity, set of interests, or tactics, in the way, for example, that early GAU work was. Rather, such intellectuals

> belong to different social groups and have loyalties to different social movements. They will possess specific professional or occupational skills and knowledges that can be applied within institutions but also in public spheres and communities. Their sense of strategy will shift from context to context, whether it involves the use of specialized knowledge in an occupational field or the use of generalized persuasion in speaking through the popular media. . . . Their ethical sense of the personal as a liberatory sphere means that their responsibility to "objective" political causes will be experientially inflected by a deeply subjective psycho-history.[52]

The fluidity Ross theorizes is responsive both to a person's multiple investments and to the demands of contexts. The new intellectual does not represent a specific constituency, as in many oppositional formulations informed by identity politics.[53] If spaces are plural, subjectivity is multiple, and the return of memory disrupts fixity, then intellectual practice must be seen as exceeding the individual subject, as movement among the ruins of the posthistorical university. Reconceptualizing the space of the university as ruins points to a multiplicity of resources and the potential for mobility in intellectuals' responses, and offers an alternative to understanding intellectual practice solely in relation to identity. Discussions of gay and lesbian academic practices, however, continue to be structured largely by identity politics.

DELIMITING LESBIAN ACADEMIC SPACES

Steven Seidman has mapped movements in gay and lesbian scholarship, and in so doing, mapped gay and lesbian intellectuals. In his delineation, from 1968 to 1975, social movement culture and politics defined scholarship as the roles of the intellectual and activist merged in efforts to establish homosexuality as natural. During the consolidation of "gay community and identity," from the mid-1970s into the 1980s, liberationist views gave way to ethnic models of identity. Even as gay and lesbian intellectuals were increasingly located in academia, they maintained ties to gay and lesbian communities, politics, and culture. However, beginning in the mid-1980s, the emergence of the university as the primary site for the production of gay and lesbian knowledge has created a situation in which "gay intellectual culture is now more divided than ever between an academic and nonacademic sector."[54] Despite the problematic tidiness of his chronology, it is suggestive of the roles of social and institutional pressures in constituting the functions and possibilities of gay and lesbian intellectuals and of increasing antagonism between "community" needs and gay and lesbian scholarship. In fact, a 1991 *Advocate* article pointed to concerns with "the effects that increasing institutionalization will have on relations between gay and lesbian academics and the mainstream scholarly world, the rest of the gay community, and other groups concerned with minority identity and oppression. At stake is not only what future students will see of openly gay professors but also what they—and the rest of us—will hear, through teaching and writing, about our lives."[55] Reminiscent of the work of the GAU, intellectual practice is framed representationally to follow three normative conflations underlying identity politics—conflation of identity and community, of identity and intellectual, and intellectual and community.

In fact, movement politics continue to define the discourses within which those who identify as "lesbian" and "intellectual" are constituted and constitute themselves. John D'Emilio situates possibilities inside and outside the academy "not simply because scholars accumulate knowledge, but because social pressures, movements of the disenfranchised, create demands for new knowledge and for the reorganization of what we already know." He attaches the role of gay and lesbian intellectuals to describing, explaining, and changing the social order: "we are involved in an effort to reshape a worldview and an intellectual tradition that has ignored, debased, and attacked same-sex relationships and that has, in the process, impoverished our understanding of human experience and human possibilities."[56] Gay and lesbian scholarship becomes a vehicle for personal and social change, defined by social and political affiliations as it seeks to produce knowledge that expands representations while remaining mindful of the struggles it may support.[57] Within the university, gay and lesbian scholarship and teaching must be understood at the intersections of society, university, discipline, and department, as what counts as knowledge is constantly redefined. Institutional recognition of marginalization can occur at the level of the official, in the form of policy, mission, and the absence or presence of events and programs of study, as well as the unofficial, in the form of attitudes, everyday exchanges, and representations. Tierney suggests that as marginalized groups "gain voice," changes occur in "communal definitions of knowledge and academic freedom": the expanded knowledges D'Emilio seeks find increasing legitimacy as the disenfranchised are recognized.[58] However, as I asked earlier, as gay men and lesbians "gain voice" or are recognized, what is seen and heard? Tierney makes the point that "[b]y voice, I mean that individuals and groups are able to seize the conditions for speaking and acting on their own, rather than having those in power set the terms on which they may speak, or be silent" (144). What conditions allow for what kinds of voices? Does one "seize" conditions or work tactically to shift them? "Speaking on one's own" implies that a voice already exists, ready to come forth. Yet conditions structure both what is said and heard. As Said has written, the question is not "its content, but its form, not what is said so much as how it is said, by whom, where and for whom."[59] Rather than positing an authentic voice, what if one adopts the stance that voice is *created* through the very conditions in which it is put to use? For example, even as social pressures create demands for new knowledges, disciplines allow scholars "to ask certain questions, to use a particular set of terms, and to study a relatively narrow set of things."[60] Despite their normalizing tendencies, disciplines are not static, as evidenced by the creation of gay and lesbian interest groups in professional organizations and interdisciplinary programs that continue to redefine acceptable topics and methods of study.[61] However, institutionalization may create new orthodoxies for scholarship whose original impetus lay in social movements.[62]

Despite poststructural challenges, identity, voice, and visibility prevail in understandings of gay and lesbian academic work,[63] Radhakrishnan has remarked, "even as an avant-garde and postrepresentational theory rages against Identity, the Voice, and the Self, myriad groups are voicing themselves with conviction into Self and Identity."[64] Particularly noteworthy are the first-person narratives by lesbian faculty in Linda Garber's edited volume *Tilting the Tower: Lesbians Teaching Queer Subjects*, which typically do not question the identity premises of their feelings of responsibility to come out in class in order to offer students a role model, to be honest to their principles, and to offer students support.[65] A number of essays encourage lesbian instructors to use their presence as a resource, to name their personal and political stakes in the subject of study and encourage students to do so as well.[66] These writers ignore the fact that while embodying oneself may in certain circumstances be an effective pedagogical tool, in others, professorial identity politics may undermine pedagogical goals. Or, given the contextual nature of the construction and use of voice, naming and voicing in the classroom may become less a means to authenticity than a rhetorical option, a gesture to produce an effect. The trope of authenticity exists equally in discussions of the research of lesbian academics. In her book about gay and lesbian faculty, Toni McNaron tells her readers, "Lesbian is an intellectual lens through which I sift all the data that enter my consciousness daily." Speaking of "coming out" and beginning to work in gay and lesbian studies, she defines the challenge for lesbians as "integrating our personal identities into our intellectual pursuits."[67] A trace of the mantra "the personal is the political," this integration assumes a scholarly perspective that can be defined by the axis of sexuality and that desires to speak itself through intellectual practice. But what if "lesbian" isn't a salient lens? Or a personal identity? What if a "lesbian" feels no need for such integration? What if she simply has other interests? These discourses of authenticity play into the problematic of creating a "place" for gay and lesbian scholars and gay and lesbian studies. As lesbian academics have gained places, new forms of work have been enabled. However, location is double-edged, for these places can result in lesbians' being called upon to be representatives or spokespersons within the university, commodified and tokenized precisely because of their status as successful minorities. This danger of containment through recognition surfaces throughout this book.

The scholarly and activist discourses I have pointed to deploy identity as central to understanding gay and lesbian oppositional work and gay and lesbian faculty's purposes and tactics in teaching and scholarship. There is a tendency for theorists and researchers to assume that collective visibility and recognition are the source of new forms of knowledge, that coming out in classrooms is inherently good, and that research that serves a community constituency is most valuable. Ignored in many discussions of academic practices and university politics are the relations of voice, visibility, identity, and knowledge—whether voice and visibility construct or are constructed by interlocutors' knowledge, and what sorts of knowledge are involved. While practices of identity politics have enabled changes in university policies, scholarship, and teaching, they reify lesbians' intellectual work by assuming their responsibility to act on identifications that may not be central to their understandings of self, their goals, or priorities. What if lesbian were understood as a practice that may have intersections with intellectual as a practice? By shifting focus to intellectual practices across institutional contexts, an understanding of the meanings of the intersections of *lesbian* and *academic* that interrogates the usefulness of tropes of voice and visibility becomes possible.

ENTERING THE INQUIRY

A central portion of this book considers the constitution of academic practices in specific domains as three women, Julie Howard, Olivia Moran, and Carol Davis, create their relationships to their roles as faculty members.[68] Through interviews with them, their students and colleagues, classroom observation, and interviews and study of university policy and social life across campus, I seek to understand their academic work within the contradictory social and institutional space of Liberal U, the university at which they work. While some themes in this text resonate across all three women's academic lives, more typically they diverge, revealing problematics specific to each woman's institutional and social locations. As the following brief introductions suggest, the narratives that unfold in this text are unique in their combinations, recombinations, and elisions of aspects of the personal, political, and intellectual.

Julie Howard, a white full professor of religious studies, is a practicing Catholic who understands her life as a spiritual and intellectual journey. She has been at Liberal U for some twenty years and is well established in the field of contemporary American Catholicism. Much of her research is born of dilemmas she has faced as a feminist and a Catholic, a fact that positions her uncomfortably in a department dedicated to the secular study of religion. Her teaching is an effort to complicate students' understandings of religion, a goal she at times pursues through "objective," yet irreverent, pedagogy and at times through sharing her self and her experiences as Catholic, as feminist, and as a woman who has had breast cancer while inviting students' personal explorations into the classroom. Julie has infrequently *voiced* her sexuality in her professional life, although in the last few years—particularly after her mastectomy and decision not to wear a prosthesis—she describes herself as more visible as lesbian to colleagues and some students.

It was the end of June when I first went to meet with Julie Howard. She had given me clear directions into town and to her house. Flowers lined the sidewalk to the front door. "Come in." We shook hands and she directed me to her back porch, where we took the same chairs we would sit in until we moved to her living room in late fall. I was disarmed by the lack of small talk—no mention of the weather, no obligatory niceties. She seemed unconcerned with consent forms and logistics, reading quickly, listening politely when I interrupted her to explicate points. "That's fine," she said, scribbling her signature where I indicated. As she looked through forms, I noticed the seeming comfort with which she stretched out in her chair and wore her clothes, an untucked Liberal U T-shirt, shorts, and Reeboks. I found myself pausing for a moment to look at the place where her breast had been.

During this first interview, Julie spoke of disembodiments she has faced throughout her professional life, first as a female teaching in a papal seminary (Dr. J. Howard, the sign on her door said), then as a lesbian entering Liberal U's Department of Religious Studies in the mid-1970s, and finally, the summer before, after a mastectomy, as a woman who refused to wear the prosthesis she was told would make her look "normal," a decision she described as something of a re-embodiment. She explained how making visible her breast cancer has led her to rethink the concealment of her sexuality in her professional and parts of her personal life. She went on to tell stories of growing up in a religion in which girls were destined to become nuns or mothers, and the few who deviated from this rule were the "career gals." Her colleagues, she said, have thought of her as like a nun. When she turned to her work at Liberal U, Julie described her research as a process of thinking through and learning from questions she encountered in her lived experience. She spoke of maintaining privacy in her relations with students, listing what she does not reveal: where she lives, her telephone number, her religious beliefs, and her sexuality. At the same time, she spoke of pedagogical situations in which sharing her religious beliefs has been helpful and in which sharing her sexual orientation could be relevant.

I was struck by her seeming candor, surely not completely unguarded, but openly reflective, confident at times and at others floundering, "I don't know, I'll have to think about that some more." What had seemed initially to be a gruffness or bluntness was complicated by the vividness with which she depicted her experiences, her gentle rendering of the contradictions she has endured, and an unexpected moment when she said, "I'm looking forward to this, this year, and this interaction. I hope I'm the kind of person you want to do this."[69] After I left Julie that first day, I was rapt by her ability to paint complex portraits in words of the felt, thought, and lived. She had an irreverent streak that combined with an earnestness in reflection that engaged me in unexpected ways.

With the exception of a six-year relationship, she has lived alone during most of her twenty years in Oasis, immersed in intellectual and spiritual work, yet not isolated from a wide circle of friends. Her words in a conversation we had toward the end of our months together present some central aspects of Julie's life. We had been talking about feminism and the Catholic church when I asked, "You've often said that the Church is lifegiving for you despite the difficulties between feminism and the Church and what you value and what you care about, and I don't think I know in what ways it's lifegiving."

> I believe in God. Teresa de Avila is not something I teach, it's something I like. I mean the only thing in my life I would change right now—I would have cancer again, I would have that stupid relationship again—if I had a year to live from right now, the only thing I would do is try to deepen my prayer life. I have no other interest. I'm not interested in finding another partner, though it would be nice. If I don't, that's fine with me. I could write another book. If I don't, I don't care. I want my friends to remember me as kind and generous, and I would like to deepen my prayer life. So religion matters to me, and this is not the kind of place to admit that any more than it's a kind of place to admit being queer. . . . There are all these closeted parts of my life. I closet my belief, closet my sex, and somehow am supposed to clothe my body in a way that I might as well put it in a closet, to deny that I've had breast cancer. I mean, it's hard to say. I think if you don't believe in religious experience, it makes no sense whatsoever. And so I don't expect it to make sense, but I believe in God, and prayer is something I want to do. Church is one of the avenues that makes prayer possible in another way. Without it, I think I would be too inclined to just sit here by myself, in my little contemplative mode.

The links between her teaching and what she cares about, her involvement with a number of communities, her connection to spiritual and religious practices, the closeting of parts of her self, the sometimes contradictory dimensions in her life—resonated throughout our conversations and my fieldwork as I learned of her relations to Liberal U, her department, her students, and the subjects she studies, and as she spoke of the meanings of cancer in her life.

Olivia Moran, a white associate professor of English, is in her second year at Liberal U. Specializing in feminist theory and lesbian studies, she is an academic "star" whose intellectual project is to debunk the category lesbian yet whose success is due to her work in lesbian studies. She thus lives an interesting contradiction, being known and in some ways hired for her work in what she calls "the commodified category" of lesbian theory, yet using the premises on which she is called to speak to challenge the category. Similarly, much of Olivia's teaching centers on denaturalizing the given, be it social categories or the organization of knowledge; in this spirit, she does not self-announce in her classes. Although she eschews connections between sexuality and her roles as faculty member, her relations with colleagues and understandings of her work in the department are mediated by her sexuality and area of scholarship.

I went to meet Olivia Moran the afternoon of the same day I first met Julie. As I turned the corner of the hallway to her office, I found her standing in the hallway chatting with her colleague Karen. After we exchanged greetings and banter, I walked with Olivia to her office, a place that fascinated me throughout our time together. Each time I came in, some things remained the same, but others changed. I wrote afterward in my research journal: "It's messy—a pile of books and papers on the floor, a tipped over lawn flamingo in the middle of them. A slinky on her desk. Bookshelves filled with small plastic super-hero-looking things and other assorted toys. Maybe showing something to those who come in, but I'm not sure I can read the message." I remember feeling a little like I had after reading Virginia Woolf's *Jacob's Room*, unsure who Jacob was but very aware of his room. In another survey, I recorded the following: "Full coke cans, orange wig, ad for her latest book, an old lunch box, a Schwarzenegger doll that throws barbells, Barbie cards strewn on the floor, a *PMLA* wrapper." At one point during the semester, the plastic pink flamingo had something that looked like someone's tenure review file underneath it.

On our first meeting, Olivia had just finished teaching a summer session class and seemed anxious to get out of her office, so we went in her sportscar for beers at a bar on the edge of campus. After we sat down, I handed her the consent form to look over, which she glanced through and proceeded, quite eloquently, to deconstruct. I initially was somewhat alarmed, not by what she was saying but by *the fact that she was saying it*; it seemed incongruous, inappropriate to acknowledge the falsity of the contract in the context of a research relationship. As I listened to her, I found myself wishing I could be taping her words; ironically, it was not until she had signed the now-acknowledged-as-meaningless consent form that I was able to audiotape. Her voiding the consent form of meaning yet willingly signing it, had the discomfiting effect, I think, if not exactly of reorganizing our positions in relation to each other, then forcing a recognition of my dependence on her. It was Olivia's first performative interview act, one of a series to which I would become accustomed. Her performances had the effect of creating a tacit yet (I think) shared acknowledgment of the constructed nature of research relationships and something of a reconstruction of ours. For example, Olivia seemed intrigued that I didn't often refer to my interview guides during our time together, and would sometimes ask what question we were on. I explained that they were groups of topics that we were indeed addressing, but that I preferred to talk through a mix of what was important to her and what was important to me—and did not want to be bound by prescribed questions. Performing the impossibility of *sustained* natural conversation in interviews, she took from time to time to saying things such as, "So are we on clump number one or clump number two?" On one occasion, in one of our last interviews, Olivia read a question from my paper upside down and proceeded to answer it, performing yet another strangely disconcerting commentary on dialogue, power, and control in interview relationships.

During our first meeting, Olivia spoke of her understandings of identity, of academia as a space that allows her her own timetable to ask and answer her questions, and of becoming a smaller fish in a bigger ocean with her upwardly mobile move the year before to Liberal U. She spoke of her preference for questioning the category lesbian rather than assuming it, her rejection of self-announcing her sexual orientation, and her dissatisfaction with lesbian communities and political activism. She located her academic work as political, suggesting that her research "infected" classrooms by introducing new questions and that her performance of "unscripted" pedagogical acts had the potential to challenge aspects of processes of teaching and learning. She spoke of her field, positioning herself in feminist and psychoanalytic traditions and in lesbian studies and rejecting alignments with gay men. As was reiterated throughout our subsequent meetings, our conversation remained primarily in the domain of the professional, with only occasional talk of Olivia's family of birth, her life with her partner, or her circles of friends. The themes that would become salient in her presentation of self and in her actions were bound up with Olivia's performance of questioning as a means to change: questioning a category of sexual identity she doesn't believe is meaningful, questioning the roles of teachers and students and naturalized orders of knowledge in her teaching, and questioning the category of "lesbian theorist" and the "discipline" of gay and lesbian studies in her work in the English department.

I was drawn into conversation with Olivia in ways different than I had been with Julie. Julie had affected me on a personal level; Olivia struck me as an intellectual puzzle. Several months later, a colleague of Olivia's said of meeting her years ago: "She's all very much there, but she's inaccessibly there, so it was both intriguing, but. . . . She's there, she's funny, she's engaged, but you're not necessarily sure who she is even then. She can talk, I mean she can perform, she can perform her presence, but you're not sure who she is. And she's smart as shit, and she's really happy in demonstrating that, and you're just like, oh my God, you know, blown away by it." As I came to understand over time, the dynamic speaker, teacher, and thinker was in many ways performing a questioning of an essential "self."

Carol Davis, in her fifth year as an assistant professor of journalism, has expertise in newspaper journalism, media history, and cultural studies. Carol is African-American, hired through an affirmative action program that had the effect of undermining her scholarly abilities and constraining colleagues' understandings of her areas of expertise. Hypervisible because of her blackness in a white institution, Carol lives in a tenuous relationship with some members of the African-American community because she is lesbian and her partner is white. As she defines her roles as faculty member, she does so primarily in relation to her race and gender, struggling with issues of authority with colleagues and students. Her race obscures her lesbianism, rendering it inscrutable to others, despite the fact that she is "out" to her colleagues and at times to students.

Carol had been away during the summer, having just returned to Oasis from a year at another institution. On the phone she had described herself as "having her teeth a bit more on edge than usual" as she braced herself for another year at Liberal U. I appeared at her office a week before the semester began. The Journalism area felt orderly—carpeting, quiet corridor, names on doors. Carol smiled, invited me to sit down, and did the perfunctory pardoning of the mess on her desk. Except for a few papers and journals to one side, it wasn't messy. She was wearing shorts and a short-sleeved button-down shirt with a pattern of donkeys and black boys that said "real native entertainment" under each picture. Throughout our time together, I often thought that her office looked like an office "should": two awards she has received hang on a bulletin board over her desk, her diploma sits to a side, books on the media, women, and African-Americans line the bookshelves, a poster about African-American women fills the wall behind her head.

Carol attended to the consent form, expressing interest in talking organizationally of various aspects of the study and fashioning a tentative calendar of interviews and observations, one that would prove annoyingly difficult to keep. We then began our first audiotaped conversation, which would introduce me only schematically to the complexities of her experiences in her academic life due to her race, gender, and sexuality. She described her decision to enter academia as rooted in her developing political consciousness and intellectual interests. Based on her experience in newsrooms, she became increasingly concerned with issues of gender and race in the practice and consumption of media, as well as with disrupting commonsense journalistic practices, such as subverting market-based assumptions in news coverage, questioning objectivity in reporting, and rethinking the journalistic canon of "newsworthiness." She entered academia with a belief that a position from the "outside" would be more efficacious in effecting change. She turned to describe her first job at a four-year college, at which, as the first black female faculty member at the college, she walked into a minefield of expectations for the roles she would take on, primarily that of "black mother" to students. She was not "out" at her first job, a fact she says complicated her relations to the small core of African-Americans, who moved between knowing and not knowing. The difficulties she had negotiating others' knowledge/ignorance precipitated her decision to be "clear" when she was invited to interview for the position at Liberal U. She described being "awkwardly" hired there under a special affirmative action line—the first person of color in the School of Journalism— and expected to "embody all their diversity" through research, work on the curriculum, and student advising. As she spoke of multiple expectations that circulate around her race and gender, Carol included difficulties she has had in classrooms, as students sometimes challenge her "authority" because she is young-looking, African-American, and female.

Our first interview introduced some themes that would resurface over the next months, such as the raced, gendered, and sexualized otherness(es) that often define(s) her interactions with colleagues and students. Carol hinted at the projects of her research and teaching, her status as valued yet devalued commodity in her department, and her mobile affinities within the university. However, it was not until subsequent interviews that she would speak of her intellectual positioning in her field or department as she gains credibility through historical work and loses credibility in some spheres for what is seen as more speculative, politicized work that draws from cultural studies. In later interviews, she would speak of the tactics she has used to survive in predominantly white environments and to gain authority in her department. She would also speak of the ways the salience of her race erases both her sexuality and her professional expertise; she is granted provisional authority in her department in issues of race and gender, but not in the history of journalism. Like most, but not all of our interviews, the first interview stayed within the frame of the expected. There is something deceptively "clear" about Carol; as she spoke, she did not wander from topic to topic but focused on particular themes. She had a tendency to make a point, follow it with a narrative example, and offer analysis of the situation she had described (a journalistic habit?). The linearity of her talk often belied her complex understandings of the intersections of academic politics and the politics of race, gender, and sexuality; it was only by unsmoothing the lines myself that I was able to locate the nuances of her understandings. There is a similar clarity in her teaching that appears to simplify the complex; yet, understood in the context of her goals and the interpersonal dynamics of her classrooms, her pedagogy retains much of the complexity of her understandings. As I began my interactions with her, I was absorbed by her narratives, yet unable to move beyond them as transparent texts. I carried my naive readings into her classrooms, which initially dissatisfied me as unexciting, traditional, and authoritative. It was not until I began to reorganize her transparent texts and to juxtapose them to the texts of her classrooms that I began to listen to the complexities underlying Carol's practices.

On leaving her office after our first meeting, I wrote of her situation in her department, imagining colleagues' responses to her: "She strikes me as an 'acceptable black.' She's well-spoken, articulate, uses 'standard English' and doesn't slip into jargon or threatening dialects. . . . She's not scary in appearance, either as black or as lesbian—autonomous body movement but not dykey." Hers is an interesting acceptability, however, for she tactfully reminds spectators that she will not accept the status of "real native entertainment"—or "higher educational entertainment," as Hazel Carby[70] has said—that they might ascribe to her.

As may be imagined through these brief introductions, Julie, Olivia, and Carol each complicate the meanings *lesbian* and *academic* can carry. Coming to know them as I did demanded that I rethink the meanings of voice, visibility, knowledge, and practice. I have not always been able to resolve the relations of these terms neatly, and have become convinced that the lack of resolution constitutes the importance of this inquiry. Each woman's opening words in our first interviews begin to suggest the impossibility of fixing the meanings of *lesbian* and *intellectual*, and of voice and visibility in practice. I began each interview by asking, "Could you talk to me a little bit about your decision to participate in this project?"[71]

JULIE. I think I told you on the phone I had breast cancer last summer, had a mastectomy, and there was something about the whole process of getting a prosthesis—they start early. A friend of mine took me over to a place called Beautiful Creations. It was awful. I spent the entire time in that place crying, and I think said "Fuck" about five hundred and fifty times. And my friend kept saying to this nurse person, "She's not usually like this, she's not usually like this." But I just didn't want to do this, I didn't want to hide this, but I actually went to Vermont—about six weeks after surgery last summer—and I wore this goddamn bra with a fake boob. I was traveling with this good friend of mine who thought this was really nifty, but I felt worse and worse and worse about it, and I came home and took the whole contraption and put it in the garage and said, "Screw it, I'm not ever wearing this again." And the more I started thinking about that experience, in terms of hiding, the more I began to think about closets. . . . I was in a reading group, we were reading *Epistemology of the Closet*. I had sort of been thinking about it anyway, and lately I had been much more comfortable, I think, with being more, I don't know, being more dykey looking, kind of out in the department. Part of this is because of a friend in another department who's been, I call her my fairy godmother, and part of it is because I have a young colleague in the department now who's gay and who started taking me to gay/lesbian faculty cocktail parties which I had never gone to before. My life has been very, very different because of these people. And because of cancer. So anyway, I'm going to write an essay about being queer and about not wearing a prosthesis, and so in the context of thinking about that project. . . . The person who got me in touch with you to begin with told me it might help me think about some of the issues I want to bring up in the essay. So I think that was what piqued my interest. . . . I'm a scholar-writer, if I can't get something out of what I'm doing, I don't really want to do it. A lot of my work very much is tied up with certain kinds of things I do or think. I write about contemporary issues for the most part. If I were just doing this and I were not somehow going to get something out of it for my own writing, I wouldn't do it. . . . Since I'm going to be writing about myself as a lesbian, I thought, why not? It would kind of be interesting. I think it'll be a whole new experience level for me, too, to think about this aspect of myself in ways that are much more overt and connected with a whole lot of different things. I feel like an evolving person on this particular plane.

OLIVIA. Actually, I was intrigued by the way you had formulated this, and I was really curious to see how it played out, particularly around the identification of people in a particular identity category, which I actually don't take too seriously. So I was curious to see how this would play out—I had a kind of intellectual curiosity about what you were going to do with this. And I was also interested to see how your ideas about this would change as you talked to three disparate people, . . . so that's, it's kind of an intellectual, intriguing interest. . . . I see it [invoking a category of identity] as a way of starting, I'm not sure that's where you're going to end up. So, that's what I'm interested in watching, is the process, I'm interested to see where you're going to get with this, because if you're going to do what you propose, which is to look at the work that the three of us do, to watch us teach class, and to watch us behave, I'm wondering how much that category is going to actually define much of anything or whether it defines things we don't know it's defining—which would be equally useful to know, for me. Or, in which case, we might want to alter or redefine that category in other ways. So, in any case, it seemed to me sort of an evolutionary, progenitive project, and that's why I was kind of interested in it. . . . It's like who knows, I might find something out about myself, too. I don't know, but I was curious to see what would happen here.

CAROL. I've been through this process [participating in a research project] before. On the one hand, the process last time was time consuming, but I found it insightful for myself in a lot of ways, to talk through some of the things I had been thinking but perhaps hadn't expressed verbally, put into context some of the political issues in the academy that I had been feeling. And so, from a personal standpoint I knew it wouldn't be an ordeal or an unpleasant experience and that it could certainly be positive. And, I guess there were some small altruistic reasons, I'm close enough to having been a graduate student myself to know how hard it is, you know, and I did some ethnographic work in graduate school, . . . and so I wanted to help another graduate student whom Karen spoke very highly of. Karen said something like this, "Now this isn't your basic stupid graduate student." You know, Karen can be very blunt. She said, "You know, she's very bright and I think you'll like her." So I guess there were a variety of factors. It wasn't something I agonized over, I talked to you, I saw your stuff, I said okay. It was a simple straightforward decision. You know, this is sort of part of the job, helping facilitate people's research, particularly if you find the person interesting and the project interesting, that's part of being an academic, being a scholar. Wanting to help a feminist, a lesbian, get her work done, that becomes part of it also. I joked with Karen about how I'm becoming this big object of study, but in a lot of respects I'm used to that as a black lesbian. As a black woman, I've been scrutinized in so many ways for so long in every aspect of my professional life, my adult life really, that it's become par for the course, that there's some reason why somebody finds me interesting. Sometimes it's an exploitive kind of situation, sometimes it's very problematic, but there are times when it's important. There aren't a lot of black women in the academy, and our perspectives are very unique, and I think very much imbued with the politics of race and gender and sexuality and so forth, not only in higher education but also in national discourse, so we, I think it's important for us to put that out there. And in a lot of ways this is a lot easier than my writing an article about my personal experiences.

Each woman's presentation of self, her interests or struggles, whether inflected with the personal, the intellectual, or the political, immediately decenters any singular perspective about how sexuality operates in academic lives. *Lesbian* is present (it was the premise of our coming together), yet is not central. Personal experience, scholarship, cancer, and unconcealment are bound up with structures of the closet and a desire to explore those structures; intellectual curiosity (or perhaps "project" would be a better word) in how the category *lesbian* might (d)evolve in the course of the study form a basis for interest; race, gender, and sexuality, but most saliently race and gender, create a set of experiences and a specific perspective that desires to be voiced. Although it would be reductive to align the women's words with social and intellectual developments of the past several decades by saying that they "represent" specific strands of thought, the themes that emerge in their opening words point to some of the tensions that structure discourse around lesbian academics: the relations of the personal to the intellectual, of a social category to one's actions and sense of self-identity, and of individuals to institutions.

NARRATIVE KNOWING AS PRACTICE

As I have said, it is difficult to know what meanings *lesbian* carries and what it means to be seen or heard. In discussing concepts that are impossible to stabilize, I find that I implicitly define them in my textualization. I do so with the hope that my text offers a means to learn from and about lesbian academics' practices that will open categories and terms such as *lesbian, knowledge,* and *identity* and their interrelations to multiple interpretations. Despite the awkwardness of invoking a category whose meanings at once seem overdetermined and at other moments elusive, I try to speak beyond it.[72] I am made hopeful by Gayatri Spivak's contention that representation necessitates a degree of essentializing, a tactic that can be deployed to strategic ends.[73]

The core dilemmas that define this study revolve around the relations of identity, knowledge, and academic practice within and beyond a university setting. I am interested in the ways Julie, Olivia, and Carol are defined by and (re)define the discursive spaces they inhabit. Centered on a fall semester, my fieldwork included ongoing interviews, class observation, and readings of their research. I also conducted research related to the social and institutional contexts of the university and the women's disciplines and departments, such as analyses of mission statements, policies, campus and local newspapers, and interviews with colleagues, students, teaching assistants, and staff. Through analysis, I integrate as I can this seeming dichotomy of "text" (what the women do and say) and "context" (the places and times in which they act), for their actions and the contexts in which they are performed are in a mutually constitutive relations.[74] As the narratives unfold, I address how, through practice, the women variously challenge or adapt to the discourses in which they are implicated. Embedded in the narratives are a number of questions: How do the individuals and groups who constitute university, discipline, and department define and redefine knowledge, identity, and lesbian at Liberal U? For these women, how do knowledge and identity relate to each other in academic practice? What personal, professional, explicit and tacit meanings do *lesbian* and *academic* take on as they pursue their teaching and research? The narratives are unique to each woman and her circumstances in order to offer insight into the particular. Diane Brunner has defined narrative as "tak[ing] on the presence of persons engaged with and situated in the world in a variety of ways."[75] The narratives, however, do not *render* presence as such, but *evoke* presences. They may be thought of as what Norman Denzin has called "truthful fictions," which combine facts (events that are believed to have occurred) and facticities (descriptions of how those events were experienced). Within the limits of the partiality of representation, I endeavor to offer a text that "is faithful to facticities and facts. It creates verisimilitude, or what are for the reader believable experiences."[76]

To acknowledge the constructed, perspectival nature of narratives it to partake of what Marcus and Fischer have called an experimental moment in the human sciences, characterized by Lyotard's oft-cited definition of postmodernism as "incredulity toward metanarratives."[77] The experimental moment foregrounds "the essential indeterminacy of human experiencing"[78] and the contingent nature of knowing. Although in the chapters that follow I offer what are decidedly my interpretations, I acknowledge their contingency and make no claim to final answers. My interpretations are situated, constituted by the detours and specificities of the happening of events and their retelling, whether the women's retelling, my retelling, or my retelling of their retelling.

As a process of human deliberation that offers depictions of lived human realities and concerns, narrative constitutes and reconstitutes choices for action. Jerome Bruner has written of paradigmatic and narrative modes of knowing. Paradigmatic, or logicoscientific, knowing is related to systematic description and explanation: "It is based upon categorization or conceptualization and the operations by which categories are established, instantiated, idealized, and related one to the other to form a system." Narrative knowing, on the other hand, "deals in human or human-like intention and action and the vicissitudes and consequences that mark their course."[79] Paradigmatic knowing is timeless and predicated on Popperian falsifiability; narrative knowing is temporally situated and rests on believability, precluding verification. Bruner's conceptualization (paradigmatic as it is) resonates with Lyotard's contrast of the metanarratives of science and the local narratives of communities. Lyotard places narrative knowledge in opposition to instrumental knowledge, which he says increasingly characterizes the scientific age and seeks to displace narrative knowing. As he describes it, the stories told in communities grant legitimacy to institutions and represent positive or negative models of integration into those institutions: "narratives allow the society in which they are told, on the one hand, to define its criteria of competence and, on the other, to evaluate according to those criteria what is performed or can be performed within it."[80] As researchers endeavor to speak of the vicissitudes of human intentions and actions, their narratives may reorganize the fixity metanarratives would impose. Narratives, as de Certeau says, "organize the play of changing relationships between places and spaces."[81]

Narratives of lived experience offer new ways of looking at and thinking about the situations they present. Attention to the construction of differing practices in differing situations expands persons' narrative knowledge and becomes less a representation of reality than a means of "coping with reality."[82] The challenge is to move beyond representation, as Kamala Visweswaran argues, to create narratives that read and open up ideological contradictions that constitute the construction of experience, to move from the indicative to the subjunctive in order to create a speculative narrative that enables new forms of thought.[83] The generation of new narratives that question the identities of which they ostensibly speak is critical in the ongoing redefinition of social knowledges and possibilities for action. In this sense, I follow de Certeau's thinking that "stories 'go in a procession' ahead of social practices in order to open a field for them."[84] Like spaces, stories are to be used and inhabited by readers who bring to them their own interests, meanings, and memories, so that they may appropriate them for altogether new opportunities. My emphasis on the speculative nature of narrative is intended to displace Lincoln and Guba's concept of the transferability of ethnographic data and other criteria of generalizability. They liken transferability to a kind of "fittingness,"[85] the degree of similarity between two situations that, when thickly described, will enable readers to determine the applicability of one context to another. I question the concept of "fit." The narratives and interpretation I provide are not necessarily intended for like situations, but for readers to develop their own senses of possibilities. The addition of varying actions in specific situations to communities' conversations becomes part of persons' narrative knowledge. Because persons dwell in multiple communities, or occupy numerous times and spaces, their knowledges move with them from context to context to create novel actions. Thus, contexts need not bear "objectively" apparent similarities. Narrative as a form of knowing finds its strength in the specificity of time and location, not as a transcendental text to be transported across situations for purposes of "application." I leave the appropriation of these narratives to the reader, to take from them what she will in the contexts she chooses.

In the following chapter, I turn to the multiple spaces that comprise Liberal U. Liberal U is a confounding university, for on the surface it offers "high-quality" academic programs and speaks in plural terms of academic work and social relations. Yet a close analysis reveals that policy and practice are characterized by limited and limiting understandings of the meanings of "diversity," the purposes of higher education, and the roles of faculty. In presenting Liberal U as an institution that is socially formed, I focus on definitions of knowledge and identities that are set forth officially and unofficially. In doing so, I begin to highlight themes that surface in later chapters pertaining to the pedagogical practices of Julie, Olivia, and Carol, their social and academic positionings in their departments, and their understandings of *lesbian* and *intellectual*. The topics that surfaced in the women's initial presentations of self—Julie's commentary that she has to closet her body and her beliefs, Olivia's refusal to be disciplined socially or academically, and Carol's struggles relating to her race and gender as subject and object of knowledge—are produced in specifically embodied ways in the social and institutional space of Liberal U. Celia Kitzinger has remarked that "[a]cademia is neither uniquely corrupt, nor uniquely liberating: it offers a set of possibilities."[86] The possibilities and the boundaries as they are put in motion in the context of the lives and work of three women at one institution unfold in the chapters that follow.

CHAPTER 2

Social and Institutional
Places and Spaces

We're out here in hobbitland.
—Staff member at Liberal U

In commemoration of a founding anniversary, Liberal U published a brochure describing the history of its trajectory to a respected status. The brochure's cover contains two drawings, one of a bear sauntering in the woods, the other of six squirrels collecting nuts beneath a tree. Large print between the pictures informs the reader: "At the time of its founding it pierced farther into the wilderness than any other state institution of higher learning at the time. The state was largely populated by wild animals, and forests covered a large part of the land." This institutional presentation of self, with its penetrative imagery and language inflected with colonialism, offers a way of thinking about Liberal U that I heard reiterated in various forms by individuals across campus and in town. Although there is no singular characterization of Liberal U that can be distilled from conversations with members of its communities or from official documents, oral and written characterizations, positive and negative, officially sanctioned and not, suggest an institutional identity that is internally contradictory.[1] Liberal U is in many ways defined by what is around it, by what it is not. The wilderness it has pierced is not yet tamed, and thus easily contrasted with the university. Self-definition through opposition with what is outside it, however, constitutes only one part of Liberal U's institutional identity. As a public institution, it has as its goal the civilization of what lies beyond it. In the logic of twentieth-century liberalism in education, the university represents and serves the very people, its constituencies, against whom it defines itself. Thus, while distinct from the wilderness, Liberal U's function is to represent and civilize that wilderness. As I will explain, Liberal U's social and academic distinction from the surroundings it has penetrated is in many ways constitutive of persons' experiences of the town and campus. At the same time, the drive to represent constituencies defines a number of discourses, both official and unofficial, that structure life and work at the university. The intersection of these definitions—different from yet representing what is outside—creates a number of tensions as Liberal U seeks to justify and enact its mission as a public research institution.

In this chapter, I offer an overview of two components of life at Liberal U. I begin with the constitution of discrete populations in the town and the university, followed by a discussion of official statements of Liberal U's goals and social relations on campus as they are constructed by diversity discourses. The juxtaposition of what is outside Liberal U with a discussion of policy statements and campus life may at first glance seem a strange choice, yet these domains situate crucial aspects of life at the university as it bears on the construction of faculty work. A strange encounter between diversity and tenets of liberal education is intertwined with reason, culture, and excellence to produce understandings of who faculty are and what they do. Yet the social and the institutional are not isomorphic: what is set forth in policy and what I present as prevailing social and academic discourses are interpreted and enacted differently in specific locations across the campus. The contradictory discourses that circulate to construct the social-institutional space of Liberal U serve as points of reference for the idiosyncratic places Julie, Olivia, and Carol inhabit.

ENTERING OASIS AND LIBERAL U: ISLAND COMMUNITIES

As one drives into the town of Oasis, it looks like yet another Midwestern town of some 50,000 people. Service roads lined with Burger Kings, Econolodges, modernized strip malls, and other standard features of the American landscape lead to the center of town and the adjacent university campus. Numerous churches of a variety of denominations, as well as a synagogue, can be found along these roads. Approaching campus, the atmosphere changes: new and used bookstores, pizza places, bars advertising Tuesday night shooter specials, cafés, and Asian restaurants predominate. Pedestrian and bicycle traffic become heavy. Most of those walking and bicycling are young white people, although it is not unusual to spot an Asian or African-American along the sidewalk. Next to the university is the "heart" of downtown Oasis, a mix of new shops and restaurants that call themselves "grilles" interspersed with car part stores and "collectibles" shops. Several Woolworth-esque stores have recently closed to make way for coffee bars and a music pub. My usual route to the university took me along a main thoroughfare, one side of which is lined with rather handsome, somehow stately, fraternity and sorority houses that face a row of academic buildings on the opposite side of the street. Although there is a mix of new and old buildings throughout the campus, as well as discrepancies in height, from towers to two-story buildings to houses that have been absorbed into university property, there is a uniformity in the color of the stone that gives a soothing sameness and seriousness to the feel of the campus.

Liberal U is a public research university, highly nationally ranked in many departments and professional schools, with a population of between 30,000 and 40,000 students.[2] Several histories of the university describe its development as a trajectory of continuous expansion and betterment, as the university has forged new departments and programs of study, built new buildings, and attracted an increasingly credentialed and cosmopolitan faculty. The first female and African-American students were admitted in the latter part of the last century, a fact highlighted in university brochures. In the mid-twentieth century, as one history describes, the university crystallized its move from "its parochial limitations" to the status of a "respectable research university." The parochial limitations may be understood in the context of the "wilderness" that surrounds the university. Liberal U is not near an urban, artistic, or industrial center. It is safe to say that the university's presence sustains many of the arts and businesses in Oasis.

The university is situated in a politically and socially conservative Midwestern state whose primary industries lie in manufacturing, retail trade, and the service industry. The state is strikingly racially homogeneous: white people constitute nearly 90 percent of the population, African-Americans under 8 percent, Asian-Americans under 1 percent, and Hispanics under 2 percent. African-Americans are clustered primarily in two urban centers in the state, and are thus not a presence in the daily lives of many of the state's white inhabitants. The county in which Liberal U is located, for example, is nearly 95 percent white, with African-Americans comprising less than 3 percent of the population. Asian-Americans comprise nearly 3 percent of the population and Hispanics just over 1 percent. Although statewide unemployment rates have ranged from 4 to 6 percent during the 1990s, 1993 statistics reveal that over 16 percent of the state's population lives in poverty (as federally defined). While statewide voting patterns are predominantly Republican, the town of Oasis has a strong pattern of Democratic voting in local, state, and national elections.

As a public institution charged with serving its constituency, Liberal U has a student body that is approximately 92 percent white, 4 percent African-American, 2.5 percent Asian, and 1.5 percent Hispanic. In other words, over 30,000 students are white; some 1,500 are African-American. There are between 6,000 and 7,000 graduate students, approximately 20 percent of Liberal U's student body. A significant percentage of students come from the state in which Liberal U is located. The students who enter Liberal U's domain are perceived by some who work at the university as conservative. One staff member commented, "Our students are relatively conservative, a lot of them are from the state, and the state is not a bastion of liberalism." A faculty member asserted, "This is a rural state, so you've got a lot of first-time college attendees in the family, and I think coming to Oasis was a major move for them. So to come from a very sheltered environment where people are NRA supporters and very conservative Republicans, to come into an environment where they're hit all of a sudden with radical movement can be overwhelming." These students, however, can find a place for themselves at Liberal U. Myriad organizations include fraternities and sororities, religious groups, activities clubs, political groups, and multicultural organizations. Carol suggested that a thread of normalcy characterizes campus life:

> I find the undergraduate culture here in general very conservative, not so much politically, but conservative from a cultural and ideological standpoint. It's very heterosexist, and they're not even conscious of the fact that it's heterosexist. It's very middle America, very bourgeois, and that crosses racial categories and class categories, and black students are just as middle of the road as white students. I think a lot of that has to do with the dominance of Midwestern culture and ethos. It's very white bread, and it's not confrontive. It's very passive, it's very middle class in terms of aspiration and lifestyle and cultural interests. The dominance of fraternities and sororities on this campus really affects undergraduate culture, so that is the central mode of social life and community organization on campus. The whole social orientation is around heterosexual dating and partying.

Even as social life echoes what lies beyond Liberal U, the university constitutes something of a community apart from the community that surrounds it. Although persons may affiliate with different communities, each constitutes a distinct enclave, or "niche," a term I frequently heard, with clearly delineated borders, both imaginary and tangible, that define individuals' affiliations, activities, and often, ways of speaking about others. These demarcations exist most predominantly along lines of race, class, and sexuality. They are at the same time geographic. The maps imagined by those within the university generally place Liberal U at the center, parts of Oasis directly adjacent to Liberal U as a concentric circle around it, and unknown or non-university-related parts of Oasis as outside, part of the wilderness. Almost invariably, people described Oasis as an island, a protective sphere, often referring to the town's history of social compassion and activism. A faculty member who does antihomophobic work on campus and in town contentedly declared, "Oasis is a caring place, a sort of a liberal island in a fairly conservative environment." Others, however, questioned the positive dimensions of this refuge. A lesbian student explained:

Oasis is an island. I've been told by people not to drive alone out in the country, because this is KKK territory. It's an island, if you cross a certain line. People can feel really "out" here in Oasis, but it's not real, it's just an artificial set-up, situation. There's nothing inherently gay/lesbian friendly in Oasis, the gay/lesbian population in Oasis can feel out because of the university. I don't know what the community would be like without the university. The frats are a swamp, a tarpit in the island.

She was able to map the town and university, both ideologically and geographically, speaking of those beyond her sphere in totalizing terms:

When you get into the townies section, outside the university section, it turns into standard conservative redneck, . . . right-wing conservative, low-middle-class, low-class people who've been brought up in racist, homophobic, anti-Semitic homes, and that clashes incredibly with the university. I used to work at a townie supermarket and would hear a lot of negative comments, like "I'm so sick of all those niggers and all those damn fags." I'd get called sir a lot. . . . Most of my friends don't care, you can't hold hands when you walk on the street, but my friend wears his sissy shirt downtown and that's okay. Once you stay within a certain block area and you cross it you should be afraid.

While university members define their locations apart from but in relation to the native environment, townspeople locate them apart from the life of local communities. Terry, the owner of the local women's bookstore, described borders in which "the university community, the faculty, are kind of, they kind of keep themselves apart. A lot of people who don't work at the university just think about them being in another world or another sphere."

With its small African-American population, Oasis is not an environment in which blacks and whites routinely associate and was consistently described as unwelcoming to African-Americans. "It's not an integrated community at all," said one woman. As Terry suggested, African-Americans' social movement is defined by the wider regional conservatism: "Even though Oasis being a university town is more liberal than the surrounding countryside, after all . . . it's pretty conservative. I think that African-Americans still have a certain amount of caution when they go out." An African-American male who works at the university described "the sacrifices that people of color make to live in a place like this. Our kids lack a sense of our culture, there's a lack of social life, I don't go out socially. Where am I going to go? Unless you're involved in mainstream activities, there's not much social life." While incidents of overt racism were not named as central concerns, an ethos that rarely extends beyond tolerance relegates black persons to distinct enclaves. Carol spoke of her frustrations: "We have friends, colleagues, straight couples with kids who argue about how Oasis is such a wonderful place to raise your kids. So, my partner and I argue, we say, bullshit, it's lily white. Is that why it's such a wonderful place to raise kids? Think about that, the fact that your kids are not going to encounter difference. Is that why? I think that people don't question that. They just feel very secure and very happy."

In contrast to the lack of interracial exchange, Oasis has a reputation as a positive environment for gay men and lesbians. Several years ago, the Democratic City Council passed an ordinance that includes nondiscrimination on the basis of sexual orientation. The event suggests the disjunctures among liberal groups in Oasis and its surroundings. Terry remembered:

> There was an uproar. The fundamentalist Christians got bused in *from all around*, there were so many people the meeting had to be moved from the city hall to a church. While it was being set up, they sang hymns till two or three o'clock in the morning. These people were calling us diseased and pedophiles and necrophiliacs and drug users. It was horrible, there were people from the Ku Klux Klan there with their shirts, so out there in the community at a certain level, there's a tremendous amount of homophobia.

Although Oasis has, by all reports, a significant, if not highly visible, gay and lesbian population, living in Oasis requires a degree of caution. Barbara, a university staff member, commented, "The community beyond Oasis is pretty redneck, conservative, homophobic. . . . It's not like it's unsafe. A lot of people who are very conservative, if you start talking to them, Liberal U's a hotbed of communism, their views are scary, they're things I haven't thought about since the fifties. But if you don't call attention to yourself [as lesbian] they don't bother you." The difficulties overt political statements and individual openness bring on suggest a precarious balance between liberal tolerance and homophobia.

Reflecting the town's segregated culture, lesbian communities form along racial and socioeconomic lines, as Terry described: "Across the board, the African-American and the Caucasian community do not mix that much. . . . I kind of regret that the lesbian community has a white face." I was told repeatedly that lesbian networks are "fragmented, divided." Barbara's characterization of divisions "between the professional and the blue-collar lesbians" was echoed in Terry's description of groups forming around specific activities, such as softball, bowling, potlucks, a dinner group for professional women, church, a theater group, a coffeehouse, dances, or events at a local bar. Neither woman mentioned the participation of faculty.[3]

A portrait that emerges of Oasis is that of a relatively homogeneous town comprised of smaller homogeneous groups—or, alternatively, that of a town in which certain types of heterogeneity are submerged by the limits of liberal pluralism. Marked identities, singular in their construction, serve as the basis for affiliation. Difference puts people and groups into place. The dangers to those who are not white and heterosexual are not so overwhelming that Oasis is "unlivable." In fact, as persons find their niches, they can lead rather pleasant lives. In her critique of Oasis, Carol described a "degree of complacency" among gays and lesbians that suggests that these enclaves, combined with the town's ethic of civility, may breed contentment:

> When you're not in a place where you feel hounded all the time, it's very easy to lapse into a feeling of security and safety. It's a very bourgeois, very liberal kind of attitude, where if I'm not personally threatened, then it's okay, and there's no analysis about the larger issues. So I think many of the queer people in this town, who are predominantly white, are just as guilty as the straight people, in terms of lapsing into this realm of comfort.

Place may ease daily life, but neutralize movement and change. Although Olivia and Julie were less critical of Oasis, the bounded nature of communities and of lesbian social, political, and cultural practices in town and beyond resonated with their disidentifications with the category lesbian, as I discuss in chapter 5. At the same time, the conservatism students bring from the wilderness plays a part in the pedagogical scenes I depict, as do campus discourses of diversity.

FINDING A PLACE FOR DIVERSITY

> The fate of minority students, the university, the state, and the country are intertwined.
> —Administrator quoted in the student newspaper

The president has explained that because Liberal U constitutes "a microcosm of the values and ideals of the state and the nation, [it is] uniquely situated to influence the development of our students by exposing them to a truly diverse educational experience." As Liberal U institutes social and academic programs meant to enrich students' perspectives, however, it is caught in a peculiar situation. Although *accountable* to the state, Liberal U is not a microcosm, embodiment, or reflection of its "values and ideals." In an epoch of antifeminist and affirmative action backlash, there is no reason to believe that the state or the nation holds "diversity" as a value. Rather, the current trend in cultural politics constructs a focus on diversities as dangerous to national unity.[4]

The university's support for diversity in official statements reveals a tension between academic excellence and social access: "There is much to be done, much that requires creative balancing. The campus must ensure, for example, that it attracts the best students in the state and nation and also supports and aggressively seeks out disadvantaged students" (Strategic Plan). A tenuous balance between quality and democracy is set out in policy. This duality must be read in light of offensives nationwide to campus diversity programs and affirmative action by both neoconservatives and traditional liberals who argue that public education's goals are, first, to promote economic growth, second, to teach basic American values, and last, to support equity.[5] Symptomatic of the fraught nature of educational equity in public discourse, policy justifications for diversifying students and faculty lie in a confusing combination of academic and social development: "The campus is committed to the belief that opportunities to interact with others from diverse backgrounds can result in increased understanding and appreciation of differences, immeasurably enriching the perspective of all members of the academic community." Diversity becomes commodified as socially enriching for those (middle- and upper-class whites?) who would not otherwise have contact with persons different from themselves. Conversely, Liberal U "recognizes a need within the state for youths from all ethnic and social groups to achieve their intellectual potential" and proposes "early intervention programs," revealing an assumption of deficit and a need for academic enrichment for marked ethnic and social groups. Liberal U will bring elements of the wilderness into its space, yet assumptions define, and thus create places for, those who differ from the institution's identity.

As an institution funded and regulated by its constituencies, Liberal U is bound to operate within the dictates of a liberal politics that conceives of individuals abstractly and of public institutions as neutral in sociopolitical relations.[6] With a policy focus on numerical representation and diversity as social interaction, university programs inadequately address material and structural factors that block easy incorporation of "diversity." Instead, the underlying ethos is accommodation in response to external social change. Meg, a graduate student activist and member of the Lesbian Avengers, asserted in a conversation about various diversity initiatives:

> I don't know how much the university can do because it's so much the norm. University administrations are middle America, they have to be, they're public institutions. If Liberal U has instituted a diversity program, that means it has become part of American consciousness, that means it's like *Newsweek* culture. I can't imagine asking the Liberal U administration to do things that *Newsweek* wouldn't do. Or that *Time*

wouldn't do. What else can you say? It is the system, it loves the system, it will be the system, and it won't be radical, that's it by definition, which doesn't mean there aren't things that can't be done that will make life more livable for people.

Although the numerous diversity programs instituted are largely reactive—that is, instituted in response to social demands—their increasing presence at Liberal U suggests that what "the system" will do is open to pressure and change. Officially, diversity is a managed and measured numbers game of representation, in which efficient performance is won through programs for faculty and student recruitment and retention. The university becomes excellent at "doing diversity." Meanwhile, unofficially, groups may use the resources provided by such programs for purposes not officially codified, much as de Certeau figures "consumers" of social spaces as productive, as putting those spaces to new uses. In this way, although representational politics has limitations, it constitutes a process of ongoing negotiation and change.

With increasing institutional recognition of difference, Chandra Mohanty has argued, "[t]he central issue, then, is not one of merely *acknowledging* difference; rather, the more difficult question concerns the kind of difference that is acknowledged and engaged."[7] Furthermore, *how* those differences are attended to is significant. Both in policy and social structures, race, gender, and sexuality are constructed as discrete entities that do not intersect, a practice that fails to take into account the meanings of the intersections of multiple differences. Diversity is constructed primarily in terms of racial groups, secondarily in terms of gender and ethnicity, and peripherally, sexual orientation. Class is either unspoken or absorbed into the category of race. Officially, diversity is attended to at the level of students and faculty; administration and staff are mentioned only sporadically in official documents and by members of the university community.

Despite, or perhaps because of, Liberal U's small nonwhite population, issues of race confound many at the university. Statistics for the retention of African-American students are low; few African-Americans can be found among the faculty and even fewer in the administration. Students, faculty, and staff consistently state that Liberal U is not a positive "climate" for African-Americans. Throughout several years of campus newspapers, incidents recurred: a student demonstration over racial discrimination in a local store; "nigger" written on dormitory walls; Black History Month announcements torn down and defaced. In letters in the newspaper, African-American students complain of their low numbers, the lack of role models, and white students' treatment of them "as if we were here under some kind of special admit program."

Many members of the university attribute problems attracting students and faculty of color to the isolation, insulation, and homogeneity of Oasis. Thus, while Liberal U endeavors to represent its constituencies by bringing "diversity" under its aegis, there are pervasive views that institutional demographic change is thwarted by local demographics. The predominantly white administration regularly expresses concern that representation of African-American faculty and students is low. An administrator explained in the newspaper, "For Liberal U to be among the top universities in the world it must continue to attract the best and brightest African-American students and faculty." Toward this end, Liberal U has committed significant resources—specifically, several decentralized offices and an array of programs—to the recruitment and retention of students, which the coordinator of diversity efforts nonetheless described as "skeletal" and inadequately funded.[8] "They pay and we're supposed to provide a service, and we have a history of not providing that service," he told me. He described his task: "When I tell people I do diversity, I tell them it is a dialogue about cultural differences, it is hearing a variety of perspectives, and it is helping people see its value and appreciating and nurturing folks and hearing those different perspectives." When I asked him what the university environment might be like were differing perspectives nurtured, he was unable to respond, except to tell me that recruitment and retention were the "bottom line." Similar to responses I heard in many "advocacy" offices, his thinking is symptomatic of a depoliticized approach to the management of diversity that stresses input and output in a representational model that does not address the quality, content, and effects of institutional and social structures.[9] For example, as part of its recruitment and retention push, the administration recently enhanced the Black Cultural Center, which includes a library, tutoring center, and other resources. As a dean explained, it is a place for "African-American students to feel at home," and gives them "an extra hand in coping with a white campus." Although its function is more than ornamental, the creation of a specific place for difference reveals that Liberal U understands itself as continuing to be a white social space that others must "cope with."

The much-publicized concern with racial diversity results in ongoing polemics on campus, particularly among students, around affirmative action, ethnic and racial centers, and student organizations. Campus programs are said to be divisive, to exacerbate racial tensions by calling attention to differences that should not be relevant in a meritocratic system, and to discriminate against those who excel. Promoting diversity involves a lessening of standards and a lowering of what excellence means. The campus newspaper regularly contains columns and letters to the editor that vilify affirmative action as racist, arguing that there will be racial equality "the day we have scholarships based only on ability and talent." A characteristic of the ongoing diversity talk is some white students', most notably white male self-identified conservatives, description of themselves as ridiculed, forced (in an interesting appropriation of the term) to "remain closeted." According to them, "Diversity Police" hold the campus hostage to diversity training and programming. One columnist explained that the PC administration was encouraging "whining" and "complaining" on the part of minority students, who should "smile more," "be excellent like Colin Powell," and "associate with people of other races." Anger toward "special privileges" combines with racist images of sullen, lazy blacks in the suggestion that the administration is fomenting a culture of complaint by promoting access over excellence. Underlying this resentment are beliefs that without a meritocratic system, whites are denied their due rights as institutions redress vague injustices from the "past." Damage control enters with the heads of offices setting forth defensive responses in the student paper: cultural centers are not forms of affirmative action, affirmative action includes race, sex, disabilities, and Vietnam veteran status, financial awards are not linked to affirmative action, and affirmative action fosters a diverse learning environment and helps "level the playing field." What is missing, as Troy Duster has described at Berkeley, "is strong morally, historically, and politically informed language that justifies affirmative action."[10]

In an environment in which talk of the need for diversity is more evident than diversity itself, a strange contradiction is evident in administrative rhetoric. On one hand, Liberal U is diverse and needs programs to accommodate its populations; on the other hand, Liberal U is not diverse enough and needs programs to attract more adequate representation. Numerical concerns generate attention to programs that might enable the university to attract isolated individuals; however, they abstract individuals from social, political, and institutional contexts. Although the perspectives of persons with dark skin are said to be valued, those perspectives are not attended to as they relate to structures of the university. At the same time, the administration, probably defensively, perpetuates the opposition of excellence versus access by repeatedly juxtaposing its high standards to its desire to increase representation of all racial, social, and ethnic groups in public statements. Talk of race creates a false dichotomy of diversity and excellence in which the two cannot be seen as coexisting.[11] It further constructs equality as the opposite of difference, mistakenly confusing sameness and equality and ignoring the fact that "the political notion of equality thus includes, indeed depends on, an acknowledgment of the existence of difference."[12]

In contrast to the number of programs for students, and despite the administration's talk about the importance of diversifying faculty, statistics are problematic and programs few. Of 1,500 faculty members, 91 percent are white, 3 percent African-American, 4 percent Asian, and 1.5 percent Hispanic. These percentages mean that there are some 1,400 white and some 50 black faculty members (26 male and 24 female). Three hundred women comprise less than 25 percent of the total faculty, 13 percent of faculty at the rank of full professor, 32 percent of associate professors, and 61 percent of assistant professors.[13] The most significant faculty recruitment program beyond affirmative action compliance is a hiring program instituted in the 1980s that allocates funds to hire two "minority" faculty at the assistant or associate level and one senior (white?) woman each year. Since departments do not incur the cost of the faculty line, they have an incentive to "bring these folks in," as one staff member told me. However, misuse of this program has occurred, as suggested by the president's concern that "emphasis should be placed on hiring faculty for demonstrated needs in departments, not hiring minorities to increase resources for a department." A staff member in the Office of Affirmative Action explained that her office's "lack of resources" renders it unable to work with departments for recruitment, monitor searches effectively, "prepare departments for the idea of having a woman or a black, . . . or to see that even if the person's research may not be in your stuff, it's really good." In addition, faculty in two professional schools explained that external exigencies, specifically accreditation concerns, had been the impetus for attention to hiring practices and departmental curriculum review. In fact, Carol was hired as the first African-American faculty member in the School of Journalism under this program, which she described as poorly implemented by a department pressured by accreditation concerns yet unprepared procedurally and psychically to recruit "diverse" faculty.

As becomes clear in Carol's case, little attention is given to the fact that simply adding minorities to departments is unlikely to alter their status without changing power relations.[14] Only one staff member complained of the decontextualized additive model: "We think that if we just got twenty-four more black faculty, that would bring our percents, and that would be fine. And that doesn't do it. . . . You've got to do something to make them feel a part of it, to influence decisions, to influence the culture of the campus." The commodification of persons of color gives them "place but not importance."[15] In fact, place can neutralize the meanings of representation in the larger social space, for it is symptomatic of a pervasive pattern of thinking that the university should be "realistic" in its hiring expectations, since Oasis is such a white community. This stance creates a particular dilemma, as one faculty member remarked, "Intellectual culture can say on one hand, 'Well we're doing everything we can to hire as many black people as we can because we understand that this is a racist society,' but then on the other hand, 'but they don't want to come here. You know, we can't keep them, we try to get them here, but they don't like it here, there are just no black people here.'" A staff member described an unwillingness or inability to alter the space of Liberal U by embracing difference as an element of "excellence": "I think it's a combination of the prejudice of the university but also the superiority of the university, that they're not good enough. So the claim would always be well they're not good enough academically."

In a system that does not consider the quality of human interactions and the underlying reasons for its homogeneity (or problematic heterogeneity), the addition of offices and programs relieves colleges and departments of responsibility for changes that would enable more than numerical representation, as a staff member remarked: "We have this attitude that we aren't racist, we're integrated, we accept anybody, we have all these centers and diversity offices and we're just fine. And yet when you look at the representation of people, particularly groups of color, they're not here." A director of a multicultural organization described administrative attitudes:

> If we have [an office], we must be doing okay with issues of diversity. But institutionally, I think the institution welcomed the office. Now they don't always pay a great deal of attention to us and they don't give us adequate funding to do what we need to do, but it looks good. . . . We find that the Institution, capital I, sometimes expects us to deal with all of those problems. . . . So we've kind of had to fight this notion that once we had the office in place, we can shift everything to them and we can wash our hands of it.

The creation of places stands in for excellent efforts at diversity.

The proliferation of discourses and offices illustrates a vexing problem at Liberal U. In the national context of equity and access, the university seeks to make itself available to "all." Yet, the university space is understood as singular, reified as excellent, meritocratic, and democratic. Policy does not encourage the pluralization of its space, but seeks to create places for those not internal to the space. A constituency logic constructs specific groups as presenting specific problems—and situates these problems (and solutions) in discrete locations. In this context, the representation of African-American students and faculty becomes a central concern; Latinos, Native Americans, and gay men and lesbians, however, do not. The location of women faculty at senior rather than junior levels becomes an institutional problem. However, the conditions of female faculty placed in junior ranks, those who could come to occupy senior positions, are not attended to. The containment of problems and solutions in these places may allow Liberal U to maintain the integrity and singularity of its space. Or does it? As I explained in chapter 1, I am interested in how individuals and groups who would be put into place use their places to disrupt the logic of the institutional space. A helpful example of the play of place and spaces—one that contextualizes the social discourses within which Julie, Carol, and Olivia enact their academic work—is the entry of gay men and lesbians, a newly vocal group to be served, into this liberal system of representation and access. By adopting tactics of identity politics, the group put to use the constituency logic of the university, which allowed for talk of serving its needs. At the same time, the problems gays and lesbians were seen as bringing to the campus were articulated through the prism of diversity discourses, which created a specific place, literally and figuratively, for them.

CENTERING GAYS AND LESBIANS

Everybody knows it's [lesbianism] there, but it doesn't really have a representation in some respects.

—Carol

This is a WASP university, and they don't talk about these things. Meanwhile, everybody knows that there are lesbians, and a lot of them. This is not a small category.

—Olivia

It's a campus that talks about these things.

—Another faculty member

Despite Olivia and Carol's statements to the contrary, Liberal U could indeed be characterized "as a campus that talks about these things." Student activism and external social pressures have caused "these things" to surface increasingly in official and unofficial conversations. Yet there is an incoherence in the talk that fluctuates between acknowledgment and disacknowledgment, as Olivia described: "Everybody knows that all these feminists are in fact lesbians, but no one's going to say it, which is real interesting, when the manifest and the latent are together—the manifest being the one that's uncertain already and the latent the one that's actually sure they're there—it creates this kind of bizarre sort of, it allows the university to sort of recognize and ignore at the same time a phenomenon. This place is rife with them."

Until the formation of an activist group several years ago, gay and lesbian organizing at Liberal U had been, if not submerged, then "behind the scenes." While some undergraduate and graduate students are "out" on campus, few gay and lesbian faculty are open about their sexuality. Despite incidents of harassment, faculty and students consistently explained that homophobia was subtle. One faculty member explained, "With faculty, it's still the same don't talk about it and it's okay kind of stuff. But I don't think anybody's actively harassing. I don't think it fits their image of being liberal. We're open-minded individuals here." Despite an environment in which "don't ask-don't tell" relegates sexuality to private domains, pockets of activism have contributed to such changes as the inclusion of sexual orientation in the university's nondiscrimination clause several years ago. Actually, it was added gradually, first in student handbooks, then in faculty handbooks, and finally in hiring policies. Domestic partnership benefits, however, have yet to gain acceptance. Although the Faculty Council passed the proposal, the Board of Trustees tabled it, citing economic viability and problematic proof of partnership, thus constructing same-sex relationships as exceptions to the rule (special privileges) and as unverifiable.[16]

Kitzinger has argued that policies are psychically comforting to lesbian faculty: "Few academic institutions have written policies about combating heterosexism; in the absence of any such explicit statements the onus for discovering whether one will be accepted or not lies with the individual lesbian."[17] On the contrary, what is institutionally codified is not isomorphic with social and collegial campus relations. Because legal statements and personal judgments exist in separate spheres in liberalism, the onus may stay with the "individual lesbian." In fact, Olivia, Carol, and Julie's responses to my questions about the meanings of these policies did not indicate a sense of "acceptance." Olivia explained: "There's no federal law that you can sue under for job discrimination if you're gay. But if the university has a policy of nondiscrimination, that gives you a leg to stand on. It's symbolic, it works. So it has meaning in tenure, it has meaning in promotion, it has meaning in all of this stuff. They can't fuck you over. Even if they do, you've got a way to go." Julie expressed utter disinterest: "I don't even know anything about it. . . . I know they were talking about domestic partnership a couple of years ago, and it got all the way up to the Trustees. I find all these things mildly interesting, but I'm really not interested in them." Carol responded with an analysis of Liberal U's institutional need for the policy:

> They have some symbolic meaning for me. And I think that those things are important in telling me that the problem of lesbian and gay discrimination is taken seriously here. I think that most of those responses are sort of token responses and not really substantive responses. I think this university in general is very good at constructing messages that are, for lack of a better term, sort of politically correct without really getting at the roots of most of the problems. . . . The uni-

versity is smart enough as an institution, and the leadership is smart enough to know that in the world of academia, it's very important to make those symbolic gestures. In terms of the national reputation of the school, in terms of being able to recruit faculty, staff, and students, and all those kinds of things. It means that they're not completely clueless, it means that the school subscribes to basic sort of liberal values.

Carol's framing of official recognition of gay men and lesbians as responsive symbolic gestures that are increasingly necessary in the context of internal and external pressures is in many ways consonant with my analysis of the opening of a support office for gay and lesbian students a year prior to my research. I offer an in-depth analysis of this event as a way of inquiring into the limitations and possibilities of the uses of identity in the interplay of place and space.

Because of the polemics around the office's creation and its galvanization of a number of communities, talk of homosexuality predominated in the student and local newspapers for several months. The activities surrounding its inception dramatize the intersections of gay and lesbian identity politics, campus diversity discourses, and liberal democratic educational policy and practice. The propaganda created by the multiple "sides" claiming stakes in the debate and the events that occurred reveal the operations of what Eve Sedgwick has identified as minoritarian and majoritarian discourses around (homo)sexuality. As she describes these contradictory yet simultaneously circulating sets of beliefs, the minoritizing view holds "that there is a distinct population of persons who 'really are' gay" and that homosexuality is "an issue of active importance primarily for a small, distinct, relatively fixed homosexual minority."[18] The universalizing, or majoritarian, view maintains "that sexual desire is an unpredictably powerful solvent of stable identities" (85), and thus homosexuality is "an issue of continuing, determinative importance in the lives of people across the spectrum of sexualities" (1). These incoherent stances intersect with rhetorics of identity politics, minority rights, and diversity to produce multiple effects. I begin with a chronicle of the events leading to the campuswide controversy.

After staff documented numerous incidents of gay and lesbian harassment in the late 1980s, Liberal U formed a task force that eventually recommended an office for educational and support services. The proposal was approved in the spring of 1994. After the administration announced that the office would be allocated $50,000 a year, letters from the local constituency and from within the university reached the administration protesting this use of university (public) money. In newspaper interviews, administrators described the letters as arguing that the center was intended for a special interest group and would be a social club (recruitment center) that promoted a "homosexual lifestyle." Basing its rhetorical stance on equity issues of creating a safe learning environment for all students through support and education, the administration pointed to the reports of gay harassment to defend the office. Thus, the polemic began around three discursive strands: (1) a liberal rights discourse suggesting that a minority population was not receiving educational equity; (2) an unwitting invocation of majoritarian discourse that recognized the instability of sexuality and implicitly denaturalized heterosexuality through the fear that homosexuality can be promoted; (3) a minoritarian discourse of gays and lesbians as victims in need of institutional support and a general public in need of education about a discrete population.

When the following academic year began, a state representative entered the fray, combining morality, money, and willful ignorance in an argument that the university was promoting an immoral, private lifestyle by publicly recognizing homosexuality. The legislator threatened to hold the university's budget hostage in the next legislative session if the office were funded. Student and local papers printed articles, editorials, and letters to the editor, as protests began and events unfolded. Gay and lesbian student groups formed a coalition, mounted protests, undertook letter writing campaigns, and met with the legislator and administration.[19] Concurrently, but with more than the usual fanfare, the "traditional" gay and lesbian fall events at the university took place: a kiss-in (complete with two front-page newspaper photos) and a rally for National Coming Out Day. To counter these events, a group held a "Straight Pride Week," during which its members staged a hug-in, wore T-shirts that said "Damn Straight," and held a "debate" over the existence of the gay and lesbian office. Finally, the university announced that the office would be funded privately by an anonymous donor, thus leaving intact the goal of having the office while escaping budgetary threats. The ability of a single legislator, external to Liberal U (from a different district, in fact) yet representing the university's constituencies, to shape the administration's actions offers an example of constraints on Liberal U to respond to social changes. Students' responses also constitute part of the process of change, in this case a proliferation of campus talk and mobilization. Although groups continued to protest the delegitimation implicit in the change of funding, with the office's existence assured, interest waned and protests slowed.

The stances and tactics marshalled in favor of the office reveal discourses that circulated throughout the events. The arguments posed by gays and lesbians, their supporters, and the administration, combined three elements.[20] First, identity politics was employed to argue that gay men and lesbians are a preconstituted minority group that pays taxes, is discriminated against, and merits its own office. In the logic of rights, this discourse argued that the administration had a responsibility to represent the needs of gay and lesbian students. In addition, liberalism was invoked to defend the separation of "private" judgments of groups and individuals from the domain of public affairs.[21] "*You are not regarding a population that should be your constituency.*" "*As a public university, we both lead and respond to concerns expressed throughout the state. Sometimes our multiple constituencies come into conflict.*" "*Liberal U is a secular institution. The goal of the University is not to make moral judgments, but to educate.*" Second, the pathology model of gay and lesbian needs attributable to harassment was expanded as a justificatory rationale, displacing the political implications in the office's creation. In this defensive posture, support and counseling neutralized politics. "*Our energies should be focused on providing services to the gay and lesbian community. In the last four years, the incidence of harassment against gays, lesbians, and bisexuals more than doubled.*" "*The intent is to provide a safe learning environment and not to advocate a lifestyle or political agenda.*" "*The office is not a political statement, but a support service to a population of students in need.*" "*It's important for people to know this isn't going to be a hotbed of political activity.*" Third, identity politics, educational equity, and pathology combined to form an argument for the symbolic importance of institutional legitimation of the gay and lesbian population by funding the office. Thus, gay and lesbian identity politics became intertwined with rhetoric of the purposes of education and the role of the university in allowing equal access to learning, educating the general public, and validating a population. "*The first problem is that education can only take place in an environment in which everyone has free access to educational resources.*" "*The university's unwillingness to publicly fund the center sets up an official closet and suggests gays and lesbians are not of equal value.*" "*Our university appears on the brink of denying identity to a large number of students based on their sexuality.*" "*The university should provide support to the sexual minority community and increase awareness within the general population.*" Fourth, academia, separate from the "real" world, was figured as both responsible for leading and responding to social change. "*Tolerance and diversity are 'in' and the university will appear to be a backwater if it does not acknowledge gay men and lesbians by funding the office.*" "*It is unethical . . . for a university to extend the closet mentality of the general world to the campus.*"

Stances against the center operated within a similar discursive field with four identifiable strands. First, minoritarian discourses stated that public funds should be spent on services that concern all students rather than a small minority. Paradoxically, majoritarian discourse, in the form of fear of promotion and recruitment, intersected with this outrage at the legitimation of the minority. *"Tax money should not pay for the agendas of special interest groups." "Many of the majority feel alienated and ask themselves why there are no 'special' funds designated for them." "I believe it's going to be used as a tool to say, 'the state university promotes us, so that gives us an excuse to promote our lifestyle.'" "It's still promoting a certain lifestyle above all others." "It gives credence to an immoral lifestyle and may sway people on the fence about which way to go." "Why should the majority be forced to pay for an office they will never step foot in?"* Second, public acknowledgment and display of difference were said to increase hostility and homophobic acts, augment separatism, and limit possibilities of acceptance. *"If they're trying to get all this equality, why make such a big deal?" "They aren't going to be accepted if they insist on being different." "It's strange they're showing their emotions to prove something [at the kiss-in]." "The office will just further exclude homosexuals from the mainstream campus." "When people are going to do things that aren't mainstream American, they're going to be discriminated against more." "I don't have any problem with them personally, but the way they are going about it is disruptive to the campus. They should just talk to each other about it."* Third, ethnic models of identity politics were challenged in arguments that (dangerous) gay men and lesbians are not a legitimate minority because they choose homosexuality as well as whether to conceal or reveal it. *"Gays and lesbians can avoid discrimination if they want to, not like racial minorities." "They elect to make it public or private." "True minorities are different than special interest groups because they look different." "It is only a matter of time before the bathrooms of —— Hall will be used nonstop for activities that defy the original purposes of bathrooms." "There are health hazards associated with the gay lifestyle."* Fourth, diversity was said to take priority over academics as the university was bowing to political correctness pressures, creating an academic culture of victims and oppressed groups whose ideas matter without regard to their content. *"It's just part of an effort to bring liberal ideas to the Liberal U campus." "Once again Liberal U has sold its soul to diversity. Once again it has designated a disproportionate amount of student funds to promote the different lifestyle of a small student group. Once again, the university has attempted to assuage tensions by promoting the very differences that created them." "The office shows just how far the administration has been distracted from the true mission of the university: the education of great ideas. [They are] letting standards decline from the exposure of students to great ideas to the ideas of the latest group to achieve 'victim' or 'oppressed' status." "I don't need to be educated. I know what homosexuality is, that there are many homosexuals, and that it's wrong to hate someone because he or she is gay." "Support? What ever happened to emotional self-sufficiency?"*

Many of the arguments for and against the office revolved around issues of minority status—defining, recognizing, and legitimating a minority, and invoking or arguing against its rights. Although constituting themselves as an aggrieved group seeking educational equity is consonant with the constituency logic of Liberal U and ultimately won students the office, it played into negative discourses of sexuality and may very well have reinscribed them. Tenuous minority status, "special interest" hostilities, and the binary opposition of equality/difference remain unchallenged. On the other hand, the upheaval did have the effect of chipping away at institutionalized ignorance. As Michael Warner has observed, "Because being queer necessarily involves and is defined by a drama of acknowledgment, a theater of knowledge and publicization, the institutions that transmit and certify knowledge take on special importance."[22] At Liberal U, gay and lesbian presence was certified on the institutional stage; gay and lesbian identity received quasi-legitimation in the institutional public sphere through private money. But precisely what is acknowledged, where it is acknowledged, is an identity, *from* which differences are presumed to emanate. In other words, identity is thought to precede difference rather than the other way around. Acknowledgment of gay men and lesbians at Liberal U is less acknowledgment of the construction of queerness or of the effects of institutionalized heterosexism and homophobia than acknowledgment of individualized problems emanating from a preexisting homosexual identity. Furthermore, the negative differences thought to follow from this identity are embodied in the existence of the office, which accommodates through counseling the special problems of this group. Difference as produced in relations of power is displaced by a liberal conception of difference as a surface-level problem.[23] The role of public/private and knowledge/ignorance thus shifted only slightly, in the form of talk of equity, personal support, and education.

There are some interesting points of comparison between the Black Cultural Center and the Gay and Lesbian Office. Both are meant to accommodate a specific population with specific needs by offering a library and a communal space. The Black Cultural Center is justified by the need to recruit and retain a population the administration purports to value and to which it wishes to extend democratic access. The Gay and Lesbian Office, on the other hand, is justified by the need for individualized counseling, support, and education for purposes of educational equity. The needs, or deficits, in the two populations differ: blacks need academic help; gays need personal help.[24] Although representational politics demands that the institution address the needs of groups, the form that recognition takes is limited by equating identity with place. The fixity of identities rather than their construction through relations of difference is symbolized in the fixity of the places that represent them and serve their needs. I do not wish to minimize the importance of either location as a resource, but to point to the strategies of space in maintaining institutional order.

The values embraced in supporting the office reveal its distance from activism and academics and its focus on individuals. The function of the office is, as the director told me, "a space to hang out," a place to get personal support in coming out, and a source for information. In the newspaper, he explained, "We are not an office for activists. We are really an office for students who are struggling in a *personal* way with issues, students doing research and students who need information or referral. It is not as glamorous as organizing kiss-ins." Whether his disavowals were intended to justify the office's continued funding or earnest descriptions of his intentions is difficult to evaluate, though my conversation with him suggested the latter.

After the office had existed for a year, a number of faculty, staff, and students described it positively, saying that it was "a form of recognition that gay and lesbian students are important" and that the office conferred credibility through "a space, a sign." As a lesbian undergraduate explained, "It's a real source of pride. It legitimizes it for a lot of people. We're accepted by the university, and that's true for straight people and people coming out." Although the explicit function of the office, in keeping with the functions of other diversity offices at Liberal U, is less to promote institutional change than to support individuals, some members of the university understand it as representing and promising institutional transformation. Not all, however, agree that the office's importance lies in recognition and support. Meg, who organized protests in favor of the office, spoke of the importance of uncovering the workings of institutional homophobia:

> I'm not invested in the final product. I was invested in the struggle and making a lot of noise about the wheeling and dealing that was happening in terms of the ways that state governments and big business are involved in university affairs and the very pernicious kinds of—it's disturbing to me the discrepancy between what people think is going on and what's really going on. . . . And the kinds of interests that determine university policies in a number of ways, this was just a particularly ugly incarnation of it.

Her concerns lay in activists' failure to take into account external pressures on the administration. A faculty member remarked on the dangers of psychologizing gay and lesbian students:

I have mixed feelings about it. I'm glad if there's a student organization, I think that that's important. When I hear that they've got peer counseling over there and they're trying to get a library of coming out novels and stuff like that, I start to worry a little bit that they're adopting the medical model and understanding the job of the institution as nurturing somebody through a deep and dark and painful psychological experience. And I don't think that that's what the university's job is in relation to this cohort of students. And I think it's dangerous in the long run to pathologize gay and lesbian students. I think what they should be doing instead, and what I'm in favor of, is culture-building, the office sponsoring events that allow students to network, that allow students to explore questions of sexuality and cultural difference in a variety of ways, reading groups, drag shows, dances, bringing in gay and lesbian performers to campus, or speakers, or things that would be defined as more cultural. I think that that's another way of dealing actually with the difficulty of coming out. It's a way of providing forums and community for people in order for them to work through that, . . . you know, the cultural and intellectual thing, that's not like the medical model that says you need to be counseled because we don't want you to kill yourself sort of thing.

One year after the office's opening, gay and lesbian activism was less prevalent on campus. However, messages I received from its e-mail distribution list indicate that the office was enabling new forms of community-building at Liberal U and in Oasis. Notices ranged from announcements of movie series, speakers, dances, and picnics, to a new course in gay and lesbian studies, to meetings of new groups at a local coffeehouse, and to local, state, and national political news, rallies, and conferences. In addition, several students spoke to me of groups they had formed or were planning to form that would meet in the office's space. These groups went beyond support and coming out to consider the political implications of queer sexualities, to advocate for gay and lesbian studies courses, and to explore the intersections of race and sexuality. There were thus signs that the office may be put to new uses as a resource for social, cultural, academic, and political networking beyond its institutionally sanctioned purposes.

Given Liberal U's institutionalization of diversity, the constitution of a visible gay and lesbian group made equitable educational access imperative. By the logic of identity politics, an institutional shift occurred at Liberal U. In his ethnographic study of gay males at one campus Rhoads suggests that students' creation of a group identity "enabled them to enter their agenda into the political terrain of the University."[25] Although Rhoads cautions against essentialism, he attributes changes in policy to the students' intertwined uses of politics, visibility, and education in the context of a positive queer identity. While the changes at Liberal U resemble those Rhoads identifies, and were also made possible by identity politics, those changes are limited in a system that circumscribes forms and locations of recognition and that is predicated on granting (and taking away) services and rights to narrowly defined groups. It may be more helpful to consider the recognition and resources won through group identity as just one aspect of ongoing negotiation that may enable the expansion of new practices. Codification in social or academic spheres can function as placement, containment, or a Foucauldian disciplining—and is not an end in itself. Policies and offices, however significant, should be understood less as final products of change and more as vehicles for ongoing change within liberalism, as offering resources open to new interpretations. They are elements of space that allow for tactical appropriation.

Thus far, I have depicted the curious relations of Liberal U to Oasis and the surrounding wilderness and the rather fraught nature of relations of difference in town, on campus, and between the campus and what surrounds it. While communities have been naturalized on the basis of identities, their deployment in the institutional space has made room for a degree of change, which carries both the dangers that inhere in the disciplining of specified identities and the possibilities that are created when something new enters a space. If what I have represented could be described as the "social," it is not far from the "academic," but intertwined with it. I would like to turn specifically to Liberal U's mission, its presentation of its goals as an academic institution, and to read them in light, first, of the troubling nature of difference at Liberal U, and, second, of their implications for the work of faculty. Because statements of institutional mission address themselves both to constituencies and to those charged with carrying out the university's goals, I look closely at assumptions underlying Liberal U's most recent strategic plan, which outlines initiatives for the 1990s. I consider both how policy reveals the ways the university must account for itself to its public and how campus discourses embody and contradict those goals.

A tension created by the disjunctures among the state, town, and university and the paradox of Liberal U's defining itself against its constituencies lies in legislative and budgetary constraints on the university: Liberal U must define its mission with an eye to the public's responses to its purposes and methods.[26] In fact, the administration has been succumbing to what Joan Scott describes as the "rhetoric of crisis in higher education,"[27] allowing public dissatisfaction to dictate much of its policy talk. Nationally, partisan attacks that decry politicized university curricula and admissions procedures have combined with nonpartisan critiques that proclaim the failure of universities to educate and credential, creating "a climate in which universities are vulnerable and in which public resistance to [funding] cuts is almost non-existent."[28] Although the state legislature has granted funding increases to Liberal U throughout the 1990s, they have been more modest than the university has requested. In this context, the administration seeks credibility by defining the university's purposes in terms of individual and economic development. It has appropriated the language and practices of business and industry in projecting an image defined by accountability, efficiency, and productivity: input, output, and excellence form the basis of the university's public justification of self. Symptomatic of the rising "managerial culture"[29] that must control and market its products in a culture of excellence, accountability represents learning, research, teaching, and service in tangible, measurable forms.[30]

David Trend has remarked that administrative documents "never assert a virtual authority. Their meanings are constructed in communicative exchange, so they are always open to subversion or revision."[31] This exchange, in which neither policies nor their enactment are products, but processes, offers an understanding of how diversity and academic and social life are defined and redefined in practice, and what interventions those definitions allow. Individual and collective understandings of the goals of the university and of what constitutes knowledge are in interplay with policy, social contexts, disciplines, and departments to construct the meanings of academic practices.[32] The elaboration of the university's mission and social practices that reconstruct it leads to my exploration of the locations Julie, Carol, and Olivia occupy in the social and institutional space of Liberal U. Each woman's pedagogy, research, and departmental relations can be understood as an example of the dilemmas the university presents and the uses to which it may be put, particularly as their practices are consonant with some norms and outside others.

CENTERING LIBERAL U:
"THE CIRCLES IN WHICH WE MOVE"

> As we strive to create a new idea of the public university, the circles in which we move expand in size and complexity. But always at the center of these many circles, firmly rooted in honorable traditions and civilizing activities, remains the campus.
> —Closing sentences of Liberal U's strategic plan

Spatial metaphors abound in official and unofficial descriptions of Liberal U, its relations to what is external, and relations internal to its space. Its placement as the central, civilizing circle locates it as a disciplinary apparatus of normalization and as the essential site of truth.[33]

The circle, as in Foucault's analysis of the Panopticon, is a mechanism of visualizing and spatializing strategies that orders and distributes individuals through the creation of proper places to be incorporated into its space.[34] Consonant with the timelessness of spatialization, Liberal U does not leave readers of its strategic plan altogether clear about what is "new" in its idea of a public university. The document begins by invoking thirteenth-century European models of the university and the transmission of knowledge in its attempt to resolve a duality of excellence and access in the university's role as a public research institution. As a *research* institution, the university "produces the next generation of society's elite." It is committed to the preservation of past knowledge and the creation of new knowledge in order to serve the state and the nation. As a *public* institution, the university "focuses on mobility from the bottom of the socioeconomic ladder to the top as a central part of its reason for being." Its public mission conflates democracy and economics: "Education . . . is and always has been the engine of economic mobility in our society; it remains the foundation of democracy." The university figures itself as an equalizing force in society, "open[ing] paths from every corner of the state . . . to the highest and best things which man can achieve." The wilderness may enter the circle of civilization.

Liberal U's mission is predicated on what Torres describes as a "liberal view [that] suggests that the state is the collective creation of its members, providing a set of common social goods."[35] The knowledge produced at Liberal U, for example, is defined in terms of both the general public interest and individual economic interests. The goal of educating students, "not solely to certify them for professional employment, but to leave them with a sense of ethical and social vision, a love of learning, and a complex, nimble intellect," reflects what Torres defines as three principal functions of liberal education: "cognitive and moral socialization, skills training, and certification" (277), or what could more crudely be described as providing academic, social, and economic goods to constituents. Multiple centers of culture, reason, and excellence define the university's allegiances to the economics of the nation-state and the "best" of civilization.

CONFESSING SINS: THE WORK OF FACULTY

In a newspaper interview, the dean of the College of Arts and Sciences described a sign in his office: "Research is to teaching as sin is to confession: without the one, you have nothing to talk about in the other." Without placing inordinate emphasis on one mention of university kitsch, I cannot resist commenting on the analogy the Dean chooses to share with members of the university: research is an indulgence, until absolved in and through the act of talking about it. To confess one's research, in a quasi-Foucauldian[36] framework, suggests the promise of a truth to be imparted to one's audience. This is not a truth of the self that is revealed, but a truth in knowledge itself, stated in the sacred sphere of the classroom. In this telling of truth, faculty speak and students listen: talk (teaching) and truth are born of prior acts of inquiry. Yet the audience (the consumer?) has the power to elicit the confession (knowledge? information?) and confirm its worth. However, faculty work at Liberal U is more than an indulgent finding and telling of truth to consumers. How does the university construct faculty roles in research, teaching, and service?

The university is "at once a conservator of past knowledge" and an "incubator for creativity and innovation" as it produces knowledge that advances individuals and the state that it represents. Thus, it is not only students who confirm the worth of knowledge. Research at Liberal U "involves the acquisition of new knowledge and new awareness," a formulation that suggests that knowledge and awareness are things independent of knowers.[37] Basic research, "focused on discovering the rules which govern nature and human behavior," and applied research "applied to the solution of current problems," are emphasized in policy. Constructing a teleological sequence of research, from basic to developmental to applied, culminating in "technological productivity," the university explains that "any reduction of the early steps in this sequence will hamper the economic progress of the state and nation." In policy, knowledge becomes an instrumental commodity to be safeguarded, passed on, acquired, or discovered. Ignored is the possibility that not all research seeks to discover universal rules, that research may seek to interpret the particular, or that the questions asked in research do not have a direct utilitarian aim, but may serve purposes that cannot be known in advance. As Derrida has demonstrated, because their uses are constantly deferred, basic and applied research are increasingly indistinguishable.[38]

Knowledge in the curriculum is organized by subject areas "which, though constantly changing, are delineated by custom, necessity, and tradition." Whose customs, necessities, and traditions remains unclear.[39] This appeal to the organization of knowledge as customary obscures the political and social nature of knowledge and disciplinary formations. Although change is acknowledged, a center holds. For example, revealing what knowledge is of value, the strategic plan states that Liberal U "dedicates itself strongly to basic instruction in the arts and sciences as the foundation of undergraduate education" at the same time that it "is committed to the maintenance of quality academic degree and nonde-gree programs that focus on the cultures of ethnic and racial minorities and other groups that have experienced disadvantage and discrimina-tion." Tradition defines a basic "core" and necessity (perhaps the mul-ticultural imperative) defines a periphery added on to the core, placed as a supplement to what is central.[40]

In this system, education should enable students "to develop the attitudes and skills necessary to assume their places as responsible citi-zens in an increasingly complex world." Faculty should "teach [stu-dents] to open their minds to new ideas, to analyze complex issues, to think critically and creatively and to communicate effectively with their fellow citizens." Liberal U's citizenship model of education reveals intriguing slippages that dramatize the simultaneity of reason, culture, and excellence as the university seeks to produce autonomous subjects, civilize students into American culture, and provide excellent skills for workers in the global information economy. In one moment, students are mobile, climbing a socioeconomic ladder; in another moment, they are molded and formed to have the attitudes and skills that enable them to take their places in society. On one hand, the university invokes Enlightenment narratives of emancipation through education and the creation of autonomous subjects that will result in progress through rea-son, culture, and communication. On the other hand, it draws on what Readings defines as "a technocratic mode of training," in which auton-omy is accorded to content "and the autonomy the student gains is the freedom to occupy a preconstituted place in the system" (157). The uni-versity's social and ideological mission—that of producing national citi-zen-subjects—is confused with its economic mission—that of producing workers for the transnational economy.[41]

Despite the connection between research and teaching that the administration would like to highlight, students perceive faculty research to be separate from their experiences at Liberal U. Symptomatic of public skepticism of higher education, student commentators in the campus newspaper complain that faculty are aloof, detached, and inac-cessible. One editorial protested that professors' research interests are arcane, removed from what undergraduates "can relate to," and that faculty make little effort to make their thinking accessible to "the regu-lar, average undergraduate." Although students complain that instruc-tors are detached from them, faculty are not properly detached from the ideas they present in classrooms. One editorial commented that by teaching their opinions rather than a range of perspectives, faculty "rob students of a complete education." Citing Liberal U's Code of Academic Ethics, that "a scholar recognizes a primary responsibility to seek and state the truth without bias," the student argued that "one of the greatest disservices an instructor can administer to an undergraduate student is to ignore his or her role as objective teacher." Letters to the editor frequently claim that faculty's opinions are left unchallenged, particularly in "classes with controversial themes such as race, gender, and political ideology." Thus, the truth and knowledge to be imparted are marred by personal, idiosyncratic inflection and interpretation, a critique that finds support in policy.

Liberal U's strategic plan divides its discussion of service into "economic" and "social development," with the former receiving more attention. Consonant with its status as a highly ranked research institution, faculty are to maintain "a visible, active presence in national and international university activities, associations, and consortia." Faculty prestige brings esteem, graduate students, and continuing financial support to the university. Service "involves the application of faculty expertise that can benefit society" and is "an essential element of faculty development . . . which often generates new ideas for teaching and research." Faculty are "to take more active roles as advocates for the state's economic growth" through partnerships, advisory roles, and sharing their skills with industry, business, the region, and the state. Service is cycled back into the teaching-research missions of the university (and the need to demonstrate utility to the public), thus having an instrumental purpose that belies its altruistic rationale. Service as social development pertains to the education of "the whole student through a tightly interwoven fabric of both classroom and extracurricular experiences." The document mentions such things as recruitment, retention, student involvement in campus life, advising, campus safety, and encouraging interactions among diverse groups. While activities for economic development are external, social development is internal to campus life. An interesting manifestation of this dichotomy lies in the placement of a statement that "discrimination on the basis of race, gender, age, sexual orientation, nationality or any other such arbitrary criteria will not be tolerated on the Liberal U campus" in the section on social development. The elision of discrimination from the realm of economic development suggests a policy logic in which "discrimination" is unrelated to material and economic concerns, relegated instead to the social, interpersonal.

What do these statements suggest about the work of faculty? The organic relationships Liberal U would depict among research, teaching, and service are unidirectional. Service is depicted as feeding into teaching and research; research feeds into teaching. Instruction as the transmission of knowledge and development of critical thought suggests that research is to be *brought* into the classroom in the form of knowledge to be imparted or skills to be cultivated. Faculty do not participate in classroom inquiry but transmit, or confess, knowledge to students. However, beyond the bureaucratic tone of consensus created by policies lie alternative understandings of the university's purposes. As I turn to Julie's, Olivia's, and Carol's enactments of intellectual in academic practice, I underscore the disjunctures between discourses of objectivity and the rhetoric of valuing diversity, the unstable nature of subject areas, and the unpredictable nature of pedagogy. I ask, what forms do the transmission of knowledge, the opening of minds, and the development of critical thinking take on in classrooms? What effects do their understandings of subject areas have on teaching, disciplinary organization, and research? How do they understand their relationships to the questions they pursue in their research? What meanings does service take on? Intellectual work, as they pursue it, is not bound by disciplinary organization or the tangible functional aims suggested in policy. Their teaching, research, and relations with colleagues, however, are lived within the space Liberal U would construct for faculty work. What happens in their specific places is a reinterpretation of that space. For example, their research, while appropriate to the university's quest for national visibility and resources, runs counter to norms that invoke the disinterested pursuit of truth. Although mediated by university policy, it is in social and academic departmental relations that the value of their scholarship is negotiated. Similarly, while their pedagogies draw on the cultivation of skills, reason, and culture, they confuse these goals in the specificities of their commitments. Discourses of objectivity play a part in constructing their pedagogies, particularly as problems of diversity and perspective intersect with social and institutional understandings of faculty work such that feminist, lesbian, and black create particular dilemmas.

The Specter of Feminist Perspective

Because the institution is indeed "liberal," as faculty members were quick to point out, blatant misogyny is infrequent; discrimination is subtle. One faculty member explained: "There's a self-consciousness in current discourse that would make it very difficult for faculty to just go blunderbussing around saying really stupid sexist, racist things, though this doesn't stop some people from doing it. It's more difficult. But what's interesting is the difference between the talk and the practice." In fact, gender concerns surface frequently among female faculty, who describe the "climate" as "male," the persistence of salary inequities despite "progress," and the paucity of women in key decision-making positions. The assistant director of women's affairs explained, "you can find a few women who are chairs or deans, but that is still a climate issue, that we're not finding them in the upper chairs, you'll find them in middle management. You have to look at the assistant or associate dean level." According to her, female faculty grapple with "being accepted within your department, the male-isms that exist within your department. . . . The climate is still feeling uncomfortable and unwanted, not being taken care of." An associate dean described women as "trying to get a fair shake" amidst these "subtle" sexist practices.[42]

What comes less subtly to the fore are ambivalent constructions of feminist research and teaching. Under excellence, feminism is at once a marketable commodity—a "must" for a respectable research institution—as well as a potential contaminant of disciplinary work. Women consistently identified concerns about departmental responses to work that might be perceived as feminist: "If you're doing research on women, if you're doing feminist research, that's not respected. I've heard people's comments, 'Well that's feminist stuff, we can't consider that in your tenure.'" A woman who has served as director of Women's Studies and is jointly appointed in another department explained, "In most departments there are still not very many women, there are even fewer feminists. Any lesbian who is also a feminist would have to be extraordinarily cautious before she got tenure." She offered her own difficulties with tenure as an example of the potential consequences of engaging in teaching and research pertaining to gender and sexuality:

> I get away with it because I'm heterosexual. They know I teach about all kinds of sexuality and they know that I do these kinds of postmodernish courses and I do all kinds of stuff about transsexuals and lesbians and teach lesbian feminist theory and so on, but somehow I get away with it, . . . it kind of overcomes it. But when I came up for tenure there was a big battle over the kinds of research and teaching I do. I got tenure. They didn't want to count my Women's Studies teaching, they didn't want to count graduate students who had worked with me in Women's Studies. . . . The way they said it, it wasn't political science, so they weren't going to count it for political science, even though my appointment started out being a joint appointment and then it switched to being full-time political science with the understanding I would continue doing women and gender issues. But anything they wanted to define as being outside the realm of political science, they, not they, that's not fair, a small proportion of senior faculty didn't want to count.

Several factors come into play to determine hostility to or acceptance of feminist work. For example, in the College of Arts and Sciences, "The dean recognizes that women's studies is a major field for publications, he thinks it's kind of cutting edge . . . and has made it clear to the tenure committee that doing women's studies research and teaching is fine." Administrators see women's studies as both a source of publication and "a source of enrollment, and additionally as a source of funding from women professionals who have graduated." Administrative support, however, is mediated by departmental factors. Disciplinary location along a continuum from empirical-analytic sciences to cultural studies affects the degree to which feminist scholars are actively sought or marginalized. Disciplines that have traditionally valorized objectivity have more propensity for resistance to feminist work, which is perceived as inherently subjective and antithetical to its methods and purposes. In addition, feminist gains have often been due to idiosyncratic factors, such as a department head who supports feminism or a nationally visible feminist in a department. Thus, despite an official, centralized message, feminism has established itself primarily in local contexts. Because feminism, though embodied in the location of Women's Studies, makes idiosyncratic appearances in new locations at Liberal U, I read it as something of a specter, a word that carries two definitions: "1. A visible incorporeal spirit, esp. one of a terrifying nature; ghost; phantom; apparition. 2. Some object or source of terror or dread: *the specter of disease.*"[43] A feminist perspective, and associated difficulties of homosexuality, radicalism, and interdisciplinarity, carries threats of unforeseeable contamination and contagion that must be contained. On the other hand, homosexuality is less visibly embodied in academic life at Liberal U and is curiously defined by the dynamics of knowledge and ignorance.

"That Lesbian Lens"

> Liberal U as a whole, like what I perceive Oasis to be, is very much of a kind of monogamous heterosexual, reproductive child-bearing community. White, very white, bourgeois, seriously bourgeois, so that its forms of sociality are all predicated on certain kinds of institutional structures.
> —Faculty member, speaking of faculty

> You really need to be a man, a married heterosexual man with children to make it, not to have certain questions asked at tenure time. And they're about personality, they're about being professional, about why you chose to do the work you did in terms of research, they're about why students like you, whole ranges of things that I think are part of this package of Midwestern liberal institution.
> —Faculty member

Despite the purported push to "diversify" faculty, Liberal U's norms for faculty behaviors are dominated by not-so-subtle ideals of the disembodied (white, male, heterosexual) professor. Although I was repeatedly told that there is a "large" number of gay and lesbian faculty at Liberal U, they did not constitute themselves as a visible presence, individually or collectively. A long-time staff member explained, "There's a perception of how safe is it, is it safe to be out on campus? People make it clear that even as tenured faculty, they are not certain how safe it is to be out. It's easier to be part of the hidden network." The dangers are intangible, due precisely to the subtlety of much homophobia on campus. One tangible concern faculty identified was "credibility with other faculty, students, administration." A woman who teaches courses that include diversity issues commented, "I've always thought it would kind of discount what I'm working on if I talked about it in a personal way." A faculty member's homosexuality can make him or her in-credible, not to be believed; a *perspective* that deauthorizes the speaker is attached to sexuality.

"Don't ask, don't tell" is connected to tacit expectations of who faculty are and what they do, playing itself out in definitions of acceptable or unacceptable behavior. One woman remarked, "This is a kind of homophobic campus, there's that there, I think you get some liberal-minded people who would say, 'Yeah, I don't mind working on the same faculty as [a lesbian], but gee, I hope she doesn't embarrass me in front of my friends.'" A faculty member described "this odd combination of conservative Midwestern and liberal at the same time. We're going to let you be what you want to be as long as you do it in a way that we find inoffensive."[44] The liberal ethos depends on gay and lesbian faculty members' collusion with structures of willful ignorance to maintain the private-public dichotomy necessary for the illusion of tolerance. Highlighting one's sexual orientation forces acknowledgment of the "open secret," which "may have nothing to do with the acquisition of new information"[45] but disrupts accepted mores. In this environment, those who are able or willing to conform to the unspoken rules of the open secret may be able to maintain successful careers, as described by the assistant director of Women's Affairs:

> The people that I know, this is going to sound real positive, and maybe it is, they seem to be able to slide under. They can do their job, they can do their work, they can get by. I think there's this sort of nonspoken, "don't tell me you're a lesbian and it's okay," you know, "and then I'm just going to look at you and actually what I'm going to look at is another white woman," because quite honestly I don't know women of color who are lesbians on our faculty. So I don't know how the color issue blends in there. But my impression has been that, "Okay, fine you're an excellent scholar, we really want you here, you're a lesbian, well let's just not talk about it."

Those who cannot "blend" by maintaining invisibility or silence due to their research and teaching, their appearance, or other reasons, are excluded from "sliding under," a term that reinscribes the power of willful ignorance and the open secret. It further suggests visual normalization: "I'm just going to look at you and actually what I'm going to look at is another white woman." Persons are understood in a single binary relation to the norm: lesbians who are not white do not exist.[46]

In this atmosphere of normalization and in-credibility, faculty across campus who are known as lesbian in their departments or colleges described a self-protective strategy of making their academic credentials unassailable. One woman in the social sciences said: "Ten years ago, it was just come in there, do your job, as people get to know you, you let them know things about you. They've already made their professional judgments about me. So my notion was that if I come in and announce this thing people will make judgments and then it'll be difficult to prove myself. . . . I wanted a compelling vita, so they had to vote for me to get tenure. So that's what I set out to do." When I asked a recently tenured woman in the humanities if she had had concerns about being active in lesbian studies, she responded:

> If they denied me tenure, I had a suit that was unassailable. I could sue them and win. That's the way I wanted it, and that's why I have been obsessed for years and overproductive and all those things. I mean, they could not have denied me tenure without being sued and me winning. That was my feeling about it, I thought whatever issues they had, they had to get over them, and they had to know that that would be the case. But I think that that's what you have to do. I personally think you have to try not to allow yourself to get into a situation where their homophobia can be justified, so that it's not a matter of thinking, "will they?" So that it's better, and I think that's just one of the things you have to know. That's about being a woman. . . . Everybody knows you have to have a book, so have a book. Whatever it is the institution says you have to have, you have it and you have more. And there's a particular burden. I think liberalism works in a certain way that people might applaud themselves when they can do the right thing and feel that they're doing it because you measure up to what their standards are and it has nothing to do with your color or your sexuality.

In contrast to the potential for "sexual-orientation blindness" among faculty, in the realm of teaching, faculty continue to exercise caution, as one woman explained:

> Faculty sort of hide in their shadows a little more, but I think with students they'll be much more blatant about "I don't like queers, I don't want them on my campus, I don't want money going to them, I don't want to have to live in the same residence hall, I don't want to have to

hear about gay literature or history in my classes, I shouldn't have to hear about that stuff." So I think students are much more honest about it. I think they're more honest about their restrictions and prejudices. I think faculty feel, not all of them, some of them certainly will be outspoken, but I think they feel given less privilege to openly comment on their prejudices or show their prejudices.

One woman described faculty perceptions that open identification as a lesbian has the potential to undermine one's pedagogy: "A lot of walls go up around the students, that you're constantly chipping at that barrier that they've put up in order to educate them. *It puts some kind of lens on them that everything you say gets distorted through that lesbian lens and they just can't see what you're talking about.* So I think it's a real dilemma. . . . I think most, the women I know on faculty just wouldn't bring it up, they would not come out in class." In this striking conflation of sensory modalities, a lens, typically for viewing, distorts what is said: students are unable to *see* what is *spoken.* Visibility can render voice incoherent. Foucault has commented, "The fact that a teacher is a homosexual can only have electrifying and intense effects on the students *to the extent that* the rest of society refuses to admit the existence of homosexuality."[47] Pedagogy operates in the context of the will to suppress public acknowledgment of homosexuality—"don't tell me about it and it's okay"—in order to maintain credibility.

While the conversations I was engaged in offer an amalgam of idiosyncratic reflections and experiences, they begin to point to the dynamics of knowledge and ignorance in constructing the academic practices of Julie, Carol, and Olivia. As I turn to their research and pedagogy, these homosexual and feminist specters haunt, in different ways, their work. Credibility and authority comprise a part of their choices (not) to announce their lesbianism in their classrooms. However, their choices are complicated by their subject matter and their political, intellectual, theoretical, and personal commitments. Each of the women, in her pedagogy and her collegial relations, works within and against expectations that might be attached to her as scholar or teacher due to perspectives she may be assumed to have, whether attached to her race, sexuality, or religion.

LOCATING KNOWLEDGES AND IDENTITIES

To speak of Liberal U as a singular space is impossible, for the contradictory discourses that comprise it do not constitute a seamless whole. Different from its surroundings, the university represents those surroundings in a constituency-based logic. The rhetoric constructed around its mission demonstrates that the university is caught between discourses of higher education as producing functional skills and knowledges, private goods in the individual consumer's interest, and public goods that benefit society and the economy. With the function of the university aligned with maximizing the production of knowledge, faculty become purveyors of skills and knowledge. This production of knowledge as private and public good becomes intertwined with the problem of Liberal U's representation of its constituency, for while Liberal U must provide goods to all it represents, becoming similar to what lies beyond it will dilute the value of those goods.

Liberal U pursues its efforts to offer equitable access and distribute knowledge and skills in the service of individuals and society without substantive regard for the contexts of those it would represent. Acknowledging the structures that determine persons' access to the university is not an easy task, for it admits difference into the fixity of space. Thus, singular categories of "diversity" come to form the basis of needs and responses from the institution. Diversity is placed, managed in a system Michael Warner calls corporate multiculturalism, "a pluralist affirmation of cultures, where cultures are conceived on a racial or ethnic model . . . in which irreconcilable demands are dealt with by giving every constituency its own course or, if necessary, program."[48] By such logic, African-American students and faculty members are sought by the administration, which employs rhetorics of perspective enrichment and democratic access. At the same time, they pose a potential danger to meritocracy, standards of excellence, and the unbiased pursuit of knowledge. Women faculty are needed for equitable representation, but pose threats to academic knowledge if they bring a feminist perspective. Because gay men and lesbians are not a group codified in many spheres, recruitment, retention, and the valuing of perspectives are nonissues. Instead, the results of gaining a semicodified status have been heightened talk of educational equity and of problems stemming from their identities, including psychology, disease, and the flaunting of immorality.

Both identity and knowledge at Liberal U are understood separately from the social, political, and institutional contexts in which they are produced. As set forth in policy, knowledge is objective, discovered in research and presented without bias in teaching, and is naturalized along self-evident disciplinary lines. In this way, the perspectives valued in the rhetoric of diversity are in direct conflict with the mission of Liberal U. Closely related to the fixing of knowledge in a proper place is the naturalization of identity as a preexisting category. As groups become constituted and acknowledged, identities carry specific meanings in relation to unquestioned norms and become construed as problems to be dealt with through centers and programs. While both identity and knowledge would be located in their proper places, there is a perpetual threat that they may become unruly, refuse to be put in place.

In moving from a discussion of Liberal U to the practices of the three women whose work embodies instances of the dilemmas posed by living in this setting, I focus on local renegotiations of the social and academic in the professional lives of Carol, Olivia, and Julie. I have organized the chapters thematically in order to place their understandings and practices side by side to some degree. Such organization at times makes for an uneven text, as the themes in their lives do not align neatly; it further makes for a recursive text, as certain strands in each woman's narrative are reconstructed in various domains. In the next chapter, I discuss the construction of Olivia's, Carol's, and Julie's pedagogical uses of existing norms relating to knowledge and identity as articulations of their intellectual lives, yet mediated by institutional and social structures. In chapter 4, I turn to their departmental positionings, which can be understood in terms of official policy and ideals for faculty work as well as official and unofficial recognitions of social identities that are specific to their departments, disciplines, and interpersonal relations. In the final chapter, I consider *lesbian* and *intellectual* as practices the women create, both as they relate to Liberal U and to prevailing oppositional logics, such as identity politics. Even as they draw on communities and identities, their habits of affiliation, their understandings and enactments of lesbian and intellectual, complicate attaching either construct to identity. Throughout all three chapters, I seek to understand how the women's self-identifications and commitments, social norms and knowledges, the (mis)recognition of others, and the contexts of Liberal U, their departments, and disciplines shape their practices and the tactics they employ to pursue their work. As I focus on what it means to live in academia for these three women, I do not seek to represent individual heroes. As Michel de Certeau explains, a study of practice is not a return to the individual, but a turn to the social: "a relation (always social) determines its terms, and not the reverse, and that each individual is a locus in which an incoherent (and often contradictory) plurality of such relational determinations interact."[49] Practices are responses to the space in which one finds oneself, and this space is never about any one thing or person.

CHAPTER 3

Displacing
Pedagogical Positionings

I begin with two scenes from the first day of class. The depictions offer representations of the tones with which Olivia and Julie began to present their relations to students and to encourage thought and engagement. The class meetings are, superficially, quite different, for in "Mystical Prayer and Western Spirituality" there is a focus on selves in relation to knowledge, whereas in "American Fiction" there seem to be not selves but subject positions that perform relations to knowledge. Unfortunately, because of overlapping class schedules and Carol's reticence, I did not attend her opening classes, and am unable to represent her initial presentation to her students.[1]

OPENING SCENES

Julie sits, not speaking or smiling, in a chair at the front of a classroom filled with rows of desks, handing students syllabi as they enter. One young man goes directly to a seat, gets a "Yo," turns around, and takes the syllabus she is holding out. Students read their syllabi in silence. Two students begin to whisper. Sixteen white students are in the room, twelve men and four women, mostly juniors and seniors. Julie closes the door, "Let's move into a kind of semicircle so we can all see each other." She returns to her chair. "I wanted to see what it would be like just to read Teresa of Avila, her most mature work, so I've sort of clustered things around her. I decided not to do a Great Books approach. A few of you e-mailed me, what did you think of the light readings I suggested?"[2] David says, "I liked them, they were on the level of everyday life." A few students nod. Julie continues, "*Virgin Time* is like a TV show, a woman looking for spirituality. The first book, *Way of a Pilgrim*, Zooey was reading that book in *Franny and Zooey*. / / They drink martinis at ten a.m. I know we can't relate to that, but that's what they do at Yale." She looks into students' faces and tells a bit of the pilgrim's journey, as though telling a story over dinner. Students listen, rapt. Julie describes the required readings, concluding, "I looked around for a definition of mysticism, but I found twenty-five, so I thought that we as a class could see if we could come up with one over time." She sits on the corner of a desk to speak of student reports, steps to the board to list texts and dates, then passes books around for students to select for class presentations. She describes each text, saying Julian of Norwich is a mystic she enjoys: "She's happier than most. She went to be a nun, then got sick, as we'll see happened to a lot of women."

"Do you have mechanical questions?" "Could you comment on the journal?" "I've never done that, but because we're not reading much and it's difficult, I thought you could write a bit to have a record. You don't have to write a lot or anything profound. We may find this too nuts and need to make changes. But I'd like to see it. The journal will be a diary of how the course acted on you and you on it. . . . I'm just trying to get you to keep personal notes on this class. I don't know if it'll work. We'll take a pulse on that. Maybe it'll work for some of you and not for others. I don't care what you do, but just some way you're really engaged with it."

Julie, in an interview: "*I sort of hate journals. But they kind of like it. I'm not all that into the journal stuff. That for me is more of a kind of disciplinary tool to get them to do a bit of reading every day. I guess I'd kind of like to see whether they think this makes sense, how many times they've read it, stuff like that. So I'm going to look at their journals, but I'm going to read a distillation of their journals. I don't need to read every little bit of every thing that they have to say. . . . I think it was an experiment. . . . I really frankly am not interested in reading them. I should be, and I will take them /up/ and so forth, but I don't care that much. Some people do, they're really into journals and a sort of personal approach and all that, but I'm really not.*"

She calls roll, careful to see what name students prefer and to check the pronunciation of last names. "While you look at the books, think of one interesting thing or significant thing about yourself to say to the class to remember you, or to remember that you don't like to talk about yourself. I don't like talking about myself very much either. A small class like this is going to work best if we know each other." Students choose books to present. A few jump at their choices; others take whatever. Julie helps several according to their majors or interests.

Rebecca, explaining her choice of the class: "*It said prayer and mysticism. I thought, well I don't know anything about mysticism, but it has a focus on Christianity so it doesn't do anything too weird for me. When I walked in I was hesitant, but she immediately warmed me up to it that first day, where she passed the books around and said which books would you like to have your outside project be on. And I was like, this is cool, she seems really responsive to the class.*"

"Let's do something else. This housekeeping stuff is—if we think about words like mysticism, contemplation, prayer, spirituality, what gets conjured up in your head? Take a couple of minutes—let me pick one. If you had to define prayer, how would you?"

STUDENT. Communicating with a higher power.

STUDENT. Relating your energy to a supreme power.

JULIE. Not communicate but relate?

BILL. Prayer is release, of your hopes and wishes.

JULIE. Is it verbal?

STUDENT. / /

JULIE. Sounds like prayer takes you out of chaos. Anyone want to argue or add to that?

DAWN. It's more communication, connection, listening.

DAVID. I relate to all of these, but prayer is a practice that allows for change. People work with their habits or with their thoughts—it's hard to say.

JULIE. When this resonates with your personal experience, it's hard to put into words.

She interjects with a question about mystics' talk of sex, "a man and woman, man and man, woman and woman, whatever, why do they use this metaphor to talk about union in mystical experience?" There is no visible verbal or nonverbal response to her inclusion of same-sex unions. Jim responds that it speaks of simplicity, human reduction. Julie: "Simple is a funny word to use, because it evokes simple-minded, and self-emptying and self-knowledge are a complicated process. Teresa of Avila's insight is that God is in the deepest center of the self."

"Is prayer something you do? What does it mean to pray for someone else, for example, someone who is dying of cancer? Does prayer change the gravitational force of the universe?" The question is asked rhetorically; no one answers. "Let me tell you why I'm teaching this. A year ago this summer I had cancer surgery. I'm a cancer survivor. You know, you look at death far off, when you recover yourself from that, you need to get into a less stressed mood. And university teaching is a process of constantly producing and being judged. And I read this book, Steven Levine, *Healing into Life and Death*, and I started to do his meditation and / /. One way to stay stress-free is to teach a course I'm interested in and want to talk through." Students listen. A man asks if she has read *Quantum Healing*. Julie and several students speak of learning to move heat around in the body. Julie returns to the class plan, "So who are these mystics, just some people who learned a few tricks to fool people?" She concludes, "For Thursday, if you have a particular book or a shtick or whatever you can bring to this, do. I'm going to talk about a book."[3]

Three months later, David, a Catholic, recalling his expectations: "*I knew if this class was going to be worth a shit, we were going to have to have some kind of a laid-back teacher. But this woman shocked me, I thought we'd have some Western sadhu with long hair and wrinkles on his face, meditating all the time, but we get this Catholic woman who just went through cancer treatment. But it really has changed her life, it makes her an expert in this field, because she has had to face her existential dilemma right then and there. And even though she's a Catholic and she doesn't understand a lot of the ascetic and mysterious things, it still is a very passionate class. There's an interest you can just feel in the class, a real want and need and desire for knowledge.*"

Twelve white graduate students, a nearly even mix of men and women, most of whom are in their twenties, are gathered around a seminar table. It is the first day of American Fiction, a class Olivia has dubbed "Performativity Paranoia." Olivia is not present. Each student is opening a large envelope with a sticker on it that bears the course number and the words "Do It Yourself Syllabus Kit." There are occasional laughs. "Cool." "No way." Quiet predominates as students sort through the contents of the envelopes, although several students speak in low voices at the far end of the table. Meg comes in and takes an envelope. "My, my, she is getting more creative." She sits, looks at its contents, picks up her envelope and bag, and leaves the room.

Meg, four weeks later: "*I sat in the hallway. Everyone in there was annoying the fuck out of me. I'm tired of graduate students not taking responsibility for their intellects, for their professional lives, for the classroom situations they're in. I'm so fucking tired of this constant deferral to authority that you hope people would have a more kind of critical relationship to at this point. There's just a slavish mentality. I mean even on the first day, I mean you saw it, you were in the room, I couldn't stand it. 'What do you think she wants us to do, what do you think she wants us to do?' . . . It's frustrating as a student who doesn't want to participate in that model and yet we all know the potential negative ramifications of upsetting that system too much, it can just come back in your face if you question that authority model too much.*"

Students have papers and sheets of stickers in front of them. Some mark things on their papers. A group at one end of the table, four females and a male, begins to work together. The male does most of the talking. "I've got it in this order: alternarrative, politics, desire, paranoia." A female responds, "Maybe you're supposed to arrange them like this." "No, politics has to come before desire." "I'm not really sure

what she wants." Rather than attempt consensus, they share their interpretations of the task at hand. The end of the table where Meg has left
a space, is quiet, working individually. After little more than half an
hour, students begin to talk. "I wonder if she has a microphone in the
room." "Think she's standing right outside the door?" "You're really
paranoid." Two students talk about what to do. "Do you think she's
coming?" "Is she up there?"

Robert, recalling class several months later: *"I realize that everybody is reading intention, they want to know why is she doing this, what
does she hope to accomplish by it, that sort of thing. I immediately realized, because I knew the class was about performativity, whatever that
is, that we were doing it, and I grinned to myself. We were putting the
class together within certain authorized limits, so there's that paradox,
you're in charge but you're sort of not in charge, and of course the
author is absent. . . . Part of me thought do I want to do this, why do it
at all? I finished, and pulled out a book, and somebody was like what
do we do with these now, and that was great, that was part of the point,
there is no authority that you can appeal to for intention here, so you do
it independently sort of, and then you ask for validation from somebody
else. Then it occurred to me, do I leave and assert authority or do I stay
in case she comes?"* He stayed.

The Envelope: Do It Yourself Syllabus Kit.   The envelope contained
five items. (1) A page titled "Syllabus" that listed class meeting dates.
The first date said "Intro"; the second, "La Jetée, Limited, Inc., Selec-
tions from Searle." The rest of the dates were blank. (2) A piece of
paper that listed Olivia's office hours, the course number, and required
texts.[4] (3) A paper titled "Instructions": "Construct a syllabus from the
elements included in this kit. Contents include: 1 partial syllabus. 1
instruction sheet. 1 blank syllabus form. 1 list of rules. 1 chart of paper
assignments. 1 set of paper assignment stickers. 1 set of reading assignment stickers." (4) A "Paper Assignment Chart": "Set the dates for the
following paper assignments by affixing the attached stickers to the
date you wish the paper to be due: 1 short (5 page) paper within first
four classes. 1 abstract within first 6 weeks. 1 proposal within first 8
weeks. 1 paper (10 pages) within 10 weeks. Final paper at end of
course. With the exception of the first paper, all writing assignments
may (should) work toward the final paper." (5) "Rules of the Game,"
ten rules:

1. The course is divided into four topics: Desire, Politics, Alternarrative, Paranoia (not necessarily in that order).
2. Works to be considered are not divided equally among sections.

3. "Theoretical" works are paired with literary works as follows:

Barthes, *Nightwood*   Freud, *White Noise*
Butler, *Lover*   Mellard, Bertens, Federman,
                                 New York Trilogy
O'Donell, *Crying of Lot 49*   Baudrillard, *The Assignment*
Lyotard, *Portrait of an Eye*   Lacan, *Lolita*
Artaud, *Naked Lunch*

4. Lyotard must precede *Picture Theory*.

5. Butler must precede *The Malady of Death*.

6. Barthes must precede Nabokov.

7. Desire must precede paranoia.

8. Desire includes Nabokov, Duras, Brossard; Politics includes Harris, Dürrenmatt; Alternarrative includes Barnes, Acker; Paranoia includes DeLillo, Burroughs, Auster.

9. Politics cannot be first.

10. Politics cannot be last.

Frank, six weeks later: "*It just had that stink of a GRE question, the logic section. Ambassador A can't sit next to Ambassador B but Ambassador C. . . . It seemed to me the point of that little exercise was to show how syllabi are performative, and it seems that could have been handled in a more straightforward manner that would have been more readily comprehensible. It was just a little too much like a kindergarten thing with little cardboard and that sort of thing. It seemed silly to me. I don't remember the discussion, I remember being annoyed that whole hour, because it seemed to me that the syllabus was set, given her guidelines, it was set.*"

Enter Olivia.   "Did you do it? Why didn't you declare it bullshit?" Meg follows her in. "I don't know everybody's names. We need performative rosters too. So let's see what you've come up with. What you make is what goes." Marsha tells her, "We have different ones."

OLIVIA. How do we rectify the differences, or should we all follow our own?

MARSHA. I'd like to discuss the books with others.

OLIVIA. So you took that seriously? Did you do it alone?

MEG. I was outside.

BILL. We sort of cooperated.

OLIVIA. You're good, you're trained. Okay, we've got alternarrative, politics, desire and paranoia. Paranoia should be first. You must be paranoid now.

Olivia suggests they vote. "How many people have Barnes first?" Five hands. "Acker?" Four hands. "Pynchon?" One hand. She writes the number of votes for each author on the board. "We'll talk about why you're all so far off, not from a standard but from each other."

OLIVIA. Why did you put Barnes first?

JIM. Because of your order.

OLIVIA. If you haven't read it, you can't know. It's a performative eroticism. It's superficial, that's why it's performative. Did you use a historical line?

TERESA. Who cares about history?

Olivia. That's my line. History doesn't work that way. Acker is the end of something. It could be instructional to put her at the beginning. Do you prefer the historical or would you like to twirl around it?

BILL. I assume you won't do Pynchon first.

OLIVIA. Pynchon is a performative postmodern text. We can use it, a canonized postmodern white male text first. We can do that.

MEG. I'd like a light load, just one text, when the papers are due.

OLIVIA. And [a literary theorist] is coming to speak on October 20. Should we do his stuff before he gets here? This is how we make a syllabus. Does it seem deeply intellectual with a theory? The logic is where do things fit, who's visiting?

JIM. I was looking for an intention.

OLIVIA. [big laugh] What do they say about the intentional fallacy?

ROBERT. Sounds paranoid.

OLIVIA. Who would like to challenge the linear model? Must we talk about the syllabus from day to day?

CHORUS OF VOICES. Yes.

OLIVIA. What do you have second? I'll assume this is not a linear trajectory but a dynamic inflectional, interflectional trajectory. There are limits to free exercise, we don't want the course to be nonsensical. Is there any theory that accounts for one of the groupings being better than the others? The idea of a syllabus is that you perform what you're studying.

ROBERT. A historical trajectory makes the most sense to us, but it's an arbitrary role of sensibility.

MEG. Are we trying to upset all preexisting systems?

ROBERT. We're within the rules that she has stated for us.

OLIVIA. Don't follow any of my rules except for papers and grades. If you throw out the rules, what would you be doing in relation to the classroom dynamic? I know you followed the rules, but if not. What if you reject the terms and categories? Alternarrative, that's stupid. Politics, what's that? Desire, that's too big.

MARSHA. We'd be performing an act of resistance or deviation.

OLIVIA. Performing a takeover of your intellectual future. That was an alternative.

MEG. If you're willing to pay the consequences.

OLIVIA. I'll grade this?

JIM. That's paranoid.

OLIVIA. You would shift the power relations between faculty and students at the seminar level. That would be good. How are you going to move from the level of student to faculty? Beat me up as long as you think about it.

MEG. We don't know enough to challenge you.

Olivia. What pedagogical principles can we apply here, go from the easiest to the hardest, as in the rules of the Western world? Or should we use a chronology, as in history as the answer to the present? Why are there foreign people here? This is a class in American.

TERESA. It questions the notion of boundaries.[5]

Olivia, in response to my query, "Talk to me about what went on": "*I had an absolutely fail-safe trick. It didn't matter what they did, no matter what they did would illustrate the point. If they tried to come up with a syllabus, then they essentially did a performative act, because they made their own syllabus. You can still talk about the intentional business and the fact that they were trying to read the text behind that text as a way of sort of backing themselves up. It wouldn't have mattered, had they gotten sort of rebellious or sort of changed things around, that would have made the point too. We still would have ended up with a syllabus and they would have seen the basic premise. Actually the point of it is to talk about power relations and performativity and to bring into issue the whole relation between the student and the teacher in the classroom.*"

IM/PERSONAL PEDAGOGIES

I have chosen these scenes as they begin to dramatize themes that recurred, with different valences, in Olivia's, Julie's, and Carol's classrooms and participants' reflections on processes of teaching and learning: the locations of authority, the meanings of knowledge, identity, experience, and, for lack of a better term, the role of "the personal." These two classrooms might be thought of as offering different qualities of experience, one "personalized" and another "intellectualized." Despite her initial gruffness, Julie's actions showed concern for her students, their potential interrelations, and relations to the material to be studied. Small gestures, such as her care with students' names, helping students identify books consonant with their interests, inviting them to speak (or not) of themselves, and asking them to bring something (flippantly called a shtick) to the next class, cumulatively set an inclusive tone that was not intrusive. Her sharing her cancer offered insight into her intellectual and lived relations to prayer and spirituality, a "personalization" that could have had disparate pedagogical effects. David, for example, referred to her cancer as making her an expert, granting the experiential a place of authority. Olivia's classroom, on the other hand, might be read as devoid of the personal. In fact, *the person* was not even present during the first hour, in which embodied authority was visibly absent, present only in the task assigned. When Olivia appeared, she related herself and her students to the construction of knowledge, focusing not on individuals but on subjects who are institutionally and disciplinarily positioned in relation to knowledge, authority, and the power to question. It was not until the last five minutes of class that Olivia asked students their names.

I wish to trouble a reading of Julie's pedagogy as personal and Olivia's as impersonal, for Julie resisted centering herself, or using the "personal" as a form of self-authorization, instead encouraging students to create their own connections to the process and content of the course. On the other hand, Olivia engaged in something of a centering of self, particularly as she established her knowledge and authority—even as her declared intentions were to call her authority into question. Olivia's pedagogical "trick," for example, enabled a conversation on knowledge and authority even as it reinscribed her authority as the person who had set the guidelines and could dictate which rules were and were not appropriate to question. Although thus far unrepresented, Carol's pedagogical practices also entail complex relations of classroom authority and knowledges. As an African-American woman, she is acutely conscious of students' multiple assumptions regarding her positioning, knowledge, and authority, and enacts her pedagogy within and against these assumptions in order to reauthor understandings of her subject matter and herself as subject. Seeking to encourage critical reflection on issues of race, gender, and journalistic practice, she alternately invokes and conceals her lived, scholarly, and professional experiences as they relate to the material of her courses, performing a questioning of meanings attached to her visible identities.

I ask of their classrooms, what forms do their pedagogical goals and practices take? How do they relate themselves to students and subjects? What forms do knowledge and authority take on? What are the places of identity and experience in constituting knowledge and authority? In order to understand how their pedagogical practices are mediated by and find meaning in context, I have turned to theories of performance. Performance suggests that teaching is a process in which instructors do not author but perform identity, authority, and relations to knowledge in intersubjective relations that are constructed contextually. Pineau has argued that actor-centered conceptualizations of performance in teaching "isolate the performer from the performance context, [and] privilege communicative behaviors over communicative interaction." However, her assertion that "actors construct their audiences"[6] ignores the multidirectionality of performance by relegating students to passive roles. If performance is understood as an instantiation of self in interaction, what Gallop refers to as im-personation, "appearing as a person,"[7] the converse is true: the "audience" participates in constructing the (actions of the) actor. Appearing as a person becomes a representation rather than a presentation, for appearance is transactional, constituted by the (mis)recognitions of others. The performances of Olivia, Julie, and Carol are defined in part by the authority conferred by their institutional positions; however, the ways they appear in relation to students and subject matter reshape the meanings of that authority. Their performances are at times performative, in that they iterate pedagogical norms, what Butler calls "conventions," yet refigure those norms in practice, as what is normative is articulated with what is not. As I described, prevailing pedagogical norms at Liberal U, codified in policy and represented in campus talk, invoke the unbiased transmission of knowledge that is neutral in its implications. Even though objectivity is not a uniform ideal or practice, its collides with discourses of valuing perspectives to create contradictory expectations for teaching. Julie, Olivia, and Carol, marked in different ways in relation to their subject matters, seek efficacy within these discourses.

As I suggested in chapter 1, social knowledges play a role in constituting actors' use of voice and visibility, as well as the meanings they take on in interaction. Michael Lynch has linked the gaze of students to instructors' concealments and revelations: "By definition, a teacher is watched. Closely. By necessity, teaching—often thought of as simply giving information—is just as much a withholding of information."[8]

With issues of the management of information in mind, before turning to represent elements of each woman's classrooms, I should highlight that lesbian is largely, though not entirely, irrelevant to their pedagogical actions. Although sexuality circulates in some evident and not-so-evident forms, with the exception of Carol, who does so at strategic moments, none of the women "comes out" in her classrooms. They do not use their lesbianism as a classroom text, enacting choices that stand in opposition to pedagogical treatises that urge instructors to come out in order to represent homosexuality and to have a place from which to speak.[9] I return to this theme, or its present absence, at the conclusion of this chapter. However, it is interesting to note that the logic of taking a gay or lesbian subject position is linked to oppositional pedagogies that would challenge the sorts of ideologies that circulate at Liberal U—the instructor as universal bearer of truth, knowledge as disinterested, and pedagogy as properly detached from political concerns. Broadly construed, these pedagogies urge instructors to name their subject positions and personal stakes in the subject matter in order to demonstrate the situated relations of knowers and known: "By assuming a position in the classroom, on the contrary, the teacher makes it possible for the student to become aware of his position, of his own relations to power/knowledge formations."[10] A primary impetus behind such stances has been the feminist mantra "the personal is the political" as it has been translated into an emphasis on the personal in the classroom. For the gay or lesbian academic, the personal becomes the sexual; sexual identity becomes the political. Presumably, a sort of osmotic modelling occurs: see my personal-sexual-political position and you will know yours. However, as becomes clear in the representations of their pedagogies, and as I discuss in detail in chapter 5, the women's intellectual, academic, and political commitments are not based in the representation of self as lesbian but in making possible alternative forms of thought and practice. Furthermore, given the minoritizing discourses of identity and objectivity at Liberal U, overtly foregrounding their lesbianism could undermine these pedagogical goals. Thus, their choices offer a nuanced counterbalance to the imperatives of what are often decontextualized calls for professorial identity politics. Overt naming of self is not the only means to enact a pedagogy that is personal or political.

The representations that follow include moments from each woman's classrooms and participants' reflections on their experiences. While disparate, these scenes offer insights into the limits and possibilities of teaching in the haunted spaces of universities. I begin with dilemmas that arise in Carol's pedagogy due to meanings students attach to her race and gender.

CAROL: CRITICAL ENLIGHTENMENT

> I have a political goal, which is to sort of enlighten, prepare these
> people, create some kind of consciousness that wouldn't ordinarily
> be there, . . . it doesn't have to be about this subject, but shake
> them up, push them, make them think.
>
> —Carol

Because Race, Gender and the Media is an elective, students are presumably not hostile to its topics. "I want students to take it for granted that this is a subject matter that is worth sitting for a semester through, and that doesn't mean that they're all in the same place. It is likely to hit a nerve in different students for different reasons throughout the semester."[11] Carol spoke of her goals developmentally, gauging success by "what the students are thinking about, what their knowledge level is at the end of the semester is important. But also, have I really gotten them to another step intellectually, another layer of analytical thinking, basically, or if it's in a skills class, have they reached another stage in terms of their own professional practice?" Location played a part in defining her goals:

> CAROL. There are some very pragmatic goals because this is a Journalism School. . . . Part of my reason for leaving the newsroom was that I really began to think that the ways to sort of enlighten people in communications had to begin much earlier, that once they're actually doing this on a daily basis and the habits and routines become embedded, it's very difficult to change, but if you can, some of it is basic consciousness raising, some of it is getting at intellectual content also. So the goal for me and the primary goal is simply that I make them more critical in the ways that they think of the media.
>
> SUSAN. You say that here [in the syllabus], "critical analysts," what does that mean?
>
> CAROL. I hope that after they take my class they'll never be able to go to the movies and just sit through a movie and veg out, that it will be difficult or impossible for them not to critique the film, particularly from the standpoints of the things that we talk about in class in terms of race and gender and representation. There might be other things as well, that they be analytical, that they not take mass media for granted, that they not be passive consumers of mass media, and most people are.

Enlightenment was to be achieved by providing historical information, modelling analytical frameworks, and engaging students' everyday lives as consumers of media. Rationalism and lived experience were intertwined as a fulcrum to effect change in professional practice:

> Some of it simply is giving them information with which to critically analyze things, and also to model for them the way to be an analyst, both through reading other people's work, through looking at films or videotapes in class or looking at slides of advertisements, to say, "What does this suggest to you? What is it that's being sold in this ad? How is everything from body language and bodies, both male and female gender identity, how is that used to sell a product? How are these things manipulated? What are the subtleties here?" And if you talk about it a few times in class, people start to think about it differently. Students in journalism are already trained in some respects to do that. Part of what they learn in an advertising class, for example, is to analyze an ad, part of what reporting and broadcast students do learn is how to take apart a television show or a newspaper story and analyze it, but they haven't done it in this way and with these objectives in mind. So part of it is to build on the skills they've learned in other courses but also to teach them how to do that.

In Public Affairs Reporting, a graduate class of fourteen students, Carol followed conventions of mass communications educational practice "as a subversive way to influence journalists." Some students, she explained, had instrumental goals of seeking credentials for the job market, while others who have worked in journalism often had more intellectual interests but could be "very set in the ways that they think or in the ways that they behave as journalists, and are very resistant to changing." Within the functional curricular demands imposed on the course, Carol sought to upset assumptions through her treatment of "canonical" topics:[12]

> The syllabus is fairly typical in some respects in terms of categories and areas, and some of it is utilitarian. But I get them from the very beginning to think about journalism differently from a traditional white male model that's based on authority as primary sources, to focus only on familiar subjects and familiar people, to only think in terms of seeking a mass audience, of making particular presumptions about particular groups, about what they're going to be interested in, what they're going to want to read about. Probably the most subversive part is that there's a canon in journalism about newsworthiness, and I completely break that down and tell them to forget what they've learned and to rethink that, and to make it their business never to rely on official sources, the authoritative white guy.

Comprised of five white women, three white men, two Asian women, three Asian men, and one black woman, the class met in a seminar format that functioned as a topical workshop, in which Carol provided information and students solved problems related to the stories they wrote for the beats they reported on weekly throughout the semester. During the second week of class, Carol invited students to reflect on criteria for selecting stories:

CAROL. For the next hour, I'd like to talk about how to come up with good stories. What is a good story? You are all readers.

STUDENT. Something that's interesting.

STUDENT. Or timely.

CAROL. Well, there are ways to get around that, you can take another kind of angle.

STUDENT. You can tie a story to an issue or an event.

CAROL. I'm glad you mentioned those, because we tend to think of timeliness as a recent event, but timeliness may not warrant a story. Or it could be that an issue may make something that at first glance doesn't seem like a story a story. . . . A good question might be who cares, so what? What else?

STUDENT. Something that provides useful information.

CAROL. You're getting into the idea of public information, not operating in the realm of traditional criteria but thinking of ways that information may be used or helpful in people's lives. Some stories will not change people's lives but must be told. Other stories may change lives, if only in small ways. You all are readers, what do you read first? Think of yourselves as producers and consumers of the news.

STUDENT. I look at weather.

STUDENT. International news.

STUDENT. If I'm looking for a job, want ads.

STUDENT. Newsworthiness.

STUDENT. Proximity.

CAROL. Sometimes I'd like to rip those pages out of those textbooks. Proximity isn't the most important thing. We need to think about proximity differently. There are national and international connections you can make with each story. You say to the reader, "Hey, this is you I'm talking about."[13]

Carol's questioning of timeliness and proximity and her emphasis on the uses to which stories may be put was part of a challenge to what Meg Morgan calls the "BIG VOICE" of journalism, which offers "the daily *recording*" of events that are thought of as hard news due to their time-liness. This voice of objectivity asks readers to "buy into a static picture of the world emphasizing continuity and concreteness; they give up change and ambiguity."[14] Rather than focus on using multiple sources to legitimate stories, Carol emphasized multiple sources' potential to complicate stories, a move that politicizes journalistic practice by admitting complexity into the linear time and singular space of reported events. She routinely challenged students to take into account audience, stressing, as she did in one class in which she offered demographic statistics pertaining to the local and statewide population, that "things take on meaning when you know the populations." During an exchange of ideas for stories, Carol asked students to consider community relations:

> CAROL. Women's affairs, both of you have identified issues, what are potential stories?
>
> STUDENT. Low-income families, I think.
>
> CAROL. Good, you don't just want to do PR. You might look at how it relates to the preoccupation with crime in Oasis.
>
> OTHER STUDENT. I'm interested in looking at children at youth shelters, not only if there's relief, but what are they doing to help for the future?
>
> CAROL. That's an important perspective, we as a nation tend to use stop-gap measures. There's a lot to look at, there's a large hidden poor community in town. Social services and welfare aren't used only by poor and minorities, but a strata of working poor at the end of the month.[15]

In order to develop students' understandings of communities as contexts for communicating, Carol highlighted the need to draw on multiple sources in order to document the multiperspectival nature of events and their impact on local communities: "The way I've observed journalism being practiced is that people don't necessarily know shit about the communities they work in, they don't feel like they have to have any deep understanding of history or social networks or anything, that all they have to do is go out, go to the press conference and call the mayor on the phone, and get the facts from the police department, and write the story, and that's sufficient." Despite several students' complaints to me that the course, like the Journalism School, was "too local" in its emphasis, these students recognized that they were "becom[ing] more complete reporters," or that learning interviewing techniques and the use of multiple sources had been "surprisingly helpful."

Although Carol sat at the head of the table and directed the class topically, students' exchange of advice and information created a cooperative environment of shared expertise, which students referred to as "an open community," "a forum, not a class," "a place for exchange," and a "minicommunity." "I'm pretty laid back and casual, not quite as formal as I am in the other class," Carol explained. "I take the position that you've had all kinds of interesting professional experiences, while I'm the teacher I'm not necessarily the authority on all accounts, so I call on other people to talk about their experience. I'm trying to make it more of a collective, interactive process because I want them to learn from each other."

Barbara: "*She lets us navigate our own course, she doesn't say you have to do this this way. We're free to explore and make our own mistakes, so she guides but doesn't direct. She'll give more direction if we need it, but after we've already started, and then we'll discuss different ways of doing things.*" Chuck: "*Her knowledge and her experience come through, but it doesn't come off as like a snob, I know this and I'm right. You can learn from it, you benefit from her experience. But also, she's good at getting us to tell about ideas, instead of her doing it.*"

The classes I observed had well-established patterns. Public Affairs Reporting included talking through stories before and after students wrote them, brief lectures on topics in journalistic practice that Carol connected to students' beats, and cooperatively solving problems students encountered on their beats. The classroom was a pleasant, if not exciting, space in which participation was well-distributed. Carol was indeed enacting the goals she described, which surfaced, although not prominently, in students' descriptions of their learning. Although students did not articulate direct answers to my questions about how they were coming to think differently about reporting, their descriptions of their work in class intimated that they were gaining complex, if not critical, views of communities and their responsibilities to those communities as reporters.

The routine in Race, Gender, and the Media, a class of twenty students (twelve white women, two black women, two black men, two Latinos, one Asian man, and one white man) usually began with a thirty to forty-five minute lecture pertaining to the day's readings, during which Carol expanded on main points and provided historical background. Her lectures were monologic, although she did pause to ask for questions, open issues for brief discussion, or ask inductive questions. She focused on the intersections of race and gender in media representations, and occasionally included issues of class and sexuality. In three classes I attended, the lecture led directly to a documentary concerned with race and gender in the media, which the class discussed afterward as time allowed. Student participation was uneven: the four black and two white female students asked and answered questions most frequently, with contributions by the Asian and one Latino. With the exception of one African-American woman's participation, a surprising element of the class was the lack of palpable passion.[16] Despite occasional interjections of students' responses to films, music, or advertising, few personal connections or affective responses to the material were made, although students were riveted during what I thought were powerful, well-chosen videos. The puzzle for me, the place of "unsmoothing" the linearity of Carol's narratives and teaching that I referred to in chapter 1, has been to understand the seeming objectivity of the classroom. I have tried to reread what I perceive to be a disjuncture between passionate topics and dispassionate subjects in the context of Carol's struggles with authority. The persistent inflection of her descriptions of teaching with a self-consciousness of her race and gender leads me to understand this "objectivity" as part of an effort to legitimize herself and her subject matter, to appear to students *as* and *not-as* her visible identities in order to gain pedagogical efficacy.

CROSS-DIRECTIONS: CAROL'S PERFORMANCES OF AUTHORITY AND IDENTITY

> I tend to be the kind of teacher who establishes a distanced relationship with my students, because I've had so many troubles with authority as a black woman. Because I look young, they always assume that I'm much younger than I am. Most of my students in the university have never had a black teacher before. . . . They're also very socialized to only ascribe authority to male professors, so the combination is that there are a lot of students who really just don't know what to do with me. As soon as I walk into the classroom, they just look at me, particularly white males who are totally resistant to ascribing me authority. So I frequently have to take a hard-ass position, you don't know me, you're not calling me by first name, you don't need to know anything about me personally, I'm the teacher, I'm the one with authority here, and shut up and listen. And I have to do that and then I can soften that position as I get to know the students, and frequently I do the friend thing, I get to know them, I come out to the gay students frequently, so they have a sense that I'm there for them.
>
> —Carol

What Carol calls her visible "age, race, and gender factors" function as a priori sources of (de)authorization, and have the effect of making her "already known, *in personal terms*."[17] These "factors" are mediated by the type of class she is teaching (academic, vocational) and its content, as well as students' professional backgrounds and race, gender, and sexuality. For example, about her skills classes, Carol commented, "I have these people in their late twenties in the class who have worked in journalism for a few years whose basic attitude is 'What can you teach me?' A lot of it is they don't really believe that this young black woman who's sitting here really has any authority or expertise from which they can learn." In a past Reporting class, she said:

> It was just a weird interaction with that whole class. For example, they were always trying to figure out how old I was, and those kinds of conversations, and they really sort of questioned my authority. . . . Two [white males] wrote these pretty nasty comments on the evaluations, basically trying to argue that I wasn't qualified to teach the class. To me, that is all about what I represent to them, not about who I am or what I actually taught in the class. . . . In the Race and Gender course, I always get a few random white boys who don't know why they're in the course, and are sort of sorry that they've taken it. One classic example, it was a really good group and we enjoyed the class, one of the three white men in the group clearly seemed alienated because he would never talk, he wouldn't engage in class discussions. And on the evaluations, there were all these evaluations, Professor Davis is so fair, she's so supportive, dadadada, and one person said Professor Davis is very aloof, very distant, and so it was all again about himself.

Patricia Williams, an African-American law professor, has written of her teaching evaluations, "The substantive ones say that what I teach is 'not law.' The nonsubstantive evaluations are about either my personality or my physical features. I am deified, reified, and vilified *in all sorts of cross-directions*. I am condescending, earthy, approachable, and arrogant." Carol has a paradoxical position in that, as Williams says, she is institutionally placed under a "shield of respectability [that] shelters me even as I am disrespected." [18] The difficulty Williams points to is the contradictory location of a black female body in a position of authority, a location that creates multiple readings. For Carol, these cross-directed readings structured a self-conscious pedagogy that cited a distanced stance in order to reconfigure students' (mis)recognitions of her and her relations to the subject matter. My interviews with students confirmed the scrutiny she suspected. Ralph reflected, "She's a charismatic person, elegant, the way she does the lectures is so confident. I'm not sure, people say African-Americans tend to be more confident than other people because not many can climb to that level. The way she talks is so persuasive, so professional, different than white professors. A lot of white professors are just casual, jeans, T-shirts and sandals, just doesn't look like a professor." Chuck's discussion of her "command of the class" betrayed his consciousness of Carol's "personal" authority: "I have to admit that I am a little intimidated by her, just because I'm covering minority affairs and she's a black woman, and I'm scared I'm going to do something un-PC and piss her off. But I just think that the way she carries herself is very good, it draws my attention in. She's very confident and assured."

Students' propensities to read Carol, as well as her self-consciousness of being read, were heightened by the content of Race, Gender, and the Media, in which her and students' potential implications in the material were seemingly more visible. Carol's efforts to engage students and to minimize resistances and identifications with her and the material made for a busy pedagogy. Cross-directions, real or imagined, played a role in shaping a pedagogy that responded to students' different positionings related to gender, race, sexual orientation, and ideology. For example, Carol sought to include white males by not focusing study of gender exclusively on women: "The resentment among the white males is that they feel excluded from the conversation about gender and when they begin to see that it has something to do with them, sometimes it makes them very uncomfortable, but it is also something that they can identify with and understand." In contrast to their disaffection, Carol struggled with the identifications of women and students of color:

> There are dangers to making the girls feel like this is a girls' club, and that this isn't work and this isn't an intellectual project. Great, yeah, I want you to feel comfortable with me, feel like I'm a teacher you can identify with, that I'm younger and I'm hipper and I'm not one of these old stodgy white guys. But that can also make them lazy, and so I try to resist some of that, that they're very anxious to heap on me, so it's a strategy, a balancing act. It's true for students of color, too, they see me and they're, you know, refuge, but also "Hey, Professor Davis, aren't you going to give me some slack, you know, you understand how rough it is being a black student on this campus." And I'm like, "No."

The circulations of disaffections and identifications in relation to identities and course content make it difficult, if not impossible, to distinguish the effects of Carol's and the course content's race and gender: "For some it is who I am, what I am, that I'm a black woman and, the black students in particular, they're just so glad to have me as a teacher that they sometimes overidentify with me. . . . I think also the sort of activist students and political left students, for whom I articulate a category of knowledge that they don't hear in other classes, particularly in the Journalism School." As revealed by Carol's language, her perception of being conflated with the material played a part in constructing her pedagogical stances:

> I have some [white women] who are totally *devoted to me*, I have others who are pretty hostile. And many who are just somewhere in

between. There are a lot of white women, straight white women in particular, who do not want to have their assumptions about gender and so forth in conflict. They don't want to be challenged about those issues, and they're always the ones that I think are still struggling themselves, and have internalized all kinds of sexist notions. . . . They want to be able to believe that they have an equal right, equal access to whatever, professions and so forth, but they don't want any sort of strong critical engagement with questions of gender because it very quickly sort of melts down this very elaborate world that they've constructed. And some of them sort of come around and I try to tread fairly lightly with them because I don't want to turn them off.

Difficulties with white women were evident in my observations, as several sat silently, sometimes exchanging glances. Resistances to the analysis were acted out as resistances to Carol:

Some of these little sorority girls, they just bug *on me* every once in a while, and I've had it slightly in this class this semester. I don't know if it's been the days you've been there. They say, "I just don't see these images in these films, well those women were powerful figures. I mean, she was a professional," talking about *Disclosure*. They were content to simply read her as a strong woman because she was a professional . . . but I think a lot of them don't want any more analysis than that. . . . *So I make them very uncomfortable.*

White women's responses, however, were unpredictable: "Sometimes the sorority girls I would never pick as being engaged, you know, made-up and blonde, bleached hair and the pony tail and the uniform, the bangs, major bangs, and the light bulb comes on and they're tripping on stuff and they're articulating things."

Struggling with the interplay of being granted too little professional and too much personal authority, Carol sought not to have her or the content's legitimacy undermined through the conflation of the content and her race and gender. The distanced, or "hard-ass," position Carol adopted in response to these readings can function, as Karamcheti has described, as a performative tactic: "The minority teacher can cast himself or herself as the traditional authoritarian personality, the hard-driving, brilliant, no-nonsense professional for whom the personal has nothing to do with anything: John Houseman in racial drag."[19] The performative nature of this stance, which works against multiple social knowledges, lies in its avoidance of the personalization of knowledge, of standing in as a metonym for an area of study. Rather than succumb to a fixed location, Carol sought to disentangle essential connections students may have wished to make between her and the subject matter. Fuss has described problems of classroom identity politics, in which identities "are treated as fixed, accessible, and determinative, conferring upon the subject's speech an aura of predictability."[20] By citing conventions of faculty as neutral bearers of information and presenting herself as authority rather than personalized representative of her subject matter, Carol played against predictability. Her confusion of visual and epistemological assumptions by refusing positioning as an "authentic" black female subject[21] highlights race itself as performance.

Barbara: "*She's the first female African-American professor I've had as a communications instructor, so to see someone who looks like me in a leadership role, they have the experience, the knowledge, the way she presents herself, it's from a universal standpoint, . . . like sometimes when people are minorities they concentrate on that aspect, but she can talk about anything.*"

Carol did not present herself as singularly distanced, for even as she adopted a "universal" stance, she put herself into her lessons as scholar and historicized body.

> I want them to know that there are people who are thinking about things that they are thinking about, too, who have been engaging in ways to analyze it. So sometimes I'll say, "Hey, when I was researching this or interviewing this person, I came across some phenomenon that's very similar to what we're talking about." Sometimes I use my own personal experience. I talk about what it was like to be a black woman in the newsroom, or sometimes I talk about my family. Particularly in a historical context I think it's sometimes interesting for them to understand that we're not talking about abstracts here, we're talking about people's lives and their quote history and cultural history and social history.

Carol's stepping in and out of, appearing *against* and *as*, her visible identities by connecting and disconnecting herself from the course content could be said to be a tactic that does not fully succumb to the university's rationalism but uses it in new ways. Even with the unruliness of the identities and identifications in her classroom, however, there are dangers that reliance on the authority of information and analytical procedures allows students to ignore their own connections to and implications in the material, a topic I take up below.

Although Carol did not problematize her sexuality as an ongoing dilemma, it too entered her balancing of pedagogical relations. Carol voiced her sexuality, which was less readily apparent than her race or gender, situationally, also with a caution about identifications students may form:

> I have lesbian students sometimes who when they figure out that I'm a dyke, they're just so happy, they're beside themselves, they can hardly stand it. "Oh, she's a dyke, oh thank God." . . . I certainly am sympathetic to that and understanding, but in other ways, I think it's some-

what problematic. There's a real danger for lesbian and gay students, just because a professor is queer, doesn't mean that they're going to share the same politics, or the same experience. There's not immediately some sort of affinity or political mobilization or solidarity that occurs. Sometimes there is, but there may not be. So I think it's very dangerous for students to leap to those kinds of conclusions. They better get hip to the fact that there are a lot of lesbians and gays out there who are not on their side, whatever they think on their side is.

Sexuality differs from race in that students do not have an obvious object to fix onto, and seems, in Carol's language, to be a more tenuous source of affinity than race. However, as with race, Carol wanted the subject matter to have legitimacy independent of her subject position:

> I don't have to reveal my sexuality to teach about it any more than a straight person. That burden is never on heterosexuals, why should it be on me to proclaim my sexuality? I claim the position of it being part of a discourse, and part of it is I want my sexuality to be ambiguous, because I want students not to think the only reason I raise it is that I'm queer and I've got some sort of ax to grind or some political agenda. Let them think perhaps that I'm straight. Even better if they think I'm a straight black woman who raises the subject because it is crucial to our understanding of whatever we're talking about.

Joseph Litvak has critiqued his own practices of "masquerading" in classrooms, explaining, "I was trying to speak out of both sides of my mouth at once, obliquely making certain gay-affirmative points while counting on a vague presumption of my heterosexuality to legitimate them but also, frankly, to make *me*, well, more desirable as their purveyor."[22] Like Carol's, his practices aim for legitimation of gay subject matter, but unlike Carol's, his are bound up with receiving personal validation. Carol's response to circumstances suggest that visibility, or overt personal mediation, is not the only desirable strategy. Ambiguity as well can combat heterosexism and homophobia. At times, though, and according to her understanding of context, Carol put her institutional authority into play with her unauthorized lesbian position:

> When there's been what I would consider to be some dangerously homophobic exchange going on in the class, a student says something, and the students might be going back and forth, and that's a moment in which it's really important for them to know that this symbol of authority standing up in front of the room is queer. . . . And I've decided that this person really needs to understand that we're not talking about theory here, we're talking about real people's lives, and that they have in fact come into contact with lesbians and gays, and they're professors. It's usually a pretty spontaneous reaction.

She contradicted her claim of spontaneity in another interview, explaining, "I'm very calculated about it," a slippage that suggests that Carol's choices to self-disclose are temporal, a tacit tactic of interrupting homophobia as she deems efficacious.

Carol's pedagogy could be thought of as a management of information, both about herself and her subject matter, that responds to students' multiple readings. As she sought to provide new ways of thinking about journalistic practice, media consumption, and their relations to race and gender, Carol appeared as authority, in contradiction to her visible identities, yet occasionally embodied herself verbally. By doing so, she preserved her ability to speak on a range of topics. Spivak has commented, "'Who should speak?' is less crucial than 'Who will listen?'"[23] I would add: "How will they listen?" When one speaks *as* something, one is defined, placed, by those who listen. To shift positions, to undo location, particularly for those who would be a priori positioned, may perform a rescripting of sedimented meanings of race, gender, and sexuality. Hoodfar points out that critical pedagogical writing has largely failed to account for the position of the "raced" instructor, explaining, "students responded more positively to 'critical thinking' when I distanced myself from them . . . and act[ed] the more powerful and knowledgeable teacher, delivering lectures and answering questions." Calls for politicizing one's positioning led her to wonder, "to what extent I can call this method of teaching 'critical pedagogy,' since my success stems in part from asserting my authority as teacher."[24] The "political" may not merely be a rejection of "neutral" teaching to be replaced by overt positioning but the tactical use of resources at hand, such as the university's rationalism, to effect changes in thinking and practice.

As I mentioned earlier, however, even as performing an authoritative role may legitimate instructor and subject matter, I am concerned that a dependency on information shuts down other possibilities for learning. Carol's developmental view of learning belies an alignment with the university's rationalistic belief in "building incremental knowledge upon the edifice of the learner," as Britzman has described. She says, "the myth is that 'information' neutralizes ignorance and that learners and their teachers will rationally accept new thoughts without having to grapple with unlearning the old ones."[25] Race, gender, class, sexuality, and the media do not lend themselves easily to rational dialogue. The information and analysis Carol offered do not acknowledge that students' resistance may be, as Penley describes, "not so much a refusal of information as a refusal to acknowledge *one's own implication* in that information."[26] Information may not change thought, for a change of thought occurs through recognition of one's implication in what one is learning. To understand pedagogy as a psychic event is to understand a need to create conditions that enable, as Britzman says, "the proliferation of identifications as a means to exceed—as opposed to return to—the self" (85). Through multiple identifications students encounter themselves relationally, as implicated subjects. If communicative dialogue would offer a realist text to transparent subjects in a neat developmental teleology of knowledge and skills, in which, as Elizabeth Ellsworth says, "education is a success when the difference between a curriculum and a student's understanding is eliminated,"[27] a pedagogy that invites engagement and implication allows for the creation of new, indeterminate meanings, relations to knowledge, and imaginings of self. Enabling and disenabling, the "return of the repressed"—rationalism, information, culture, and the progressive development of student minds—haunts a pedagogy that turns its critique on institutions the university's rational and cultural centers were once intended to uphold. This haunting is both the condition of the possibility and impossibility of Carol's pedagogy.

In Julie's classrooms, issues of students' implications in knowledge arose in slightly different forms as she sought to create conditions for them to connect the study of religion to social, political, and personal practices. Neither the unlocated stance she performed in Introduction to Christianity nor her located stance in Mystical Prayer functioned as transparent representations of self or subject, for each was complicated by students' readings of what they saw and heard.

JULIE: COMPLICATIONS AS RESPONSE

Another scene from the first day of class: At the door of a lecture hall in which Introduction to Christianity will be held, students stand in line chatting. Julie and her two TAs, Lydia and Kevin, greet them, "How are you? What discussion section are you in? See the chart on the board? That's how we want you to sit in this room, so if you're in A you'd sit in the front left corner." Students look at their registration papers, make sense of the board, and find corresponding seats in the auditorium. After everyone is seated, Julie stands at the lectern, introduces herself, names the course, and describes drop/add. She peers out over her half-glasses, telling students to get the reader, which contains policies and the syllabus. "You said when you came in here, it's real big. This is a lecture, but it's a lecture with a twist. It's not just somebody standing up here, but we'll be discussing one day a week." She writes on the board: "lecture (twist)." "I saw a lecture called the best course I never taught." She writes "(n)ever" on the board and describes a talk she attended about teaching through interactive problem solving: "I could talk to you and you'd learn more and forget it faster than if you do things. The more of this you do, you might learn less facts and stuff, but you'll remember more and be more engaged with it."

Students are sorted within their discussion groups into groups of four to five. TAs walk around. Julie writes instructions on the board: "name your group, exchange names and phone numbers, make a list of your group." TAs circulate and write down names. Julie waves her arms, "Everyone ready?" She explains the point system, broken down by lecture and discussion participation, group and individual projects, and exams. "Students like what they're doing, they've read, they're into what'll happen in class. Is this your experience?" Silence. "This is a joke. You don't do it however much I want. So my way to help you is with five unannounced reading quizzes." She defines discussion sections: "If I'm not clear, that's my problem. I'll clarify for you. That's not the purpose of the discussion sections. It's also not a place to prepare for the exam. You need to learn how to do that. Discussion is a place where you engage what we're doing." The TAs give points for participation in discussion; students can earn extra points for activities outside of class: "You can come to me and say, I saw *Angels in America* and I'm interested in learning about Mormon underwear." Students mutter, snicker. "You can lose points if you're not here. We do a spot attendance check. This is one of those structured 100-level classes. It's like a pyramid, we lay a groundwork and build up to the end of class."

After checking for logistical questions, Julie says, "You have five minutes to come up with one essential characteristic of a religion in your small groups." Groups lean in to confer. "Are you ready?" "Ready." Hands go up. Julie points and groups call out words, "doctrine, faith, symbols, followers, good and evil," which she puts on the board. "These are all great answers." She occasionally asks for an example or clarification. After almost two dozen terms are up, she asks, "In order to be a religion you have to have some of these things. My colleagues in Chinese or Asian religions might argue that Buddhists have no doctrine. Some communitarians have no leaders. Are they a religion? Or fundamentalists and Quakers don't want liturgy. Are they a religion?" She pauses. "We find all these concepts in a lot of religions. Can we put them together in any way?" Another pause. "Today Christians aren't killing each other over their religious beliefs so much, but have split off in their political beliefs. . . . Conservative Catholics are more aligned with fundamentalist Christians because of abortion than they are with liberal Catholics." She points at the terms, explaining that during the semester most will come up in different ways: "Every concept is arguable depending on who you're talking to." She recounts that a reporter called to ask her impressions for a story he was writing on college students and religion: "I notice that you can't generalize any more. I do notice that fewer people have religious backgrounds. This course may be easier for those with no background than for those with background." She tells students to pick up the reader and sit in the same places next class. They file out.[28]

On this first day of class, Julie appeared differently to her students than in the seemingly more personal space of Mystical Prayer. However, even in the distance of a lecture hall, her efforts to encourage academic and worldly engagement and her awareness of students' multiple investments were evident. She demonstrated a respectful authoritative stance as she explained her rationale for the course design. In introducing the content, she drew on students' knowledges to identify elements of a religion, which she complicated by pointing to the diversity of religious practices and the intertwining of religion with politics. She expressed, although somewhat obliquely, her awareness of the potential difficulties students' religious backgrounds may cause them during the semester. She gently began to enact what she had articulated as her goals:

> I just want them to see that Christianity is a helluva lot more complicated than they think it is, and that religion is worth thinking about as an intellectual, social, and political issue. Religion's not a private matter. Religion is in the mix of country and its background and the assumptions that people have about life and how it ought to be lived. It's right in the thick of debates about abortion, euthanasia, capital punishment, national debt, and all this kind of stuff. There's no clear way to read the Bible. I think that's an important thing for them to learn, too. Ten different people can read the same passage and come up with radically different conclusions about what that means. And Christians of good will can disagree radically on dramatic things like slavery. So it's that sort of thing, and show how these evolutions, the coalition of religion and politics, that's always been, religion's always been involved in politics, really from the fourth century on.

Kevin, speaking of TAing for Julie: *Something I thought intuitively is now something I think consciously, the tradition is a tradition of argument and interpretation much more than it is a coherent body of thought which lapsed from time to time. I tend to think of history using the key words that she does, like diversity and plurality . . . in terms of responses to social and historical contingencies, and that's come from Howard's course. She's shaken me out of some of my assumptions just like she has most of the students, which is, I think, a testimony to the course.*

Julie recently began using what she calls "interactive teaching" to interest herself and engage students: "I get tired of going over the same old ground. Especially in a large introductory course the trick there is to keep yourself from getting bored out of your gourd with this material that you know inside and out." Activities are intended to lend coherence to lecture and discussion, and include readings that problematize religion: "We'll give them this one, 'How the Bible made America,' which is a very pro-fundamentalist thing and then this thing by Barbara Ehrenreich, saying that the Bible is a piece of crap, none of the founding fathers liked it, and all of the best things about America are anti-Bible." She explained the coordination of lecture and discussion:

> We'll try to design the discussion section so it'll have six parts, or six opinions or six facets or something like that, and we'll give each one during this day some particular thing. Let's say they need to kind of on the basis of certain clues and evidence construct an image of God as found in the Hebrew Bible, so we'll give them something like in the Book of Numbers when God said, "I'm sick of this goddamn complaining so I'm going to send you poison bread," they'll get this kind of angry stuff, then something very compassionate, something vulnerable, something very controlling, something bellicose, something peaceful, and out of those, and let them talk about it among themselves, and do a little report [in lecture].

Tim: "*It's [discussion] kind of fun because there's, you never know what you're going to do, you get into a lot of arguments and debates that are kind of fun.*" Stephanie: "*This is the best discussion section I've ever been in, it's not just going over stuff for tests. You explore things in depth, clarify things, create your own opinions. I usually skip discussion sections, but not here.*"

These students' mention of debate and exploration were consonant with Julie's goals:

> What I'm trying to show them is that groups of Christians can use the Bible to justify almost anything, so that some of them are for poverty, some of them are against it, some are for heavy-duty capitalism, some of them are not, some of them are for war, some of them think you have to be against all war. I don't want them to think there's a kind of a clear way to do this. It's something that people have to figure out in their own community or their own conscience or whatever.

In fact, students' descriptions of their evolving understandings revealed an intertwining of academic and personal dimensions. Tim, the only self-identified fundamentalist Christian with whom I spoke, described class: "The history of Christianity in America and altogether really, before there even was Christianity, the Jews, and along with that you get a history of the world. Wars are involved, politics, so it's not just set to religion totally. Feminism, abortion, anything. So religion has its views on everything." When I asked if he was coming to think differently about the course topics, he said, "I have some very concrete opinions about Christianity and things like that, so it really hasn't changed my attitude but it opens up your eyes to things where you can see, well I kind of understand where these people believe this or that, but I don't feel the same way, but it still broadens your horizons to get other opinions." Stephanie offered another perspective: "The outside forces on Christianity, the impact of Judaism on Christianity, how it developed and branched out, and different doctrines, deism and theism. . . . In a personal way it helps me realize what my heritage is and also how other people think, why they might be so conservative, I don't fly off the cuff as much anymore toward the Christian Right."

In Mystical Prayer and Western Spirituality, Julie's goal of complicating understandings made for a course that, although structured by readings and student presentations, was open to detour: "I'm just letting the class evolve. . . . I have a kind of a plan, but I'm willing for it to be disrupted if something better happens." Julie wished to focus on the connections of students' experiences to the content rather than structuring the course through a priori definitions of mysticism: "I think I know what [mysticism] means for me, but I think there are just tons of ways, I think the spiritual journey such as it is, is very personal and mysterious, and arrived at in lots of different directions, so I'm kind of interested in that, what people perceive in these readings, or in their background, or out of their head, or wherever they're coming from." Multiple approaches to and practices of spirituality and prayer formed a basis for content and process:

> It's the combination of skepticism and belief that I'm always playing with with my students. If they're very credulous, I find a lot of undermining things to say, if they're very skeptical I find a lot of little witnessy things to say, so that they're always just a little bit off balance. I only want them to know that nothing is very simple, that there is no simple definition of mysticism, there isn't any one way to do anything. Talk about God, do prayer, write a paper, go to school, anything.

Julie's focus on multiple ways of doing things, on diversity and contingency, suggests an understanding of pedagogy itself as a response to context, to others. Her very engagement with mysticism underscores her concern with the uses to which others put traditions to create new ways of doing things. It is an unsurprising coincidence that Michel de Certeau had an ongoing interest in mystical practices as they arose within and responded to historical contexts. He writes that mystics

> did not basically set out to pioneer new systems of knowledge, topographies, or complementary or substitutive powers; rather, they defined a different treatment of the Christian tradition. . . . What is

essential, then, is not a body of doctrines, . . . but the epistemic foundation of a domain within which specific procedures are followed: a new space, with new mechanisms. . . . The mystics' reinterpretation of the tradition is characterized by a set of procedures allowing a new treatment of language—of all contemporary language, not only the area delimited by theological knowledge or the corpus of patristic and scriptural works.[29]

As mystical practice is the creation of new spaces (and, in another unsurprising coincidence, based in knowing through the body), Julie's pedagogy sought to enable appropriations of what she, the readings, and students offered the classroom space. In both of her classes, her teaching was shaped by the content as well as her understandings of her students and their relationships to the material. In her introductory course, which included a range of Christian thought and practice, Julie sought to locate herself nowhere, concerned instead with locating religious traditions and their complexities, whereas in her upper-level course on mysticism, Julie positioned herself in relation to readings and discussion, embodying herself as Catholic and as a woman with breast cancer.

STIRRING THEM UP:
JULIE'S "PARTICULAR KIND OF EMBODIMENT"

All it [self-disclosure as lesbian] would do to those poor little freshmen sitting in my Introduction to Christianity class would just make them all upset. It wouldn't help their learning experience, it wouldn't do anything. The best thing to do there is to be as entertaining and as intellectually challenging and as good a teacher as I could be and if some of them figure out in the course of the semester that I'm Catholic or I'm queer, I think that's fine. But I think leading with either of those things just sets up certain kinds of resistances that they then have to get over.

—Julie

Howard is very aware of things that are going to hurt them. I've watched her, she knows what's going to stir them up, and she wants to stir them up, but it's not to assert herself as grand paradigm of knowledge, scholarship, and teaching. It's about them. It's not Howard up there going, "I'm trying to be a really good teacher and stand out always." This is about getting them to sort of come up out of their world view. It's very respectful, even though it's confrontational, it's directed to them. It's not directed to get them to look at her, it's to get them to look at themselves.

—Lydia

Julie's consciousness of students' knowledges of Christianity led her to perform an objective stance in her introductory class:

> I just like to hide religion period. Because there are a lot of kids in there who want me to be a born-again Christian, there's a lot of kids in there who don't understand why we would be studying Catholics in a course on Christianity, or Mormons, or Unitarians. Sort of what I'm trying to do in that class is to be as Baptist, as Pentecostal, as whatever it is I'm teaching, to try to be in such sympathy with that point of view. I do a whole section in there on what Christians have done to Jews and how Jesus was a, and all this anti-Semitism and stuff like that, and invariably I get kids saying, "I thought this was a course on Christianity. I didn't know it was going to be pro-Jewish."

As Lydia described, she performed the practices she was explicating to students: "She's quite remarkable. She takes on different voices quite well, and they don't see this. She will wear a fundamentalist tone, she'll wear a scientist tone, a historical critic's tone, and they miss it."

Her pedagogy entailed movement between irreverence and earnest respect for Christian practices. In the space of one lecture, for example, she would shift from talk of the beauty of religious practice to a less respectful, playful tone. For example, when reviewing a quiz, she asked, "What did they do when they came to the Red Sea? They bitched and moaned and complained. What did God do? He parted the waters." In a discussion of the twelve tribes of Israel, a student asked, "What does the name change [from Isaac to Jacob] mean?" "If I say your name isn't X, it's Y, either I'm some kind of nut or it means I have some sort of power. So, Jacob has twelve sons and they reproduce like crazy." At times, Julie intertwined issues of gender with her irreverence, as in her discussion of the burning bush: "Moses asks, 'Who are you?' 'I am who I am.' There's a help. He said, 'I'm God of Noah, Abraham, and Isaac.' If this God had been a feminist, he'd have said, 'I'm God of Sarah, Rachel, and / /.'" Or, in a lecture on medieval Christianity, she pointed out, "In your book are Thomas Aquinas and Peter Abelard. Abelard is famous for his love affair with his student Heloise. A case of sexual harassment. His uncle had him castrated. People did not mess around with these things then."

As I will highlight in the following chapter, Julie's concealment of her religion is called for by religious studies' precarious position at a public university that is suspicious of the nonsecular, and by the pervasive presence of conservative religious views among undergraduates. Julie's colleague Michael spoke of his struggles with "how much to come out as atheist, or Christian, or Hindu, or Buddhist. . . . In my class students come up to me and say, 'Do you believe what Paul said?' And my answer to that question will determine whether they accept or don't accept what I talk about." However, despite Julie's concealments, a number of students persisted in scrutinizing her and her relations to the course content. What Lydia described as students' "missing" the multiple voices Julie adopted suggests that something was at work besides the transmission of knowledge. Other knowledges circulated in this classroom. Kevin explained:

> People take this course with a very predetermined idea of what Christianity is, and a lot of people react instantly to Dr. Howard because she immediately doesn't conform to what their definition of Christianity is. I don't know what gives them that impression so quickly, but I do a lot of damage control in my discussion sections. . . . I tell them that their concerns are concerns about the tradition, not concerns about Dr. Howard. I say she is a faithful representative of the tradition. . . . For one reason or another, it does happen more in Howard's class than any others.

Mired in an uncertainty that may be more certain than he would reveal, Kevin's words point to students' religious and social knowledges as forms of resistance: their knowledge of the subject matter intermingled with their readings of Julie Howard as subject who matters. The slippage in what it means to be a "faithful representative of the tradition"— is it in the telling of tradition or its embodiment?—suggests shifts between knowledges of Christian tradition and knowledges of Julie Howard that structured teaching and learning in this classroom. In this sense, ignorance and knowledge are not opposites, but, as Britzman and others have argued, "they mutually implicate each other, structuring and enforcing particular forms of knowledge and forms of ignorance."[30]

Like Carol, Julie was aware of students' displacing difficulties with her analysis on her:

> Some of them think I'm anti-Catholic because I'm pretty hard on the pope. So I try to make whatever it is I believe not obvious to them in any way, or what I believe is so quirky, /such a/ mix of things that it would be hard for them to identify me. All these Catholic kids have these naive views, so to hear that there were these pervert popes or warrior popes really bothers them. They think this is an attack on the Church, rather than an historical statement.

In order to assuage students, Julie constructed her lectures as a back and forth movement that shifted according to her perceptions of the dynamics of students' responses: "When I'm being too skeptical, and they're getting nervous, I will move back into a little rhapsody on belief or liturgy or something like that and how important religion has been in everybody's lives. . . . I tend to move along a spectrum, I'm trying to undercut some of their rigidities, and at the same time not destroy them in some way, open up their minds to certain things, and yet at the same time I don't want to trash religion." Lydia emphasized Julie's desire to unsettle, but with sensitivity to context:

> She knows what she's holding up is radical, and she puts it out there and says, "I know this is intense for you," she'll say, "I know this is hard, it's different." So it's sort of in-your-face but it's not. She puts out how hard a view is, its roughest edges, to get them stirred, and then she backs off and softens. It's an interesting technique, it seems almost like queer politics but not, because she's putting a thing out there that is so radically different for them to be confronted with, to shake them up and shatter, and then she pulls back and starts filling in.

These dynamics suggest an intertextual dynamic at play, in which students read Julie and Julie read students' readings of her and her relations to the course content.

Kevin's description of Julie's not conforming to students' definitions of Christianity, as well as Julie's awareness of students' responses to her, suggests several elements, difficult to separate, at work. The emphasis on the diversity of traditions, in which none is standard, eternal or univocal, posed a direct, often personal, challenge to students as knowers. Lydia commented:

> They were freaked out when she was trying to let them see that the New Testament was not a unity, that there are different voices within, and they had the hardest time seeing it. And she was talking about it, that there were different historical strands and events. They just, I have a section that is like eight out of thirty are fundamentalists, and they just get right to the core and say to me, *she*'s threatening our beliefs, and *she*'s asking us to give up our Christianity.

As Julie's historical analysis challenged students' knowledges and beliefs, they read Julie as context to understand the texts presented despite her efforts to avoid conflation with the material.[31] Her movement between earnestness and irreverence rendered some students unable to reconcile the contradictions she presented and represented, as Kevin suggested:

> Humor and religion do not mix, irony and religion do not mix for a lot of these kids. . . . One of the biggest problems with my students is getting across the idea that there is diversity, there is plurality in this tradition, there are Christians who think radically different things from what they think. And I think their discomfort with that sort of parallels their discomfort with humor and irreverence and the idea that there is basically more than one attitude towards these things. And I think the seriousness confuses them, because when she talks about the beauty of a medieval cathedral or the beauty and simplicity of prayer,

I think a lot of them suspect she's being disingenuous, because they can't reconcile that with the humor, they can't reconcile that with the playfulness.[32]

In addition to the contradictions she voices, Julie's appearance may have played into students' readings of her as (con)text for the course content. Lydia spoke of Julie's embodiment:

The way she moves in her body, it's not really feminine, I don't see it as butch either, so she's kind of in this space that I have a lot of respect for that I watch. It's hard to articulate. . . . She's rooted in [her body]. That's why I don't think a prosthesis is important to her. Maybe because they're uncomfortable, and I can't imagine she would do something that's uncomfortable for appearance. . . . It's like [my body] is comfort, and I take care of this, and this is sort of my expression and it's going to be mine. I can't even articulate it, she puts herself out there in ways that, it's a particular kind of embodiment.

In a culture that demands visual normalcy after a mastectomy, Julie's rejection of a prosthesis marks a refusal to conform to appropriate gendered appearances.[33] Neither her body, her words, nor her authoritarian demeanor correspond to understandings of Christianity or womanhood. Students may have read her through what Urla and Terry have called *embodied deviance*, "the historically and culturally specific belief that deviant social behavior . . . manifests in the materiality of the body, as a cause or an effect, or perhaps merely a suggestive trace."[34] Bodies are thought to be evidence to be interpreted, encoded with (homo)sexuality, which is "written immodestly on the face and body because it was *a secret that always gave itself away.*"[35] Following Miller and Sedgwick, I would call it an open secret, particularly given the notable absence of talk of Julie's embodiment and the preponderance of religious speculation.[36]

As an example of students' desire for knowledge of Julie, Tim praised her neutrality, yet revealed a preoccupation with her beliefs: "She's just basically stating the facts, this church believes this, this church believes that, there's conflict between churches, and she's just giving you the facts and telling you how it is. She doesn't really say I think this is right, she gives kind of an unbiased opinion on the thing. I have no idea what she believes officially. *She doesn't say it, and that's good.*" Despite his pleasure in being allowed to remain ignorant via a religious "don't ask–don't tell," Tim actively sought knowledge of Julie: "We talked about feminism and using the right tenses [sic], don't say mankind if you talk to her, say humankind. She talks about how the Bible is sexist, and things like that. I was raised, I really don't think it was sexist at all. . . . She's a firm believer in that, I think, *she doesn't say, but you can just kind of tell.* . . . I just thought there was maybe a little bit of a bias." Although Kevin and Lydia had more intimate and frequent contact with students, they were not asked about their religious affiliations, whereas Julie's were a persistent object of speculation. When I asked Kevin, "Is there anything about her sexuality that's circulating?" he emphasized unspoken (dis)acknowledgments: "No one talks about it, but it is. It's just there, you can feel it. People are almost about to say something, and you know what they're almost about to say, but they sort of, it gets cut off. I know that's there. *You can just tell.*" He elaborated, "It's like gnats or something. It's not the greatest of problems, it doesn't prevent me from carrying out my tasks or anything, but you wish you didn't have to deal with it because it just doesn't seem that important. I think a lot more of it is on the religion end than the sexuality end, that sort of feeds the religion end, it's like it's evidence that they're right about religion, or something. It's just funky."

Gnats is a particularly apt metaphor for talking about the circulation of the open secret, which Miller has described as knowledge that is omnipresent yet unarticulated, a "secret that everyone hides because everyone holds."[37] In classrooms, this circulation creates a space of paradoxical uncertainty, in which knowledges are never absolute but performative, productive of other knowledges and ignorances. Lydia disacknowledged, even as she confirmed, knowledges students sought: "I think they're clueless about her being lesbian. They don't react to her that way, it doesn't come up. And I'm sure, because I pastor to them when I've seen that their feathers have been ruffled, I do a pulse take and sort of assuage, and I know they would talk about it. Because they ask about other things. Is she Catholic? *Is she married?*" Empowered by the open secret, students validated their own knowledges by looking to Julie as a lens through which to read the content and analysis of the class in order to resist new, disruptive knowledges. However, "constructed by students as *one who never says what they want [her] to say,*"[38] Julie worked under but did not succumb to their gaze. Her self-conscious pedagogy responded to students' responses as she could. Her voice was constructed by what appeared to be visible; reciprocally, the visible was constructed by what appeared to be heard. Neither, however, offered denial or affirmation of knowledges. Rather, both unfixed knowledges such that, even with resistances enabled by the open secret, students had to take positions in relation to the subject matter.

Without the same pressures to conceal her Catholicism in Mystical Prayer, Julie's appearances functioned differently. For example, her irreverence took on a different character in the context of her openly embracing Catholicism. Rather than representing a belief system, Julie presented herself as appropriating aspects of a religious tradition for her own spiritual practices, thus inviting rethinkings about what Catholic might mean. Roger Simon's discussion of "teaching as a Jew," in which he cites multiple forms of Jewishness in order to displace preconceptions of its meanings, offers insight into the dynamics of Julie's performances: "Neither an 'ethnic' recovery nor testimony, such pedagogy will challenge students to forego closure on their conceptions of Jewish identity while I visibly reproduce myself as a Jew through an engagement with contemporary, historical, and traditional 'texts' which inform Jewish life."[39] Julie's references to engaging some practices and struggling with others enacted an unfixed positionality suggestive of individual responsibility for recreating traditions. In fact, David's description of Julie's tone in addressing the class suggests a use of the academic to explore one's implications in knowledges: "We're not talking about objective things in this class, we're talking about mystical prayer. It's an intimate topic. I really like it when a teacher can say 'crap.' If it's crap, that's what it is. Express it, there's a certain emotionality in the vernacular that needs to be expressed. And when she says things like 'goddamn,' she's expressing something. This is an academic class, but since she has an interest in it and the class does too, she can elicit that." Movement characterized the class, which alternated between lecture, particularly when texts were difficult or historical background was needed, and open discussion. David described the movement as spatial as well as topical:

> It's great when she just sits on the edge of the desk and just chills out. . . . It's like breaking down roles. We all know that she is the instructor, the expert. . . . After she's done on the board, she sits on the desk and we get in a circle, and she says what did you think about this, what did you gather from this, she'll hit the general and particular questions. And you can't get out of it, she doesn't pry, but you have to think through what you're saying. The other nice thing about Professor Howard is, as an educator you're supposed to be interested in this stuff, you're not supposed to be actually in it, where she reads Teresa, it's changed her life. In this type of class, where this is a personal issue, there'd really be a wall if you didn't address some of these things.

As I read Julie's motivations in sharing her cancer with her students, they were bound up precisely with breaking down detachment in order to demonstrate to students the possibilities of engaging in multiple ways the texts under study. After the first class, I asked her, "What was it like talking to your students in the Mysticism class, explaining that you'd had breast cancer?"

> I wanted them to know that because it was my way of kind of explaining why I was interested in particular kinds of things that they were doing. I would be more interested in what their reactions were to it, because I didn't watch them for their reactions, I just kind of told them,

and kept my eyes down, on purpose. I didn't want that to be confrontational at all, I wanted that to be kind of like a fact. . . . To me it
was something I wanted to tell them. . . . Because I think it's obvious
by the way I look, and I think it's made a difference in my life. I think
it's important, that to me is *more important than telling them other
things*, which I wouldn't tell them probably, because I don't see that
that's important. But this seems like such a shaping thing for me and
has changed things for me in so many ways. Of course, that is in no
way obvious to them, I suspect, and it might not be important to them
to know that at all.

Or was it? Claire, speaking of Julie's sharing her cancer: "*It gives you a
context, her state of mind. It helps you as a guide through the course,
because it helps you understand the human side of how she put it
together. It's nice not to have just a lecturer standing at a podium.
They're just this role, they're not who they are, they are what they do,
and she introduces more than what she does. . . . It adds personality,
context, it gives the whole class personality, a face, a sense of having a
life of its own. . . . She embodies her whole self, she says, 'I have these
physical frailties, I have this mental ability, I have this experience, and
I have this knowledge.'*"

As I suggested, there are dangers that Julie's sharing her cancer
could have placed her in a position of authority on the basis of lived
experience. For example, reflecting on teaching with AIDS, Michael
Lynch commented on the "Oracular Expectations" his illness engendered in him and his students.[40] However, the open-ended nature of the
course, the movement between the academic and the lived, and Julie's
multiple citations appear to have positioned her less as the subject-pre-
sumed-to-know than as one whose questioning and search for alternatives encouraged others to do the same. Patricia interpreted Julie's cancer as creating this openness: "She's just placed more priorities on what
she thinks would actually help students, not just, 'I'll teach this, blah
blah blah.' I think she sincerely believes, like here's a book that gives
you an idea of what other people do, you can change it a little and incor-
porate it into your life and that kind of thing." Claire used the course
for just such appropriations:

> We can discover the material as being new to us, pertinent to us, we
> can take off with our own imaginations about what it means. We're
> free to explore the text, to bring new meaning to it, to bring ourselves
> to it as a welcome feature of the class. . . . It's been a big transition to
> look at my religious past critically without saying fuck this, fuck that,
> denial of it, starting to respect how it had an impact on me from an
> objective point of view and how I care to read the Scriptures now, how
> I care to deal with my spiritual life now.

As Lydia said of Introduction to Christianity, Julie's classroom practices invited students to look at themselves rather than at her. A pedagogy that appears to be "personal" but that self-discloses performatively rather than confesses representationally enabled students to respond to the course as implicated subjects by creating new knowledges and positions in relation to those knowledges.

Julie's "personal depersonalization" extends beyond the classroom: "I'm not interested in being friends with students, I never have been. Graduate students too—I'm not their buddy, I'm somebody that's going to make important judgments about their lives. . . . I make them call me Professor Howard. I'm not on this first name shit." However, in her tacit visibility, Julie has made herself available to students struggling with sexuality and religious affiliation: "I've been pastorally aware, if that's a way to put it, of a lot of this with kids, on a one-to-one level I'm perfectly happy to do it, but I have no intention or desire to be public about this." She explained:

> The kids who are queer know that I am, they just know it and they can sense it, and they may come and talk to me and so forth. And we have these conversations where I don't have to be confessional and tell them anything, but they can talk to me, lots of kids talk to me, and feel confident about that, and I think that's enough. . . . I'm kind of a little voice of realism for some of them, things aren't really going to change very much, and you just have to learn to live with certain inequities in your life because of this. Especially kids that are in a religious tradition, Baptist or Catholic or something like that, that's pretty hostile on those issues. Those religious traditions aren't going to change. You can leave or try to somehow finesse the situation. I can tell them what both of those things mean.[41]

Lesbian is not a place to occupy, but a point of identification to use to enable students to consider their choices for ways to live in the traditions and communities in which they find themselves.

As response, Julie's teaching refused location and enacted movement, whether between respect and irreverence, the academic and the personal, or the taking up and questioning of positions. Traditions became inheritances whose implications were to be understood and evaluated in order to be put to new uses. The complications of Julie's presentation of self and subject matter responded to students' responses to what they saw and heard, and formed a representation in which voice and visibility were intertwined, dynamic, never transparent. Some students responded by assigning Julie and her content a place in order to resist new learning, whereas others engaged the responsibility of creating their relations to knowledges.

While issues of subjects' implications in knowledge played a role in

Olivia's classrooms, she framed much of her pedagogy as a response to institutional and social structures that place representational demands on her as subject. In refusing to represent a position, Olivia's pedagogy sought to place in crisis the relations of authority on which the ends of education depend.

OLIVIA: IS THERE A TEXT IN THIS CLASS?

> About the change, the effect in the classroom, it wouldn't be around any specific theme of particular thought about something. . . . I think teaching is teaching them to ask questions, because I'm not sure they do, or if they do, they're not posing them. So the change comes in simply asking questions.
>
> —Olivia

> I think she perceives students' function as taking material that's almost a nonsequitur and to constantly question it, up to and including her own authority in the class.
>
> —Frank, a student in Olivia's graduate seminar

> She has this unspoken aura that people are drawn to. She walks in and people shut up. It's the way she carries herself, she's confident or cocky. When she comes into the room, her presence is just known. It's like a president walking into the room, it's just like boom, she's there, we stop talking and focus in.
>
> —Roger, a student in her undergraduate class

As Olivia described it, her "do-it-yourself syllabus kit" functioned as a prelude to a set of pedagogical tactics intended to perform, rather than to speak or tell, a questioning of pedagogical relations, authority, and orders of knowledge. She wished from the outset to "set the class as different in terms of its dynamic and its mode of investigation from other classes, . . . an exploration rather than something that's an accomplished fact." The dynamic she sought was for students to "perform a model of inquiry, a particular kind of questioning that I want them to be able to do in their own fashion." Integral to the performance was the interrogation of orders of knowledge: "The last thing you want is for them to think there's some sort of a preset order here and that they're just sort of imbibing it. They're not imbibing an order, it doesn't exist." Rather than transmitting a body of knowledge, at stake was a process of questioning that would proliferate questions whose answers and effects could not be known in advance. A necessary, and, in fact, performative tension of her pedagogy was its reliance on the very knowledge and authority it questioned. "Do-it-yourself" functioned as both imperative and impossibility.

A metapedagogical moment from the penultimate class meeting of "Performativity Paranoia" reveals how Olivia's questioning formed a response to social and institutional structures of teaching and learning. During a discussion of *White Noise* and the rise of commodity culture in the United States after the Second World War, Olivia turned to the commodification of education:

> OLIVIA. Even as we resist what we think of as commodity culture in academe, at the same time we're affected by it every moment, in the choice of materials we can teach, in the ways that we're allowed to do things, and the way the university begins to adopt the consumer model as being education. What? Since when was education a consumer thing? Since when was anybody who walked into the classroom not expected to put out as much as they were being given? Except in a consumer model where one can go in like a tanning bed. And when that model takes off, you're in trouble.
>
> ROBERT. It is admittedly odd, but . . . You're exchanging money for a good, an education.
>
> OLIVIA. It's not a good. That's following the commodity model. It doesn't belong in the commodity model.
>
> MEG. Well, because they're paying . . .
>
> OLIVIA. There's nothing to exchange. You are buying the opportunity to engage in a dynamic, and you must engage in that dynamic in order to get the benefit of that dynamic. You can't walk in there expecting that somebody is giving you, purveying information that you then take out in some little form.[43]

Olivia's critique of the pedagogical implications of the commodification of education vivifies analyses such as Jean-François Lyotard's theorization of "the postmodern condition," in which knowledge becomes operational "only if learning is translated into quantities of information." [44] As a technological system displaces the metanarratives that have traditionally legitimated knowledge, such as speculative philosophy or the emancipation of the subject, "[k]nowledge is and will be produced in order to be sold, it is and will be consumed in order to be valorized in a new production: in both cases, the goal is exchange" (4). Under what Lyotard calls "the principle of optimal performance: maximizing output . . . and minimizing input" (44), knowledge production is located in a system in which the efficient transmission of information and skills "becomes the optimal contribution of higher education to the best performativity of the social system" (48). Whereas in the Kantian and Humboldtian universities literary studies took on the "social and socializing project"[45] of forming citizen-subjects for the nation-state, in the

University of Excellence, reason and culture become contemporaneous with the commodification of knowledge-information in a performative economy. The state of knowledge maps directly onto student-professor relations. In a performative (efficient) system of literary studies, the teaching of canonical literary texts and theoretical "methods" becomes an exchange, with the teacher-as-proprietor-of-information occupying a distinct place "in the economy, in production."[46] Space positions teachers and students hierarchically in relation to subject matter: the professor becomes the "certified bearer of the Word,"[47] the authority acceded to in exchange for knowledge-information. Efficient knowledge transmission depends on the professor's epistemic authority and is predicated on a teleology of teaching and learning as having fixed outcomes.[48] Olivia responded to this positioning by seeking to redefine the terms of the exchange through a pedagogy whose effects could not be predicted in order to challenge the reification of knowledge and pedagogy.

Two interrelated elements are central to Olivia's pedagogical performance. First, its improvisational nature should engage students in shaping the inquiry that emerges. Second, the spontaneity she sought hinged on her not, as she says, "being the text," for the text is the process of inquiry rather than her "authorial" intentions. A pedagogy that questions the very norms it must invoke for its efficacy within the circumscribed structures of university classrooms can never fully refuse the structures that make it possible. As I discuss, her efforts to detextualize herself as author(ity) in the classroom did not ultimately displace pedagogical teleologies but created forms of exchange that to some extent shifted the time and space of teaching.

For Olivia, to reject authorship is to create conditions for a pedagogical "authenticity" that does not have predetermined ends:

> There are moments of actual excitement, and that comes when there is actually a question, and they know when I really don't know the answer to a question. . . . You can't fake that, maybe you can fake an orgasm, but you can't fake that. So if you go in there and try to play that, it really is improv in the sense that it happens at the moment and it's not preplanned. I think what happens with me is that there is very much a plan, but I don't know it, I will not tell myself what the plan is, so I maintain this disavowal stance.

Her intentional disavowal is consonant with the pedagogy of psychoanalysis in which the instructor is "pedagogically ignorant of her own deliberately suspended knowledge and actually ignorant of the knowledge the analysand/learner presumes her to possess."[49] However, her acknowledgment of her knowledges suggests that this spontaneity may be illusory: "I may have on some level a larger understanding of what's going on, so I can push it in ways, it's not a total free-for-all, there's no illusion of that." Signifying (either her mastery of the texts or) the lack of a plan, she did not bring notes to her classes:

> I never go into class with a script, I may have a trick or something, but I don't have a script. I have, maybe some notion in the back of my mind where I want this to go or what I think they should be getting from it, but it often changes depending on what they say. . . . I can't stick to a script even if I wanted to. I don't think you can have real interactions with people if you've got it scripted already because people know that you're looking for the answers that you want and they're reluctant to play that game.

Nonetheless, Olivia authored and guided classroom exchanges, using "tricks" to set the limits of the stage for improvisational speech and action. For example, the "do-it-yourself syllabus kit," while enabling a conversation on knowledge and authority, paradoxically reinscribed her authority as the person who could dictate which rules were and were not appropriate to question.

Her performance of *tabula rasa* was intended to perform the absence of intentions in order to create spontaneity and shift responsibility to students: "If you want the students to be active in a classroom, you have to be active, too. You can't go in there with preconceived ideas about what you want, because they know, they know when you have certain things in mind, and it limits what they're going to do. It also limits what you do, so you can't be active in relation to what they're saying, and let it push you." A displacement of authority unfixes the ends of pedagogy:

> [Graduate students'] whole project is figuring out what the teacher's agenda is. It's a game, they'll figure out the teacher's agenda and then play along, and if you flip it on them and make the agenda based on their questions, it shifts the balance. . . . It enables them to be part of a community that's working together in relation to certain texts, where there are not preconceived ideas about how these texts work, and where everyone in the class should come out having learned something, including me.

Speaking of her undergraduate teaching, Olivia explained:

> By taking their questions seriously and following through with their queries, you teach that questioning is a viable thing, but also by leaving the questions open. You don't ask a question because you'll get an answer to it. You ask a question because there are too many answers to it. You don't interpret a poem because there's a single reading, you interpret it because you want to see how many readings there are. . . . The trick is to come up with multiple possibilities and see how they work together and play off the richness rather than the limitation.

A generative process reorganizes the linear time of the "ends" of education, for it defies the reduction of interpretation to a quantity of information and the certitude of final authority.

The seeming neutrality Olivia performed was also intended to allay resistances to what students may perceive as political goals. Regarding her introductory class, she explained, "You can never actually aim at a political agenda because students pick that up and dismiss it. They read it as political and they dismiss it. It has to be a by-product, you have to actually teach so that it's a by-product, which means that you have to tell yourself that you are really teaching issues of genre and literary interpretation." In order to minimize students' reading her pedagogical intentions or politics, Olivia shared few aspects of self, although she was aware that graduate students drew conclusions about her sexuality based on her work in lesbian studies. In both of her classes, she performed herself as a dynamic presence, yet shared little more than her theoretical dexterity in her graduate class and her humor and familiarity with American literature and popular culture in her undergraduate class. She repeated emphatically several times, "I am not the text in my class":

> I make no secret. I make no point. My sexual preferences aren't a text in any class I teach, just as I'm not a text in any class I teach, except for what I have to say that is relevant to that course. . . . I don't find it necessary whatsoever to announce it, just like I don't find it necessary to announce my religious upbringing, my tastes in pasta, or my political leanings. I think they all might be deeply evident, but I'm not going to announce them.

A "personal," lesbian or otherwise, was not only irrelevant, but would mediate the subject matter and undermine the dissolution of pedagogical ends that depended on Olivia's authorial absence. She explained, "you can't be a text in a class that aims to eradicate you":

> People are studying you instead of, they study whatever the subject matter is through you. Their total lens is, it's more like, "What does she want here?" To a certain extent it's unavoidable given the pedagogical circumstances, but you really have to work against that because to some extent, yeah, that's exactly what they're getting, is my version of this, and if you say that it tends to sort of debunk it. But what you want them to do is to begin to think independently and as long as they're reading you as the text they won't do that.

Her rejection of textuality may be read in relation to Foucault's critique of the "author-function," in which the author's presence and intentions allow a text to be understood.[50] To read the author (teacher) as text is to surrender responsibility for encountering the subject of the class as text. Unwilling to accept teaching and learning as mimetic, Olivia understood the "personal" as text as representing closure in the form of conformity to professorial intentions, whereas "process of inquiry" as text represents openness in the form of the appropriation of questioning for new uses.[51]

In the graduate seminar on American Fiction and the undergraduate Introduction to Writing and the Study of Literature, Olivia's performances took different forms and had different goals, although questioning was paramount in each. In her undergraduate class, Olivia focused her questioning on literary and television representations of the family. As I discuss below, her design of the class and her appropriation of the lecture format for a large discussion had performative effects that called into question the dynamics of teaching and learning and idealized images of American families. In the graduate seminar, in which an explicit theme was performativity, much of the class was designed to perform a questioning of academic practices, such as area definitions (including Duras and Brossard in an American class), generic divisions (in at least one class, the literary text showed itself to be theoretical and the theoretical text literary), and the authority of students and teachers. The performances became vehicles for ongoing metacommentaries on the process of instruction, similar to what Brecht called the "A-effect" (alienation effect) in his epic theater, in which the actor is a "demonstrator" who portrays an event as "striking, something that calls for explanation, is not to be taken for granted, not just natural."[52] In Brechtian theater, as in Olivia's pedagogy, spectators are not to submit uncritically to their experiences but are mobilized as producers of the text; through the alienation of the familiar, an otherwise is suggested.

I return to her graduate seminar, four weeks into the semester. The assigned texts were Judith Butler's *Gender Trouble* and Bertha Harris' *Lover*.[53] Traces of the performative syllabus lingered, as the actor/director and actor/spectators had redefined the stage somewhat.

> OLIVIA. I passed out, at the bottom of that sheet there are two quotes, a true or false test. Did you check one? Check one. [Students read] You'll never fill out forms again, will you? Are you done? How many of you checked one or the other?
>
> JIM. Would you answer true or false?
>
> OLIVIA. Sure.
>
> JONATHAN. True or false in relation to what?
>
> OLIVIA. True or false.
>
> OLIVIA. What would it mean to check one in a post-Butlerian age?
>
> TERESA. A consciousness that you're performing.

FRANK. You could just perform something by doing it.

OLIVIA. Yeah, as we know from Butler, we're all placed that way anyway. The first, which you might recognize from Butler, how many said true? [some hands] False? [some hands, but not all of the class has responded] Why not?

JIM. I said true according to Butler.

JONATHAN. I marked both.

MEG. Actually, I was following the rule of not following the rule.

OLIVIA. All right. Tom, why not you?

TOM. I didn't want to explain why I put true or false.

OLIVIA. And now you have to explain anyway.

BOB. I put two checks, I was following the rule of not following the rule.

OLIVIA. You're becoming sick people. True or false is a particular kind of a binary that forces, by simply asking you to do this, I'm forcing you to perform, so by refusing that performance you're performing something. You can't get away from it. What about the second one? True, false, anyone not say anything?

ROBERT. It's false. I'm trying to work with the speech act thing.

OLIVIA. Okay, what does this sentence say? Let's start there.

ROBERT. It's a tautology. That gender is an attribute.

OLIVIA. This is a true tautology.

MEG. I don't think so. The sentence may explode existing tautologies.

OLIVIA. What is a gender attribute?[54]

In this scene, Olivia and her students commented on the new norm that had been instituted in the class, the paradoxical norm of breaking the norm. Urged by Olivia, students articulated their options for performance within given structures while she commented on her own actions and the nature of binaries, performing content and process to initiate a discussion of gender. Although Olivia as person may not have been the text, her performance was center stage, as she directed the flow of events by shifting questioning from the content to the process of the course.

Frank: "*She sort of repeatedly cuts the floor out from under you, just so you have to find your own bearings yourself. For example, she will offer a question and you think you're studying that question and in fact what is going on is she's trying to get you to think about the degree to which you accept somebody's directions or you just say fuck this, this is nuts. She gave us this assignment in class, true or false, everybody in the class said either true or false, and I think that was what she was getting at. People were answering this question sort of honestly, and she was saying, 'No, there's not a true or false,' I think. So she can give you an assignment and you think you're answering honestly and intelligently and she says, 'You don't get it, do you?' She's trying to show how the question performs."*

As with her "do-it-yourself syllabus kit," Olivia's use of self-conscious conversations about performativity, combined with her positioning persons to perform, alienated the familiar. The performance of performativity, in which process itself becomes a metacommentary on pedagogy and performativity rather than a didactic lesson, is akin to psychoanalytic pedagogy in which psychoanalysis is not the object but the subject of teaching. A lesson of psychoanalysis is that there is not a content to be learned, but a process that allows for what Felman calls "the creation of a new *condition* of knowledge." In the dynamics of this process, the transmission of knowledge is not at stake but its use: "Textual or analytic knowledge is, in other words, that peculiarly specific knowledge which, unlike any commodity, is subsumed by its *use* value, having no exchange value whatsoever."[55]

Robert: *"She seems to be more interested, well, in method. I don't think it's content-based, it's more a matter of negotiating what we already have but is constantly being augmented or altered in some fashion, both knowledge and the process. . . . If there's an ideal class, it's that one, because we go in and converse, and it's not all located in one power source, Olivia. I mean, she is a guiding force."*

Olivia, however, spoke of "a contradiction, . . . which is that while I'm bringing into question the teacher-student power relationship, I will take tremendous power in the classroom. I'm just waiting for them to challenge it." Her power lay less in her status as "personal text" than in her use of questions to direct classroom scenes as "intellectual text." In a moment from the same class session, students had been discussing the location of the performative, whether it depends on the knowledges of readers or actors. Following Butler, they used drag as their example.

MEG. You have to already believe that gender is imitation in order to see how it is imitative.

OLIVIA. Because there are other people who are going to read drag as "Look at that pervert, that's a man dressed as a woman."

MEG. Either that or "Wow, what a good-looking woman," says a straight man. Big deal, so what, nothing changes.

OLIVIA. In other words, it reifies.

MEG. There's no troublemaking.

BOB. If we see someone in drag and we're aware it's artificial, in that case how would what we would construct as normal gender, how does that show that to be imitative?

OLIVIA. You bring up a good point between the two of you, that in order for drag to work you have to know that there are two different genders being performed there. Drag is not the performance of one, but the performance of both. Drag's no good if you don't know that the person doing it is a different gender than they're performing, which becomes then a performance of the so-called underlying gender.

BOB. The first gender.

OLIVIA. There's a double performance going on. Which imitative quality of gender is being performed / /? To make one look like the real gender, it has to reiterate this structure.

FRANK. It's like that true false business, both genders / /.

MARSHA. That's my problem with Butler, the one person who's noticing or doing any of this is the only person who's bringing anything into question, and there's no audience for it, and for me there has to be an audience.

OLIVIA. Yeah, that goes back to what Robert was saying. . . .

TERESA. So performative depends on a certain knowledge—is it performative for you? If there's a text that's meant to perform something, but you don't understand what it's performing, is it performative?

ROBERT. Hasn't that been our discussion the past six weeks, it could be or it couldn't be performative for certain readers in the abstract?

OLIVIA. Can something be performative if someone doesn't know it's being performative? There may be another way to look at this, and that may be that texts themselves will announce—that's what enables drag. It announces it semiotically. That consciousness is already in the signifying system. Someone who weighs two hundred and fifty pounds, has heavy five o'clock shadow, and is mouthing the words to *Somewhere Over the Rainbow*, you know that this is drag. It's saying, "I'm drag, this is drag, and I love it."[56]

As in this exchange, Olivia routinely responded to and integrated students' concerns and questions. She ostensibly performed a mediating role, yet her use of students' points to pursue a line of questioning continued to position her as director—a contradiction announced semiotically by her position at the head of the table. Olivia lacks the weight and facial hair, yet demonstrated institutional and epistemic authorities as she pushed the conversation in certain directions even as she offered "another way to look at this." There were challenges to Judith Butler, yet each time Olivia spoke, students offered little challenge. Despite the rule she authored of challenging the rule, her authority remained intact. Questioning had proliferated, but not reached to her authority.

Although she endeavored to dissolve her authorial presence, her intentions became a necessary element of class. Olivia became a text if not in terms of content, then in terms of process. However, her textual presence was, as Barthes has distinguished, less that of a "work," a site of cultural *reproduction* in which authorized meanings reside in the author/text to be interpreted and consumed, than it was that of a "text," a site of cultural *production*, in which meanings are open to multiple readings that become a field of "play, activity, production, practice."[57] Olivia's contradictory position as author at the center of the stage was performative of multiple institutional inscriptions of knowledge and authority at work in teaching and learning, as it both enabled and limited the creation of new meanings. Although students followed her lead in reading against authority even as they conformed to it—in order, paradoxically, that they take more authority, their articulated awarenesses and questioning of structures of knowledge and authority did not alter significantly *practices* of classroom relations.

"WE CAN'T REDUCE THE PLAY [OR OLIVIA] TO ONE MESSAGE"

> If I hit two people, I'm doing good. You could even hit five people, they start to see the world a little differently, they start to ask questions about the status quo. That's political. They grow up, they do something a little differently. That's political, I think. That's activism. It's just as much activism as having a kiss-in in a fucking mall in New Jersey. You can either annoy housewives or educate them. I prefer the education part.
>
> —Olivia

Olivia's emphasis on questioning, propensity for running metacommentaries on instructional processes, and dramatized teaching were also evident in her undergraduate class, whose content and process were structured by her choice of the theme of the American family:

> Families are a recurring paradigm in literature and literary interpretation, and, unfortunately, in the American public sphere right now, and one of the curious things about American literature is that most of the literary and filmic representations of family are not good, and yet the

public sphere keeps appealing to this wonderful thing that we call the family. There's a real contradiction going on, which I hope to have them discover for themselves. I'm not going to lecture that way.

Her syllabus, heavily based in performance genres, with four plays and five weeks of television, two novels, and a few short stories and essays,[58] suggests a loose interpretation of the course title, Introduction to Writing and the Study of Literature. Her choice of genres reflects part of her goal, a project consonant with moves in cultural studies to cultivate media literacy: "They're bombarded with media, they have no other reason to read, why would they? And I think that we're culturally shifting away from the medium anyway. So we might as well become intelligent readers of the media." The intelligent readings she sought pertained to television's representations of the family:

> [TV shows] don't paint an entirely rosy portrait, they give hints to non-rosiness, but they're hints that deflect from the fact that it may be the institution that's the problem into sort of individual quirks, like *The Brady Bunch*. . . . The kids of course disobey their parents, that's the whole crux of that, Beaver disobeying and getting in trouble. So the dysfunctionality is displaced into individual actions that are seen as not deriving from the family but from the individual within the family.

Avoiding textuality, Olivia carefully chose and placed readings and films to create a "framework" for the "discoveries" students would make. Her authority was located behind the scenes, visible in the structure she had built into the course and at times in the questions she pressed in class.

A last scene from the first day of class: A noisy auditorium packed with some 150 students, with only a few scattered seats open. Olivia enters, followed by three TAs. She walks across the stage, chewing gum in an exaggerated manner. She chews for a good fifteen to twenty seconds as she scans the audience, then makes a sharp whistling sound. Silence. "That did it. What power." She smiles and looks at them. A number of loud mutters, "Oh, God." She takes a step, "This is like a mill, such individualized attention. I'm Olivia Moran. I won't ask who you are. These are the TAs for the course. I'm the person paid to bellow. They're paid to talk. And we have a multimedia surround-sound effect for your pleasure." A few laughs. The TAs pass syllabi to the ends of the rows. Mimicking a British accent, Olivia says, "You'll learn to interpret literature and to write critically. The course is organized by genre, drama, short story, and novel. There is a larger thematic." She drops the British accent. "Yeah? No? Sound familiar? Nod your heads, look like you're alive. The thematic is the 'Family in the Nuclear Age,' how the paradigm of the family informs paradigms of literature and how literature informs American conceptions of self. It's a way into the literature, we'll be looking at terms and principles of literary interpretation, expository writing. . . . Does everybody have the syllabus? The dead people didn't get a syllabus." The TAs distribute more syllabi. "How much do you want to talk back?" A number of shouts, "A lot." "Okay, we'll discuss. I'm happier if you discuss, you have to be active, then you learn." She details policies on the syllabus. About attendance, she says, "like I'll read 150 names. But there shouldn't be empty seats. You make the choice to be in class. Discipline yourself or I'll have to." She puts her hand to her ear, pauses, then says, "Ten second response time for voices to go back and forth. . . . Discussions: you push me, I push you. We get somewhere new. Don't leave me up here alone. I can tell you what that's like, but they'd censor it."

OLIVIA. Are there more questions about the syllabus?

STUDENT [in front row]. No.

OLIVIA. She speaks from the first row for the whole class.

STUDENT. Is there a final exam?

OLIVIA. How would I give you a final exam in literature? . . . Are there other questions about the material or about life? I want to open it up to larger issues.

STUDENT. If the lecture is discussion, and the other is discussion, what's the difference?

OLIVIA. They'll know your writing better than I will. This is the university's answer to economics. One professor, three TAs.

STUDENT. Are you going to / /, so I'll know what you're looking for?

OLIVIA. [shouts] WHAT DOES SHE WANT? The goal is to be cagey, strategic writers. We'll talk more about those strategies.[59]

Her self-conscious theatrics took on a Brechtian character of performing commentaries to denaturalize the roles in which she and her students were placed as Olivia refused the information-giving mode implicit in a lecture course by creating a dialogic space that included commentary on institutionalized structures of teaching and learning. Her references to the multimedia surround-sound effect, voice-response time, the effect of institutional economics on instructional structure, her directing students to nod their heads, and her insistence that students not abdicate active roles functioned as embedded critiques of instructional processes at the same time that they signaled, as do Brechtian "learning-plays," that such processes may be changed. Spectators, to paraphrase Brecht, are not to be hypnotized by the performance but are to adopt a critical attitude.[60] These commentaries continued throughout the semester, particularly during breakdowns in the flow of class. When students did not respond or talked among themselves, Olivia would say such things as, "Yes, what are they? Sea of hands, please," or, "Are you getting again the lovely image of the happy American family here? What's wrong with this family, she says waving the book around in front of the class, as if it will suggest answers to you."

Describing the class's quick evolution into a discussion led by Olivia, Jane, a TA, said, "Her extemporaneity, and her facility at winging it is something I would really love to do more. I'm not comfortable with doing what Olivia does, which is pretty much going in there, raising a couple of very big questions and seeing where it goes." The class usually "went somewhere," although at times it became noisy and unfocused, "controlled chaos," as another TA remarked. Olivia would recenter students' attention by throwing out commentaries on recent sporting events and then returning to the discussion. At other moments, waves of chaos were beyond her control. Olivia led the discussion by asking general questions and using students' responses to further her questioning of the family. In the following excerpt, the class was discussing *Death of a Salesman*:

OLIVIA. We can't reduce the play to one message—it tells us a lot of things, many of which contradict each other. Tell me what the play is saying or doing and give an example of your point. That's your paper, so why not practice it in here?

STUDENT. Biff /knowing yourself/.

OLIVIA. That's like Polonius. Are you familiar with *Hamlet*? [She looks pointedly at students and nods her head affirmatively in an exaggerated motion; a number of students nod back.] He's the fool in *Hamlet*. Should we take that seriously? / / Anything else?

STUDENT. / /

OLIVIA. [bellows] BELLOW. YOU GOTTA BELLOW.

STUDENT. [bellows] It talks about increasing industrialization and the decline of the family.

OLIVIA. Okay. Why?

STUDENT. Nothing works, how technology is taking over life and how it doesn't even work.

STUDENT. How women should be passive and patient.

OLIVIA. What do you think that means that both plays portray women as—think of the mother in *Long Day's Journey*.

STUDENT. Because it's written in the past and those are the stereotypes of women, not like now.

OLIVIA. What you say suggests two things. First, that plays reflect life at the time they were written. You bring up a problem in the relation between drama and reality. Did Shakespeare's plays reflect Elizabethan life? They're like it and they're not. / /. The fifties aren't so happy and gentle as we're told. This consumer boom comes in and placates people. We'll see shows, think of June Cleaver. Did women really wear heels and pearls at home? Don't trust plays to directly reflect reality.

STUDENT. Do you think those shows are how people would like life to be?

OLIVIA. *The Honeymooners* is like that. And Beaver's father seems to work and have money. With no effort. What else does this tell us?

STUDENT. How the generations are different.

OLIVIA. Do you all believe in the concept of a generation? [A lot of yeahs.] But since people are born every year, where are they?[61]

As in this scene, Olivia used students' comments tactically to continue her line of questioning. By connecting issues of realism to her questioning of the family, she foreshadowed the differences between television and literary representations of the family.

Although the TAs reported that some students were concerned that they were not learning content, students with whom I spoke commented enthusiastically about the process, saying such things as "It's more interactive, it has more audience participation," "We get to have input, she doesn't just dictate," "We have the opportunity to make the class," or, "I don't see her so much as a teacher as a questioner. She asks questions, she doesn't dictate what our answers will be, . . . I like this class because I feel like student input is just as important as teacher lecture. How can you feel you're getting anything out of a class if you can't put anything into it?" When I asked four students to describe Olivia's role, they bounced terms back and forth: "Mediator." "Referee." "Translator, she translates what people say to make it sound eloquent and intelligible." "Catalyst, she stimulates the discussions. She'll start by dropping a bombshell that has two different sides, like semicontroversial and see if we'll do something with it, and if we don't she'll do something else." "She gets rid of that pedestal where teachers are placed, it's almost like she's a student herself." "She's very informal, the way she dresses, she just puts you at ease. She's not going to come in there with her briefcase and her little suit, here's my projector."

Although Olivia appeared to place herself in dialogue with students, her questioning was indeed directive: "I ask questions that make them draw certain conclusions, whereas I could ask them other questions that would make them draw the opposite conclusion, so it's a rhetorical, a Socratic tool, yeah. That way they think it's theirs." Socrates' educational goals were to instill in his interlocutors a desire to pursue truth and to offer a method for doing so through a dialectic that "demands activity and thought from the learner" by posing questions that draw on "the autonomous intellectual capacities of the answerer."[62] Olivia demonstrates that skillful use of Socratic dialogue can be put to the didactic purposes underlying Brechtian performance. Socrates, not unlike Olivia, claimed to be an inquirer who possessed no knowledge. In a discussion of contemporary analyses of Socratic dialogue, Rob Reich identifies some writers who depict the profession of ignorance as a "pedagogical ruse" to draw others into dialogue, and others who see it as a sincere attempt to enable students to bring ideas to birth. Reich holds that "postmodernists and historicists who believe truth to be contingent appropriate the sincerely ignorant version of Socrates." This pedagogue does not purvey truth but has an "openness to dialogue and questioning."[63] However, Olivia's questioning is marked by elements of control implied in her language and actions and could be said, as Finke argues of Socratic dialogue as pedagogical mastery, to be aligned with a "banking" metaphor of education in that it "function[s] to manage the flow of knowledge (defined as finite information) as a bank manages the flow of currency."[64]

To be placed at the podium in a lecture hall, a location Canaan aptly calls "the key area for the production and transmission of knowledge,"[65] is to be placed in a position of authority and control. Debbie Epstein has suggested that the instructor so positioned use interactive teaching to "reduc[e] the distance between the expertise of the lecturer and the apprenticeship of the student" so that "students' knowledge can be validated and the lecturer's knowledge can become (appear) more provisional."[66] "Appear" may indeed be the operative word. Rather than a maieutic drawing out of students' ideas, interactive questioning can guide the development of students' knowledge in ways that are less than innocent. Despite the appearance of a pedagogy in which, as Wright argues of Brecht, "the author is no longer just a hidden persuader, but openly solicits the collaboration of the spectator,"[67] the nature of that collaboration may be predetermined and the persuasion may remain hidden. Such a method may ultimately fail students, for rather than engaging in the task of thinking to change the self, they are directed developmentally toward the mastery of prespecified knowledges and skills.[68] Open-ended questioning that purports to cultivate student autonomy is haunted by the return of the repressed of the cultivation of reasoning subjects, the structures of universities, and disavowed intentions.

In this scene, the class was discussing *The American Dream*. Students had just identified Mary Tyrone as the only "good" parent in the plays they had read.

OLIVIA. Isn't it odd that out of the eight parents we've seen there's only one that seems good, normal? [Murmurs of no.] What does this tell you? I didn't pick the four plays because they're bad portraits of families but because they were about families. Why isn't that odd?

STUDENT. They're a realist style.

OLIVIA. Well, just because it's realist in style, doesn't mean it's reality. Are you saying this is like reality? If that's true, and we're reading plays from 1945 to 1978 and none of them has a good family, why are we using that as the model for what we think is good in this country?

STUDENT. Like *The Simpsons*, the plays portray bad families to show how not to be.

OLIVIA. So you're going to give the plays a didactic purpose, to show what we're not supposed to do. That's an interesting way to read it. Yeah?

STUDENT. Maybe dysfunctional is normal.

OLIVIA. Well, that raises a question about where our definition of normal comes from. Where do we get the idea of normal in the first place? Yeah?

STUDENT. I can't answer the idea of normal, but—

OLIVIA. You don't have to answer that question.

STUDENT. I guess it's to tell you that not anyone can play the perfect parent, that's just a vision that we seem to have, but it's out of reach.

STUDENT. They're based on reality and they like pick one thing where they see something wrong and intensify the bad things. And then *The Brady Bunch* intensifies the good things.

OLIVIA. That's interesting, because that goes back to what you said, that this is about what's unsaid but everyone knows. [Increasingly noisy murmurs.] We were talking about, where do we get the idea of a normal family? If it's easier to find the abnormal than the normal, does that make the normal abnormal?[69]

After this class, Olivia was frustrated by students' lack of engagement with the question of normalcy and frequent side discussions: "There are times, like today, God, we came to a rest stop. . . . I think, well am I asking them the right questions? The questions are designed to bring out more than the play. I want them to talk about style, genre, and where do we get these stereotypes of family, and all that stuff, and they don't want to talk about that." The reasons for students' resistance are impossible to identify—they may have stemmed from a refusal to be led by Olivia's questions, desires not to engage difficult analyses of the family, or disengagement in a large lecture hall. Regardless, despite some refusals to engage with the spoken or asked, the structure of the course enacted, and thus reinforced, the purposes underlying her questioning. During the weeks devoted to television, watching the shows occupied the bulk of class time and left little room for discussion. Students would watch, for example, *The Brady Bunch* on a twelve-foot-high screen, sing along to the opening music amidst murmurs of "Oh, this is the one where . . . ," and talk over the ads as if they were in a living room. In a group interview, Cathy remarked, "I'm getting bored with the monotony of watching TV TV TV."

SARA. It's getting tedious.

CATHY. It's like the McDonaldization of society.

ROGER. It's a good break.

CATHY. That bothers me, the point of watching TV isn't to be a break, and that's what people see it as. It's to know how this is different from the representations we see in literature. But we're not having time to discuss it, we see the same themes over and over.

ROGER. I used to say to my mom, why can't we be like the Brady Bunch, and the answer is because Mr. Brady died of AIDS.

CATHY. The TV doesn't affect me emotionally. With a book you read it and think about it, but with TV you don't think, you just plug in, eyes glazed.

SARA. I think that's the point, what society has become and maybe more of what we learn comes from TV than it does from literature. I mean, they're trying to stress that how TV is now is how our generation is interpreting how ideal families should be.

Their complaints about the nondialogic nature of TV, as opposed to thoughtful engagement with literature, underscore how the structure of classroom experiences performed a commentary on television's role in creating uncritical viewers. Where discussion did not lead students, process did. One young woman explained, "I'm getting a new perspective on TV and how it's written, and how they influence people. . . . I never realized that dramas showed unhappy families and sitcoms are so happy, but then when you watch them and analyze them they really aren't happy."

Olivia's "Brechtian-Socratic" performance of questioning and structuring experiences cited a norm of objectivity as she turned the university's rationalism to cultural critique rather than culture-building. Her questioning alternately obscured and highlighted her textuality in terms of content and process. The illusory student agency in this not-so-non-teleological pedagogy parallels that of her graduate class, in which her disavowed authorial intentions became a necessary element of classroom processes. Yet, although her performances were not without contradictions, even the contradictions had performative effects, particularly as the talked-about and the experienced merged and collided. These tensions highlight the impossibility of completely rescripting space and the dependence, both enabling and constraining, of alternative practices on dominant structures.

LESS EUCLIDEAN SPACES

Traditional geometry

One of the principle functions of teaching was that the formation
of the individual be accompanied by the determination of his place
in society. Today we ought to conceive it in such a way that it
would permit the individual to modify himself according to his
own will, which is possible only on the condition that teaching be
a "permanently open" possibility. . . . The connection people
make with culture must be continuous and as polymorphic as people are. There ought not to be this formation that one submits to
on the one hand and this information one is exposed to on the
other.
—Michel Foucault, "Masked Philosopher"

Conscious of the difficulties of "concluding" a chapter that represents the dilemmas of the teaching of Carol, Julie, and Olivia, I highlight several intertwined themes from their classrooms: identity, social and academic knowledges, and the haunted nature of pedagogical practices. Distinctions between place and space and the citation of convention help to understand their responses to the places in which they and the knowledges they engage would be put. Because knowledges played multiple roles in what it means to be a subject that matters who teaches content that matters, I begin with what has been alternately present and absent throughout this chapter—"lesbian" positioning—as a point of entry to inquire into authority and knowledge as they relate to pedagogical actions and their effects.

In the classroom of Olivia, Julie, and Carol and in their reflections on their teaching, issues pertaining to lesbianism surfaced only infrequently—in the form of the open secret, ministering to students, tactically coming out, and refusing sexual textuality. Instead, what is paramount are the contextual translations of their intellectual, personal, and political projects into classroom practices. For these women, the significance of their pedagogy does not lie in effecting change through articulating or representing *lesbian identity* as such but in encouraging alternative forms of thought and practice. Although Carol may "come out" to interrupt homophobia, her choices are made in the context of her commitments to effecting critical consciousness and practice. Julie's understanding of her responsibilities to students replaces a "personal is the political" with a "pastoral awareness" of helping students evaluate their choices for action. Olivia's desire to interrupt the authority on which the ends of education depend leads her to disavow a role as personal text that demands that she not reveal herself as sexual text. Their actions suggest that "coming out" in classrooms is not a simple either-or dichotomy, but an idiosyncratic act performed in the context of social and academic knowledges, intellectual and political commitments, and specific pedagogical goals.

As I discussed in chapter 1 and at the outset of this chapter, in response to ideologies that frame instructors as universal bearers of truth, oppositional norms that call for overt pedagogical positioning have been constituted. This move to the "personal as political" is predicated on beliefs that voicing the self disrupts the "mind/body split" in academia: "Once we start talking in the classroom about the body and about how we live in our bodies, we're automatically challenging the way power has orchestrated itself in that particular institutionalized space."[70] Following feminist and critical pedagogies' calls for positioning as well as identity politics' calls for voice and visibility, gay and lesbian writing on pedagogy has created its own incitement for instructors to "come out." By its logic, "out" instructors combat heterosexism and homophobia, offer gay and lesbian students role models, and counter institutionalized silencing of gays and lesbians. George Haggerty has gone so far as to argue that gay and lesbian faculty have a "duty" to be open about their sexuality so that it might be "reinvested with personal and cultural meaning."[71] Such calls for voice and visibility have created an imperative—indeed, an obligation—for faculty to figure themselves as classroom texts, to embody a category of sexuality so that their very presence is pedagogical. Julie, Olivia, and Carol refuse this pedagogical obligation, which leads to what may seem an obvious proposition: identity is not all that is at stake in teaching and learning. Their choices not to teach "as lesbian," not to represent a category that can be constraining, may be thought of as performative responses to coming out manifestos that call for professorial identity politics. To talk about the body may not be an automatic challenge to power, but a reinscription of it.

Beyond decentering identity, they suggest that what McNaron refers to as "integrating our personal identities into our intellectual pursuits"[72] is in need of reconceptualization. That integration may not be a realist representation of self, but an occasional representation, a tacit enactment, or a performance of anti-essentialism.

Pressures to "take a position" through the "personal" break down, as sexuality may not be a "personal" to reveal. Litvak's assertion that "the closeted gay or lesbian teacher's compulsory ambiguity seems, like all compulsions, forced on him or her"[73] places a singularly negative valence on ambiguity, which might be better understood as refusal of the fixity of place. Khayatt has remarked, "To come out is not simply to inform others of one's sexuality; it is a process whereby the speaker reiterates a certain relation, and perhaps a commitment to an identity, even if momentarily, and always in context."[74] Is a refusal to commit to lesbian identity tantamount to capitulating to compulsory ambiguity? Or might it be a performance of other commitments? To be placed as lesbian is to be put into place. Although a refusal of fixity is a response constructed within minoritizing discourses that fix places, it may be less forced than an effect of multiple personal and pedagogical commitments. To put relations to ideas into play, rather than invoking identities is to challenge the placement of the sexuality-identity nexus and to dwell in spaces that may be endlessly expanded and changed. To reject the "duties" of the lesbian instructor is akin to Agamben's understanding of ethics as born of irreducible singularity: "there is no essence, no historical or spiritual vocation, no biological destiny that humans must enact or realize. This is the only reason why something like an ethics can exist, because it is clear that if humans were or had to be this or that substance, this or that destiny, no ethical experience would be possible— there would only be tasks to be done."[75] To perform "lesbian" nonrepresentationally may create unpredictable relations to what can seem an all-too-predictable subject position. Rather than the closure of a "lesbian personal," new actions may be made possible by a "lesbian impersonal."

Identities were in fact not all that was at stake in these classrooms. Dramas of identification, knowledge and ignorance, resistance, and implication were played out in these pedagogical spaces. Goffman has commented that "the wider world of structures and positions is bled into [lectures]."[76] This world made for the circulation of social and academic knowledges that included, but were not limited to, identities. Julie, Olivia, and Carol held knowledges about their students and their subject matter at the same time that students came to hold knowledges about their professors and the subject matter. Their consciousness of students' knowledges played a part in constructing their (re)presentations of self and subject, which students scrutinized as part of a sub-merged process of accepting and refusing new knowledges. This inter-play of knowledge and ignorance can overdetermine pedagogical situa-tions, in which, as Deborah Britzman has written, "receiving knowledge is a problem for the learner and the teacher, particularly when the knowledge one already possesses or is possessed by works as an entitle-ment to one's ignorance or when the knowledge encountered cannot be incorporated because it disrupts how the self might imagine itself and others."[77] The abilities of Julie, Carol, and Olivia to create new imagin-ings of selves and others were based in their responses to their readings of students' readings: they performed what Goffman calls a "self-con-struing at the podium" (194). Their (re)presentations of self and their effects, as I have suggested throughout this chapter, depended on the interplay of what is and is not seen, heard, voiced, or made visible within social and academic knowledges and ignorances.

It is difficult to evaluate the three women's pedagogical effects, pre-cisely because they seek less to transmit information than to offer alter-native ways of thinking, questioning, and acting that reach beyond the classroom. These goals are neither quantifiable nor efficient, as Liberal U's accountability plans would have it, and actually call into question the congruence of the time of education and the time of learning—a con-gruence on which accountability depends. The uses to which students put their learning and the meanings they created are multiple and unpre-dictable. Grossberg's description of pedagogy as suggesting "a different organization of the space of possibilities"[78] underscores this open-ended nature of teaching and learning. Yet, because the reorganization of space occurs from a place within space, pedagogy is indeed contextually constrained. This is not to say, however, that it is overdetermined. The rearrangement of the space of possibilities occurs through unpredictable articulations of social and academic structures. In this sense, pedagogi-cal "agency" is not a property one possesses but is produced as an effect, or consequence, of knowledges and ignorances, of social and institu-tional space.

As demonstrated in Carol's course on Race and Gender, Julie's Introduction to Christianity, and Olivia's undergraduate course, the knowledges the women offered met with knowledges that formed a basis for student resistance, which was at times exacerbated by their very appearances to students. Present in Julie's and Carol's classrooms were complications of authority, distance, and objectivity, for Julie and Carol both carry visible differences and placed elements of the lived in their classrooms. Whether seemingly reverent or irreverent or seemingly objective or personal, Julie created connections among intellectual and personal understandings of religious practices to offer her students alternative ways of thinking and acting. Despite the sometimes confounding nature of her appearances, and some students' unwillingness to alter their worldviews, Julie structured her classes in such a way that students had to engage their own and others' beliefs *at some level*. Carol shifted between authoritative and occasional personalized stances as she enacted her goals of engendering students' critical consciousness regarding the social and political implications of race, gender, and the practice of journalism. Although I have little evidence that reveals how students received, constructed, or acted on new knowledges, her performance of pedagogies whose objectivity did not match her visibly raced and gendered appearance must have inserted some dissonance into a space that might otherwise have organized itself and its disruptions seamlessly. Olivia sidestepped personal social knowledges more explicitly than Carol or Julie, challenging instead academic and social knowledges without overtly figuring her relation to either. However, even as she avoided a "personal," her presence was more directive than either Carol's or Julie's. Julie's "personal" pedagogy in Mystical Prayer, for example, enabled students' creation of meanings. Within Olivia's performance of a quasi-objective pedagogical practice, even when her introductory students resisted the didacticism implicit in her questioning, the structure of class performed her goals. Conversely, she and her graduate students questioned orders of knowledge and authority despite the lack of tangible evidence of change in the *practices* Olivia was calling into question. Indeed, Olivia's performances may have functioned to reinscribe her authority and, in contrast to Julie's and Carol's classrooms, circumscribe the spaces she offered students for reconstituting meaning. Nonetheless, even within resistances to their teaching and course content, students were confronted with new ways of thinking. Yet the contours of knowledges and ignorances suggest multiple, rather than monolithic, pedagogical effects, which are ultimately unknowable. Each woman's contextual engagement of working within and stepping outside existing norms, such as citations of objective/authoritative stances, functioned as specific articulations that subtly refigured those very norms in ineffable ways.

I view the indeterminacy of their pedagogies optimistically. Radhakrishnan has asked, "If the revolution in pedagogy consists in the loss of pedagogical certitude, in what cause can one teach such a pedagogy?"[79] If professorial intentionality is problematic, knowledge per se is not exchanged, and readings are multiple and often contrary to actions, what is the value of tactical performativity in relation to the performativity of the system? The value may be located precisely in the loss of certitude, and with it, the efficient transfer of information and skills. For example, Olivia's performances in her graduate seminar, constructed in response to her understandings of institutional exigencies, reorganized the time and space of the pedagogical scene. By keeping knowledge "from reverting back into a known thing,"[80] her pedagogy did not abolish the functions of teachers and students but enacted a disruption, however incomplete, of their reproduction. To incite questions rather than conclusions and to understand knowledge as producing the unknown destabilizes a system predicated on the transfer of information. Space is reauthored as new forms of exchange are inserted into existing sets of norms.

Although the disruption to the performative economy of Liberal U was most evident (and contradictory) in Olivia's pedagogy, Carol and Julie also refused the terms of a neat exchange. By not offering up a black female identity, a Catholic identity, or a cancerous body for consumption, and, particularly in Carol's case, by performing contrary to raced and gendered expectations, they responded to tacit questions with a tacit refusal to offer answers. Through the movements of their classrooms and the contradictions they performed, they called on students to create new knowledges—citing social and institutional norms in order to do so. Such pedagogies, in which the conventional and the unconventional intermingle, do not offer complete knowledges of subjects or subject matter. Rather, they contribute to creating what Barthes calls "a less upright, less Euclidean space where no one, neither teacher nor students would ever be *in his final place*. One would then be able to see that what must be made reversible are not social 'roles' . . . but the regions of speech. Where is speech? In locution? In listening? In the *returns* of the one and the other?"[81] Authority and knowledge are displaced through exchange, through the contradictions of pedagogies that cite the Euclidean axioms they challenge. If questions are not closed but open to multiple readings and knowledge as such is never finally produced, the commodity logic of classroom exchanges is temporarily suspended. The effects of that suspension are unknowable, yet make possible the constitution of alternative practices that exceed accepted axioms of teaching and learning.

In considering how space becomes less Euclidean, I return to de Certeau's formulation of consumers as active users of space who participate in redefining its meanings. An accountable university such as Liberal U is predicated on a rational system of production whose efficiency is confused by "an entirely different kind of production, called 'consumption,' and characterized by its ruses, its fragmentation (the result of circumstances), its poaching, its clandestine nature, its tireless but quiet activity, in short by its quasi-invisibility, since it shows itself not in its own products (where would it place them?) but in an art of using those imposed on it."[82] Consumption is creative as it moves production from its intended purposes. As what de Certeau calls "the ghosts" (35) of society, practices of consumption recombine past and present conventions to put them to new uses. In short, they confuse linear time. I wish to hold onto this understanding of consumer practices as productive while extending Readings' claim that students in the University of Excellence are consumers to faculty as well. As consumers of Liberal U's space, Julie, Olivia, Carol, *and* their students actualize its possibilities. If "the University [is] a *ruined* institution, one that has lost its historical raison d'être,"[83] it becomes the task of faculty and students to invent through practice multiple reasons for its being, multiple uses to which it may be put. The indeterminacy of Excellence, its lack of referent, demands response, for it opens possibilities for teachers and students to pluralize cultural spaces in ways that are not immediately visible. Because culture is plural and educational institutions are one site of cultural production among many, teaching and learning "can form a critical crux where teachers and students develop their own practices from information that has come from different sources."[84]

Time articulates itself in the organized space of Liberal U's classrooms as the past—be it the repressed of pedagogical methods and goals, the centers of reason and culture, or the sedimented meanings of identities—returns in new forms in the present. De Certeau calls this return of the repressed "a permanently dangerous underground," for new meaning created through the recombination of elements "eliminates all 'sacred' value to which a given sign would be accredited."[85] This danger may be double-edged, both enabling and constraining. A Foucauldian reading of the return of the university's rationalism would suggest, as de Certeau remarks, that "a past model of organization is coming back and 'colonizing' the revolutionary projects of a new time."[86] Yet even as this return signals a repetition of sorts, this repetition is never a faithful copy, but necessary for the creation of new possibilities. Following Butler's formulation of citationality, a break with context allows acts to "acquire non-ordinary meanings [and] constitutes their continuing political promise."[87] Rearrangements of space through the articulation of past and present and unexpected combinations of identities and practices represent displacements that open new possibilities. I attribute some negative weight to legacies in what I read as moments in which I wondered what might have been different had rationalism or developmentalism not formed elements of classroom processes. However, in a posthistorical university, the past may become a resource, however imposed, whose return enables the recreation of space according to what is propitious in a given moment. The time of teaching and learning, in which the repressed returns in the form of identifications, disavowals, resistances, and repetitions may make it impossible to put pedagogy in its place. If education would make a space between teacher and learner, between teacher and subject matter, between learner and subject matter, the time of teaching and learning and the return of the repressed replace these separations with implications that take participants in education beyond the self, fixed identities, known places. The ruins of the university enable the creation of non-Euclidean spaces that demand ever-changing responses to situations and relations.

CHAPTER 4

Departmental Academic and Social Knowledges

In this chapter, I consider how the academic practices of Julie, Carol, and Olivia are articulated within, rather than determined by, the departmental social and academic spaces they inhabit. As locations, their departments are in unique interplay with social and academic norms at Liberal U. Shifts in the social and academic serve as resources for them to use in redefining their departmental roles and the spaces in which they work. My analysis is informed by an understanding of academic knowledge as structured by divisions that normalize. Speaking not of academic discipline but of the disciplining, or division, of *subjects* through knowledge, Foucault has offered the image of knowledge as formed spatially. Discipline, he argues, "individualizes bodies by a location that does not give them a fixed position, but distributes them and circulates them in a network of relations." Disciplinary tactics enable observation, judgment, and measurement in relation to norms as well as in relation to the gaps between persons, allowing "the characterization of the individual as individual and the ordering of a given multiplicity. It is the first condition for the control and use of an ensemble of distinct elements."[1] In terms of academic knowledge, discipline legitimates methods and topics of inquiry in which practitioners gain expertise and credibility. Although disciplines are not stable, they can have the effect of "overdetermining practitioners' identities."[2] Social knowledge disciplines, or locates, individuals on the basis of social norms, which, like academic norms, shift according to relations within as well as among networks. However, as I suggested in chapter 1, a fixed disciplinary grid does not account for disciplinary changes as new practices shift the standards and practices of disciplinary milieu. As de Certeau maintains, even as analyses of technologies of power-knowledge have enabled new insights, their focus on institutional strategies has neglected "other, equally infinitesimal procedures that have remained unprivileged by history yet which continue to flourish in the interstices of the institutional technologies."[3] Those procedures are the everyday practices of the inhabitants of disciplinary spaces, whose use of the relations of social knowledges and academic

137

norms both organizes their practice and reorganizes space. While many discussions of academic change rightly focus on the impact of larger social changes on academia, they fail to consider the role of local, internal social dynamics in defining the constraints and possibilities of academic work, and thus do not account for the relations of social positionings within departmental spaces to intellectual possibilities in practice. Although writers have sought to connect persons' social and academic positionings in order to demonstrate the mutually constitutive nature of individuals' actions and institutional structures, these efforts have been either wholly theoretical, or, when empirical, studies of macro-level disciplinary trends.[4] The "infinitesimal procedures" of everyday social life affect academic disciplinary places and spaces.

As I examine the academic and social contexts of Olivia's, Julie's, and Carol's departments, I consider how the women are alternately valued and devalued, and theorize their departmental practices as forms of agency. Of interest are the ways each woman's departmental "usefulness" creates for her a proper place, which becomes a location against which she works and a resource that enables her work. While all three are in some ways situated at the "center" in terms of recognition and rewards, they could also be said to work from positions at the margins, either due to social identities that are imposed on them or the sorts of academic work they value. However, rather than reinscribe the static spatial trope of center/margins to describe the interrelations of their academic and social positionings, it is more appropriate to speak of them as occupying multiple contemporaneous positions and to examine how this contemporaneity is enabling.

As portions of the women's professional lives are presented as texts, the texts must be read with an understanding that by "standard" academic measures, all three are "successful" in their careers. Carol is finishing a manuscript for which she has a prepublication contract with a university press, and has completed a postdoctoral fellowship during which she began research for her second book. Olivia was hired as an associate professor with tenure at Liberal U a year ago with one sole-authored and one co-edited book, and has since co-edited a book and sole-authored two books that are in press: "This is a woman with three books. Am I going to worry about promotion?" Julie is well-established in her field: "I just got my eighth book coming out this fall, and I've got two books in press right now, . . . I'm revising a textbook, that'll be out next summer. I'm just about to get another major grant to proceed with the next leg of my project on American Catholicism. I'm 53, I have breast cancer, I don't have to sort of prove anything." It is not their "success" per se that interests me. Rather, what does location in university departmental structures mean as they seek to engage themselves and others intellectually, to create and offer new ways of thinking and acting? What effects have they had in the domains in which they work and how have those domains shaped the resources they have drawn on to pursue work that they value?

OTHER/SAME

I've watched interdepartmental politics, people's behaviors and responses, [and learned] not to take any of it in terms of my own ego. It's not about me. Actually, that's a good thing to know about academe, it's never about you anyway, it's always about something else, so don't get your dander up about it. It's very tempting to get your dander up in academe. It's very tempting to get caught in sibling rivalry scenarios in academe because academe works like a big stupid family.

—Olivia

If you're a reproductive lesbian or an extraordinarily bourgeois lesbian, in terms of being monogamous, you know, replicating a married thing, it's easier, just in the same way that I think heterosexuals who are single have a much more difficult time being located in this community and in the culture.

—Karen, Olivia's colleague

Although I do not wish to advance Olivia's academic family metaphor more than it merits, an interesting thread throughout my interviews was the intrusion of the model of the family on social understandings of academic departments in two distinct, yet related, ways. Faculty spoke of all three departments as families: faculty were "wedded" to the department, faculty were grouped generationally, senior faculty "raised" junior faculty, and faculty meetings became quintessential dysfunctional family dinners in which topics of significance were avoided. At the same time, patterns of socializing were often defined by reproductive lifestyles, in which family structures created bonds and faculty with children socialized with others with children. Within these configurations, social knowledge constructed each woman, as lesbian, as tacitly counter to the prevailing culture—strange daughters, mothers, or sisters in their departmental spaces.

"Lesbian identity," however, was not central to the women's understandings of self or the constitution of their departmental positionings: multiple factors came into play as social (mis)recognitions and disciplinary definitions of academic knowledge contributed to locating them. Nonetheless, their consciousness of social knowledges' role in defining the categories they occupy constructed to some extent their departmental tactics. I discuss each woman's location separately, and conclude this chapter by pointing to what I find to be illuminating thematic convergences and divergences. However, I pause first on one element that surfaces, albeit differently, in each woman's departmental relations, her (in)appropriateness. Three anecdotes begin to reveal the complex intertwinings of social and academic norms and what their interruptions can entail.

OLIVIA. Oh, you're queer, well, there are certain expectations that carries. Like the surprise when the associate chair and chair, when they walked into Karen's house and thought it was normal. Like, "Oh, you have a house." What did you expect me to do, live in a tent? It's been very educational for people here, because both Karen and I have real houses, we have nice houses, they look like normal places. They look like bourgeois places, because they are bourgeois places. You try to explain that I'm a bourgeois kid, I came from a bourgeois family in a bourgeois neighborhood. So on some level that's really scary to them because how could a really good bourgeois turn out to be a freak? On the other hand, it's really comforting that the freaks are bourgeois. If we weren't bourgeois, we wouldn't be here basically. So you know, we're safe freaks.

CAROL. They really operated through an old boys' network to hire me, because that's the way the culture of this school operates. I was getting my doctorate at State U, many of the faculty here went to State U, many of the faculty at State U went to school here, so there's this real network. So the dean here called up the dean at State U, and asked, I think, in general terms who among your doctoral students are going to be on the market, and I had gotten lots of support from the dean at State U, and he said, "Carol." And so they started salivating: "She's one of us, but she's one of them too, you know, she's an Other, but she's one of us." And that's what they want, they don't want an alien. They want to diversify the faculty but they still want people who are essentially them, who they think are educated in the same way, and who they believe share the same values and do the same kinds of research and participate in the same professional societies and so forth and so on.

MICHAEL, JULIE'S COLLEAGUE. We had the possibility of getting an extra position from the dean, . . . so we're talking [in a faculty meeting] about what kind of person this would be. I mean, many of us feel that it probably should be someone who's interested in some sort of liberationist perspective, whether that's Latin American or feminist, . . . even that is controversial to many. So here comes Julie who could not attend, I think she was sick at the time, but she sends this e-mail for the chair to read to the meeting that talks about getting someone that does queer theory, and on she goes about this. Well, the word queer would never be used at any faculty meeting that we would ever have, I couldn't imagine such a thing. Queer perhaps in the sense of odd or strange. Well, anyway, you might as well, I mean, a pin dropped when people heard that.

SUSAN. He reads this out?

MICHAEL. YES, he reads this out, and I'm just sitting there, oh God, and I can feel certain members of the department just staring at me, "Oh, it's you people waving your banners in our department." So, anyway, I think she's felt more free to just say these things. But, you know, she knew this would never be what they would do, so she's just saying this to get a rise out of them. So, on one hand, I think her sense of humor and her irreverence about things really means she fits in with a group that might even have been suspicious of her. We all know that lesbian feminists have no sense of humor, so now we know they do, isn't that great—or at least ours does. But a couple of other times, it does, it can be counterproductive, but many times it just means that she fits in.

Both inside and outside, safe, yet dangerous, same, yet different, domesticated, yet possibly not tame. This contradictory movement is suggested by Trinh Minh-ha's "Inappropriate Other/Same," who has no pure essence, who is locatable as neither inside nor outside:

> Not quite the Same, not quite the Other, she stands in that undetermined *threshold* place where she constantly drifts in and out. Undercutting the inside/outside opposition, her intervention is necessarily that of both a deceptive insider and a deceptive outsider. She is this Inappropriate Other/Same who moves about with always at least two/four gestures: that of affirming "I am like you" while persisting in her difference; and that of reminding "I am different" while unsettling every definition of otherness arrived at.[6]

Olivia speaks of herself as a bourgeois freak, assumed to be different, yet unsettlingly same; Carol is culturally alien yet appropriately socialized into the values of her profession; Julie's humor positions her as one of, yet different from, the group. Like the Inappropriate Other/Same, their performances confuse the rules by which differences are located and contained.

Trinh's formulation suggests that it may be useful to expand de Certeau's theory of practice with an understanding of transgression that does not essentialize it as a position outside a single norm, but conceptualizes it as temporal movement back and forth, in and out, across multiple dimensions. In *The Politics and Poetics of Transgression*, Stallybras and White describe relational classifications as fundamental to ordering and sense-making in the Renaissance in a "complex cultural process whereby the human body, psychic forms, geographical space and the social formation are all constructed within interrelating and dependent hierarchies of high and low."[7] Borrowing Barbara Babcock's formulation of symbolic inversion, they define transgression "as any act of expressive behaviour which inverts, contradicts, abrogates, or in some fashion presents an alternative to commonly held cultural codes, values and norms be they linguistic, literary or artistic, religious, social and political."[8] Their focus on "acts of expressive behaviors" rather than identity (such as lesbian) or a position outside a norm underscores the dynamic, transactional nature of transgression as a "doing" that is inscribed in and reinscribes norms for new uses. Because norms and hierarchies are interdependent, Stallybras and White explain, "transgressing the rules of hierarchy and order in any one of the domains may have major consequences in the others" (3). However, these acts have "no a priori revolutionary vector" (16) but create their effects contextually. Part of their contextual effect comes about through "being" other/same. "Doing," or expressive acts, may contradict or complicate what is assumed to attach to "being." Social knowledge highlights marked differences *among* persons in a network and ignores differences *within* persons. In this sense, assumptions attached to lesbian, feminist, African-American, and Catholic offer colleagues knowledges of "social facts" that leads them to attend to limited dimensions of the women. Their resulting knowledge/ignorance is productive of the women's interactions as they at times act out and act against their marked social identities. "Identity" and "expressive acts" combine to rescript places and spaces.

Throughout this chapter, I argue that it is in practice that their positions and departmental norms are constructed and reconstructed through this interplay of positioning and acting. Carol, for example, steps in and out of social identities in order to authorize herself academically among her colleagues. Olivia performs herself as departmental good citizen rather than departmental lesbian theorist as she gains authority in multiple arenas and seeks to locate lesbian and feminist inquiry in multiple spheres. Julie's national recognition and local irreverence lend her academic and social credibility in a department that would otherwise be skeptical of her practical, committed scholarship. I begin with Julie's department, and seek to understand her positioning in terms of a fluidity of movement that may be characterized spatially and temporally.

JULIE AND THE LIMINAL GAP

It's like I went to the gospel jamboree at the —— church. It's a
great thing, I go over there every year. I go over there for church
periodically. But you see these choirs, all these black choirs, black
Baptists, black Pentecostals, they're singing, moving around,
stomping their feet, and then they have this Lutheran choir, white,
they didn't move, disembodied, they sang very nicely, but they just
didn't fit into what they're doing. That's sort of me, I think, I
don't exactly fit into what we're doing here.

—Julie

Julie in many ways does not exactly fit into what her department is
doing. However, to reverse her analogy, it is her refusal of disembodi-
ment of her subjectivity and spirituality in her scholarship and, to some
extent, her "visible embodiment" of herself as a lesbian and as a woman
who has had breast cancer that sets her apart from her colleagues. She
is not the lone disembodied Lutheran choir but the lone black choir who
sings, stomps, moves, and claps. Elements of this "visibility" have to
some extent historically defined Julie's interactions with her colleagues,
yet her use of "voice" in practice has mediated its meanings within her
tightly knit department.

The Department of Religious Studies, which has under twenty faculty members, was formed in the late 1960s amidst acrimonious university debate over the role of religious studies in a public university.[9] Julie
entered the department a few years after its formation. Bob Kirkland, a
former chair of the department, recalled the circumstances of its founding: "Everyone sort of looking at us, that kind of hovered over, that we
were being particularly evaluated to see what we, a lot of faculty just
don't know what it is, what are you doing in the study of religion. . . . I
think part of the culture is to lean over backwards to separate ourselves
from any theological engagement, to make a very clear wall between
what goes on in a seminary and what goes on in a state university." In
addition to this historical legacy of objectivity—one consonant with the
exigencies of Liberal U's status as a secular public institution devoted to
the objective pursuit of truth—the external scrutiny, as Bob described it,
contributed to creating internal unity: "When you feel a questioning outside the group, it formed a real sense of cohesiveness. We were founding
the department, we were building it, there was no long history of bick-
ering or anything like that, and that has remained pretty much throughout. But from the very beginning it almost developed the feeling of a
family. We really felt very closely bonded together." As I spoke with faculty and graduate students, I heard few complaints, detected little bit-
terness, and listened to frequent expressions of contentment with the

department. Julie also spoke positively of it: "Some of my colleagues I don't particularly like, and others I like very much. But I'm in a very good department in terms of kind of friendly relationships that people maintain. We've got two or three parties we have a year, we do colloquia, we read each others' work, we talk about it, it's a very congenial kind of department."

After two decades of little hiring, a number of new faculty positions were filled in the 1990s, creating something of a generational split in the minds of faculty. Bob characterized disparate approaches to "what is religion and how is it best studied" as a central departmental question that has shifted generationally: "One of the big issues is what role does the teaching of theology have in a state university, and that for many years was a very divisive issue, and I think we're now into a sort of live and let live. I don't think the younger generation has quite such an ax to grind on that issue." When I asked Michael, Julie's younger colleague, to describe the culture of the department, he turned immediately to speak of generations:

> MICHAEL. I would say the most outstanding thing about our department right now is the generational difference, in which we have a group of people who are in their mid-fifties to mid-sixties who have been in this department for many, many years, and who came mostly in the late sixties, early seventies and have been mostly together for all that time. And then there is a group of us who arrived here in the last five or six years, there's a whole bunch of us, most of whom are in our thirties, even late twenties. There's not real tension between these groups, but I think it's the most interesting part of who we are, and it's kind of a difference in culture between the one group and the other. And then there are the people who fall in between, who fall in between or into some sort of liminal gap between these places, and interestingly, Julie, although she technically falls into the older category, kind of falls into that liminal gap.
>
> SUSAN. How would you describe the two different cultures?
>
> MICHAEL. I'd say, in a crude way, the older culture is more male, more straight, more dedicated to the notions of seeking objective truth and this kind of thing that characterize liberal academic scholarship. . . . I would say the younger group is not as male, more diverse in their family living situations, and profoundly less optimistic about things such as going out and finding the truth, whatever that may be. More formed by recent developments in the academy, the postmodern side of things, interested in things like gender. . . .

SUSAN. So talk to me about the liminal gap, what's going on in the liminal gap?

MICHAEL. Part of it has to due with age, . . . there are cores of people who socialize together in each of these groups, and in the gap fall some people who I don't think belong to either core group of people socially, or who, for one reason or another, would seem to belong to the one group but has more affinities with the other. Julie falls into this category, she has been here almost as long as everybody else, but in terms of the way she does things, her personal life, who she bonds with in the department, belongs to this other group.

Liminal, *of or pertaining to the threshold,* is derived from *limen* (Latin for boundary or limit). To dwell in the liminal gap is to occupy a space that is relational yet not specifically locatable *within* boundaries. Julie's internal differences, her differences from the category in which she seemingly resides, and her "expressive acts" place her in multiple simultaneous relations rather than inside or outside a single group. Giorgio Agamben has written of threshold:

> 'outside' is expressed in many European languages by a word that means 'at the door'. . . . The outside is not another space that resides beyond a determinate space, but rather, it is the passage, the exteriority that gives it access—in a word, it is its face, its *eidos*. The threshold is not, in this sense, another thing with respect to the limit; it is, so to speak, the experience of the limit itself, the experience of being-*within* an *outside*.[10]

If borders mark differences between *this* and *not-this,* Julie's liminality could be, as Kal Alston has said, a means by which she, intentionally or not, uses her position "in, between, and beyond to resist and subvert the taken for granted relations of the world."[11] The thresholds in which she dwells, comprised of shifting boundaries and spaces, may be an enactment of a questioning of fixed place and location. The changing social and academic landscape of Julie's department, the shifting networks of relations, have been constitutive of her positioning, the meanings and possibilities of her actions and interactions, and of the limits themselves.

Julie has participated actively over the years in building the department, publishing, serving on departmental, college, and university committees, and developing new courses. Although scholarship has recently taken on increasing importance, teaching continues to be valued, and is an area in which Julie has excelled, having received consistently high student evaluations and a universitywide teaching award. Moreover, the areas in which she teaches have pragmatic utility:

> I teach a lot of different stuff, which is another difference between me and my colleagues, I'm much broader but less deep than any of them,

so they just teach in one little area. See, I've taught Religion and Literature, Mysticism, Christianity, I've taught Judaism, Christianity, and Islam, I've taught Women and Religion, I've taught Fundamentalism and Gender, I teach Modern American Catholicism, so I've got a really broad kind of range of stuff. I'm very useful. Useful is my word for myself.

Julie is trained in Patristics and theology (the only faculty member whose graduate education was not secular), yet teaches neither in Liberal U's nontheological setting. She is primarily "self-trained" in her teaching areas, surrounded by colleagues who teach in their areas of specialty, which are consonant with the objective study of religion. Despite the significant role Julie has played as a teacher and mentor,[12] it is her research that is salient in terms of what she values and how she is received and positioned by colleagues. The domain from which she derives the most satisfaction is precisely that which is least understood, creating a sort of scholarly liminality.

Inside/Outside Academic Knowledge

> When I read Julie's things—I find [her book] very suggestive, it opens up ideas to me, but that's regarded as, *if not right at the edge, then over the edge.*
>
> —Bob

> Most of the stuff I've written is useful. It has some ideas in it, but I would say that the bottom line is it's useful. I wouldn't say that much of any of the stuff my colleagues have written is useful to a general audience. It's probably useful in a scholarly way, and, you know, I've never been interested in that.
>
> —Julie

Michael emphasized the department's drive to preserve a secular identity as playing a large part in determining what sort of scholarship is valued:

> Historical study that seems to have nothing to do with contemporary communities of faith or other commitments, written in peer-reviewed journals and published in university presses. Work that comes from a clear position of advocacy, of spirituality, of wanting to speak to a contemporary community, and as a part of that community, is often devalued, and I think a lot of people in the department don't know how to evaluate it, it's not objective. There aren't objective criteria by which to measure the value of such work.

Julie described colleagues' perceptions of her scholarship: "Some of the old men in my department see my stuff as way too popular, too simple, way too accessible, because I do sort of broad cultural analysis. A lot of these guys, especially the historians, are miniaturists, I mean, they work on some guy's thought from 1671 to 1673. I've never been good at that, I've never liked that." Speaking of the effect of their responses to her work on her, she explained, "I think for a long time, I felt a lot of, and I may have construed this all in my head, but I felt a lot of negativity from those guys, you know, like what they did was great, what I did was not. I think what I do is skillful, but it's not always kind of valued in a way. . . . People read my stuff. So, anyway, all of that kind of makes my colleagues happy and not happy at the same time."

Although Julie has engaged in historical analysis that could be construed as appropriate, she has framed her scholarship as stemming from her position as a member of a religious community concerned with practical dilemmas. In a department that seeks to erase theological and practical engagement, Julie's work walks edges. Bob explained:

> Anything that has a practical orientation, that is written for the benefit of, well I've done a lot of stuff for the public schools, or even worse, for the church, is just discounted, basically. But anything written for, that was primarily of use to the church, and we've had several colleagues who've done that, including Julie, was put under the service column, was not scholarship. This was material that was interesting, it's helping other groups, and we benefit from that.

The benefits he went on to refer to were Julie's national visibility with "regular" church members, Bishops, and National Public Radio, and the resulting recognition the department has received—recognition, however, that is not in and of itself "scholarly," and may contribute to making her "colleagues happy and not happy at the same time."

The privileging of historical analysis, objectivity, and detachment over contemporary concerns, subjectivity, and commitment results in a not-so-benign neglect of Julie's work:

> The last time I was evaluated, I think [a book] had just come out, and basically what they said was, "We don't know how to evaluate this. This should really be evaluated by the people for whom it was written." It's like the only people who could say whether this was a good book or not were Catholic women who were struggling with their identity in the contemporary Church, that somehow my colleagues weren't able to judge. And I was disappointed, if not pissed off, by that response. I mean, I just thought, you weenies, why can't you just say one thing or another thing?

Despite the unknowable loss when new ways of thinking and communicating are not nurtured locally, others may gain from Julie's presence. Her thought may contribute to shifting what is understood as *at* or *right over the edge*; her colleagues may come, as Patricia Williams has said, "to wonder about the things I wonder about, and to think about some of the things that trouble me."[13]

This shift of limits, or edges, may be made possible by the significant external support, recognition, and awards Julie has received: "I don't think they like this more popular stuff quite so much, and I don't really care anymore, and by the time I retire I will have pulled in more than a million dollars in grant money, and that's more than any of them. And they can't figure that out, why did she get all that money. . . . They don't know why this is happening." This is "happening" because outside the space of Liberal U and the Department of Religious Studies, there is a need, or demand, for what Julie values—addressing contemporary dilemmas facing the Church. While this recognition does not necessarily internally validate the form and content of her scholarship, it at least creates an acknowledgment of its legitimacy, if only in other spheres. In an ironic twist, Liberal U's quest for external funds to enhance its reputation[14] and prove its external relevance institutionally legitimates what is departmentally marginal:

> To get that kind of grant . . . you do have to have your finger on a more popular pulse, I think, and you have to be willing to do stuff that's going to make some kind of actual practical difference for the way churches look at themselves, because that's what they're interested in. My stuff, I hope, will lead American Catholic Bishops and activists to some new dimensions that might actually change the Church. Well, we're not supposed to be interested in the Church. We're just not. As I always am telling people, people in Religious Studies don't believe anything, they think we just study people who do, we think they're neat. Also I think you're at a slight disadvantage if you're Christian. I mean, there's this veiled orientalism that's still around in the department, in some of these old boys. They'll go on and on about how great it is that Gary is a practicing Buddhist, they would vomit at the thought of somebody being a practicing Catholic or an observant Jew. They go on and on about how he went on this pilgrimage, he walked a hundred miles looking at all these Buddhists, his feet got blisters. This is like Norman Mailer. But if some woman, some Christian, if I had gone to England and walked on the pilgrimage for Our Lady of Walsingham, and wrote a book about it, they would be embarrassed. They don't realize how offensive this is, of thinking this is okay and somehow cute for people as long as they're doing something as "bizarre" as Hinduism or Buddhism, but it would be really awful if they were doing "real" religion, like Christianity.[15]

There are hints of departmental shifts in the valuing of objectivity and the devaluing of practical issues of faith. Bob suggested that the younger generation doesn't have such an "ax to grind"; Julie described the veiled orientalism as "still" around, locating it in "some of these old boys."

Somewhat parallel to Julie's "practical" work, her involvement in feminist scholarship has not always "fit" her department or discipline. As Michael commented, "She was interested in things like women and gender long before it was particularly hip or cool in the academy."

> When I first started doing this, in the early seventies, and I was doing some of it when I got here, they sort of thought this would go away, or Mary Daly was a nut,[16] or various things like that. I think in [a book she published in the mid-1980s] I said, I hoped that I could make feminism more accessible to my religious studies colleagues and religion more accessible to my feminist colleagues. I mean, one of the places where I get stuck in this is that most feminists think that religion sucks the big one, and the whole idea that God, church, religious community, prayer, would even be a problem, just totally eludes them. The real problems are representation or hegemonic blah blahs or abortion. So I think most feminists don't find religion an interesting problem and most religious studies at that point didn't find feminism an interesting problem. They thought it was faddish, secular, and not particularly interesting. I think now we have a whole new generation who sees the kinds of things you can do just in scholarship once you take into account this whole other half of the human race, and it's really interesting. It will change the way we look at the Gospels and the way we look at late antiquity and the way we look at history, the way we look at other things. So I think it's made its way into the academy in that particular kind of way.

An additional liminal gap becomes apparent: a space between religious studies and feminism, in which there was little intellectual community within or beyond Julie's department that nurtured her bringing them together. However, since the late 1970s, disciplinary shifts encouraged by feminist activism and the subsequent development of women's studies and feminist scholarship have made gender a part of inquiry in religious studies, as in other domains at Liberal U. Nonetheless, as recently as 1995, Judith Plaskow wrote of the difficulty of feminist religious studies: "Working within a system that rarely rewards, and sometimes punishes, engaged scholarship, how do we maintain our commitment to engagement? Working within a system that values preciousness and jargon above clarity and reach, how do we maintain a commitment to speak to a broad audience about issues that make a difference in ordinary people's lives?"[17] As with her "practical" writing, enabling to Julie has been the internal validation of her feminist work through external pressures:

> I wouldn't say I've gotten tons of support inside the department to do feminist work. It wasn't as though there was someone who ever threat-

ened me in some way, or said this is just going to lead to no good end. Our former chair, I think, thought it was frivolous and a little odd, why would anybody want to do this, but, you know, once I got an NEH that muted a lot of those guys who wondered what in the hell this was all about. And then when the book came out, I got a lot of support, and it won an award, and I think I got promoted on this book, to full professor. I've put some stuff in the curriculum on this, a Women and Religion class at the graduate and undergraduate level, and that's been useful for us. . . . They now know that we have to do that, that if we're a department with no women in it, or a department that does no feminist stuff at all, we just look really weird. So, and they all have tried to mainstream some of it into their classes, some of them with more success than others. Some of them with more interest than others.

The institutionalization of inquiry into gender and external demands for practical knowledge place her scholarship in an unfixed position at the threshold, neither at the edge nor in the center.

In depicting the skepticism some colleagues have expressed of her work, I do not mean to suggest that Julie is not an integral part of the department, for faculty and graduate students consistently spoke of her with respect and affection. In many ways, Julie's social interactions mediate what could be her tenuous academic positioning. Michael spoke of her irreverence about religion as softening the impact of the impropriety her Catholicism:

> It fits in exactly perfectly because this older generation, one of their great virtues was, and still is, their total commitment to the secular study of religion in this environment, so that there is a freedom about irreverence about religious studies and so on that is just fine. Everyone in this department is distanced enough from what we're studying that I think that irreverence about religion is perfectly appropriate. . . . Her humor and so on makes her able to function in that group of people without difficulties.[18]

Julie's social interactions confuse her otherness by performing a sameness, making a fixed location impossible, instead enacting a liminality at once inside and outside, appropriate and inappropriate.

Even with the enlarged network of collegial relations and attendant shifts in academic norms that I have described, Julie's scholarship is but one source of social/academic liminality. Her sexuality and her breast cancer should remain unspoken. I have chosen to discuss Julie's sexuality somewhat separately from her scholarship, for until recently it has had little overt bearing on her intellectual work or relations with colleagues. However, to say that it has had little bearing seems an impossible statement, for the energies, meanings, and consequences that concealment entails are unknowable. Like her academic work, Julie's sexuality has taken on shifting meanings within the shifting limits in the department. It has been her perception that social knowledge of her sexuality would affect colleagues' perceptions of her relation to academic knowledge.

Social Unknowing

> I think partly because of Karen, partly because of the cancer last summer, I've been more flamboyant, I think, in my own terms, in the way that I dress and act and talk around the department and the classroom.
>
> —Julie

Julie's concealment and unconcealment of her sexuality have largely depended on the relations of seeing and knowing among colleagues who have historically chosen not (or perhaps been unable) to see or know. Julie and Michael's descriptions suggest that although the department as a whole has historically denied the presence of homosexuality in its midst, faculty members are not overtly homophobic: "They're liberally tolerant for the most part, and I think the young people are quite accepting and queer-friendly. I think the older ones would like to think they're not bigoted in any way." Michael echoed Julie's thinking, "That older generation, there is certainly no prejudice or anything. It's, however, not something that normally fits into their normal life. I can tell that the way they think about me and my relationship is in fact somewhat different from the way they think about my married colleagues' relationships."

Julie says she expended "a lot of energy around obscuring it when I first got here." During her first decade at Liberal U, she used her actions and the visual to avoid the (mis)recognitions that knowledge of her sexuality might have brought:

> I was into a lot of sort of public denial about that, and at that point, I didn't think, as I do now, that lesbians have a look. I don't know if it's really true, but there is a way that I have about me, so there's something really funny when I think about myself tromping around there trying to look like a suburban housewife. . . . I had this little hairDO, rather than a hairCUT. . . . [Before], when I first came here I had real long hair all the way down my back. I was very thin. I was sort of a character of a different sort. I was not opposed to being a kind of a character or slightly eccentric, but I never cast it in sexual terms. It always had to do with—I mean, I had this amazing kind of denim jacket that somebody had embroidered the whole kind of Muslim creation myth on the back. I would wear that with this long hair, and I smoked, but no, never, it was probably designed in some ways to divert people from thinking about anything else.

Julie figured herself as visibly different, yet not sexually different, for the "lesbian" look to which she referred is bound up with gender norms and styles of dress. Urla and Terry's notion of *embodied deviance*,[19] in which the gendered body is constructed as material evidence of deviant social behavior or sexuality, was operative in Julie's management of information about herself. Gender nonconformity is encoded with sexuality, as Kath Weston has remarked:

> In the United States, the shifting sands of gender are sculpted, in part, by the widespread belief that lesbians can be identified at a glance. "Is she or isn't she?" people wonder. To back up their speculations, they look for clues, confident in their ability to infer sexual identity directly from bodies. . . . In most cases the clues people seek are not about sexuality per se but about gender. Rather than ask whether anyone has ever spotted So-and-So kissing another woman, people are more likely to assess her gay potential based upon the timbre of her voice, the way she occupies space in a room, the boyish cut of her clothing, or her "nontraditional" job.[20]

Julie's "degendering" of her nonconformity offered (mis)representations that enabled colleagues' ignorance in that she did not fit with social knowledge of what a lesbian is. In other words, persons create assumptions based on what they see; conversely, these assumptions dictate what can be seen. In this way, she has been cast as a blank page:

> If you live alone, which I have done many of the years I've been here, and have not had a girlfriend, I mean, there isn't anything, there's nobody sort of *seeing*. Those people who *want* to are free to think of this as an unenacted tendency or something like that. . . . I think that was true of my colleagues when I was living with Linda and we would go to these parties. Several of them just didn't, they don't tend to think that way. I mean, I think that's true of my generation and older, you don't *look* at somebody and immediately speculate about their sexuality in a way that you do now.

To see, to look, is to have evidence, to know, yet the visual allows and perpetuates ignorance. Julie and her partner of six years were "in evidence" at departmental parties, yet discreetly so, for it was during her years with Linda—when there might have been tangible evidence—that Julie adopted the "suburban housewife" hairstyle and dress: "We appeared socially as a couple [at department gatherings], that didn't seem to bother anybody. And she was very into dressing, very chi-chi, good-looking and all that, so I don't think anybody would have figured this out. Plus, she was a convert, she'd been married twice." What is seen does not conform to knowledge of what a lesbian looks like; what is known—that Linda has been married—prevents seeing a lesbian, as it does not conform to what a lesbian is or does. A reciprocity was at work in which the visual constructed knowledge/ignorance at the same time that knowledge/ignorance constructed what was possible within the visual. These convoluted dynamics of knowledge and ignorance extended to Julie as well, for she lived in a sort of unknowing, assuming that her colleagues had a tacit knowledge of her sexuality, when they in fact did not: "When I broke up with Linda . . . I was just devastated. So we [Julie and a "favorite" colleague] went out to lunch and I told him about this and he said, 'I had no idea you were in that kind of relationship.' And I think that's sort of how my colleagues were, and I think I assumed that's how the students were, that they didn't know, they didn't particularly want to know, and there was no particular reason to tell them."

Julie recounted an incident from only three years ago with a colleague whom she has described as antifeminist and homophobic that reveals the links persons can imagine between sexuality and positioning in relation to academic knowledge:

> I was on a search committee with her, and a couple of people we interviewed were obviously gay, and she said, "Well, we can't hire him, I think he's gay." And I said, "So what?" "Well, you know, gay people have this political agenda," and blah, blah, blah. So she was just difficult. We did hire a gay man. I think what she didn't know was that we interviewed ten people, and nine of them were gay. I knew that. She didn't know that. . . . I was saying to a younger colleague later, "She's saying that to me." And then this other woman said, "Well maybe she doesn't know about you." And I said, "Oh, come on." And then the guy said, "Well, why don't you tell her?" And I said, "Well, why should I come out to a homophobe?" I have no investment in that. Screw her.

Visual (mis)recognition has shaped Julie's use of voice in her choice not to constitute new forms of being seen and known for those who would prefer not to have such knowledge. Unwilling to speak "a truth of herself" in order to reconfigure ignorance, or pessimistic that such a voicing would reconfigure ignorance, Julie refused to present herself as lesbian.

Julie described herself as more flamboyant, "in my own terms," in her dress, actions, and speech in the department. However, even as she has come to worry less about others' perceptions, the visual has not had a uniform effect of divulging her sexuality. Julie's "terms" are clearly in flux, as she comes to know herself as a person who does not deny or conceal her embodiments but does not claim them as representing an essential self. The visual may be self-referential, though not, I believe, a transparent representation of self. However, it is impossible to know, as Abena Busia has asked of dress that breaks with expectations, "how much of it is internal and how much a construction of the self in the face of external gazes?"[21] As Elizabeth Wilson has pointed out, "In our hairstyles, our choice of clothes and our use (or not) of cosmetics we create an 'appearance' for public and private consumption; an image whose relationship with some implied 'reality' beneath it is not so straightforward as it might seem."[22] Not prone to "voicing" her sexuality representationally, Julie's recent openness is enacted through a tacit visual representation of self and an insertion of queer topics into the department through her actions and speech. Julie's use of "voice" is not (self-)representational, "denot[ing] the public expression of a particular perspective on self and social life, the effort to represent one's own experience."[23] Rather, she uses her voice to disrupt the taken-for-granted, for example, by placing queerness in the realm of academic knowledge. Michael described in Julie "a change . . . that I'm still seeing something that's going on. What I mean by that, I think there is a greater willingness to be herself and not do things that are false. And this has led to a certain more emboldened character in the department to simply say what she thinks, or simply to say things that she knows will freak out people in the department." In describing her willingness to articulate the unspeakable, Julie referred to the same example I drew from Michael's depiction at the beginning of this chapter:

JULIE. I've just started to say little things like queer theory, you know, it just makes these people, they don't even know that such a thing exists. So I think as I get more daring and as I retool myself in the next year about what some of that means, I am going to start bringing that into meetings. I am going to start saying, if looking at religion, looking at women, looking at all this can give us a different slice through these things, so can this perspective, and I think I'll get some support, not just from Michael but from a couple of other people on the faculty.

SUSAN. So what's the effect around you as this stuff comes up or as you say things?

JULIE. The effect? I don't know. Danielle is consternated, but she's easily consternated. The old guys, I've been living with these guys for twenty years, and I'm not going away, they're not going away. Nothing's going to happen with this, we're not going to hire somebody in queer theory, so they don't have to worry and they know that. It'll give the young people a kind of chance to have a reaction. I do it mostly I think to bother some of them. . . . It's a joke for me right now. And when it gets to be real, I want to get to the point where I'm like Karen, I know what these texts are, I know what kind of arguments they're making, I know how valuable somebody like Judith Butler is, I know how to raise some of those arguments. And so if we see somebody coming through here on a job application or something, who's got some expertise in that, I'll know how to evaluate that.

The contradiction between Julie's statement that the department will not hire a queer theorist and her desire to be able to evaluate applicants suggests that her mentions of queer theory may be disingenuous. Or, given the departmental context, she may have been acting out the family role of "bad girl." Yet underneath the humor or role play lies a seriousness to her mention of queer theory. Breaking with the appropriate to "name" it in department meetings, she disrupted her colleagues' academic ignorance of a burgeoning area of scholarship that could reshape aspects of inquiry in their field. Her social and academic liminality enabled a pressing at the edges of departmental limits. A form of acknowledgment entered the departmental space.

Julie's voice is by no means unitary, for in the complicated intertwinings of social and academic knowledges, she at times disrupted assumptions and at times softened the impact of others' (mis)recognitions. Her refusal to conceal her mastectomy (euphemized as her "surgery" by nearly everyone with whom I spoke) visually announces a refusal to conform to gendered expectations through concealment of the loss of a symbol of femaleness.[24] However, Michael suggested that Julie's humor may actually defuse the recognition that the visual invites:

> Sometimes for this older generation humor can function as a way of avoiding or putting at a distance sensitive personal issues that they might find uncomfortable to talk about or deal with. I think Julie's surgery and the way she's chosen to deal with that makes people face this is a person who's had this kind of surgery, and I think some of them sometimes mistake her willingness to joke about it to mean that this is not a painful thing. I don't know, but I think all men of any age, sexual orientation, whatever, find this an extremely uncomfortable topic, it's just difficult.

It is difficult to know if Julie's humor deflected conversation about her breast cancer or, given the interpersonal dynamics of the department, offered a means for its verbal acknowledgment, even if in the distanced way Michael described. Although Julie consistently intertwined her breast cancer with what she felt was increasing openness about her sexuality, she did not speak of a need to *voice* their meanings with colleagues. The presence or absence of a single breast is a visual reminder, an embodiment, of the border between illness and health, life and death, a liminal space that does and does not speak for itself. This personalized visibility may create knowledges in a context that does not easily acknowledge its knowledges. Her visual challenges are not those of transparent presence, but are mediated by and mediate her use of voice in social and academic interactions as the contradictions she embodies and enacts position her in multiple simultaneous sets of relations.

In contrast to the shifting mixtures of social and academic knowledges that constituted Julie's departmental positioning, the salience of Carol's racialized visibility in the School of Journalism placed her in a confined academic positioning, which she had to combat in order to gain broad-based academic authority aligned with her areas of expertise. I begin with the academic context of the department, moving to discuss Carol's entrance into the departmental social and her means of establishing herself academically.

CAROL AND SHIFTING AUTHORITY

The School of Journalism, comprised of some thirty faculty, built its reputation on the basis of its empirical research as well as its preparation of practitioners for media industries. This legacy of disciplinary and professional norms was beginning to shift when Carol came to Liberal U. If one were to follow a generational model, the school is on its first generation beyond the tenure of a dean who developed the school's reputation and whose name continues to be "invoked when people talk about the ways things should be done, would have been done," as Sara Brookes, a senior faculty member, described. Since his departure, the school has not lost its strong empirical and positivist base, but has been complemented by new faculty who conduct qualitative research. In addition, it is in the midst of a shift from a focus on preparing practitioners to increasing recognition of scholarship, although teaching continues to be highly valued. Carol identified herself among the new faculty, who "are more scholars or writers. We've been more influenced or socialized by the way academia is today than were many of the senior faculty, most of whom have never published a book, most of whom have developed their reputations on a series of journal articles, and a lot of it is pretty boring and not very exciting stuff."

Despite this shift to scholarship, the school maintains a priority in hiring faculty according to their teaching credentials, as all faculty teach one vocational and one "academic" course each semester. Sara explained, "It's not terribly unusual, but a lot of schools found after a while that hiring people with that kind of mix became harder and harder, and started hiring professors on different tracks. It really does become frustrating to find people with strong credentials in both." Carol emphasized the importance of teaching: "The Journalism School is somewhat different in its value system about teaching than the rest of the university because historically as a professional program, up until a few years ago, scholarship was not always the dominant paradigm. The discourse and the history of the school is that teaching is very important, and so people here can still get tenure, and have gotten tenure, on the basis of teaching as opposed to research." However, definitions of faculty work have taken on multiple valences, as Ben, a junior colleague, explained:

> There is a large contingent of people who place a lot of emphasis on teaching, consider that their primary function, their primary activity, and devote most of their energy to it. . . . I think everybody shares these values, so maybe it's a question of the degree to which, or the strength of their orientation. There would be a set of people who would see our role as far more academic, that what we're about is understanding communication, mass communication, or mass media, their role in society, and they would probably see us as less oriented toward or less concerned with creating semiprofessionals.

Ben described rapid changes in media industries and technologies, such as cable television and on-line news delivery, as bringing about a rethinking of curriculum away from programs of study organized along industry lines toward study of communications to "train students more broadly." The tensions these changes created among faculty often remained unarticulated, as Sara described:

> We talk endlessly over petty issues and tend to avoid talking about larger philosophical issues, so they never really get aired, they stay submerged. We've never really finished talking about changes in the undergraduate curriculum, the role of the school in the profession, whether we want to continue to have accreditation. We don't address these issues because people, I think, are afraid to deepen divisions. Sometimes if we approach these issues, and see that there are serious cleavages, you can imagine what it would be like if we really got into it.

Curricular shifts, moves to recognize faculty as scholars, and the advent of multiple forms of scholarship have created a mix of goals and sources of authority in the school. As I spoke with faculty, there did not appear to be distinct "groups" in which espoused values were coextensive with positions of power. Rather, Carol commented that positioning was unclear, as teaching, scholarship, and longevity combined to grant faculty differing levels and types of authority:

> Power is determined by a lot of factors. One is how much status you have in the profession generally, and sort of how much, I would say in the Journalism School it has a lot to do with longevity, this is a department that is all about history and hierarchy, and so people who have

been here longest and sort of climbed the ranks and see themselves as
having paid a certain amount of dues tend to have the most influence.
They claim the most power. . . . They completely are about authorizing their own true position. And then status in the profession, the ones
who are better known, who are real published and all of that, that
gives them more voice and more authority. . . . Not everyone, simply
being a senior faculty member doesn't ascribe to oneself a modicum of
power. This is still a place in which teaching is pretty highly valued, so
that makes a difference.

In contrast to the school's crisis of academic authority, social norms
are more stable (though not uniform), as suggested by what Carol called
the "fallacy" of having anticipated entering an "intellectual and social
community." Patterns of socializing are based less on intellectual affinities than on social bonds external to academic departmental concerns:

My social life does not revolve around my colleagues. And in some
respects that's a source of disappointment for me, although that's the
way it is, and that's the way it had to be . . . because you also have to
be in a department with people with whom you have something in
common on other levels. And a lot of it has to do with age. I'm the
youngest person in the department. But the average, two years ago, the
average age of the department was something like fifty-six or fifty-
seven.[25] People are older than me and in a different place in their lives,
they've got kids who've gone off to college, and then, they're very heterosexual, and their lives are really oriented around their kids, they've
been here, they're very established in Oasis. I think there are, some of
my colleagues are clearly uncomfortable with the fact that I'm a
dyke. . . . But this is not a unit of people that socialize for the most
part. They really draw a line between work and social life, and so they
go home and their world is a different world, it's oriented around their
kids and their neighbors and their schools and so forth and not around
their friendship units with other people in the department.[26]

It is interesting that in describing social patterns, Carol did not highlight
race, but age, sexuality, and outside interests. Based on cues she has, it
appears that her openly naming herself lesbian breaks with departmental heteronormativity, causing some colleagues to feign ignorance
through verbal nonrecognition, what Patricia Williams, speaking of
race, has referred to as "setting up regions of conversational taboo and
rigidified politeness."[27] More than rigidified politeness, colleagues use
what Sedgwick calls the "privilege of unknowing" in which the interlocutor who has or pretends to have less knowledge is able to "define
the terms of the exchange":[28]

It doesn't come up as much now because the pattern is sort of established, we don't socialize, they don't invite me, I don't invite them,

that's fine. But before the pattern was established early on, and they would ask me about myself for example, they would never include how are you guys doing, or have you gotten settled, or any of those things. They were always talking to me as if I were single, so the sort of erasure of my sexuality was one strategy. Another was to make inappropriate invitations to invite me to their house and not invite Laura [her partner]. Others would, they'd sort of want to ask me things, but they couldn't quite because it might get into that subject and they wouldn't know how to handle it, and so you know there would just be these awkward moments in the conversation. So there's a couple of people who I don't particularly like and they don't particularly like me, and it could be for any number of reasons why, but I suspect that one of the factors might be my sexuality. I mean, there's lots, you know, lots of reasons why. They also think I'm a raving feminist, this radical, whatever, Marxist, postmodernist, whatever they want to think. . . . Black nationalist. What else? I press every single button that they have.

Others' privileged ignorance structures the space Carol lives in as one of unknowing: "That's always something that I wonder about. I will always wonder, I'm sure this is true for most queer people, whether or not the people with whom I have sort of strained or uncomfortable relations, if that's the basis of it or if it's something else."[29]

The need for collegial socializing has been stressed by researchers concerned that African-American and female faculty are cut out of departmental networks and put at a disadvantage in that they have less access to mentoring, national and international networks, information regarding tenure and promotion, and research collaboration.[30] However, Carol did not identify tangible professional disadvantages due to her lack of departmental social ties. This is due, I believe, to the fact that her interdisciplinarity has enabled her to create networks with persons at other universities and in other departments at Liberal U, such as English, History, and African-American Studies.

How do Carol's categories of social otherness and intellectual stances combine to position her in relation to her all-white, predominantly heterosexual colleagues? A significant facet of the intertwining of Carol's race, gender, class, and sexuality is the normalization and erasure of her sexuality in interaction. At the same time, the hypervisibility of the "social fact" of her race, a significant concern at Liberal U, obscures her academic and intellectual abilities.

Salient Visibilities

I've probably said this before, but I'm the first person of color to be hired in a tenure track position in this school. Ever.

—Carol

> The market is awful, but we also haven't been as aggressive as we could have been. We were aggressive in getting Carol here. She resisted for a long time. We kept talking to her. It took a long time.
>
> —Sara

> Once I was hired it gave the school the opportunity to collectively breathe a sigh of relief, now they didn't need to worry about this diversity stuff anymore. I was here, they could go on about the business of what they're really about.
>
> —Carol

Eight years ago, the Journalism School's accrediting council implemented a standard that journalism schools must diversify their faculty, integrate issues of diversity into the curriculum, and work to recruit and retain minority students. Carol described the social and academic context she entered: "It has been a lily-white male bastion for sixty-some-odd years. There had never been a person of color on tenure track on faculty, it's pathetic the number of students of color in this school, and there was nothing, not one course in the curriculum, that addressed these issues." In response to accrediting pressures, the school recruited Carol through the universitywide minority hiring program I described in chapter 2, which she described ambivalently: "In many respects it's a good strategy because it puts the onus on departments and schools to think about this and make a commitment to it. But of course, it immediately raises the specter that whoever was hired in those positions didn't have to go through regular channels and go through the regular rigmarole and scrutiny and competition." Carol felt she was "set up" from the beginning:

> I didn't have to apply for the job, my qualifications didn't have to measure up against other people's qualifications. So I think that that *tarnished* me in the view of a good number of my colleagues the moment I walked in the door. It affected the way, the Journalism School is incredibly inept at this process. Some of the other departments are much better at it, take it much more seriously, understand the kinds of pressures and double standards that influence candidates, and I think handle it quite well.

Tarnish, *to dull the luster of*, suggests that the implementation of affirmative action in Carol's department created a situation in which, in the eyes of colleagues, Carol's color obscured her other qualities, which became difficult to see. Several elements of the hiring process are noteworthy. Although there were other candidates for the position, no formal job description was offered to Carol. While her qualifications may have been measured against others', they were not measured against formal criteria. And, as I explain below, although the department was gaining a free line, senior faculty were gaining competition for courses in Journalism History, a significant area of Carol's expertise.

The mishandling of Carol's hire began with her invitation to campus by the dean, who "said to me on the phone, 'We'd like for you to come to Liberal U to look us over, check out the program, and we're very interested in you,' and so forth and so on, and he asked me to send a vita, I did all of that, . . . I get here and I find out I'm expected to give a job talk. He hadn't even told me. I didn't know that this was in fact a bona fide job interview." She continued, "Essentially what then happens is that sets up a degree of mistrust among the faculty, because if I had been one of the faculty members and saw that this was the way that somebody was brought in, I would have been skeptical, too. I would have said, 'who is this person, and what is the deal here?'" This practice effectively constructed Carol according to one dimension of her social being, her race, and erased her academic credentials in the minds of some faculty members.

Carol attributes her hiring less to her professional expertise than to her ability to perform her blackness appropriately. She remarked, "I felt like that it's very much sort of a white cultural environment, they were looking for a black person who wouldn't make them uncomfortable essentially, or wasn't going to make them feel threatened. And whatever my abilities are at being able to negotiate white social structures, I did a little bit better than those other two people." She explained:

> I speak the white man's English, you know, there's no, there doesn't have to be any sign of colloquialisms or Southernisms in my voice, for example. I think I'm confident without being, I can be confident and sort of forthright and direct, without being threatening, without being arrogant. . . . Because of my background, a lot of it having to do with the way my parents raised me and so forth, and my education, I'm very different *in the eyes of* white colleagues from a black person who came perhaps from a more sheltered black environment, who talks black *to their ear*, who is not as comfortable, or who sort of displays perhaps even more arrogance or what would be *seen* as aggressiveness. And so I think that gender plays a dramatic role in that also, the perception of a black female as being less threatening than a black male is very much deeply ensconced in the white psyche.

As she understands it, her credentials consisted of her abilities to appear as an appropriate other who can be seen and heard as familiar rather than as alien or uppity. Her performance within social constructions of gendered blackness contributed to making her an acceptable diversification.

Coming into the department as socially other due to her race and academically "tarnished," Carol also put forward her not-so-visible difference in order to avoid "never-never land, that quasi-scary place" of being neither "in" nor "out" as lesbian: "I also came out to the dean at the end of the interview. I wanted it to be very clear. I found out later that he presented it in a sensitive and straightforward manner to the faculty because there had been some problems in terms of homophobia in the department with other faculty before. And he essentially said, 'I don't want this to happen again, I don't want this to be a problem.' So now I'm coming in not only as a black person but as a lesbian." Although her sexuality has socially othered her, it has not *identifiably* academically positioned her. Social and academic expectations around her black femaleness, however, have had a continuing impact on her departmental work, an experience that is not new for Carol: "the *visibility* of my race and my gender have always placed me in positions where there are a lot of assumptions and judgments made about my ability and so forth, regardless of what my actual performance is."

In the minoritizing context of Liberal U, Carol's work can be located in its proper place, as suggested by the school's highlighting the area of her professional background thought to inhere in her *visible* identities and downplaying those that do not: "I was hired to be the black person and the feminist. And they had no clue about that, they wanted me to develop some kind of course like [Race and Gender in the Media]." Although issues of race and gender are an area of Carol's scholarly expertise, her work in media history has largely been discounted in her teaching assignments: "I have not, up until this year, even though my primary area of expertise is media history, been able to teach a history course, sort of a straight media history course." However, not all of Carol's colleagues ignored her scholarship, as "one of the other historians on the faculty didn't want to hire me, because he saw me as being competition for his courses, and while . . . I dislike this person intensely, I respect his honesty, because he was right that we didn't need another historian on the faculty." Sara explained: "She may not feel she gets to teach in all the areas she wants to, but that happens to everybody from time to time. I know she feels strongly about not wanting to be the only person holding up certain areas, she'd like back-up and we have to work harder to do that. It's pretty hard when you're a faculty the size we are and you have to cover so many areas." In practice, Carol has had to challenge this role of "covering" race and gender: "Last year I had a massive fit on e-mail, I just blew the dean's ears off, and I said, 'What is this shit, I've been on the faculty for four years, three white boys that were just hired are all getting the courses that fulfill their area of expertise, why is it that I'm sort of consistently'—they finally grudgingly gave in, so finally I'll be able to teach a history course next semester." The location of Carol as embodying a diversity mandate through the inappropriate use of affirmative action created a containment that she has worked against in order to gain authority beyond her visible differences.

Although Carol has been academically relegated to diversity, there is a curious way in which, as across Liberal U's campus, diversity was not located in the academic but in the social, in something of a parallel to the ways that Carol felt her credentials for hiring were more social than academic. In speaking with her colleagues, it became clear that transformations of knowledge were not what was at stake but social interaction, as suggested in Ben's language:

> I think everybody believes that the department be as culturally diverse as possible. I tend to view what happens to our students here as an opportunity to interact with people from a lot of different backgrounds. It doesn't matter in what setting they *bump up against* Carol or they *bump up against* a Mormon or a gay person or an Asian-American, but they should do that some time, it provides a different perspective for looking at the world. Unless we have a diverse faculty, the value sets students are *bumping up against* are pretty similar to theirs.

How this "bumping up against" might become more than a tourism of social perspectives that entails a substantive change of perspective related to academic and professional practice remains unspoken. Sara's talk of the faculty's lack of understanding of race further revealed a relegation of diversity to the social rather than the academic and a reification of "diverse" faculty as role models:

> A good portion of the faculty have not spent much of their lives interacting with people of other races or cultures. They have difficulty confronting their own feelings about certain issues. And I know that Carol feels that she's alone a lot of the time here, and I think that's an awful position to be in, . . . I really don't think they understand it, they want us to have role models for the minority student population, I think they would like to see that taken on by someone else because they don't understand it at all. It would be nice if we can find one or two more faculty members in our next search, but nobody's going to work very hard at it, as an imperative to keeping Carol, as an imperative to experiencing diversity.[31]

This disjuncture between white faculty's verbal support for and their actions in recruitment of new faculty is evidenced by the results of six searches in the past three years, in which all faculty hired have been white. The department's "structured preference"[32] of finding the "right" combination of professional and scholarly background (not to mention graduate work at the "right" schools) acts as a self-fulfilling prophecy of the difficulty of hiring nonwhite candidates. Carol explained, "the rationale is that it's not about race but it's about that person'll come in and won't be able to get tenure because they don't have the right kind of education and they won't be able to cut the mustard and it'll just be a frustrating experience for them."

The objectification of Carol on the basis of her race is symptomatic of what Reyes and Halcón have referred to as covert racism in academia, in which minority candidates are only seriously considered under pressure to diversify faculty, and must then dispel the "stigma" of their hiring. What they call "the typecasting syndrome," or the creation of minority-related positions, relieves others of responsibility for issues of diversity and simultaneously limits minority faculty's ability to bring their perspectives to bear on a range of issues.[33] This commodification of visible black bodies produces certain silences even as it would pretend to give voice to the perspectives thought to be immanent in those bodies. Evelynn Hammonds has remarked, "The hypervisibility of black women academics means that visibility too can be used to control the intellectual issues that black women can and cannot speak about."[34] Located as representative, token, and role model, Carol is not readily conferred authority to speak about a range of issues. A seeming opening represents closure through placement. Homi Bhabha has described this contradiction in educational institutions: "although there is always an entertainment and encouragement of cultural diversity, there is also a corresponding containment of it. A transparent norm is constituted, a norm given by the host society or dominant culture, which says that 'these other cultures are fine, but we must be able to locate them within our own grid.'"[35] It is this placement by the norms and assumptions of the departmental social and academic space that Carol has had to work against.

Reyes and Halcón enumerate four responses of minority academics to institutional(ized) behaviors: (1) giving in to the demands of the environment and assimilating; (2) combatting injustices, often at the expense of scholarship and professional status; (3) fighting racism, maintaining strong community ties, and leaving the institution "when they recognize that the price of the struggle is not worth their efforts *in that particular environment*"; and, (4) fighting back within the system by "play[ing] the game, without compromising either their integrity or their ethnicity" (310). Cornel West has offered a somewhat similar delineation: (1) assimilating to the mainstream for legitimacy; (2) maintaining group insularity; (3) adopting extreme individualism, rejecting both the mainstream and the group; and, (4) taking on a role of "Critical Organic Catalyst" by appropriating what the mainstream offers while maintaining a grounding in subcultures of critique and resistance.[36] These ideal classifications reflect much current thinking about the work of black academics. Yet Carol renders these typologies, which leave little room for ambivalence, irrelevant, if not meaningless. Their limitation lies in their assumption of an underlying black "authenticity," in which subjectivity is unitary (or, at best, split between resistance and assimilation). African-American academics can be understood only in terms of singular relations to dominant or subcultural groups, a construction that locates a black subject in ways parallel to those of the problematic institutional and social structures in which Carol lives. To assume a proper black subject and locate that subject within a grid dependent on insider/outsider status fails to account for practices that exceed binary locations. Carol is not fully inside or outside a single community, set of practices, or norms. While she is undoubtedly resisting racist structures that would contain her, this resistance is by no means a response organic to a singular positioning, raced or otherwise.

"Maneuvering the Structure as It Exists"

> If I were a white woman, would my sexuality be more visible, would that be the way that I was categorized? Because I'm a black woman, race becomes the dominant characteristic.
>
> —Carol

> The expectation that I was going to embody the entire Journalism School's efforts at diversity, I was going to do the things that they wanted to do in the curriculum, I was going to be here as a physical statement. Of course that is pure bullshit. . . . I've been associated with this school for five years, and I'm totally pissed off at it. I'm in a very bad mood about the whole thing and I'm letting it be known.
>
> —Carol

> It's what people of color have to do in a white world. . . . I like the notion of adjustments and negotiation because what you have to do is not give up yourself but figure out how to maneuver the structure as it exists. It's a set of skills that one acquires all the time.
>
> —Carol, speaking of Marlon Riggs' film *Color Adjustment*

Carol's movement to establish multiple scholarly authorities has been enabled by her actions, such as gaining external recognition for her scholarship that includes a prestigious dissertation award and a fellowship at another university, and by her use of voice in interactions, particularly challenging colleagues' assumptions about diversity in academic contexts. Her tenuous authorities and acceptabilities become resources to be put to use in order to shift the relations of academic and social knowledge that would locate her academic work. The location of authority, in fact, was a recurring theme throughout our conversations. After Carol spoke one day of authority in the department, I asked about her sources of authority:

> Obviously my visible identities. I am the authority on race, and that is sort of the dominant authority. . . . I become the immediate authority that everyone sort of acquiesces to, and that's really problematic, not only because I'm tokenized but because it's this sort of naive white position in which they don't believe that they could have some authority too if they just did a little bit of work, read a few books. . . . When I first came I was not ascribed much authority in terms of being a scholar. I think that's changed. I think I've earned a fair amount of their respect because I have been an active scholar, I've gotten lots of public recognition for my research, and in the arenas in which they feel comfortable. So I think some of them grudgingly have ascribed to me more intellectual and scholarly authority than when I first came here. One thing I sort of didn't realize . . . was I am one of the highest ranked people in terms of teaching in the school, but what I realized was that other people knew that, particularly senior colleagues. . . . I think I have now been ascribed more authority, not the highest authority obviously, that belongs to some other people in the school, but high authority in terms of being recognized as a good teacher, not just a popular teacher, but a good teacher, someone who sort of takes teaching seriously.

Carol's sources of academic legitimacy correspond to departmental norms of externally recognized scholarship and high teaching evaluations. She has moved from a quasi-authoritative status on the basis of her race to what she calls "legitimated authority" in domains in which, consonant with an academic model of individual competition, she can be judged in relation to her colleagues.

Whereas the locus of Carol's authority has shifted to some extent from the social to the academic, issues of race and gender continue to be academically peripheral among her colleagues, undermined as an area of scholarship even as they are purportedly valued:

> One of my colleagues sent me an e-mail a couple of years ago who said, in this sort of benevolent, liberal way, "I just think what you're doing in the Race, Gender, and Media class is just so important, and I think I'd like to teach that class too, and maybe we could get together for coffee and talk about it." And just spare me, spare me. So I wrote back a really nasty e-mail, I tried really hard not to make it too nasty, but I said, "This is not a game, I've spent years studying this material, and this is an area of scholarly attention, and it takes a lot of work, and you can't just sort of brush up for a few weeks and decide that you're going to offer a course on this too."

Even as Carol may have gained legitimacy, the areas she would be seen as representing are not understood as necessitating the rigorous study other academic areas require. Although Carol said "students are clamoring for material," colleagues refused responsibility for knowledge: "I have to be the consultant to all the other people in the department who don't know shit about race, but they want to talk about it in class. So for the Intro to Reporting class for a couple of years they kept coming to me and asking if I would organize the lecture on race or minority issues or something, and finally I just said no." In an incoherence that reveals social and academic assumptions, Carol has had to challenge beliefs that race and gender are not areas of serious scholarship while paradoxically forcing recognition that she is not the only person who may (or should) speak about them. The lesson she must teach is that phenotype does not create knowledge; study and engagement do. Her actions seek to detach social categories of identity from what one can do.[37]

Although she has gained national scholarly awards in appropriate arenas, her work is both inside and outside the values and understandings of her local colleagues. Compounding the peripheral nature of the content of Carol's scholarship are her interdisciplinary work and her forays into cultural studies, which go beyond the boundaries of traditional journalistic scholarship:

> I'm on the fringe. Well, in some ways I'm not on the fringe because my work is historical for the most part. There are several very established historians in the department, and they're some of the most influential people in the department, so they know the kind of work that I'm doing and they respect it. But I don't sort of stop there and I engage in other kinds of research and I also integrate theoretical arguments into my historical work, and into my teaching, and they're not comfortable with that. There are a couple of other people who sort of dabble in cultural studies in the department, but they don't really take it very seriously. They do it more because they know that the graduate students want it.

Carol has forged her scholarship in an academic context that is strangely multiple, as she works within a field that draws on multiple disciplinary traditions within a department that has an ambivalent relationship to those traditions. Carol thus lives in a dual space of (in)appropriateness. First, her academic qualifications are recognized in the legitimate areas of teaching and scholarship. Yet her subject matter is locally devalued, as persons do not engage with her work or understand it as an area of scholarly expertise. Second, methodologically and theoretically, Carol's research incorporates elements of what is locally valued as well as that which is alien. However, as in Julie's case, external validation lends it credibility. Her nationally recognized achievements and her local refusal of location in tokenized roles combine to combat the silencing that hypervisibility can bring and to confuse easy categorizations of herself as subject and of her subject matter.

Consonant with my earlier discussion of Carol's foregrounding sexuality as problematic in her social relations, race surfaced to locate her academic positioning to the exclusion of sexuality:

> Authority about being queer, since nobody talks about that, and nobody wants to see me in that category, they'd just as soon not think about it or not know, it's not a category in which authority is inscribed, at least within this environment. So instead of saying, "Well, Carol, what do you think about so and so and so and so," there isn't a conversation. So there is a conversation about race because race is part of the larger discourse, but there isn't about sexuality, because they're still in the stages of trying to understand what appropriate behavior is and become tolerant and all those kinds of things. And, also, most of them don't know much about the intellectual conversations that are going on in terms of queer theory, so it's not a category.

Carol is commodified for her visible, codified identity, ignored in terms of her less visible, less codified identity—a commodification and a denial that are institutionally sanctioned in Liberal U's rhetorical valuing of some perspectives and not others. The social and academic intertwine in curious ways as one difference is suppressed and another highlighted. This nonrecognition of her sexuality has an effect of, if not heterosexualizing Carol's blackness, then desexualizing it. Dhairyan has argued that the "contrast between the visibility of race and the invisibility of queer sexuality, then, hierarchizes queer sexuality over race by ignoring the cultural terrorism that maintains race as a stable category to contain its manifestations."[38] Meanings attached to skin color prevent the emergence of alternative manifestations of black femaleness, namely lesbian sexuality, even as Carol would assert its presence. The grid on which Carol would be located does not allow for multiple differences. However, as I describe below, she challenges this singular construction.

Although I cannot claim definitively that Carol has effected change within her department, that she has encouraged her colleagues to think differently about the implications of race, gender, and sexuality, or that she has opened a rethinking definitions of scholarship, there are signs that this is true for some faculty members. External pressures for diversification, students' request for such material, and some faculty's well-intentioned if poorly enacted interests in teaching race and gender, suggest that the relations of the social and the academic are not static. I find it difficult to think that Carol's interactions—challenging her dean about her teaching assignments, voicing discontent over faculty hires and giving her dean a list of recruiting resources, reminding faculty that hers is an area of scholarly expertise—when considered in the context of her abilities to speak within white social structures in language that can be understood, have no positive efficacy. In fact, Sara stressed the effectiveness of her voice and colleagues' respect for her:

> SARA. Carol is the strongest female faculty member who is defined as a researcher in this school in terms both of what she does but also because she is a voice. Carol speaks up, is a strong researcher, and she's a good teacher. She's a valued member of the department, in a lot of capacities. I think to a person no one would want her leaving, having nothing to do with minority status, gender or race, she would be difficult to impossible to replace.
>
> SUSAN. What do you mean by uses her voice?
>
> SARA. I am the only female full professor on faculty, and now we have a couple of associates, but a couple of them don't contribute at the level I think they're capable of, and especially before their tenure, they wouldn't say anything in faculty meetings. And Carol didn't feel she needed to be shy about stating her opinion.
>
> SUSAN. What makes her effective?
>
> SARA. She's articulate and / /, and she's mainstream. Some people can sound like they're coming from another planet. She's reasonable at meetings, so people can hear her.

Although Sara maintains that Carol is valued in ways that have *nothing to do with minority status, gender or race*, much of Carol's self-perception of her status hinged on her gender and race. Even with the apparent contradiction between their viewpoints, Sara's remarks may be consonant with Carol's perceptions that she has moved into expanded domains of legitimacy, which Sara emphasized by focusing on the multiple capacities in which Carol is valued that are no longer predicated on her minority status—but which Sara may have contradicted by mentioning at all.

In effect, Carol is aware of performing her differences in ways that challenge but that are within interactional norms, and hence, audible to others:

> There are enough people in the department, I wouldn't say they're afraid of me, but they're careful of me, of pissing me off, because they know I can hold my own, I'm not easily intimidated. . . . It's not to say that I'm intimidating but that I'm willing to confront the situation. . . . I've taken them on in faculty meetings. I've been fairly direct, and I have not been afraid to be the only one to vote in a particular way or to articulate my opposition to certain perspectives. I don't do that all

the time, I don't present myself as combative, but I'm not silent either. And I've had to, because I'm so—the way I think about things is so different from them, the way I analyze issues is just so different, just about anything we talk about, curriculum, hiring, anything, is going to be ripe for that kind of situation.

As an example, Carol gently invokes her positioning as lesbian to question heterosexual privilege:

I see the ways heterosexual people benefit in the academy and the only way to confront that is to be out and to say this is the way you're responding in this situation, you're placing me at a disadvantage because I'm not part of that network. I don't have a husband or whatever it is, I'm not into issues with childcare, so politically I think it's important, too. I don't feel like I pay any huge price, because the people who are homophobic in my department, they're going to feel uncomfortable regardless, and the discomfort is just going to be higher because I was just trying to keep silent or not let them know certain things about me.

Her manner of engaging her colleagues' assumptions is, as Sara said, "reasonable," consonant with departmental interactional styles:

Ben and I are working on the curriculum committee, and this is a classic example. We're also the two openly queer people in the school. And Ben and I are sort of the same in terms of our style, we're sort of chilled out people, we're busy, we're not going to do this sort of radical engagement constantly on every level about our gender or sexuality or something. But they also ain't getting nothing by us. So the women who are the faculty advisors, we were talking about certain exemptions to residency requirements for graduation, and they said, "One of the exemptions we often give is marriage. If a student gets married and they're moving away," and the antenna went up, and we looked at each other. And Ben said, "Well," in a sort of sweet voice, "are you trying to say that marriage is a category for exemption here?" And they still didn't get it. And, "So, what if people aren't married?" Still didn't get it. So I said, "Are we talking about giving people exemptions for moving or based on marital status and are we then?" So he and I were able to sort of coalesce and get right to it and then they sort of figured it out and their heads dropped and they said, "Oh shit." It's sort of pushing people's buttons and raising their consciousness, to use that cliché. If I didn't do it, if he didn't do it, if a few people didn't do it, it wouldn't matter, it wouldn't get done.

Simultaneously appropriate and inappropriate, Carol has created spaces for herself by speaking strategically, citing and challenging social and academic norms, drawing on the structures of her department to establish herself and to shift those structures subtly. At first glance it would appear that Carol's responses to the space in which she finds herself are akin to those of West's "Critical Organic Catalyst," who works within the system while compromising as little sense of self as possible, adjusting, as Carol says, in order to learn to manipulate the structures of which she is a part. However, as I argued, both Reyes and Halcón's and West's typologies depend for their meaning on an authentic, unitary subject whose identity and actions are derived from a group or community. Carol's actions, however, do not have a point of origin in a commitment to an African-American or lesbian identity or community but are formed by multiple identifications. Furthermore, as I discuss in the following chapter, Carol does not have a "community" as such to which she could be said to belong. Her scholarly, personal, and political commitments exceed a single subject position that could be read as mainstream or resisting. Her responses to the location that would be ascribed her are responses formed within the recognitions of others that break open both the locations her school would create for her and the locations suggested by assimilationist-resisting dichotomies, both of which depend on an inside-outside. Her multiple positionings in legitimate academic domains and her performances of peripheral, yet central, social categories set assumptions about identity, and authority, and resistance into play.

In contrast to sexuality as subtext in Julie's and Carol's departmental positionings stands Olivia's academic status as lesbian theorist. From a position of commodification, which shares some points of comparison with Carol's racialization, Olivia refuses voice and visibility as lesbian, seeking instead to perform a departmental presence that intentionally plays into and against social and academic norms in order to effect change.

OLIVIA AND THE PERFORMANCE OF LOCATIONS

The English department, with over sixty faculty members and a large graduate program, is highly ranked and has a strong, nationally visible feminist presence. The faculty could be characterized along several dimensions: a bifurcation of age groups, with few faculty in their forties, persons engaged in theoretical work and others who are not, and those dedicated to literary studies and others who work in cultural studies.[39] Over the last decade, as the faculty composition has changed from predominantly older and senior to increasingly young and junior, the declining job market has enabled the hiring of highly productive, theoretical faculty.[40] Karen, Olivia's colleague, offered an elaborate response to my question about how she would group the faculty:

Along certain kinds of intellectual lines, in terms of the discipline. I would group them according to those who would think of what an English department does as being about Western civilization, the greatest works or thoughts or writings or whatever, and that would take care of a number of them. Let's see, that'd be one group. Then I think there are people who expressly want to redo the canon, add sort of other people to it. Then there are those who don't bother to talk about the canon and aren't really interested in it but are still primarily literary in their orientation. I think that there are a few people, and not many at all, and I would count myself in this group, who are not primarily literary in orientation, not any longer anyway, and that's getting into visual and also theoretical things.

Despite these differences, there is an atmosphere of collegiality. William, Olivia's colleague, cautiously explained, "I think there is also an amicable and affectionate interaction among senior and junior faculty. There are some moments in which there is some unease between senior and junior faculty on issues of theoretical orientation or lack thereof, and these usually manifest themselves on Ph.D. exam committees. But that doesn't happen too often." He added, "We don't have anyone like Dinesh D'Souza who thinks we should only be reading Milton and Dante, but we do have colleagues who are invested heavily in traditional periods and genres of literature, and as those courses seem not to draw students in the same way that interdisciplinary courses in film, TV, and literature, the intersections of various theories, contemporary culture, then there is some tension." As Olivia described it, tensions rarely surface in direct confrontations: "This department is never vicious about anybody, they don't, you don't gain anything by doing that here. That would be my predilection anyway. But the idea is that you are basically generous and kill them quietly. And killing is very subtle in this department. As one faculty member said to me, 'A vote of twenty-six for/three against in tenure is a no vote in this department.' Kill you with kindness here." In describing her first year of observing departmental interactions, she remarked:

> The subtlety stands out, but it's deeply familiar. That's very much a WASP subtlety. I really think there is a lack of real rancor here. At State U there really was rancor, and there were people that were very professionally disappointed and upset at the profession because they felt they were being left out, and it got reflected in a lot of ways in department meetings around issues of curriculum and hiring. . . . Here, the people are much younger, they're not at the death stage, they've kept up, they're not afraid of the profession. They're more confident in themselves, they feel better about the department. Liberal U sort of sees itself as good. I wish they had more ambition than they do, they could be a helluva lot better with very little trouble. But it's taken me a year to see that, and it'll take a little while to get things rolling.

The confidence and caliber of the department were evident in conversations I had with faculty and graduate students, who demonstrated a distinct tone of professionalism and of taking the implications of their work seriously. Professional and political stakes in teaching, service, and research, but most saliently in the quantity and character of one's research, were indirectly and directly articulated in conversation after conversation. Students' and faculty's awareness of their positioning vis-à-vis colleagues, the field, and the institution were more pronounced in the English department than in the School of Journalism or the Department of Religious Studies. Combined with the ethos of amiability was something of a charged professional and political atmosphere.

As a nationally ranked department in a competitive discipline, the English department, consonant with the College of Arts and Sciences, places heavy emphasis on research, inflecting both service and teaching with publication. Publication, productivity, and national visibility overshadow, yet do not completely undermine, other faculty responsibilities. Barbara, the Director of Undergraduate Studies, complained that teaching is devalued in the department and university: "The dean of the college said several years ago, sure, you could get tenure on teaching, if you publish in pedagogy. So again not on any sort of demonstrable performance." She added, "We don't know how to talk about our teaching. Olivia is eloquent about her teaching."

Within these departmental configurations, Olivia is one of the few faculty members in her forties. Her research, not unlike the courses she teaches, is highly theoretical, interdisciplinary, and includes literary and cultural studies. Olivia's service more than fulfills the department's demands for national visibility, and is increasingly including department-level service. Having entered the department only a year before, Olivia chose roles she would perform after learning of patterns of interaction and departmental values. She self-consciously framed her actions to respond to and use departmental norms and concerns to effect changes that she sees as politically and professionally beneficial, both for her and for the department as a space in which to work.

Tactical Citizenship

> I kept my mouth shut the first year and watched what went on,
> and have this year shown pretty good savvy about what I've done.
> So I think the fact that I seem to have fairly good judgment about
> departmental politics is, has been good. I think I'm friendly, cheerful, cooperative, and I seem to be interested in students. I work
> hard.
>
> —Olivia

She's been elected to the Advisory Committee, which is a popular vote of her peers, she's on the Recruitment Committee, she's on the Graduate Studies Committee, and she's been very smart about this, she's slowly moving into the core of the department. Frankly, the department is probably run on the participation of about twenty people. And she's clearly one of those.

—William

I think it's very open, very democratic, they need some education, they're very open to ideas, there's, as in all things in America, a tendency to want to slide back into the good old days when men were men and no one else was around. And you have to kind of work against that current subtly. Systems allow lots of intervention, and you just need to figure out where to intervene and how, make it look like it's in their interest or in the interest of graduate students to do certain things. Most people will go along, because they don't realize what you're doing, because their vision isn't like that.

—Olivia

Younger women faculty who are savvy learn to have insurance policies, which means you either overachieve, which means that they can't clobber you, or you have a law degree, which means they won't touch you. . . . I have a law degree, they won't touch me, and I overachieve, both.

—Olivia

Having entered the department with the authority of her prolific publishing record behind her, Olivia also used her service to place herself at the center and to "get things rolling," as she said. Convinced that the "academic mind is inert," she described her energy as enabling her to craft an interesting environment in which to work. Service, or "doing things on your own initiative that are departmentally helpful," became a means to make changes:

> I put together a one-day seminar on publishing for graduate students, invited someone from outside, and it was on my own initiative. It was my initiative to get together the group of feminist people in the department and make up the new courses. . . . We've done the undergrad, I've put the undergraduate curriculum through and I'll put the graduate curriculum through and then we'll work on the minor. . . . Three new feminist courses on the graduate level, two new on the undergraduate level, and then the idea is to have a graduate minor in feminist critical studies. And I'm probably going to begin the revision of the department's tenure and promotion policies. There'll be other initiatives coming.

Olivia engaged the feminist curricular revision and rewriting the tenure and promotion policies with a tactical awareness of how modes of social interaction and academic values can be put to use.

During the semester I was at Liberal U, the possibility that definitions of service were gendered in nature was a source of contention in the department. William explained:

> One of my younger colleagues said that she thought [the evaluation of service] had a particular kind of gender inflection, and I think she was right. I think more than a gender inflection, it's an exceptionally narrow-minded notion of what counts as service. . . . We have had a couple of service cases recently where the question is how do you define outstanding service. The answer would appear to be a national professional visibility, holding office in professional organizations, or the editorship of journals. Well, that's okay. What about those faculty who are on twenty-five dissertation committees? What about those faculty who are on committees in the department? Recruitment committees? No matter how much of that you do, you can't be outstanding. But if I'm the secretary of the James Joyce Society and I go to two meetings a year somehow that's really important. Same with teaching. How do you know I'm an outstanding teacher? One of the first things in the definition is you must have published something on teaching or pedagogy. So that there is no such thing as outstanding teaching absent research. There's no such thing as outstanding service outside of national visibility. Those similar terms came up in a recent tenure decision, and it turned out gender was an issue in that, too. Is the unwillingness to be more supple in our definition intellectual laziness? Is it gender politics? I don't know. I've thought, and still do think, that this is a pretty amicable department. But at the same time there are these dynamics and gender politics.

Olivia's concern with tenure and promotion policies came from her observation of the evaluation of colleagues: "their standards tend to vary." In order to allay personal and political skirmishes, she drew on norms of noncontentiousness by positioning herself as a neutral believer in procedure:

> OLIVIA. [The service requirements] are inconsistent and make it almost impossible for almost anybody to get an outstanding in service in the department, so my ploy is let's rewrite these so they don't conflict with the college rules but do enable a larger kind of outstanding service. But also a certain kind of clarity about procedure, and why procedure, and it has to be maintained consistently, because if it's not, there are grounds for a suit right there if it's negative, and they're playing fast and loose with this shit. . . . I finally got it [the promotion and tenure document]. Of course I read it instantly and became the P and T document expert in the department, because I took it with me to the meeting, something nobody

ever thought of doing, and when the question of what constitutes a service thing came up, I was able to read the language out of that, and say this is what this says. The law thing, it's my way into having some say. I might as well use it, I've got it.

SUSAN. What's the underlying concern?

OLIVIA. They don't listen to girls. You should see it, they gave Karen a pretty hard time. Karen says things in such a way that she is going to get flak, and there are ways she could couch things that she wouldn't. She does it as a confrontational, deliberately confrontational mode, and confrontation does not work in this department. Au contraire, everybody has to play the fiction of the nicey-nice, so the way to do it is to go back, that's why I think the law works particularly well here, because it doesn't offend anybody. You can't really complain about the law. So that's why I'm taking that tack now. I'm still new, they won't trust me for two or three years. You just have to be a good player, a good citizen. And I am generally a good citizen. I was socialized successfully. I do my job, I'm not a crank, I do my little extra work. I figure, hell, it's better than getting dressed up. Virtues of academe, you keep your own hours and don't get dressed up.

Olivia likened her and Karen's respective roles in the department to "playing good cop, bad cop." Conscious of being perceived as lesbian—confrontive, embattled—Olivia avoided that typification through hard work, cheerfulness, and a reliance on objective procedure rather than the potentially charged realms of interpersonal relations or disciplinary politics. Olivia claimed the power to set the tone for her interactions and others' perceptions of her:

> You bring on your own paranoia. I think people will treat you para-
> noidly if you act like they should, and since I act like well what's the
> problem, I tend not to get treated the same way Karen does. . . . [It] is
> odd because I look much more the dyke than she does, but I act much
> less the dyke than she does. She's pretty good at playing with the boys,
> jollying them along and stuff, but there's something about her that's
> very confrontive. I don't do the confronting stuff, I know how to do it
> obliquely in ways that she doesn't. I've watched her. I can say stuff
> that's confrontive that always seems oblique.

This obliqueness and departmental good citizenship characterized her project of adding courses in feminist cultural and critical studies to the curriculum. Barbara, the Director of Undergraduate Studies, described the rethinking of curricular offerings as precipitated by faculty who "are into self-conscious theoretical discourse who are saying there's a mismatch between what they're doing in the classroom and what they're doing in terms of scholarship." Although Barbara understood the new courses as following "the old additive model, more cereal boxes on the shelf," Olivia had grander plans: "[The department] needs to be even more into a critical studies mode than it is. I'm not, when you say that people think you're an advocate for losing literature, I'm not, but I am more interested in what's happening to the discipline, looking at culture, reading culture textually." Her idea was to create a core of feminist faculty and students and to distribute feminist studies throughout the curriculum: "What's the difference between looking at women, which is important, and looking at other things? It's only the extent to which the method and issues are integrated into other kinds of things that they stay, become permanently imprinted, to use animal behavior language. You imprint them." Olivia mentioned the need to advertise the department's feminist strengths by naming a graduate minor in order to attract students and to facilitate the development of lesbian studies: "If we give it an institutional presence, it suddenly, you have a base from which to maneuver and in the name of which to maneuver." She attributes the vitality of feminist theory to the fact that it has become an integral part of inquiry into a number of topics, both literary and cultural. Her goal for lesbian studies is parallel: "It's just that my idea is that it needs to be like feminist theory, integrated into questions about other material, which is one of the reasons I don't like identity politics very much."

Olivia's wide range of teaching abilities enabled her to imprint feminist studies in a variety of locations: "If I can show versatility, I'm more valuable than if I can't. I'm also better for feminist studies if I'm versatile than if I'm not. I can teach, and have taught, Shakespeare, British literature, American literature, drama, critical theory, feminist theory, gay and lesbian studies, film. That's pretty versatile. You see, this is good for departments, they need all-purpose, I'm a utility infielder basically." Her versatility is not a purely altruistic tactic for "the cause," for she derives both pleasure and benefit from the variety (for example, in her recent upwardly mobile hire at Liberal U). Nevertheless, the fact that she does not work solely in feminist and lesbian studies enables her to bring inquiry into gender and sexuality into canonized period and genre courses.

Olivia's tactical citizenship and avoidance of the personal comprise a performance that created multiple positions rather than a position that may be conferred on her as lesbian/lesbian theorist. By performance, I do not mean to suggest that Olivia's actions are the enactment of a role; rather, her performances operated to transform roles and to constitute new sets of relations.[41] Conquergood's description of performance as a process in which "becoming" displaces "being" may characterize her

departmental tactics.[42] While dependent on context for their legitimation, her performances were productive precisely because they engaged
norms, ideals, and standards as they were being reconstructed in the
department. She used the assumptions by which she and her work
would be located to deconstruct and dis-locate her subject and disciplinary positions.

"I Find My Commodity Category Deeply Annoying"

> We'd have to read the hiring that the English department has done
> as having to do to some weird extent with the visibility of the stu-
> dent population, the students—there are a good number of gay
> and lesbian students—so it seems like there is a constituency there.
> So you can say, "Oh, we should have some of this, and then queer
> theory is making these inroads, so we should have some of that."
>
> —Karen[43]

> Now they think I'm an Americanist. That's fine, they've made me
> normal.
>
> —Olivia

Hired under a job description that sought a feminist theorist with expertise in gay and lesbian studies and twentieth-century literature, Olivia
has built much of her reputation on the basis of her work in lesbian theory. As I will discuss in detail in chapter 5, Olivia rejects the lesbian
identity and community that have been constituted in lesbian scholarship and writing. Much of her intellectual project is to interrogate
assumptions attached to "lesbian" and to call into question meanings
the category may be thought to carry. She thus lives and works in something of a contradiction, known for her work in "the commodity category" of lesbian theory, yet using the premises on which she is called to
speak to challenge—even decommodify—the very category that has
enabled her academic success. In this spirit, she neither teaches courses
in gay and lesbian studies nor self-announces to students: "You assume
people care because you announce. There's a bizarre assumption
attached to that announcement, like this is significant, and I don't think
it, it isn't really." Even so, Olivia is unsure of the meanings of her
departmental categorization:

> The way that they categorized that job, it was categorized as a feminist
> theorist, and the expectations from it have been nothing. What I'm
> teaching, basically I'm a regular player. . . . And yet you hear, what I
> get in a lot of the stuff that I do, disciplinarily in gay and lesbian stud-
> ies is that there is this category that is commodified, and I can certainly
> say that in a way I have taken advantage of that, I very quickly took

advantage of it, I took advantage of it at the beginning. I knew it was coming somehow, from way back, and I was in a position to do it. But I'm not sure I would say I was taking advantage of it. . . . Some of the stuff I'm doing is being published because of it. If it were earlier, it wouldn't have been published. On the other hand, I'm resistant to seeing myself as taken as only that. And I don't know if I am or not.

Olivia's work in multiple arenas makes it doubtful that she is taken only as lesbian theorist, yet the effects of a category that would position her even as she refuses its significance are unknowable.

Like Carol, not being "taken as only that" depended on Olivia's claiming authority in a number of spheres. She spoke of entering the department as a known theorist in lesbian studies:

> Initially, it can authorize you in ways that I think are not very good, like it authorizes you to speak for gay people. If you have other things to say and do other things, you outstrip it. . . . Academe is all about— if you know stuff or you're interested in stuff and you can carry on conversations about a broad range of things, you'll be seen as a broadranging person. If you only talk about gay things, you'll be seen as a gay person. It's what you do ultimately, rather than any kind of rubric that's going to count, that's going to define you. The trick is, in academe you can't control this, you have to be what you are, what you say you are. In other words, if you want to be regarded as a serious researcher, you simply do serious research, if you want to be regarded as a good teacher, you simply do good teaching. . . . The way to maintain authority is to do what you know.

Authority is achieved by "doing," through action and interaction, rather than by "being," acquiescing to a category. However, the doing can never be fully separated from the being: the two interact to constitute Olivia's performances. Although assumptions about the "narrowness" of gay and lesbian studies comprise part of Olivia's concerns, it is interesting to note that disciplinary shifts in the field of English have made gay and lesbian issues part of departmental discourse, unlike the School of Journalism and contrary to the overall ethos of Liberal U.

Olivia's "doing" seeks not only to claim multiple authorities but to disclaim "being," or the roles thought to inhere in the social/academic category lesbian/lesbian theorist. As she characterized the meanings some colleagues would attach to the category, she described the way she and Karen, who also works in lesbian theory, are treated: "We will be our countercultural figures, we will be relied upon to do certain kinds of things and we speak for all gay people, and all that kind of stereotypical association kind of crap that you get." This tokenization played itself out not only in the English department, but across the university as Olivia was granted authority to speak for gay and lesbian persons and issues. After mentioning being asked to take a lesbian job candidate in another department to dinner and to be interviewed for an article on gay and lesbian rights for an internal university publication, Olivia spoke of her use of her token position:

> I use the opportunity to debunk the notion of the category. . . . I don't know to what extent the privilege I have is because of [the category] and because I produce a helluva lot—I can't figure that, I don't know which it is. But that work has to be done. And the work means providing an interesting discussion about what these issues and categories are, in the place of an assumption about the category. And that's what Karen and I both do. I mean, neither of us will acquiesce to being the representative of the group—rather, we begin to question the notion of the group in our functions.

In a difficult contradiction, and despite her intentions, Olivia's use of token contexts to debunk the category simultaneously enables others to read her as reinforcing and embodying the category.

The goal of "breaking down the tokenism" is successful "when they forget. . . . When they don't, of course you can't tell that, but there are times when your agenda is not assumed to be gay studies." Both socially and academically, Olivia understands her actions as rewriting the interactions that others' knowledges would define: "You have to interact with a person enough to get that out of the way, the more homophobic people it'll be a lot longer. But they'll forget, eventually they'll just take it for granted. If you make a big deal out of it, they'll make a big deal out of it. People have a way of picking up from you what they're supposed to do." Although Olivia understands performance as something whose effects an actor cannot predict or control, as creating a Barthesian "writerly text" in which the reader is "no longer a consumer but a producer of the text,"[44] she claims an ability to set the stage for the readings that will be produced.

As a symptom of departmental assumptions around lesbian/lesbian theorist, Olivia and Karen are conflated: "Lesbians are equally interchangeable, it doesn't matter, we're all the same. You know, Karen, me, it doesn't matter. Karen and I are often confused, like how the hell could they do that? It's not based on physics or appearance or anything like that, it's based on that identity business. They're both lesbians, ergo they're both the same." An anecdote demonstrates how the social and academic merge, such that lesbian identity and scholarship narrow others' understandings of her and Karen:

> There is a course that is required of all incoming students in the department, which is an introduction to graduate studies course, which is deeply, deeply badly conceived. It has always been team-taught. The

teams have always . . . tended to represent the modern and historical areas, it's this bifurcation in the discipline, but they've also reflected other kinds of difference. Usually it has been male/female, often the male has been senior, the female has been junior, it's not been a terribly good thing. Occasionally they will have white male, black female or senior woman and middle man, but it's always been this hetero configuration. They have trouble finding people to teach this course, this is really badly conceived. So Karen and I decided we'd like to teach this course, and we volunteered to teach it. The Graduate Director, she's new this year, went to the former Director of Graduate Studies, who is my friend, and said, "Olivia and Karen put in for this course, should I let them teach it?" He said basically why the hell not? "Well, because they're the same, they do the same thing." Well, Karen and I don't do the same thing, we're both twentieth century, we don't do the same thing. Well, the Graduate Director e-mailed Karen and said, "Well, you and Olivia are too much the same, but would you be willing to teach this with Bob," this white guy that does twentieth-century American literature, which is what she does. And Karen said, "No, I'm not going to do this with anybody besides Olivia, and what's the difference between Bob and me?" Karen went on and said she was being homophobic. So the Graduate Director goes and gets two other groups of people to do it. Her real coup was having a white male who does nineteenth-century British teach it with another white male who does nineteenth-century British.

Karen spoke of the incident as a "homo problem, lesbo problem":

> [Olivia] must have told you this, we put in to teach a course together, and they said no, we were too alike, we weren't different enough. Which is very amusing to me, because the books we've done, articles, whatever, my work is very different than hers. Now they're acting like they're going to rethink the course that we applied to teach together. They made a mess for themselves and now they're going to have to figure out what to do, because now they've let two men of the same composition—straight white men—after we were too similar, it'll be interesting.

In fact, Karen's research is materialist and theorizes sexuality, gender, class, and race, whereas Olivia's is psychoanalytic and only infrequently engaged with issues of race and class. Nonetheless, "lesbian studies" came to stand as a monolith that does not include numerous approaches and issues. Despite their research and teaching in areas beyond lesbian studies, lesbian became salient. It is precisely the homophobia of registering Karen and Olivia as the same, and refusing to see the breadth of their scholarship, then registering two white men as different, that constitutes the delimitation of "lesbian" that Olivia performs against in her department.

In order to open up lesbian for their colleagues, Olivia explained that in committee work she and Karen "come from different angles, on purpose . . . to keep enacting the fact that we are not the same." Karen explained, "She has a different style, and in a way that's good because they, at first they were really collapsing us into each other, but we're different in how we go about things and people are starting to be able to read that." Though dissimilar in their oblique and confrontive interactional styles, they share a quest to enact a dissimilarity from the position "lesbian/lesbian theorist." Olivia reiterated a Foucauldian concern with disciplining persons as subjects—as well as with disciplining disciplines—as she performs against the predictable role of lesbian theorist who implements predictable gay and lesbian studies courses:

> If we read Foucault, why is sexuality a meaningful category in the first place? . . . Why is it that sexuality is given the prominence it is in this culture, which is a fairly modern invention, and it's politically efficacious to do that, but hell, that's a control, that's a discipline here. In what way do we delimit people by naming it—and it's just the delimitation that one wants to fight against. In other words, if you're a lesbian and you don't act like one, you're supposed to, but you don't, but you still are, do you screw up the disciplinary function? I don't know. It's an interesting question, I'm playing it out to see what happens. I have the perfect set-up for it [with Karen]. We correlate, sometimes she's bad cop, I'm good cop, or she's good cop and I'm bad cop. . . . We are not going to act according to type. We are not going to do the things you think we are supposed to do. We would never give a course on gay and lesbian studies, we would give a course called Studies in Sexuality, if you want such a thing on the books. . . . That's what the discipline has to do and it can only do it by seeping into things other than its discipline, which is what Karen and I do, seep into other things than THAT THING, that isn't really a discipline but people keep trying to call one. We're going for versatility here. . . . Given the political configurations in this department, what we need to do for ourselves, and what we think of as having intellectual integrity, and also ethics, is to not reify the categories that they want to reify via us, but rather to explode that by being anything or everything in addition to and but that. We simply show how it is always an element of interrogation, not ignore it nor overly include it, but do it in intelligent relation to other things.

Rather than accept a place as a subject or a place for a discipline, Olivia's goal is to do away with disciplinarity, to make sexuality a common part of textual and cultural interrogation by locating it through multiple discourses. Not wanting to participate in a discipline that turns in on itself as categories of identity turn in on themselves, Olivia in a sense performed the slogan "we are everywhere." "Everywhere" is undisciplined, unlocatable, unpredictable.[45]

By being everywhere, Olivia sidestepped departmental tensions between canonic literary and cultural studies by incorporating her work into both theoretical and genre-period classes. This seeping, in which identity is less at stake than the politics of texts, Karen argued, "affect[s] the issue of gay and lesbian studies directly because then you're talking about how does the study of sexuality become significant. I mean, are you just going to try to find homosexuality somewhere, are you just going to be involved in some stupid reclamation of trying to prove Shakespeare was a fag? That's a bore." Olivia engaged the structure through performances in practice, using the range of her teaching abilities to "seep" inquiry into sexuality into multiple domains:

> If you're a commodified category it gives you an entré, it's up to you to change it. You know, maybe this is idealistic, but okay, they hired me because they want someone in feminist theory that does gay and lesbian studies. But they don't really want anybody to do gay and lesbian studies, so you don't really do gay and lesbian studies in a way that anyone can understand as gay and lesbian studies, so instead you do something else that's even worse than gay and lesbian studies, which they think is more benign because it looks more traditional. Sexuality or American literature that's chock full, you saw what we did in my performativity class.

Olivia's performances of *dis*location through good citizenship challenge arguments that lesbian voice and visibility are necessary to effect change and put pressure on assumptions that a distinct field of gay and lesbian studies is wholly desirable. However, although she eschews lesbian voice and visibility in order to question the category and seep inquiry into a number of domains, Olivia is bound to the category. Her project of "being anything or everything in addition to and but that" depend precisely on a "that" not to be. By playing deliberately against that which is expected of her as "lesbian/lesbian theorist," Olivia's performances depend on visibility as lesbian and on others' social knowledge of lesbian in order to achieve their effects. She worked from a place to displace the category that would put her in place. While her performances may not be those of an essential self or an essential field, they rely on essential knowledges.

Writing of the haltingly persistent advances of gay and lesbian studies, David Román has argued that optimism regarding its rise "imagines commodity fetishism and the rhetoric of tolerance as viable sites for gay and lesbian agency. The task at hand is to critically locate sites of agency in order to challenge the commodification and depoliticization of lesbian and gay studies within institutional movements based on tolerance and market trends." Román would suggest a liminality for the field of gay and lesbian studies, such that it is perpetually in process, never fully legitimated, acculturated, or defined. The liminal is a temporal space, which "enacts the move toward canonicity: it produces the illusion of assimilation while still holding license to remain temporarily outside of disciplinary control, even as it presupposes a narrative that will conclude in the initiation of customary norms."[46] Parallel to his antidisciplinary stance, Elizabeth Grosz's caution against overtheorizing, naming, and codifying lesbian pleasure serves as a warning against regarding gay and lesbian studies as a project of representation. Resistance to transparency allows limits and boundaries to remain open. That which cannot be contained ontologically or epistemologically through disciplinary representation or canonization must be allowed free play: "To submit one's pleasures and desires to enumeration and definitive articulation is to submit processes and becomings to entities, locations, and boundaries, to become welded to an organizing nucleus of fantasy whose goal is not simply pleasure and expansion but control, the production of endless repetition, endless variations of the same."[47] Perpetual liminality may be difficult to sustain, particularly in light of both oppositional and mainstream pressures for legitimation, inclusion, and location. However, the contradictions of Olivia's performative positioning suggest that it may be possible to preclude the closure naming brings through interactions that rearrange the meanings of those names—that, in short, surprise. Projects such as Olivia's suggest that even with the limitations of disciplining, the insights of gay and lesbian studies may seep into other areas, and the disciplined subjects who work under its aegis may confuse the terms by which they would be located. Commodification allows for Olivia's presence; the challenge is to appropriate the terms of disciplined presences in order to perform alternatives to fixed categories. This appropriation may occur by moving in and out of disciplinary norms such that expectations are never fulfilled but always rearranged. Although codification, representation, and market trends contain thought and action, they may also offer resources with which to maneuver, allowing a rewriting of the terms of location by being there, nowhere, and everywhere, in and out of proper places. In this way there may be a continual shifting of limits.

APPROPRIATION AND PRACTICE

What might be learned from the (in)appropriate places these women occupy in their departmental spaces? While I have offered a necessarily partial representation, several themes emerge: the relations of individuals to departmental social and academic knowledges, the placement of individual departments in institutional academic and social spaces, and

the strange meanings identity and difference take on across these relations. I discuss these themes in the context of my concerns with knowledge and ignorance, voice and visibility, and "being" and "doing" as
they relate to (in)appropriateness, liminality, and transgression.

As I have suggested throughout this chapter, the social and academic knowledges at work in Olivia's, Julie's, and Carol's departments
were not discrete, but intertwined in unpredictable ways. Their interplay
was affected by disciplinary, institutional, and social norms, which were
themselves in shifting sets of relations. In understanding individuals'
relations to disciplines, Hartman and Messer-Davidow maintain that
"[t]hrough this social positioning, we acquire the *values* that draw us to
certain disciplines, which in turn codify the values that influence our disciplinary *judgments* about subjects to investigate, methods to employ,
knowledge to produce, and uses to which that knowledge should be
put." Their location of individuals' social positioning as external to and
prior to entrance into disciplinary milieu appears to leave disciplinary
norms and values impermeable to change through internal dynamics.
Although they acknowledge that disciplinary changes can be understood
by taking into account "how hegemonic its culture and how closed its
borders to neighboring disciplines,"[48] they ignore local context as individuals who constitute and reconstitute departments in specific institutions negotiate knowledge through academic and social interactions. In
other words, the effects of faculty members' positionings and actions are
unaccounted for. Not only are faculty changed by participation in networks of relations, but networks themselves are changed by the presence
and actions of individuals.[49] Because culture is contested and perpetually
in process, norms and positionings are not immutable, never whole,
never fully one thing or another, but part of a process of redefinition and
renegotiation. The fluidity of what is socially or academically appropriate makes room for change. Spaces and places are not so fixed as they
might seem.

Within Liberal U's ideals for academic knowledge, its efforts to
include and represent "diversity," and the demands for external funding
and recognition, each department offers specific enactments of the university's mission that underscore the effects of institutions on departments and the unpredictable workings of departments in universities.
The Departments of English and Religious Studies and the School of
Journalism represent and embody specific times and places in Liberal U's
posthistorical space. The contestation of the centers of reason and culture, combined with excellence's lack of content, allow Julie, Carol, and
Olivia room for performative play. If Liberal U could be said to need
these women's differences to prove its excellence, the women could
equally be said to be using the institution's incorporation of them to

their advantage. For example, in religious studies, anxieties about the return of theological engagement in the space of reason would determine departmental norms. In a curious rewriting of the intersections of diversity and objectivity discourses, the department commodifies practitioners of "exotic" religions while casting suspicion on practicing Christians, whose work appears to bear directly on local practices and thus seems less objective. In Julie's case, excellence intrudes to legitimate her feminist, practical, and subjective approaches to her field due to her scholarship's viability for funding, its increasing disciplinary recognition, and its responsiveness to pressures brought to bear by "diversity." As a professional school, the School of Journalism's emphasis on the preparation of practitioners (employability) and objectivity and utilitarianism in research are closely aligned with Liberal U's institutional presentation of self. The school exemplifies the institutional ethos of incorporating social diversity by making it visible in discrete locations while assuming little shared responsibility for knowledge of diversity and its academic or social implications. Carol's role has been to confuse these spatial separations and locations. The Department of English offers an instantiation of institutional publishing pressures and the present "high-stakes," competitive situation of literary studies. Disciplinary shifts within English, combined with social pressures and campus identity politics, have increasingly allowed a representational position for gay and lesbian studies and for shifts from culture-building through teaching the canon to cultural critique. Olivia has used her resulting commodified position as "lesbian/lesbian theorist" to enact cultural critiques and to "de-representationalize" her "field."

Each of the women is (in)appropriate in ways specific to her department, multiply positioned, neither fully inside or outside social and academic norms. Appropriations through practice constitute them socially and academically as subjects and objects of knowledge—and enable interventions. Their appropriations of the appropriate, intentional or not, for uses that are not always altogether appropriate enable their departmental positioning and bring about a modicum of change in their departmental spaces. It is this interplay of actions and interactions in context that is the site of agency. For example, Julie is a Catholic lesbian who speaks frankly and irreverently while she writes texts that are socially, practically, and spiritually grounded. Academically, her work is nationally acclaimed; socially, she is able to speak in languages that are shared and understood in her predominantly secular and objective department. Over time, Julie's visibility as Catholic, feminist, and lesbian has been relational and shifting—as the contexts within which she works have shifted. Julie's actions and interactions in her department could be understood as an acting out of her relations and an acting against her identities. For example, her (in)visibility as lesbian—which has been constitutive of and constituted by her colleagues' unknowing—can be understood as a performance of and against "identity" through the said and unsaid. Her queering of department meetings forces tacit recognitions that may be both academic and social—and act out a set of collegial relations within structures of knowledge and ignorance.

Similarly, Carol's and Olivia's actions and interactions entail an acting out of and against their identities, which necessarily involve voice and visibility. Carol is a black lesbian who engages in cultural studies and voices her politics. However, she has been appropriately socialized and is able to excel on familiar terms while using those terms to conduct cultural and political analysis that challenges the practices of her field. She began her departmental relations in the context of being (seen as) her race, which Patricia Williams has described as offering knowledges that would overdetermine her position: "Culturally, blackness signifies the realm of the always known, as well as the not worth knowing. A space of the entirely judged. . . . Racism is a gaze that insists upon the power to make others conform, to perform endlessly in the prison of prior expectation, circling repetitively back upon the expired utility of the entirely known."[50] Yet, through her actions and interactions—an interplay of challenging and at times deferring to the ways she and her work would be categorized—Carol complicated this social/academic location to locate herself as authority in multiple domains. Her "doing," or her performances through speech and action, combined with knowledges of her "being" to disrupt meanings attached to black femaleness. Her use of her voice acted against her objectification on the basis of her visible identities, and inserted her less visible identities and abilities strategically into the department. In this way, she challenged others' refusals of shared responsibility for curricular diversity, heterosexist departmental policies, and assumptions of her academic expertise. By not conforming to the knowledges attached to her, Carol exceeded the place into which she would be put. Olivia's performances against voice and visibility as lesbian depended on the very category she acted against. Colleagues' knowledges of her and Karen's categorizations as "lesbians/lesbian theorists" enabled her project of "debunking" and her use of Karen as a counterpoint to enact differences among lesbians and from the category lesbian. Although Olivia does not claim voice or visibility, they structure knowledges of her and her acting out against those knowledges. It is interesting that for Julie and Carol the visual was directly constitutive of how they were constructed and comprised a part of their understandings of how they were perceived, while for Olivia, the visual was less explicitly at stake, except as a trope to be overcome. Julie and Carol, corporeally marked as historicized bodies, challenge conceptions of the disembodied thinker, a fact that places their departmental authority at risk. Olivia's actions and theoretical stances place in view not an academic body but a body of knowledge, highly intellectual and depersonalized. Her theoretical, disembodied work and her anti-essentialism may function as academic strategies of legitimation in which knowledge is detached from the body, from person as social knower.

These three women's interactions suggest that the tropes of voice and visibility must be understood as mutually constitutive and relational. Sight, Martin Jay has argued, is "less temporal than other senses such as hearing or touch, [and] thus tends to elevate static Being over dynamic Becoming, fixed essences over ephemeral appearances."[51] Vision creates an illusion of knowledge, of being able to map and fix objects in a field, to organize space. These seemingly fixable objects are, however, in dynamic interplay with knowledge and ignorance. They are made visible by structures of knowledge and ignorance—indeed, become visible within structures of knowledge and ignorance—yet reorganize those structures through interaction. In this sense, voice—not a decontextualized voice, nor a voice that is a transparent representation of self, but voice that is used and constituted in action and interaction— mediates what is seen, working to unfix the static nature of vision in and through *practice*. However, voice should not be privileged over visibility nor deemed more authentic, for they are mutually implicated. As voice complicates the epistemic field of vision, visibility complicates what is spoken and heard. Voice and visibility change in their relations and effects across contexts comprised of shifting configurations of knowledge and ignorance. In this regard, Biddy Martin has offered a useful caution regarding theoretical trends that overvalorize visible outsiderness:

> Queer theory and politics necessarily celebrate transgression in the form of visible difference from norms that are then exposed to be norms, not natures or inevitabilities. Gender and sexual identities are arranged, in much of this work, around demonstrably defiant deviations and configurations. Surfaces, then, take priority over interiors and depths and even rule conventional approaches to them out of bounds as inevitably disciplinary and constraining.[52]

Her argument suggests that what might appear to be conformity is not inherently conservative, but may constitute part of a set of tactics akin to those of Trinh's Inappropriate Other/Same. Ambiguity and movement refuse absolute difference or location. Movement, or engagement in and appropriation of multiple practices, refuses singular, visible, or coherent differences, and allows room for play in departmental spaces. For example, what I have described as Julie's liminality is produced precisely in the context of the shifting of limits of her department, which include new forms of academic production and new forms of social relations, and helps to keep those limits in play. Julie's role is classifiable as neither this nor that, but draws on and breaks with differing norms for gender and sexuality, academic values, and social interactions.

The issue of the "transgressive" potential of visible outsiderness also illuminates aspects of Carol's and Olivia's work in their departments. While the institutionalization of scholarship in racial, ethnic, women's, and gay and lesbian studies is in many ways enabling, at the same time, the rhetoric of identity politics and institutional responses to it have had the social and academic effect of conflating identity with minority group affiliation. As a result, faculty can become representatives of a social position, contained in what Roof and Wiegman call "a new, deafening 'authenticity,' one that disturbingly reduces the complexity of social subjectivity."[53] As David Palumbo-Liu points out, scholars who were once asked to universalize themselves—to ignore, for example, their gendered and racialized beings—are now asked "not only to recognize the personal as racial but to foreground it particularly in their scholarly duties."[54] With Liberal U's responses to demands for multicultural subjects, Olivia and Carol could be said to have been at least partly hired on the basis of their identities or areas of "identity scholarship" as objects of exchange that fill "niches" that demonstrate institutional commitments to diversity. In the University of Excellence, the value of exchange lies in the exchange of information, such that diverse faculty in the academic market may be pleasantly poised to offer consumers informational commodities. For example, the segmentation of gay and lesbian studies into what Judith Roof calls a "consumer discipline" directly affects the work of lesbian scholars in contradictory ways: "the link between identity, epistemology, and discipline appears to open the academy, while in practice it restricts thought, limits and consolidates authority under the guise of distributing it, and sequesters individuals within manageable consumer groups with discrete market interests."[55] If, as Lauren Berlant has ventured, the public sphere is "a marketplace where people participate through consumption,"[56] it may be that blacks, feminists, and gays and lesbians are entering the academic public sphere as ostensible subjects so that they might be consumable objects of knowledge. Such is the skepticism Olivia and Carol act out about the liberatory nature of their respective disciplinary and departmental positions. Yet even with the salience of identity politics, ideologies of objectivity persist at Liberal U, creating a duality in which the erasure and the highlighting of identity are simultaneous and contradictory ideals that structure academic authority. In a sense, it is their refusal to act "informationally" or "authentically," in combination with their abilities to cite objectivity and difference in different contexts, that allows them to reconstruct this duality.

Across the women's tactics, there is an interplay of multiple samenesses and differences in relation to others and to expectations that may be said to constitute transgression. This interplay temporalizes spatial locations by creating new modes of exchange that destabilize the fixity of the networks of relations in which they find themselves. De Certeau suggests that a "cultural operation might be represented as a trajectory relating to the places that determine its conditions of possibility."[57] If social and academic structures, knowledges, and identities overburdened with meanings comprise the places from which Julie, Carol, and Olivia work, they also comprise the resources available to push at the limits of place. As I mentioned in the previous chapter, Agamben has described ethics as based not on human essences or destiny but on "possibility or potentiality."[58] What he calls "singularity" is "freed from the false dilemma that obliges knowledge to choose between the ineffability of the individual and the intelligibility of the universal. . . . [It] is reclaimed from its having this or that property, which identifies it as belonging to this or that set, to this or that class" (1). This singularity is "not a final determination of being, but an unraveling or an indetermination of its limits: a paradoxical *individuation* by *indetermination*" (56). This indetermination, which may take form as liminality, antiessentialism, ambiguity, or movement between conformity and nonconformity, is part of a process in which "[w]hat changes are not the things but their limits" (92). Transgression may be no more than a refusal of place, movement itself, the process of rearrangement.

CHAPTER 5

Lesbian/Intellectual

Lesbian is loaded in terms of stereotypes and expectations. . . . The notion of lesbian—who is it, what is it, and why aren't you one—there are all these expectations and assumptions bound up in the word. I think it's outmoded. In some ways it's lost its usefulness as a category, but in some ways we can't sort of let go of it yet.

—Carol

By centering much of my inquiry on intellectual, personal, and professional meanings of "lesbian" in the lives of Olivia, Julie, and Carol, I have invoked a category that can obscure more than it reveals. Throughout the inquiry, their words and actions have placed lesbian outside the core of their intellectual and academic work. In this sense, lesbian imposes an artificial construct on three women who do not define it as central to their experiences or understandings of self.[1] In contrast, my placing intellectual as another central element of inquiry is consonant with their understandings of self and commitments. Each woman offers a unique articulation of intellectual that makes multiple its meanings. If *lesbian* carries stereotypes, assumptions, and expectations, how do they describe their relations to and experience its meanings? What sorts of relations does *lesbian* have to their intellectual lives, if any? How do they conceptualize their intellectual work, its purposes and meanings? What can be learned from their articulations of the two categories? In this chapter, I explore the meanings of *lesbian, intellectual,* and *academic* for these three women and connect them to their pedagogical and departmental work at Liberal U.

Although each woman uses the word lesbian to speak of herself, the term is clearly not a transcendental signifier that attaches itself in predictable ways to their intellectual practices and affiliations. Olivia's theoretical approach to what a lesbian is(n't)—a verb rather than a noun, identifications rather than an identity, a source of limitation and entrapment rather than of liberation—is constitutive of much of her intellectual work, her "performance of presence," and refusal of location. Julie's historical reflections on the shifting meanings of lesbian—an element of her life that has been constructed as private, that she has not overtly problematized until recently, that has had little tangible relation to her intellectual life—are those of a person open to asking what meanings sexuality has had and continues to have in her life. Carol's dismissal of lesbian and lesbian communities as a singular identity politic insufficient to her needs and interests as an African-American and an intellectual creates a complicated dynamic in her social and intellectual affiliations, one that highlights the fact that for her there is no "inside," but provisional alliances that are formed and reformed. Lesbian identity as inherently meaningful and lesbian community as premised on assumptions of shared experiences and attitudes are at odds with each woman's intellectual life and point to the limitations of lesbian "identities" and "communities" as they have been constituted and understood. For Olivia, Julie, and Carol, an active intellectual life of questioning is paramount, and often irrelevant to or at odds with affiliations based on sexuality.

OLIVIA: "THE CRANKY LESBIAN CRITIC"

Olivia understands lesbian not as a category to represent, voice, or make visible, but as a relational process of shifting identifications. In problematizing identity, she drew on the psychoanalytic notion of an ego fiction, "the thing that deludes you into believing there's something whole that you're speaking from," something that can speak but that is usually spoken:

> This is identification, it's a process, it's not a static thing, it's not a category, it's not a thing. I prefer that as a way of understanding this because it allows flux, it allows the tensions, dynamics, and shifts, whereas identity seems to provide the fiction that there is this thing, this stable thing that's sort of unchanging through time. . . . /I/ think of this as a process of identifying and realize first of all that it's transactional and not one-sided; second of all, that it changes and is mutable and flexible, and is not a given; third of all that human relations are interactive and not sets of stable signifiers bumping against each other like bumper cars.

Not fully constituted, "identities" are situationally evoked:

> We have a legion of things that are providing identities, they're not that full, they're like attachments in some way. . . . They're always there, but they recede and they're more prominent at times and they recede at times. They're like a whole wardrobe, and sometimes, they're there, they're in the closet, you take them off and put them on, but it's more involuntary than that, I think. They come. They're called up by certain stimuli, it may be contextual, it may be environmental, . . . it has a lot to do with where you are and what's being asked of you.

Her unsettling and evocative mixture of theatrical and closet metaphors suggests not a unified subject but a highly contextual self whose actions are consonant with the discontinuities of performance. Sexuality cannot be understood as a fixed category of identity, for, like identity, it is inherently transactional. Ways of acting and interacting, wardrobes that come in and out of the closet, shift in meaning across contexts; signification, identification, and knowledge are unstable.

Olivia maintains that understanding identity as a substance is implicated in the construction of what she calls "counterpoint identities," in which the meanings of inferior terms in hierarchized oppositions (such as man/woman, white/black, straight/gay) become overdetermined in their specificity vis-à-vis the unmarked "universals" with which they are paired: "It's only the difference that has the identity, it's not the mainstream." As in practices of identity politics, counterpoint identities conflate difference and identity; what is processual and relational becomes naturalized as preexisting rather than constructed. Reified through voice and visibility, they are represented as stable rather than dynamic. Understood through a Foucauldian lens, counterpoint identities become convenient mechanisms for the location, discipline, and control of subjects.

Olivia's conceptualization of socially imposed "counterpoint identities" is closely linked to her understanding of the uses to which persons put identity *due to recognition by others*. The announcement of positionality ("As a white male heterosexual, I . . .") is a rhetorical strategy in which "identities are nouns rather than verbs, and that somehow is seen as a legitimate rhetorical move that authorizes even as it excuses. It's not just an excuse, it's a fortification. It's almost like girding themselves before battle. You know, I'm going to put on my white male suit now with words." Rhetorical strategies are dependent on context, which defines "what a relevant identity category is there." If lesbian is a shifting process, if neither sexual categories nor our relations to them are static, what are the benefits of positioning oneself categorically? To reverse the question, what might be the benefits of questioning the category in practice? As evidenced in her academic work, Olivia's response is not only to sidestep recognition by not naming a "personal" but also to enact a performance that has as its point of departure location within the category yet works against it, a performance that, as David Román describes, "due to its *discontinuity*, offers neither a fixed subject position nor an essential representation of the 'real.'"[2]

In Olivia's understanding, persons announce only positions that they perceive to be relevant or beneficial in a specific context: "I'm going to position myself here, partly because I have to admit to the visible signs of my, the visible assumptions you're going to make about me, partly because I'm going to speak from what I perceive to be the position of a white male heterosexual." The lesbian position, however, is neither beneficial, relevant, nor visible:

> Rhetorical strategies have a lot to do with what you're going to get. . . . What does a lesbian get back if she self-announces it? . . . Unless the discussion is about sexuality, you've basically just disenfranchised what you've said. But gay males don't necessarily disenfranchise themselves by what they say. I could imagine a conversation on one of those [talk] shows about child custody or something. There's a gay male, "Oh yes, the gay male says da da da." A lesbian would get up, she might as well not open her mouth.

Her emphasis on the asymmetric role of gender in defining lesbian authorization to speak finds resonance in her allegiance to feminist and lesbian studies rather than gay and lesbian studies or queer theory. Although her anti-essentialist stance may appear to contradict her rejection of queer as "an erasure category" that does not attend to the specificities of lesbian issues, it is based, I believe, in her understanding of the importance of gender in constructing the meanings of sexual categories and her intellectual connection to lesbian theory's feminist legacy.[3]

Olivia's understandings of (lesbian) identity suggest that it is not a category but a shifting process that offers at best a contingent, illusory knowledge. To invoke identity, to attempt to be seen or heard as lesbian, is to invoke a disciplining mark of difference, to incur voicelessness. In the same way that she rejects the category theoretically, Olivia says that she does not experience herself or her relations with others according to the category: "I'm not going to appeal to any kind of essentialism, but I think that one gets used to being simply, I mean, I don't walk around thinking of myself as a lesbian. I walk around thinking of myself as me, and I relate to people the way I relate to people and I don't even think about that." Despite her disavowal of the relevance of the "lesbian position" in her approaches to interacting with others, I am more than ambivalent about her claim that she does not "even think about that." Although she may not attach intrinsic significance to lesbian, her departmental positioning necessitates her thinking of herself as lesbian in her collegial interactions, as revealed by her articulated tactics for unraveling assumptions attached to "lesbian/lesbian theorist." In other words, rejecting thinking of herself as lesbian creates the paradoxical situation of thinking of herself as lesbian.

Rather than seeing her self as expanding understandings of lesbian, Olivia is concerned that lesbian as the mark of difference precludes alternative understandings of self:

> If you say that any identity category is limiting, then why isn't being lesbian limiting? But if you say that it's limiting, then somehow that's

homophobic. So you're caught in a trap, and the only way around it is to say, well, according to the way this culture defines categories of sexuality, that's a component of what my life is, but it's not, it would be very difficult for me to estimate what portion that is if one could even express it that way. But it is not the sum total and I would not want it to be the conclusion of the syllogism.

Her refusal of the category echoes Michel Foucault's claim that "[v]isibility is a trap"[4] that disciplines the subject and perpetuates itself:

> I really have a problem with the whole idea of role models and all of that stuff, particularly with sexuality, because it involves a reification of stereotypes and the entrapment of people in a particular place. So what I see as the virtue of debunking the sexual category is that it allows—not flexibility—but it allows you to move beyond that category which is a self-delimiting category. It's not an accident that you get "I am what I am" in the middle of *La Cage Aux Folles*. That's the tautological what is a gay person like, they're gay. Over and over again. . . . It's a version of narcissism but it's also a self-limiting narrative of self-discovery that keeps circling on itself and if people treat you like that's the only salient fact about you, it actually is playing on the homophobia that you would like to get rid of. In other words, there's a way in which coming out and reifying that category is exactly the opposite of what one would want to happen with that kind of emergence of category.

Inverting the efficacy of identity politics, Olivia argues that to claim the category is to become complicit with the structure of the closet and to confirm the construction of sexuality as an identity. To model a role presumes a transparent ideal to be taught and copied. To question categories of sexual identity is to refuse the foreclosed meanings of a fixed location and its repetition.

Linked to Olivia's rejection of centering sexuality as a locus of identity is her disconnection from lesbian communities and her discontent with political activism that has formed around the category. In one of our interviews, after she mentioned an uncharacteristically personal paragraph in one of her books, I asked, "Are you implicated in what you study?"

> I don't know. I have an odd position in relation to it, partly because I've never been able to be part of a lesbian community in my life. I mean, any time I was around them I was always put off by it in some way, like I don't really fit here. Nor was I actually ever allowed to fit, and it's not like a vendetta or anything, but it's more like what the hell's going on here, what are the assumptions of these communities? What is the self-portrait being drawn of lesbians? I mean, lesbian literature is a pretty dismal self-portrait. You know, maybe I don't hate

myself enough to be in these things, I don't know, but it's very kind of depressing. . . . They tend to be, well now, but then they were focused around celebrating women and then walked around sort of screwing each other over, and they were terribly anti-intellectual, and most of them never did a goddamn thing, and they'd sit around, this was during the bar years mostly, they'd sit around and drink in bars and they would never do anything. Maybe I'm just too imbued in the Protestant ethic or something. I've never seen more people do less, this is what is seen as the community. I'm sure there are lesbians that do a lot, but you don't see them there, because they've got other things to do. Now it's all twelve-step. But it's the same thing, it's the same sort of self-engaged, self-focused kind of thing. Maybe twelve-step is better than the bars, but it seems a little more tedious to me, and a kind of limited vision. . . . You know, I have made a choice that academe is the most political place that you can be.

The separation Olivia draws between herself and bar dyke and lesbian feminist communities overgeneralizes what she believes to be the solipsistic turning inward of identity-based communities and ignores individual and collective changes they have enabled, even as it raises significant questions about lesbian practices.[5] Turning outward through academia is an inversion not without its ironies, as those involved in political movements often argue that academia is a turning inward of sorts. Olivia's scholarly turn entails a response to activist constructions and representations of lesbian, a fact that leads me to read her work to some extent autobiographically, located at the intersections of lived experience and professional positioning, despite (and perhaps because of) her explicit and self-conscious performance against "lesbian" as the personal.

During my ineffectual attempts to make sense of the "origins" of Olivia's questions, I sometimes thought she would be pleased that I could not locate her life in her work in a *sustained* way, for she is a vocal critic of biographical criticism and the "intentional fallacy" in literary studies, concerned that readers not think there is a "real" against which they can read an author's work. Olivia does not often offer a real, describing her intellectual interests much as she describes her "identity": shifting, relational, situationally evoked. "I have multiple interests and they switch back and forth," she explained. "I'm always interested in the whys and the hows of anything, cultural phenomena. Why do we like vampires? How do they work? You'd be surprised where that takes you." Experience is not personal, but an artifact of sorts, an expression of culture. Olivia can speak lightly of the purposes of her intellectual projects despite their seriousness:

If you have questions that are probing enough, then you will do the thing that will enable you to answer them, so if you have questions that can be answered by art, you would be an artist. Whether you can live by it or not, academe's easier, a little easier chance of living by it. I have questions about the nature of the civilization in which we live, and this allows me to play around with answering them while getting paid. . . . Any time you just sit around and watch TV, and you go, why is that, and you see these things, and you start to notice these pattern changes for some reason, and you want to know, why does that pattern change that way? Like, for example, five or six years ago, suddenly, what appeared to be suddenly, all of these what appeared to be real-life based television series started coming on television. Well, why? . . . These are little questions—why is Arnold Schwarzennegger a phenomenon? Madonna? These seem minor, but they're symptoms. If we were to hypothesize that culture had an imaginary like a human would and that it had an unconscious sort of, then we can read these things, and follow back and try to figure out what this is all about. They're overdetermined, they're very complex things. . . . These are sort of cultural questions.

Olivia's use of the language of games—"playing around" with questions—often led me to think back to her office, to wonder about the elements of play. Yet she suggests cultural and political stakes in analyzing and theorizing cultural practices and their shifts.

Academia, as Olivia describes it, does not impose undue constraints on the content or methodology with which she wishes to engage. In fact, she sees the disciplinary openings that have occurred in English as enabling her pursuit of her intellectual interests: "I think what's happening, I'm not unusual, people are cutting across what are seen as the traditional disciplines in very different ways but that are complementary to what they do. I can do twentieth-century cultural studies, I can do it in French, American, and British, I can do it with psychoanalysis, with theory, film, painting, and visual arts." Even with the range of her scholarship, the persistent thread in lesbian studies suggests an autobiographical inflection, particularly as she connects it to her rejection of lesbian communities, forms of activism, and literature:

All the self-congratulatory activists. . . . Talk about bogus, if you want activism to have credibility, and then you end up with Rita Mae Brown, who has none, but a lot among people who are not academics. God, her novels get worse and worse. *Rubyfruit Jungle*, I don't know why, I think that started my career as the cranky lesbian critic, actually. . . . I don't celebrate. What is this trash I'm forced to read? Yuck, gag writing. This does not, very little of it is actually intellectually exciting, very little of it is titillating. Bleck.

Her expression of feeling oppressed by lesbian pop culture ("What is this trash I'm *forced* to read?") takes up June Jordan's distinction "between a common identity that has been imposed and the individual identity any one of us will choose, once she gains that chance."[6] Rather than acquiesce to anti-intellectualism or representations of lesbians perpetuated by pop culture or activist circles as representing "the community," Olivia questions assumptions underlying the production and reception of popular representations and their power to enforce labels. Through her scholarship and her "scholarly identity," an "anti-identity" that questions the knowledges representation would offer, she enacts this fluidity and refusal to conform to expectations.

This oppositional relation Olivia sets up between activist and academic work stems from her skepticism of the political uses of identity:

> There are probably more useful points of juncture [among activists and academics] than anyone would take advantage of, because there's a kind of oppositional dialogue that goes on there, a kind of adversarial dialogue. Activists, for example, won't recognize classrooms as sites of activity. Activist writing in academe would be just too small of an audience. A lot of gay and lesbian writing in academe is activist writing but who does it reach? People who are already convinced basically, so it's not politically efficacious to do that kind of writing in the academy. . . . I do think there's a different genealogy about the derivation of these things—their appearance depended on the same kinds of forces, the same kind of opening up of patriarchal metaphors at the same point in time, but they're really things that started at separate places, take off at separate places, have similar interests, but very different questions. Because activists are much more willing to reify the category and ask for political rights whereas academics are more willing to question the category as a way of trying to garner political rights.

Although she undermines the political impact of the *product* of intellectual work that critiques representations that reach mass audiences and in effect situates academics who question the category lesbian as speaking only among themselves, she places political efficacy in classroom *processes*: "The answer is not that the books are going to effect cultural change, they're not. The process of thinking through the work that you do gets translated into the classroom, and it's via the classroom that very small changes are made." Olivia's understanding that new forms of thought created through research find their effect through pedagogy could be said to resonate with Carol's desire to effect change through her teaching. However, Carol seeks specific changes in practice, whereas Olivia sees change as unpredictable, impossible to control.

Within academic traditions, Olivia situates her scholarship largely in relation to academic feminism, describing her intellectual work in relation—again, in critical opposition to—"camps" she sees emerging in lesbian studies:

There's the old criticism school . . . there's [an] outlet for that kind of material. Well, it's important material, it's not all that—it's useful, it's not going to break anything, but it's useful, that's all right. I think there is a kind of style queer group of lesbians, sort of self-styled radical, queer, not feminist, though. . . . Lipstick lezzies and leather wearing, the whole queer as intrinsically radical kind of thing, which is bullshit. And then I think there's more the line like I take, and other people take that line, people that do more cultural criticism and are a little more critical of the category. . . . Where we know that there's a debt to feminism and that feminism is still the thing in a way, and we are suspicious of alliances and basically spend all our time critiquing / /, and in it, the alliances become a lot clearer. And there are some women, too, who are sort of hooked in with the boys, that will never not be hooked in with the boys, . . . that will always be the boys' girls, who see themselves primarily as queer theorists, not as lipstick lesbians.

In her relentless questioning, Olivia critiques some of the very academic projects that have enabled her own. The "old criticism school," which, not uncoincidentally, is closely aligned with identity politics' project of recuperating lesbian texts, yet which is closely aligned with feminism, has published work that is "useful" to her. Her critiques of queer, particularly its more "stylized" and male manifestations, ignore its contributions to the disciplinary openings that facilitate her work.

The tentative biographical links I have suggested among lesbian, intellectual, and academic are not determinative, but an element of Olivia's resources for responding to what she considers important: proliferating new ways of thinking and acting that are open-ended, not bound to location. Carol and Julie do not explicitly draw on psychoanalytic and poststructural understandings of lesbian/identity. Nonetheless, their reflections similarly suggest the limitations of lesbian as a way of understanding self and its tenuous links to intellectual practice.

CAROL: "YOU DON'T JUST SORT OF STAY IN A PLACE AND WALLOW IN IT"

Carol, who embodies multiple "counterpoint identities," does not derive a static sense of self from positionings based on her race, class, gender, and sexuality. Rather, her self-identifications contain elements of, but are not limited to, her marked differences. As those differences often function as irreconcilable categories in her interactions with others, Carol expresses a desire for and a skepticism of affiliations based on race and sexuality. Her description of her spheres of affiliation begins to reveal disjunctures between identity and identifications:

CAROL. My friendship units are sort of inside and outside of lesbian networks. I don't tend to seek out friends based on who happen to be lesbians on campus. However, if I know of someone who's new and happens to be a dyke, I might be more motivated to meet that person or get to know them. And, frankly, I've been disappointed by a lot of the social networks that have been only oriented around sexuality or sexual identity. So I tend to choose my friends and allies based more on politics, sort of political affinity and cultural interests, commonalities, so we [Carol and her partner] have probably as many straight friends as we have queer friends.

SUSAN. In the networks of friends that you have, what is it that you're seeking?

CAROL. Similar attitudes and ways of looking at the world, I think. Similar ways of evaluating and critiquing, what we're eating for dinner that night or some national crisis. People that I can talk to, people who, frequently, have some shared experience with me. So it might be the shared experience of not growing up in the Midwest, of being an urban person, of living in cities. It may be more of an intellectual, in terms of the kinds of things that I study. . . . I look for affinity in at least some categories, knowing that your precious friends are the ones that you have affinities in a range of categories, so you can share and you have a lot of interests. . . .

SUSAN. What's the nature of your disappointment with networks based more around sexuality?

CAROL. If we talk specifically here, I think some of it is that sexuality doesn't transcend all those other categories, so simply the fact that I'm in a room with a bunch of other lesbians doesn't mean that I have anything else in common, and sexuality and sexual identity as a singular identity politic is insufficient for me. . . . Also, the lesbian culture here tends to be utterly white, and the way people here have a good time is to go two-stepping, but as a black person I have no affinity with that kind of music. . . . I think what happens in lesbian communities is that social life and so forth coalesce around certain cultural activities, music and the way people party and socialize and so forth, and I feel pretty alienated from most of those, in the same ways that I feel alienated in general from [the state's] culture. I feel alienated by the ways in which white lesbians in Oasis have sort of modified that culture for their own purposes, and whereas I see that that works for them and that's really important, and I'm like more power to them. They've created this culture and that's great and they're happy with it on some levels, but it doesn't do any good for me. Part of it for me is, and I think this is what makes people like us who are academics and intellectuals in general different from people who aren't, is that part of what we do as our work and our daily practice is this process of trying to move forward in a variety of ways, and that crosses all the different categories and boundaries. But our lives are really committed to this developmental process, that you don't just sort of stay in a place and wallow in it and get comfortable in it.

Carol's rejection of a singular identity politic separates identity from experience and does not presume that meanings inhere in sexuality. Her mention of the exclusionary nature of lesbians' appropriation of local white cultural practices echoes in a different key Olivia's critique of the insularity of lesbian communities.[7] In contrast to the singularity and stasis of the practices of lesbian communities, intellectual life is a dynamic process of movement forward that demands multiple affiliations. This mobility is incompatible with the visible and fixed locations created through identity-based social, political, and cultural practices.

In ways parallel but not identical to the limitations of lesbian networks, Carol has found affiliations on the basis of race problematic in minoritizing contexts. While she described universities as spaces in which race defines the ways persons organize themselves (or, I would add, are organized), this organizing rubric does not provide automatic bonds: "I've found this throughout my life, in all kinds of predominantly white situations, when you've got that small a number [of African-Americans], you throw together all these people who don't necessarily have anything in common other than their race, and it creates all kinds of ugly situations." Within the spatialized "niches" of marked categories formed at Liberal U, the inadequacy of categories to represent the fluidity of individuals' identifications and experiences becomes heightened. June Jordan has written: "Yes: race and class and gender remain as real as the weather. But what they must mean about the contact between two individuals is less obvious and, like the weather, not predictable."[8] In Carol's case, this contact resulted in "ugly situations" pertaining to her sexuality:

> There's still a sort of overarching social pressure, and that got busted wide open as soon as I got here, because there's sort of a core culture that's dictated by people in African-American studies. I find it entirely provincial, they're very tied to the black church, many of them are queer as the day is long, but very closeted. So here I show up. I'm out. My lover is white. . . . There are all these complicated things that just made them completely freaked out. Who are these people and what are they doing here?[9]

Despite the need she articulates for a black network (more so than a lesbian network), the normalizing manner in which the "core" has been constituted excludes her:

> I'm sort of constantly searching for black colleagues who can provide me with a support network and a social network that I find lacking at predominantly white institutions. And the fact that I'm a lesbian is always a complicated fact. It's less so here, so I have some black friends here, but they tend to be sort of outside of that core. . . . There are very few blacks in this town who are not in some way associated with the university. So finding a racial cohort is an overarching problematic and the ways that the politics of my sexual identity come in.

Carol's alienation from local lesbian cultural practices and her exclusion from the African-American community suggest that the practices minoritized groups adopt as responses to their circumstances, while enabling of some forms of being-together, constrain others. Lesbians' appropriation of two-stepping is a segregating gesture that reinscribes racial practices in Oasis. African-Americans' appropriation of Midwestern propriety through closeting sexuality to preserve an appearance of normalcy in their "niche" at Liberal U both perpetuates singular representations of African-Americans and limits the potential for the creation of fluid rather than bounded communities. Practice and location become dangerously intertwined.

Evelynn Hammonds has historicized African-Americans', particularly women's, responses to racialized sexual stereotyping as resistance to sexualization through codes of silence regarding sexuality. Carol's openness about her lesbianism breaks with these codes to position her as something of a "traitor to the race":[10]

> My mother exists in a world, and it's true for her generation, it's true for her class, it's true for this sort of black middle-class world in which appearances and respectability is everything, what other people think about you and what other people say about you is everything. . . . It's not just about my mother, it's sort of about the cultural category, I think one of the things I've found interesting is the way that alternative sexuality or otherness of sexuality is dealt with in the context of the black middle class. It is denied. African-Americans cannot accept queers in their midst because that is a refutation of everything that African-Americans think that they have to do in order to be accepted in our society. If the fundamental discussion about African-American sexuality is about deviance, then people like my mother spend their entire lives trying to prove they're not deviant. And so if there's a deviant in their midst, you ignore it or make it invisible because you develop this enormous value system that says that you don't exist and denies and says that it's a white construct, that homosexuality is a white problem, and black queers have spent too much time around white people.

Speaking of her own upbringing, Michele Wallace remarked, "[m]iddle class signifies ordinary to the general culture. But among blacks, middle class means special." To remain special, she says, is to "be better than everybody else."[11] The class, race, gender, and sexual structures in which Carol lives and works place her as never wholly appropriate, never fully belonging in any place. Her middle class socialization makes her acceptable in her department, whereas in the African-American community at Liberal U, which adopts Midwestern propriety as a tactic to gain acceptability, norms resulting from their responses to minoritization locate her as unacceptable.

Carol's multiple subject position(s) create for her a consciousness of the limitations of "a singular identity politic," akin to Laura Harris' description of "queer black feminism," an appropriation of stances that she says "allow me to . . . define my feminist identifications rather than have them defined for me" and to create "a practice of alliances rather than community."[12] Wary of defining herself or her relations with others on the basis of socially constructed, marked categories, Carol has adopted such a mobile conception of self, affiliations, and intellectual life, in which, as María Lugones has said, persons are "not fixed in particular constructions of ourselves, which is part of saying we are *open to self-construction*."[13] Carol embraces the norms of no single community, yet learns from her contradictory positionings in numerous locations. This openness is reflected in her pedagogical and departmental responses to students' and colleagues' recognitions and misrecognitions of her. Skeptical of differing assumptions that students—white, black, female, male, heterosexual, gay, lesbian—(may) make on the basis of her visible and not-so-visible identities, Carol alternately claims and steps back from her subject positions of African-American/female/lesbian/intellectual. Her struggles against narrow identity-based authority demonstrate her awareness that, as Hazel Carby says, "allowing black folks to play the sideshow is not threatening to the main event."[14] At stake intellectually, personally, and professionally is the possibility of exceeding location through the play of ideas. Identifications across communities and ideas make intellectual work a process of changing rather than reiterating the self: "You have, whether consciously or not, made this commitment to yourself, that I'm not content where I am in this place or where I was ten years ago intellectually and I'm going to go work on this continuum. . . . Even if you become sort of settled in your lifestyle, there's still this movement going on. . . . It's just a different way of conceiving of your life."

Her commitment is evidenced by her depiction of her movement from professional to academic practice. After some years as a newspaper reporter, Carol decided to pursue a master's degree, primarily to fill gaps in her knowledge and gain professional credentials:

The process of going to graduate school had changed me so much and had made me so much more analytical that it was much more difficult for me to take for granted the routines and the regimen and the value system of daily journalism. I found that most of my bosses, with one exception, and I said this in jest but with some truth, I really found to be my intellectual inferiors. They were these idiot white boys who were making the decisions in this newsroom. And I sort of had to participate in that and it really made me angry, and I had lots of experiences, so that was sort of, I don't want to call it an epiphany, but that was a turning point for me.

She continued:

As I became more intellectually attuned to a lot of issues about the media and about gender and race and so forth, I began to feel like what I wanted to do was critique the practice of journalism and study it rather than be a participant in it. . . . I realized that it's a very sort of tradition-bound insular institution that gives a lot of lip service to diversity and all of those kinds of issues, but it's very, very difficult to change that. So I think I made a very conscious decision that I'd be much happier and I could do more from the outside, both in terms of training journalists, sort of getting them before they've actually gone in and trying to influence the shape of it in some ways, and also engaging in some scholarship that could really ask these questions and write about it and in that way try to change our understanding about journalistic practice.

Her linear description of intellectual life as a developmental continuum—as an outgrowth of her political and professional development—resonates with the linearity of her goals of changing journalistic practice by influencing practitioners through training and scholarship. Carol's intellectual practice may be thought of as a process of changing the self and her own understandings, rooted in problems she has encountered in practice, in order to bring her new thinking back to journalistic practice: "I'm also interested in finding something that's compelling, and sort of filling gaps and doing work that is not navel-gazing and has some interest and utility to a larger audience. . . . I think my research agenda is very much a composite of who I am as a person, sort of my own personal history." The direct link Carol draws to practice makes her work more immediately tangible than Julie's or Olivia's and is at the core of the logic of professional training, consonant with location in a professional school. While both Julie's and Carol's intellectual lives are inflected with autobiography that is put to use to communicate with wider audiences, Julie offers others opportunities to rethink their assumptions for their practices, whereas Carol's efforts to change fossilized practices pertaining to race and gender seek more clearly defined results.

Carol's desire to effect change in practice does not lead to distinctly utilitarian research. Rather, much of her scholarship recuperates and theorizes activist work of African-American women in journalism.[15] Carol's early work centered on African-American female journalists in the nineteenth century, yet she has also researched contemporary representations of African-American women in television, and is moving to a project on representations of African-American social movements over the last three decades in news and entertainment media. Although bound to some extent by her location in the field of mass communication, she moves across disciplines:

> I'm about transcending those boundaries, so the way I see myself is as a person who is trained in the sort of scholarly methodological arguments in mass communication, but I've also gotten grounded in African-American history and women's history and cultural studies, as a rubric, so I sort of go at research questions with all of those things in mind. So if I'm looking at a journalistic question, I don't necessarily treat it in a narrow frame the way a lot of mass communication scholars might, only looking at media effects, for example, or looking at the role of media in political campaigns or that sort of thing. By the same token, I don't feel that I have to restrict myself to journalistic questions, because I feel that the division between news and entertainment is a real false dichotomy.

Moving across research areas is not without its problems, however:

> I'm moving much more into the world of theoretical examination and arguments about popular culture and mass culture, and that's something, because my graduate program did not specifically train me. . . . I've had to teach myself a lot of that, and so, my earlier work was not that theoretical, it wasn't really embedded in strong theoretical arguments that I was either informed by or that I was developing. I really resist the sort of postmodernist jargon, you know. I think the arguments are really important. . . . But it really eliminates, makes it very difficult to communicate with people outside of a very narrow realm of intellectuals. . . . The disciplinary boundaries again keep coming in there, so people who are in some areas of, you know, there are these divisions among mass comm and media studies, for example. In mass comm scholars are trained primarily in social science theory and methodology, media studies people tend to be informed by literary theory and philosophy. And so the media studies people pooh-pooh the mass comm people and think, "Oh well, they're really out of it, they're positivists, they don't know anything," and there's this sort of superiority thing. . . . So I've experienced that and on the other hand I've got colleagues here who argue with me because they think that all cultural studies is biased and political. I'm just like, "shoot me now."

Carol's disciplinary mobility marks a refusal to be confined to an intellectual position theoretically or methodologically and a desire to speak to a variety of scholars and practitioners. However, even as she puts multiple discourses into play and refuses a "pure" academic location, the content of her work could be said to be located by her reiterations of topics pertaining to race and gender. Her movement forward, however, is not static, but a response to the dilemmas of her lived experiences, an effort to bring new thought to bear on her own and others' practices.

Toni Morrison has posed what I think are haunting questions of the meanings of being a "raced" writer in a racialized society: "What does positioning one's writerly self, in the wholly racialized society that is the United States, as unraced and all others as raced entail? What happens to the writerly imagination of a black author who is at some level *always* conscious of representing one's own race to, or in spite of, a race of readers that understands itself to be 'universal' or race-free?"[16] It interests me that Carol has demonstrated a high degree of consciousness of representing—or not representing—black femaleness to colleagues and students. Yet, in her scholarship, issues of performing a stance in relation to her race and gender were either not at stake or left unarticulated. Could it be that she finds writing as intellectual practice, despite disciplinary normativity, to be a freer space within which to work?

JULIE: "RESPONDING TO A REAL CONCRETE PROBLEM"

Julie's understandings of self and commitments resonate with Carol's multiple affiliations and the salience of intellectual in her life, for Julie dwells in multiple communities that have been constructed as unrelated. In her historicized account of the relegation of lesbian to her private life and its separation from her intellectual life, Julie linked what is something of a new-found freedom in relation to lesbian to changing social and historical moments and her position at Liberal U:

> At this point in my life, I have operated and survived, I am successful. My book is coming out this month. I'll be fifty-three. I don't have to worry about any of this stuff anymore. And the times have changed. Maybe if I were just coming into the university at twenty-eight or something, it would be different. But believe me the 70s were not a time to be doing this. And growing up in the 40s and 50s was not a time to be running around thinking of yourself as a lesbian when you were in high school. It just didn't work.

She explained, "I started thinking about this whole thing about being in the closet, and why it is, . . . I just didn't understand what the issue was in my twenties, in my thirties I'm here working my butt off trying to get tenure, I'm not about to do it [come out], and in my forties I had sort of convinced myself I didn't need to do it, and I think it just all sort of clar- ified, gelled for the first time in some ways [on refusing to wear a pros- thesis]."

In fact, until the past few years, the privatization of her sexuality and its disconnection from other dimensions of her life were pro- nounced:

> When I got into this relationship in '85, a lot of the people that we knew here and in [a nearby city], we knew because they were gay, . . . and we hung around with these people, and I didn't like them particularly. They weren't intellectuals. Some of them were in the uni- versity but in phys. ed. or something like that. And the only thing we had in common was sexual orientation, and I thought that was really a stupid way to make friends. So when that broke up in '91 I was really more than ready to step back from some of those folks, and I did. I don't mind hanging around with, I love hanging around with Karen, she's queer and she's smart, but just to hang around with somebody who's queer, but has an eighth-grade sense of humor and reads Danielle Steele. I don't want to do that. They all want to get in their RVs and travel to all fifty states. . . . Until Karen and Michael, I just wasn't around people that were really bright and queer, and could be bright about being queer, too. I must say that a lot of these other peo- ple didn't exactly want to talk about it, it was all spoken about in euphemisms, a member of the sorority, a member of the club. No one ever talked about being a lesbian, being gay, being queer, being any of that stuff, so it was an oddly discomforting situation in a lot of ways.

This contradictory quest for normalcy that maintains the open secret through collective verbal disacknowledgment and privatizing of sexual- ity by the very individuals who congregate around sexuality has striking parallels to the practices of propriety of Liberal U's African-American core.[17]

In contrast, recent friendships with gay and lesbian faculty have contributed to tentative connections between Julie's sexuality and the "public sphere":

> For a long time, because I was uncomfortable with myself and wanted to keep myself in a sort of shadow in relation to sexuality, I don't think I paid any attention to it. I knew that there was a faculty gay/lesbian cocktail party. I didn't want to have anything to do with it. In fact, until this stuff really started popping up on TV, in the media, places like that, I don't think I paid much attention at all. I thought it was a private issue, I didn't think it was very much of a political issue. I never really thought of it as a women's movement thing, you know, "the per- sonal is the political." It took me a long time to figure out what that

meant, and then I didn't want to get involved in it. . . . I didn't really notice anything until I started thinking more about this project of yours, and a lot of that is due to Karen, I think. Just looking at Karen, what she looks like, and how kind of confident she is, changed me. . . . I think having Michael in the department changed me. I dress a lot more flamboyantly than I ever did before. I wear my hair differently. Michael said when I first met him, I looked like a suburban house-wife. . . . Now I go to these gay/lesbian cocktail parties, I'm on the distribution list of the stuff that comes out of the center here. I know that all this stuff came out about being out, gay pride, marching, all that kind of stuff, and I had no intention of doing it. . . . But at the same time, I think I'm much more visible without saying anything than I have been before.

Although lesbian is not an identity or (political) position to be "integrated" into all domains of her life, it is an aspect of self that increasingly emerges in new contexts, particularly as Julie enters networks of affiliation that include multiple identifications. However, even as her movement outside the "shadow" entails the use of cultural codes through a more flamboyant look, Julie does not claim unmediated lesbian visibility, as I discussed in the context of her departmental interactions. As her responses to students and colleagues suggest, Julie is aware of being seen differently in different domains by different persons. [18]

Julie's historicization of the meanings of lesbian in her life suggest a number of ways life practices, identifications with others and ideas, and "sexual identity" do not align neatly. Like Carol, she has developed multiple networks of affiliation during her twenty years in Oasis, what she called "friends in a lot of different venues" in speaking of support she received before, during, and after her mastectomy. Her friends include persons from feminist academic circles, church groups, lesbians and gay men, colleagues, and others in town. A significant aspect of Julie's life lies in her religious affiliation, which has been at odds with her lesbianism. I have puzzled over the relationship of Julie's Catholicism to her sexuality since meeting her. In response to my queries that she help me think through how she has been able to reconcile these dimensions of her life, Julie compared her disagreement with the Church's antihomosexual stances to those of practicing Catholics who use birth control, oppose the Church's stance on abortion, or believe in women's ordination, but who continue to find value in Catholicism. Trying to offer a context, she explained that in her young adulthood, she was conflicted by her desires and the teachings of the Church, "so guilty, so confused, wanting to do this and thinking it's deadly wrong, a sin. . . . So I had this kind of battle between the flesh and the spirit—in my head at least—for a long time." Yet Julie named no marker, no single moment of resolution:

"Leaving the Church and sort of in effect telling the Pope to fuck off was not an option for me. I like religion, but trying to put the two together is just excruciating, they don't go together, they just don't work. . . . They're [the Church] just wrong about this, but it took me a while to be able to say that and to say it sometimes to my students." I am not sure if I expected her to describe a moment of epiphany or the gradual development of a line of reasoning, but what she offers is a categorical refusal of the contradiction: "There are moral issues around almost anything, so I think you could be an immoral dyke or a moral person depending on how you treat people and whatnot, not depending on what you do sexually. So it doesn't bother me the way it used to. Could I or I can't? Is this a sin? It just isn't." The best understanding I have been able to come to is based in Julie's description of her spiritual life as private, at home, and her attendance at church as based in enjoyment of liturgy and a desire to participate in a religious community. This reconciliation of Catholicism and lesbianism is not, however, an easy split along dimensions of private/public, but, I think, a complex process in which Julie has appropriated aspects of Catholicism for her own spiritual practices.[19] This appropriation, or working through, forms a significant part of her intellectual life and of what she seeks to offer students through her pedagogy.

In yet another twist, while practicing lesbianism is at odds with practicing Catholicism, practicing Catholicism places Julie as outsider to some lesbians. She was describing responses she had gotten to a personal ad she had placed with a group for lesbians over fifty:

> I've had two or three letters from people. But when they call, you know, the two things that seem to bother them, is one, I seem rooted to Oasis, I don't want to move to Utah and grow artichokes or whatever they're doing. And the other thing is they just can't believe this religion thing. I mean, they could understand if it were the Goddess [sigh]. So, it's, "Are you deeply Catholic?" I said, "Well, yeah, but it's not what you think it is. I mean, I think it's okay to be Catholic and queer, I think it's okay to be Catholic and think women should be ordained, I think it's okay to be Catholic and not believe that Jesus was the preexistent son of God. I mean, I have a very radical kind of theological view, but yeah, I'm a deeply religious person." "Do you believe in the Goddess?" "Not really." So, you know, there we are, struck down by religion again.

Women's efforts to create nonpatriarchal religious and spiritual practices marginalize Julie in much the same way that lesbian cultural appropriations exclude Carol. In this sense, women's responses to oppressive structures that place them as "outsiders" result in the creation of practices that themselves do not allow for multiplicity and thus perpetuate the stasis of place.

Whereas contradictions between Julie's practices as Catholic and self-identifications as feminist have been at the heart of much of her intellectual work, lesbian has not. She has written extensively on women and the Church and on spiritual issues facing feminist Catholics, projects born of dilemmas she has experienced. As I began to understand that her scholarly work related to problems she encountered in life, I became increasingly aware of the fact that contradictions relating to her sexuality (or what *I* assume to be contradictions) have not been overtly present in her writing. I do not mean to suggest unselfconsciously that lesbians should place sexuality in their inquiry or to reinscribe the "personal-intellectual" integration on which formulations of lesbian intellectuals often depend. Rather, Julie's choices raise a question of what constitutes a contradiction worthy of intellectual attention for a woman whose intellectual life is centered on problems of living. I am inclined to think that the placement of sexuality apart from her religious and intellectual life has discouraged its emergence as an interesting topic of inquiry. Or, perhaps because she has refused the contradiction even as she has perceived it as impossible to reconcile, Julie has felt little compulsion to explore the topic. However, she was considering exploring issues of sexuality in writing, a change she connects to her experience of breast cancer, and which appears to take part of a moment in which Julie is acting out new relations to what surrounds her.

Much of Julie's intellectual life could be said to be about relations and dilemmas that come from and form part of her life practices. For example, her choice of an area for graduate study was born of her interest in the institution in which she was raised, the Catholic Church: "I looked at history, intellectual history and so on and so forth, and I thought, well the only history that really interests me, frankly, is the history of this particular institution. This ecclesiastical institution has survived for two thousand years through hordes of barbarians, tons of corruption, lots of stupidity, major assaults, the Enlightenment, and it's still there, it's still standing." Despite the worldly nature of her intellectual work, Julie described herself as primarily engaged with ideas: "An intellectual is somebody whose really primary motivation comes from ideas, and who wants to think about things, and argue about things and write about things, and talk about things. . . . I would much rather sit here and read a book or think a thought than go down and take back the night. My primary turn-on is with ideas, not with people and projects and activities." However, her intellectual life is not one of the lone scholar grappling with abstract thoughts. Rather, she seeks to understand self, lived experience, and the difficulties of the contemporary Catholic Church in ways that will have practical resonance for a number of audiences, including communities of faith, Church officials, and sociologists and historians of Catholicism: "I'm less interested in writing for my peers than for a broader audience. I always have been." Julie worked with a clear sense of audience and context:

> With my feminist work, I've really kind of fallen between two stools. On the one hand, it's not scholarly enough and esoteric enough to really impress some of my colleagues, not just in the department but in the field. And it's not theological enough, because I'm in a religious studies setting rather than a theological setting, so I'm not really crafting a new ecclesiology or a new way of looking at God. It's not theological enough to have made a kind of genuine difference at some kind of intellectual level. On the other hand, I'm not an activist. It doesn't come out prescribing, saying what women or women's churches or Women's Ordination Conference or stuff like that should do. So I try to float in all three of those pools in some way, and I find that kind of satisfying, and I think it speaks to women on a practical level.

Referring to her first books as "footnotes in the nineteenth century," Julie has moved beyond historical research to explore contemporary faith experiences of American Catholics, primarily women and feminists, and their relations to the Catholic Church. Her analysis is cultural, historical, and social, concerned with the implications of changing human responses to the Church and the Church's responses to the humans who inhabit it. Her historicization of changes despite the Church's seeming intractability offers rethinkings that aim to inform efforts to restructure the Church as well as women's efforts to pursue spiritual practices in an often hostile environment.

For Julie, it is location within spiritual, religious, and intellectual traditions, practices, and communities that lends meaning to her work:

> One of the things that makes me interesting to myself is that I can take these maverick views about all of these practices and beliefs, and I know all those practices and beliefs, I've lived them. And I can quote from the fathers, I can quote from tradition, I've read Thomas Aquinas, I know all of that. I know all of the bedrock that it kind of stands on, so that kind of anchors me to take certain stands or positions intellectually. Now some of these younger writers who reject it all, they don't have any of that background, so they're taking stands and positions— maybe this is an old fart reaction—I find myself sort of taken aback by them. Not because it's something I disagree with or wouldn't say myself, but I don't know where it's coming from. It's coming from a different place, and sometimes a place I don't understand.

Julie's intellectual "place" is one of movement beyond lived experience that makes use of understandings she has created through reflection and study of traditions and practices in which she has participated. She commented, "People who write, just write. If you're an intellectual, basically anything can turn into some kind of grist for your mill." However, "anything" is not grist for Julie's mill, but that which allows her to respond to spiritual and intellectual problems in ways that may be enabling for others: "The book I really love is ———, which are talks and essays about real problems for real people right now. That book just sells very well. I get lots of letters about it, how neat it is for people." She continued, "All of those things [essays] were talks, I think, given some place, where I had to respond to a real concrete problem, and I only took them if they had some resonance with something I was trying to think about at the time."

Because so much of Julie's work grapples with seeming diametric opposites and problems of living, such as feminism and the Church, I asked her why sexuality has not entered the domain of her work, why gender was an interesting problem while sexuality is not:

> Until I thought of the [essay on breast cancer and lesbianism], I've never found anything very interesting about this to write about. I do not find being gay an interesting intellectual issue. It's probably an interesting political issue. I don't tend to be a very politically inter-ested person. How women could be priests in the Catholic Church, that's an interesting historical and intellectual and liturgical issue for me. There's a lot of things to think about in that that engage me. How one can lead a spiritual life in a very busy world, I find that a kind of interesting practical problem; how to reconceptualize the deity in ways that go beyond classical theism is an interesting intellectual thought. . . . But my being queer is not interesting to me, has not been interesting to me. This only became interesting to me in light of this prosthetic issue with breast cancer. You know, I sort of started think-ing about that and ways in which that could be interesting to me per-sonally. I mean, these things don't open out into a kind of wider area that can include all kinds of people who aren't queer and haven't had cancer and stuff like that.

Although Julie would separate the political and the intellectual and thinks of queer issues as not general but narrow, the intensity of her experiences have led her to explore the relations of (not) hiding her breast cancer to her lesbianism: "Part of the exercise of thinking about and writing that is a way to investigate it, learn something about it. Most of the stuff I write, I learn something about myself. That's why I do it." In *The Cancer Journals*, Audre Lorde described her reflections on cancer and living as rooted in a new sense of self, of asking, "[H]ow do I live with myself one-breasted? What posture do I take, literally, with my physical self?"[20] The posture Julie has taken is to question and reject normalization that calls for concealment of her embodiments, to make public and visible a disease that has been constructed as private and invisible.[21] To write about her experiences as lesbian and woman with breast cancer extends her project of communicating with new audiences. I asked Julie what shape she anticipated the essay would take:

JULIE. Right now I'm just basically trying to sort of write down little things as I think about them. I kept, I didn't keep a journal, but all through that cancer thing last summer I wrote a lot of notes and letters and various things like that that I've kept, and I want to look at that again. I want to get some stuff down out of myself before I start to read anything. But I know Eve Sedgwick in her latest book has got a reflection on breast cancer, and I've read Audre Lorde's *Cancer Journals* and so we'll see, we'll see what happens. I'm kind of letting this essay live its life in me before I try to get it down on paper.

SUSAN. And how does it live a life in you?

JULIE. It just does, my work kind of, I'm a sort of broody, contemplative person. I think about things a long time before I write them down. And then when I write them down I tend to be able to get a lot. And so I'll mull around in the garden, sitting out here just looking at the trees, so it comes, I don't know how it does. It's a little process that works.

SUSAN. . . . So in a sense it sounds like your breast cancer is precipitating—

JULIE. I think it has. I think the conjunction actually between breast cancer and being hidden as a lesbian, and being mad about both those things. I mean, there's a kind of anger you get when you get this disease which is never going to go away and which will probably eventually kill you. And you don't want to think like that, I don't know. It's a real mind trip that you've got to learn, it's like a ride at a carnival and you've just got to learn how to, what the ups and downs of it are, and how to hold on, and I think that, you're right, that got me thinking about this other thing, how it's a very similar experience in some ways. A lot of people would prefer all this to be invisible. They want to hide this, they want me to put this little titty on so that they don't have to look at this flat little chest here. They don't care if you're queer, but they just really don't want to know about it. They don't want you to turn up at a department party in a tuxedo—not that I would, but I think about it now sometimes, which I find amusing. So I think being mad about sending my breast off to the landfill has probably fed the kind of anger about having to kind of deny and pretend for such a goddamn long time.

With the painful images she has evoked, Julie responds to the contradictions and agonies of her lived experiences by opening them to inquiry that may be of use to others. In a society structured on its preferences not to know, she may invite her readers to ask what is lost and what is gained through concealment of self, body, sexuality, life, disease, death. To question personal and social meanings of ignorances, to speak of how persons "hold on" and to ask perhaps why the "ride" is as it is, is to speak the unspeakable to multiple communities, not only those who have had breast cancer or who are queer. Audre Lorde said of turning to write of her breast cancer, "I am learning to speak my pieces, to inject into the living world my convictions of what is necessary and what I think is important without concern (of the enervating kind) for whether or not it is understood, tolerated, correct, or heard before" (48). Julie's responses to her circumstances might be thought of as offerings to others. Practices and experiences—related and unrelated to categories of difference—and the dilemmas they pose comprise the obligations by which she frames her intellectual and academic pursuits.

Across all three women's reflections are disjunctures and points of intersection between lesbian and intellectual. I am hesitant to make a sweeping claim that their commitments to intellectual life constitute *the* most important aspect of their lives. Similarly, I cannot say that lesbian is completely disconnected from their intellectual work, although it is indeed incompatible with their understandings of the nature of their intellectual lives. I believe "lesbian" and "intellectual" do inform each other, despite the fact that, for example, none of the three specifically and consistently placed her lived experiences as lesbian in the role of catalyst of her intellectual projects. However, what most interests me is why lesbian appears to become a site of confinement and intellectual a site of openness for recreating the self and relations to others.

EXCEEDING LOCATIONS: PRACTICES OF THE SELF

To be at once an academic and an intellectual is to try to manipulate a type of knowledge and analysis that is taught and received in the universities in such a way as to alter not only others' thoughts, but also one's own. This work of altering one's own thought and that of others seems to me to be the intellectual's raison d'être.
                    —Michel Foucault, "Concern for Truth"

A lesbian who does not reinvent the word is a lesbian in the process of disappearing.
                    —Nicole Brossard, "Kind Skin My Mind"

In thinking through how Olivia, Julie, and Carol position themselves in relation to constructs of lesbian/intellectual, I find useful Michel Foucault's idea of "practices of the self," which he describes as "the way in which the subject constitutes himself in an active fashion." He explains, "these practices are nevertheless not something that the individual invents by himself. They are patterns that he finds in his culture and which are proposed, suggested and imposed on him by his culture, his society and his social group."[22] Practices of the self make use of cultures, institutions, and their conventions as resources, much as de Certeau's tactics depend on the space in which they are deployed and Butler's agency resides in actions in context rather than in subjects per se. What Julie, Olivia, and Carol suggest to me is that *lesbian* and *intellectual* are practices rather than substances, identities, or categories. Yet, if both are practices, why does intellectual appear to offer fluidity and lesbian stasis? I am inclined to think that lesbian has been culturally constructed as a place—and, as Julie, Carol, and Olivia suggest, it is a narrow place overburdened with meanings attached to a "counterpoint identity." A conflation of sexuality, identity, and community has been constructed by both homophobic and antihomophobic forces, resulting in a propensity for insularity in lesbian communities and rigidity in defining lesbian identity. I touch only briefly on the formation of lesbian identity and community in the United States as a context for understanding their responses to placement.

Lesbian as a social category did not emerge until the end of the last century, when sexologists labeled women's romantic friendships and erotic attachments deviant, thus creating the conditions for the creation of lesbian sexuality as an identity. Faderman has argued that the sexologists "helped to make possible the establishment of lesbian communities through their theories, which separated off the lesbian from the rest of womankind and presented new concepts to describe certain feelings and preferences that had before been within the spectrum of 'normal' female experiences."[23] While their writings codified the classification of the lesbian as a "species," the sexologists did not single-handedly create the discourse of deviance; rather, their thinking and writing were products of larger social changes.[24] Demarcation through discourses of pathology encouraged congregating in secrecy, or segregation. Noteworthy regarding the formation and re-formation of lesbian communities throughout the twentieth century is the epoch after World War II, during which popularizations of Freud, virulent antihomosexual propaganda, and McCarthy-era witch-hunts created a persecutory atmosphere that necessitated increasingly covert lesbian life. Submerged social circles and bars functioned as sources of support and contact at the same time that they fomented the segregation and privatization of lesbianism. Evident in many, but not all, subcultural groups was stratification by age, class, and race.[25]

In the 1970s, as part of the epoch of the civil rights, feminist, and gay liberation movements, mostly white, young, recently politicized lesbians sought to create a visible women's culture that would be free of oppressive patriarchal structures and would rewrite pathological models of the lesbian. They undertook a project of culture-building against the backdrop of negative representations of lesbians by connecting experience, identity, and community in ways that would be affirming. Their efforts relied on the constitution of individual and collective identity through personal testimony that offered "an authentic, empirical lesbian voice, or voices, [that] debunked the so-called expert knowledge that previously defined lesbian experience."[26] When lesbian-feminist ideologies took hold as dominant representations of authentic lesbian identity and community, an underlying separatism demanded that women not engage with social forces and institutions contrary to lesbian-feminist ideals. Regarding the anti-intellectualism that Olivia, Julie, and Carol have encountered, it is interesting to note the existence of class divisions among lesbian-feminists in the 1970s and the devaluing of intellectual practice as complicit with an oppressive system.[27] In fact, many of their comments pertaining to insularity, anti-intellectualism, and exclusionary practices is symptomatic of much of the visible lesbian social and political organizing at this time, traces of which continue to return in the present.

The twentieth-century creation of lesbian identity can be read as a process in which lesbians have appropriated negative differences attached to lesbian identity to create alternative (positive) communities and cultures. While these practices are forms of resistance to definitions, they have submerged individual differences to create a normative "lesbian community," and with it, norms for "lesbian identity."[28] What appears to have happened is that lesbians, relegated to a place by spatializing practices, challenged the definition of their place but not the terms of placement itself.[29] In other words, a rewriting of definition, however affirming, also had the effect of reifying identity and closing down the fluidity of identifications and open-ended relations. Raymond Williams' contrast of two twentieth-century usages of the word *community* underscores the tensions in its signification between emerging identifications or normative sets of relations: "Community can be the warmly persuasive word to describe an existing set of relationships, or the warmly persuasive word to describe an alternative set of relationships. What is most important, perhaps, is that unlike all other terms of social organization (*state, nation, society,* etc.) it seems never to be used unfavourably, and never to be given any positive opposing or distinguishing term."[30] Read in the context of lesbian, community can take on a coercive tone, as "existing sets of relationships" (both identifications and categories imposed by the dominant order) are transformed to refer to "an alternative set of relationships" (rescripted, and, in this case, prescriptive).

Responding to the problematic nature of the construction of community on the basis of what people have in common, Walcott has pointed out that "[t]he concept of community as singular means that only two positions are possible—in or out."[31] Yet, because humans are not singular and do not live their categories as they should, they exceed their locations. In short, as Laura Harris argues, "Categories are queer." She says, "By this I do not mean that categories are useless, obviously not when they are already in place as a complex network of social meanings and bodies of knowledge." Even with their cultural salience, categories, locations, and places are open to revision: "at the place where theories and identities converge to form practice categories fall apart and practice can no longer be prescribed."[32] As the actions of Julie, Carol, and Olivia suggest, humans make themselves, their relations, and their surroundings not through what they are but through what they do. All three women enact disjunctures, rather than an ultimate separation, between identity and practice and thus pluralize the ways "lesbian" might be understood. *Doing*, rather than *being*, as well as *doing* in tandem with *being*, suggests that identities and communities are not finalities, but contingent processes whose very nongivenness places responsibility on individuals and collectivities for "the working out of what it might mean to possibly live together."[33] The limits of communities and identities are unknowable, dependent on what actors make of them and themselves. Olivia's, Carol's, and Julie's creations of self and relations, their responses to what exists around them, exceed the limits of place and open new possibilities for how lesbian and intellectual and their relations might be understood. In a sense, they follow Foucault's suggestion that "the relationships we have to have with ourselves are not ones of identity, rather they must be relationships of differentiation, of creation, of innovation. To be the same is really boring."[34]

This idea of differentiation and creation finds resonance in Blanchot's discussion of the impossibility of communities based on the common and offers a way of understanding the salience of intellectual for Olivia, Julie, and Carol: "A being does not want to be recognized, it wants to be contested: in order to exist it goes towards the other, which contests and at times negates it, so as to start being only in that privation that makes it conscious . . . of the impossibility of being itself, of subsisting as its *ipse* or, if you will, as itself as a separate individual." Existence takes place in relations of difference; we cannot put ourselves into question autonomously or in the company of sameness. He says, "An ethics is possible only when . . . the self is not content with recognizing the Other, with recognizing itself in it, but feels that the Other always puts it into question to the point of being able to respond to it only through a responsibility that cannot limit itself and that exceeds itself without exhausting itself." [35] The Other that takes beings beyond stasis and repetition of the given may be found in ideas. Encounters with ideas—thought—is a means of pressing the limits of self, of creating the self and relations to others anew. For Julie, Carol, and Olivia, there is an eros in coming to think and understand differently. Identifications with ideas, the task of thinking, allows them to exceed the given, to complicate place and space.

Intellectual becomes less an identity than a practice, more a way of relating to the world than a location in the world, a way of questioning given orders rather than acquiescing to them. In contrast to lesbian as a category that can fix meanings and overdetermine relationships, intellectual is a modality of being and acting that is transported and redefined across contexts to create new questions, understandings, and relations. These women's intellectual work is formed by personal, political, and theoretical commitments—and as lesbian enters those domains and can be put to use in ways that allow them to move beyond self and experience, they engage with lesbian in their intellectual lives. Their use of relations to ideas to craft themselves and respond to their surroundings offers a more fluid notion of intellectual than the linear relationship between lesbian identity and intellectual practice constructed by identity politics' conflation of identity, difference, and experience. In fact, the ways they live the interrelations of lesbian and intellectual suggest that each construct is more temporal than spatial, unfixed by the memories that haunt them.

Their understandings and enactments of lesbian and intellectual reveal something of the dilemmas and possibilities institutional and social spaces present. For example, the representations of lesbian identity and community at Liberal U and in Oasis are part of the larger historical practices I have discussed, for in town and on campus minoritized, or "diverse," communities have been constituted according to essential differences. However, for Julie, Carol, and Olivia, marked social identities do not imply predictable ways of being or situate one in predictable communities. In many ways they are thus unintelligible, for they do not conform to constructions—positive or negative—of what lesbians or lesbian academics are. Their enactments of academic practice are highly contextual and idiosyncratic, as each woman is defined by and (re)defines what might be meant by *lesbian* and *academic* according to the shifting academic and social contexts in which she finds herself. Each woman works within sets of norms that she participates in altering subtly through engagement with multiple discourses in her research, teaching, and departmental work. The knowledges they create and offer are located not in their "identities" per se, however, but in forms of practice in which they have participated: feminist academic, journalistic, and spiritual and religious. Julie and Carol use their academic positions to speak in ways that will be useful to communities in which they have participated and are affiliated with multiple communities of practice. Olivia, in contrast, refuses location, with the exception of her institutional location in the discourses of academia.

Their intellectual lives stand in stark contrast to functional social and institutional definitions of the roles of faculty, which are devoid of the presence and practices of living, feeling beings. As I described, a prevailing ethos in policy and among students at Liberal U is that of the unbiased pursuit and transmission of knowledge. To recall Liberal U's mission, the university values faculty who are objective, yet purports to value different perspectives. Each of the women, in different ways, cites objectivity in her teaching, research, and departmental relations while, for example, at the same time engaging in what might be termed personalized pedagogies that evoke intellectual, personal, and political responses in her students. Although feminist scholars have rightly argued against the imposition of objectivity, suggesting that knowledge and knowers are situated and should be recognized as such, given the configurations of social and academic assumptions in the university, the practices of the three women suggest that a separation of what is deemed public and private can at times have positive efficacy. This may be particularly true in Olivia's case, for although politicized in terms of its content and process, her academic work could almost "pass" for the disinterested pursuit of knowledge, in that it is not located in identity and does not name concrete, prespecified goals.

Intellectual life is more than the "acquisition of new awareness," "the discovery of knowledge," or an unbiased "application of knowledge to the solution of current problems" espoused officially and unofficially at Liberal U. What are the purposes and effects of research and teaching? Do they entail the acquisition of technical skills and knowledge? The change of life practices and habits of thinking? The transmission or production of knowledge to be applied to social problems? No definitive answers are possible, for the incessant deferral of the ends of research and teaching make it impossible to know to what uses teaching, learning, and inquiry will be put.[36] As these three women demonstrate, intellectual and academic practice change the self, the organization of knowledges, and suggest further, unknowable possibilities for change. The "usefulness" of their work is counter to Liberal U's technological and economic emphasis, as their ends are located in the *qualities* of social, professional, political, spiritual, and lived practices. Furthermore, the category of faculty member is not static, but redefined creatively in practice, whether recognized in official institutional statements and unofficial talk or not.

As I discussed in chapter 1, voice and visibility have been conceptualized as metonyms for a (lesbian) subject who seeks to represent herself and thus to exercise agency. Yet Julie, Olivia, and Carol do not seek agency through voice and visibility *as lesbians* but in the domain of their intellectual lives. A significant means through which they gain intellectual voice lies in their performative movement in and out of accepted norms to disrupt static location. It may be that a source of their agency lies in their lack of conformity to normative claims made by socially marginal groups and by dominant groups, placing them in indeterminate relations to, neither fully inside nor outside, multiple collectivities. Through their departmental, disciplinary, and pedagogical practices, they alter what might be understood by their marked social identities, the roles of faculty, and their intersections. For example, the commodification that would place them also offers a tenuous acceptability that allows them to work to change the terms by which they would be understood. Whether their actions challenge the premises of commodification itself is difficult to assess. Rather, their practices transform commodification from an individual liability to a resource and rescript the circumscription of their social and academic positions. The women's academic work suggests that rather than conceptualizing voice as a preexistent text or a realist representation of, for example, a lesbian self, and thus relegating agency to a category of social being, voice is more effectively conceptualized as part of intellectual practice and as constructed contextually in practice within the recognitions of others. Doing and being are mutually mediated, but have the effect of reconstructing voice, visibility, and social and intellectual locations. Because the women's voices and visibilities are constructed within and find their effects as consequences of lived social and institutional structures, agency that they may derive from voice and visibility, is not an origin, but an effect of practice.

Lesbian, academic, and intellectual practice may be understood as gestures of exceeding the self and present discourses, as modalities of being that are at times complementary and at other times disconnected, as identifications that are relational, that do not carry a priori meanings that come forth in predictable ways, but are brought forth as contingent articulations in social spaces. As practices rather than as destinies or identities to be fulfilled, lesbian, academic, and intellectual respond to what Readings calls the ethical imperatives of intellectual work in the ruins, in which "the University becomes one more place among others where the question of being-together is posed" (127).

QUEER ETHNOGRAPHIC SPACES

What if queer research were not merely undertaken in the interest
of action (by providing a new and improved theory or interpretation of the world according to which we would act) but were itself
an active intervention, a provocation: an interruption rather than a
reproduction?

—William Haver, "Queer Research"

The interpretations I have drawn throughout this text do not comprise
the only connections that are possible. I hope readers will find points
of disagreement, empirical representations that provoke and unsettle,
and theoretical speculations that generate new ideas. The questions I
brought to this inquiry centered around sexuality, knowledge, identity,
and academic practice and included dimensions that were social, institutional, disciplinary, departmental, and individual. Five rather simple
themes could be said to come to the fore. First, the meanings of *lesbian*, *intellectual*, and *academic* are idiosyncratic and contextual, their
intersections continually reenacted and reinterpreted in social, political, and academic spaces. Second, voice and visibility are relational,
multidimensional, implicated in structures of knowledge and ignorance, and find their effects transactionally in practice. Third, departmental and pedagogical relations and practices are created through an
interplay of personal, political, and intellectual commitments with the
social and institutional contexts that play a part in determining their
possibilities. Fourth, social and academic knowledges are intertwined,
unfixed as the relations of spaces and places change. Fifth, there are no
tidy connections between practices of identity and intellectual and academic practices.

The themes that have emerged through this inquiry lead me to suggest that ethnographic inquiry could benefit from rethinking assumptions that gay and lesbian research participants do not have voices and
that the role of research is to change that state of affairs, be it through
"making visible," "giving voice," or "uncovering voice." To uncover
voices is a laudable project, and has the potential to contribute to understandings of the lives of gay and lesbian persons, yet is predicated on *and
limited by* a belief that empirical representations of gay and lesbian subjects are inherently transformative. Rather than uncovering voices, it
may be more helpful to demonstrate how they work in specific contexts
or to challenge the binary opposition of voice and silence by uncovering
the roles of silences in practice. Julie, Olivia, and Carol, for example, are
not powerless, voiceless, or without privilege. In practice, they perform
sets of relations to social structures and disciplinary formations.

"Voice," as in *having voice as*, may be a trope of limited value, a term that is less representational than it is performative, a means of recreating positionings. Research might begin to understand its role not as rendering authentic experiences or subjects, but as inquiring into the ways and contexts in which "voices" are constructed and performed within the contours of knowledge and ignorance. Performance that is neither purely auditory nor purely visual, neither representational nor fixed, yet that may invoke the seen and the heard, then becomes a useful metaphor for identifying the shifting tactics of gay and lesbian participants whose lives and work are not always defined by or confined to gay or lesbian voice and visibility.

With queer theory's affinities with postmodernisms and poststructuralisms, scholars in the humanities frequently dismiss empirically grounded work on gay and lesbian topics in the social sciences as atheoretical, naïve positivism. In an interview with Judith Butler, Gayle Rubin cautioned against the privileging of theory and the devaluation of empirical work, arguing that "[a] lack of solid, well-researched, careful descriptive work will eventually impoverish feminism, and gay and lesbian studies, as much as a lack of rigorous conceptual scrutiny will."[37] Conversely, empirical researchers are often reticent (sometimes due to disciplinary pressures) or unprepared to engage with theoretical frameworks from the humanities that are often seen as speculative, idiosyncratic, and unverifiable as narratives of explanation. Indeed, methodological tensions surface in bringing together ethnography and poststructuralism. Ethnography relies on empirical methods and has representation as an explicit purpose in the study of *human* lives. Poststructuralism, which has evolved primarily as the study of *texts*, questions representation as inherently mediated and understands voice and experience as effects rather than origins. To engage such contradictory epistemologies can be a difficult task, particularly when voice, visibility, and performances have inherently mediated forms, and when knowledge and ignorance do not always readily offer evidence of their presence, absence, or workings. However, in order to forge scholarship that moves beyond representing to create, challenge, and refine social theories as they relate to empirical data, researchers must engage not only in descriptive work but in work that seeks to understand, however speculatively, its subjects of study. Carefully interpreted empirical data from multiple sources, when put into dialogue with poststructural theories can inform and be informed by those theories, particularly when "hard evidence" is lacking.

William Haver has argued that "it would be more useful to ask what queer research *does*, to ask what *happens* in queer research, than to ask what it *is*. . . . If queer research is less a knowledge or the production of knowledge than it is a pragmatics, an interruption in the production of knowledge, then we might begin to think the praxis of its poiesis as an interruption in the formation of cultural subjects, the identities formed in and through the production of knowledge as subjects who are supposed to know."[38] Julie, Carol, and Olivia interrupt knowledge in the domains in which they work, for their performances demand its rearrangement. If an absence of knowledge or a rearrangement of knowledge through unpredictable movement could be said to despatialize, perhaps ethnography could learn from its participants by taking on a performative role that might rearrange knowledges in ways that are never final. Victor Turner has characterized performance as "a critique, direct or veiled, of the social life it grows out of, an evaluation (with lively possibilities of rejection) of the way society handles history." He describes performance as subjunctive, a response to the mandates of the indicative mood, with its rationalism, ordering of logical relations, and refusal of ambiguity. Following this subjunctive mood, a part of anthropology's "postmodern turn," he argues, is the "processualization of space, its temporalization, as against the spatialization of process or time."[39] Such inquiry considers actors' intentions, subjectivities, and improvised everyday practices within the received social and institutional structures they inhabit as "an active process rather than a static product."[40] By not objectifying practices as given or necessary, inquiry that stresses temporality, contingency, and the impossibility of stasis invites its readers to imagine other possibilities. Inquiry, like performance, is temporal, contingent, and perhaps at its best when subjunctive. Like performance, it is a process haunted by many times and places, a process that invites readers to think differently rather than a product that offers the closure of single answers. Perhaps inquiry might learn from Haver's idea of queer research to intervene in unpredictable places by seeking less to represent authentic subjects than to understand how humans' use of seemingly fixed social, cultural, and institutional structures opens them to new interpretations and transformations. "Queerness" is not about seeing how sexuality "fits in" with or gets "integrated" into the work of intellectuals or academics, but helps to understand how queer things happen in our work and our relations to our work. The *Oxford English Dictionary* identifies "slack, not closely fitting" as having possible etymological significance to the word "gay." This may be a task of queer: not to fit categories or surroundings closely. It may also be a task of queer research, if such a thing can be named: not to fit subjects but to show what can happen when subjects don't fit.

In *The Writing of History*, de Certeau tells readers that the differentiation between past and present enables the writing of history: "It assumes a gap to exist between the silent opacity of the 'reality' that it seems to express and the place where it produces its own speech, protected by the distance established between itself and its object" (3). Space, such as the space ethnography creates between the subject and object of inquiry, creates an illusion of separation and nonimplication. However, temporality confuses the neatness of spatial separations and underscores subjects' and spaces' intertwined historicities and implications in knowledges and networks of relations. Temporality opens space, for it suggests the presence of "the ruses of other interests and desires that are neither determined nor captured by the systems in which they develop."[41] Ethnography cannot fully represent or account for the repressed that haunts institutional and social spaces, and ethnographers cannot account for the repressed of their own practices. Throughout this text I have tried to enact positions through the structure and movement of my interpretations and responses to what I have seen, heard, and experienced rather than taking part in the practice of naming a position that has become so commonplace in ethnographic texts. This naming often seems to promise readers more information than it offers. Positioning might locate an ethnographer but not explicate the time of ethnography's making.

Nonetheless, at professional meetings I have received queries about my "identity" that reveal desires to know whether my dwelling in the categories "lesbian" and "academic" defines me as an "insider" relative to Julie, Olivia, and Carol or as implicated in the subject of research. As I have explained, I began with ambivalences and curiosities about such issues as the meanings lesbian can have in intellectual and academic practice, the efficacy of "coming out" to colleagues and students, how one defines research interests, and how institutional and social structures affect one's actions. The women's initial descriptions of their reasons for agreeing to participate in my research—Julie's seeking to uncover meanings of lesbian in her life, Olivia's denial of them and curiosity to see what would happen to the category lesbian during my inquiry, and Carol's desire for the representation of a black lesbian voice—reveal contradictory commitments that drew simultaneously on my humanist and poststructuralist assumptions and on my ambivalences and wonderings about living in categories. There is a persistent irony that, despite our shared skepticisms of the category, sexuality served as the premise of our coming together. Living in a marked category of sexuality does not confer privileged access to or automatic understandings with another person. Whatever understandings are formed among participants in inquiry or by the researcher are provisional, made possible by the intermingling of time and space.[42] The intersections and points of departure among us put into question assumptions that there are easy "insider" relationships among lesbian researchers and participants in fieldwork, just as my ongoing ambivalences call into question whether a researcher can have a single "position" in relation to her inquiry. Throughout the inquiry, I have found it at once freeing in some ways and troubling in others, and resonant with much of my own experience, to think that intellectual and lesbian may be constructs with few affinities or points of connection. As I have considered the implications of my interpretations, I have been mindful of the gains that have been made through identity politics in certain contexts, yet concerned that an emphasis on identity forecloses possibilities of understanding and changing human relations in ways that allow us to exceed the given. By placing ourselves and others in research within boundaries of identity, we reify ourselves, those who participate in research, and the questions and purposes that evolve in the process of inquiry. Queer research may be less about who researches whom or what is researched than about what is and what can be done with the research.

If heterology is the introduction of the other into a familiar space, the other can defamiliarize that space, pluralize it through new and surprising practices. De Certeau explains that spaces "allow for social communication and creativity because they furnish, on the one hand, common *references*, and, on the other, *possible* paths of pursuit." However, as spaces become pluralized through the introduction of others, through the indeterminate wanderings of other times and places, they lose singular authority. This loss of final authority, he says, "demoralizes the people who still adhere to institutions through conviction. They feel they are crying in vain in the midst of ruins."[43] Perhaps ethnography, like institutions and identities, should be thought of as a ruin, a space without authority that offers its readers the task of engaging it with their memories, and thus the obligation of doing something with it themselves.

NOTES

CHAPTER 1.
HAUNTED QUESTIONS, INHABITED SPACES

1. Adrienne Rich, *What Is Found There*, 51.

2. Richard Terdiman, "Response of the Other," 37.

3. My discussion of the GAU is based primarily on research conducted at the Lesbian Herstory Archives in Brooklyn, New York.

4. Gay Academic Union, *Universities and the Gay Experience*, n.p.

5. In order to contextualize the founding moment of the GAU, I take brief note of the dominant gay and lesbian social and political movements of the early seventies. After Stonewall, the Gay Liberation Front (GLF), a New Left activist group, organized around an anti-essentialist stance that mainstream mores needed to be changed and that the hetero- or homosexual in every person needed to be released in order to transform society. The group disintegrated as reform-minded activists took the lead in gay and lesbian politics. The reformists, the Gay Activists Alliance (GAA), eschewed the GLF's coalitional politics and organized around identity as a means of gaining civil rights; they saw the creation of a minority identity and culture as integral to gaining social acceptance. Both the GLF and the GAA enjoyed the participation of women and men; however, in the heyday of separatism, women dissatisfied with males' stances toward lesbian and feminist issues broke off from both groups. The political environment, then, was characterized by tensions between identity politics and transformative politics and gay men and lesbians. (These characterizations are drawn from Marotta, *Politics of Homosexuality*.)

6. George Chauncey, Martin Duberman, and Martha Vicinus, "Introduction."

7. By 1975, the organization had formed a national network with chapters in cities including Philadelphia, Ann Arbor, Boston, and Chicago, and writers such as Kate Millet, Adrienne Rich, and Rita Mae Brown giving readings at conferences and fundraisers.

8. A number of GAU members were integral in helping to form gay/lesbian caucuses: the Modern Language Association in 1973, the American Anthropological Association in 1974, the American Sociological Association in 1974, and the American Historical Association several years later. With the political splits and the increasing move to disciplinary work, the New York GAU fell into something of a state of disarray. In 1978, GAU headquarters and leadership moved to Los Angeles, where the new director, Wayne Dynes, turned the organization's focus to interpersonal and spiritual issues and political, legisla-

tive, and electoral strategies. By 1979, GAU conference attendance had dwindled to 300 after a 1975 peak of 1,200.

9. On NOW, see Marotta, *Politics of Homosexuality*. On responses by academic feminists, see Gallop, *Around 1981*; Showalter, ed., *New Feminist Criticism*; and Spelman, *Inessential Woman*. See also Sandoval, "Feminism and Racism," on racism at the 1981 National Women's Studies Association Conference.

10. On gay and lesbian history, see Duberman, *About Time*; on literature, see Showalter, "Criticism of Our Own."

11. Caroll Smith-Rosenberg, "Female World"; Barbara Smith, "Toward a Black Feminist Criticism"; Adrienne Rich, "Compulsory Heterosexuality"; Bonnie Zimmerman, "What Has Never Been." During the same epoch, a number of definitions were set forth, defining a lesbian by criteria of her affective ties (e.g., Faderman, *Surpassing the Love of Men*), genital sexual experiences (e.g. Stimpson, "Zero Degree Deviancy"), or her politics and resistances.

12. See Escoffier, "Inside the Ivory Closet," "Generations"; S. Seidman, "Identity Politics"; Vance, ed., *Pleasure and Danger*.

13. See Escoffier's accounts of these trends in "Inside the Ivory Closet" and "Generations."

14. Steven Seidman, for example, has argued that poststructural critiques of identity politics "fail to theoretically engage the practices of individuals organized around affirmative gay and lesbian identities" and ignore the ways identities "are enabling or productive of social collectivities, moral bonds, and political agency" ("Identity Politics," 134). See Alcoff, "Cultural Feminism Versus Post-Structuralism," for a discussion of these tensions.

15. Chauncey, Duberman, and Vicinus, "Introduction"; S. Seidman, "Identity Politics."

16. bell hooks, *Teaching to Transgress*, 88–89.

17. See Scott, "Experience."

18. Judith Roof, "Lesbians and Lyotard," 51.

19. Valerie Traub, "Ambiguities of 'Lesbian' Viewing Pleasure," 305.

20. A trope (from the Greek for "turn" or "twist") is a literary or rhetorical device in which words are used "in a way different from their standard or literal usage" (Harvey, "Trope," 647), a distinction questioned by poststructuralists, who consider all language tropological, inherently unstable, constantly turning. Tropes are bound up with concepts and are shaped by and "create the shape of experience—they define what we agree to be true" (McLaughlin, "Figurative Language," 87). As tropes, voice and visibility define the logic of gay and lesbian activism.

21. Bonnie Zimmerman, "Politics of Transliteration," 262.

22. Adrienne Rich, "Invisibility in Academe," 199–200.

23. See Teresa de Lauretis, "Feminist Studies/Critical Studies," 8; Gillan, "Foucault's Philosophy," 37.

24. hooks, *Teaching to Transgress*, 41.

25. See Crosby, "Dealing with Differences."

26. Butler, *Bodies that Matter*, 226.

27. Sedgwick, *Epistemology of the Closet*, 68.

28. Erving Goffman, *Stigma*. A line of inquiry related to "identity management" has continued to the present. Through narratives and group interviews, Pat Griffin, in "Identity Management Strategies," for example, identified the strategies of thirteen K–12 gay and lesbian educators, finding that strategies her participants used with different persons in different contexts were not unified. "Passing," "covering," "implicitly coming out," and "explicitly coming out" were highly contextual, frequently defined by individual collegial relationships in the school setting. Although some writers have attached Goffman's formulations to the identity and community created in identity politics, I read his emphasis on the role of social knowledges in shaping interactions as participating in laying a groundwork for queer theorizing that understands gay and lesbian "identity" as a performance constructed in multiple layers of context. Griffin's work, for example, points to the ways the recognitions of others within an institutional context construct the actions of gay and lesbian educators.

29. Judith Butler, "Imitation and Gender Insubordination," 309.

30. Judith Butler, "For a Careful Reading," 137.

31. Judith Butler, *Gender Trouble*, 144.

32. Michel de Certeau, *Practice of Everyday Life*. Roach, for example, has suggested that "*Performance*, . . . though it frequently makes reference to theatricality as the most fecund metaphor for the social dimension of cultural production, embraces a much wider range of human behaviors. Such behaviors may include what Michel de Certeau calls 'the practice of everyday life,' in which the role of spectator expands into that of participant. De Certeau's 'practice' has itself enlarged into an open-ended category marked 'performative'" ("Culture and Performance," 46).

33. I do not dwell on de Certeau's understanding of power, which seems simplistic in its conceptualization of persons or organizations as having or not having power, particularly in light of Foucault's elaboration in *History of Sexuality* of the multiple points through which power is exercised. What I do find helpful is his identification of the evolving, interdependent relations of the spatial and temporal and the ways tactical practices elude disciplinary control. See pp. 34–39 of *The Practice of Everyday Life* for a full elaboration of tactics and strategies.

34. De Certeau, *Heterologies*, viii.

35. De Certeau, *Practice of Everyday Life*, 108.

36. Cindy Patton, "Performativity and Spatial Distinction," 182.

37. William Sewell, "Theory of Structure."

38. Bourdieu, *Outline of a Theory of Practice*; Giddens, *Constitution of Society*.

39. Ann Swidler's conceptions of "culture" as resources persons have to construct "strategies of action" and culture as fragmented is consonant with "transposability" across contexts, as strategies of action—intentional or not—can be "reappropriated and altered in new circumstances" ("Culture in Action," 273, 283).

40. Bruce Robbins, introduction to *Intellectuals*, xix.

41. Bill Readings, *University in Ruins*, 54.

42. "Yale Report of 1828," 545.

43. Culler, *Framing the Sign*, 44. In fact, between the world wars university curricula specifically turned to U.S. society as an object of study, a move counter to the ideal of disinterestedness of liberal education, yet one that underscores the role of the humanities in maintaining, or restoring, a common culture. Columbia's Contemporary Civilization proposals in 1917, Harvard's "Redbook," Hutchins' *General Education in a Free Society*, and the more recent Western Civ debates at Stanford reveal ongoing curricular preoccupation with such citizenship formation. See Carnochan, *Battleground of the Curriculum*; and Pratt, "Humanities for the Future."

44. For example, Bloom, *Closing of the American Mind*; D'Souza, *Illiberal Education*; and Kimball, *Tenured Radicals*.

45. See, for example, Association of American Colleges, *Integrity in the College Curriculum*; W. Bennett, *To Reclaim a Legacy*; and Cheney, *50 Hours*.

46. Giroux, "Academics as Public Intellectuals," 295.

47. See Spanos, *End of Education*.

48. De Certeau, *Practice of Everyday Life*, 108.

49. Kritzman, "Introduction," xiv.

50. Foucault, "Concern for Truth," 265.

51. Foucault's claim of specificity has been criticized for its lack of attachment to a cause, as Foucault himself has been criticized for not problematizing his own social and intellectual locations (see Radhakrishnan, "Toward and Effective Intellectual"). However, his articulation of the role of the specific intellectual offers a mobility in intellectual practice that is consonant with the demands of the posthistorical university.

52. Andrew Ross, *No Respect*, 230.

53. For example, see hooks and West, *Breaking Bread*; see Radhakrishnan, "Toward an Effective Intellectual," and Said, "American Intellectuals," for discussions of "representational" intellectuals.

54. Steven Seidman, "Deconstructing Queer Theory," 122.

55. Saslow, "Lavendar Academia," 66.

56. John D'Emilio, *Making Trouble*, 163, 158.

57. Adrienne Rich has spoken of lesbian feminist work: "Our theory, scholarship, and teaching must continue to refer back to flesh, blood, violence, sexuality, anger . . . : the particularity and commonality of this vast turbulence of female becoming, which is continually being erased or generalized" ("Resisting Amnesia," 154–155).

58. Tierney, "Academic Freedom," 144. Researchers contend that in institutional cultures that do not recognize gay and lesbian existence, little research and teaching on gay and lesbian topics is conducted by hetero- or homosexuals (see Bensimon, "Lesbian Existence"; D'Augelli, "Lesbians and Gay Men on Campus"; Tierney, *Building Communities of Difference*) and may be suspect as politically motivated (see Kitzinger, "Beyond the Boundaries").

59. Edward Said, "Intellectuals in the Post-Colonial World," 46.

60. Giroux, *Teachers as Intellectuals*, 146.

61. See Gumport, "Curricula as Signposts," "Feminist Scholarship as Vocation"; and O'Barr, *Feminism in Action*.

62. D'Emilio, *Making Trouble*.

63. See, for instance, the overview of issues facing lesbian university faculty by Rothblum, "Lesbians in Academia."

64. Radhakrishnan, "Toward an Effective Intellectual," 57.

65. I find the slippage in Garber's volume particularly interesting, given the postmodern inflection of a number of its essays. In contrast, Mintz and Rothblum's 1997 edited volume, *Lesbians in Academia: Degrees of Freedom*, which also includes first-person narratives, situates itself squarely in identity politics and social scientific traditions: the editors go so far as to look for variance and patterns across the narratives.

66. For example, Barale, "Romance of Class and Queers"; Chapkis, "Explicit Instruction."

67. Toni McNaron, *Poisoned Ivy*, 110, 112.

68. The names of all participants in the study, as well as institutional and geographic names, are pseudonyms.

69. In transcribed text from interviews or classroom scenes, slashes / / appear to indicate that a word or words were inaudible in transcription. A word or words appearing inside slashes indicates my best guess, based on partial audibility or my recollection of the interview. Brackets denote the addition of my words to the text, usually for clarification. A three-em dash denotes something I have omitted, such as the title of a book or article that one of the women has written, usually for the sake of confidentiality. Ellipses indicate text I have omitted, a phrase (. . .) or (a) sentence(s) (. . . .) that may be redundant, do not enhance clarity or understanding, or represent an interruption (a phone call or person stopping by an office).

70. Hazel Carby, "Politics of Difference," 84.

71. Over six months, I conducted seven interviews lasting an average of two hours with Julie and Carol, and six with Olivia. The interviews could be described in social scientific terms as semistructured. I began with the same interview guide for all three women and constructed subsequent guides with their specific concerns in mind. I made a point of asking a "core" of common questions, such as the ways they negotiate their sexuality with colleagues and students, their conceptions of themselves and goals as researchers and teachers, the connections they experience between their research and pedagogy, the types of professional service in which they are engaged, and their views of their disciplines, departments, and university. As the women's particularities emerged, the interviews became specific to their situations. For example, Julie and I spoke about the ways her cancer had affected her understandings of what it has meant to hide her sexuality; Carol and I spoke of the polite racism she faces and how her race obscures her sexuality for her colleagues; Olivia and I spoke of how her stature in lesbian studies turns her into a commodity. Although my interview guides were based in the logic of fieldwork, our interviews frequently took other courses, cycling away from and back to topics on the guides (see Hammersley and Atkinson, *Ethnography: Principles in Practice*, on flexibility in interviewing). There were times when the interviews began with spontaneous discussion of something that had occurred in class that day, or when they deviated completely from the expected. Although the origin of the interviews lay in my questions, they evolved through the negotiation that characterizes conversations (see,

for example, Clandinin and Connelly, "Personal Experience Methods"). However, as evidenced in my interactions with Olivia, there was not symmetry in the interview relationships, though the asymmetry differed from that typically documented in the research literature, which preoccupies itself with researchers' power over participants, or with differential social positions, in which the researcher is in or from a "more powerful" position than the researched (see, for example, the essays in Gitlin, ed., *Power and Method*).

72. See James Sears, "Researching the Other," for a lucid description of "the conceptual difficulties in defining people on the basis of 'sexual orientation'" (150) and the dangers of "validat[ing] spurious categories that become the very engines of oppression" (151). While I relied on self-identification as lesbian, I do not mean to suggest any meanings inhere in the term nor that "lesbian" must be a central organizing category for one's life and work.

73. Gayatri Spivak, *Post-Colonial Critic*, 109.

74. My data, which I describe more fully in footnotes in subsequent chapters, include the following: (1) transcriptions and notes from interviews with the women; (2) transcriptions and notes from interviews with the women's colleagues, students, and TAs; (3) transcriptions and notes from interviews across campus; (4) transcriptions and notes from classroom observations; (5) copies of the women's research; (6) copies of newspaper articles, course listings, statements and policies from across the campus; (7) my research journal. I mapped these sources in a variety of ways to discover interconnections and inconsistencies across them. My sympathies for what David Smith, following Gadamer's *Truth and Method*, calls a "hermeneutic imagination," or an interpretive stance that questions the assumption of "truth being ultimately a methodological affair" ("Hermeneutic Inquiry," 189), place me in tension with normative demands of social scientific inquiry that are comprised of a priori standards for conducting research and analysis. While techniques are an important part of social scientific inquiry, they can never reveal the ways a researcher has dwelled in her inquiry, at what moments the "creepy detours" (Britzman, "Could This Be Your Story," 6) have created new clearings, or what ineffable resources have been called upon for conversation and understanding. For example, I am wary of overreliance on "coding," which I see as valuable only insofar as it enables researchers to know texts from a variety of angles, but that, as Kleinman and Copp point out in *Emotions and Fieldwork*, has an underlying positivist verificationist epistemology ("I've got it all") that can block holistic, intuitive approaches to interpretation. Instead, analytic techniques offer a place within and beyond which interpretation occurs, creating no more than a path that offers possibilities for detour. As I understand inquiry, it is a process of sharing with others the understandings and knowledges one is able to create. Throughout the study, I attended carefully to the interpretations underlying my observations, the sources of my questions, the events and interactions that puzzled or moved me. I constructed a portrait of questions that recurred, were displaced or transformed, of uncertainties and dissonances. Although I explicate my analytic procedures here, I am aware that the process of coming to understand cannot easily be enumerated, and hope that my understandings reveal themselves in the movement of the narratives.

In one component of analysis, I analyzed the interviews I had conducted with faculty, staff, and students across the campus, finding themes and anomalies within and across interviews. Basic categories that emerged from the transcripts included: communities (subdivided into race, class, gender, sexuality, university, and nonuniversity), diversity (also subdivided), gay/lesbian (subdivided into policy, student perceptions, classrooms, faculty, colleagues, visibility/voice), and so on. I studied documents I had collected across the campus, constructing categories and narratives that I considered in relation to the interviews. I sought to understand documents first internally, and then, in relation to other sources of information. In a second task, I turned to the interviews with the women, which I read in a number of ways. During fieldwork, I identified topics that were salient either in their repetition or in the significance the women ascribed to them, sought tentative connections among them, and formulated conjectures as to their possible meanings. After the fieldwork was complete, I undertook a second form of analysis in which I imposed a set of categories based on areas of interest I had brought to the study. The eleven categories included: conceptions of research, conceptions of teaching, conceptions of service, professional support, perceptions of external expectations for research, perceptions of external expectations for teaching, perceptions of official representations of lesbians (link to work), perceptions of unofficial representations of lesbians, meanings of sexuality as teachers, meanings of sexuality as researchers, meanings of sexuality as colleagues. Throughout the processes, I checked the interview transcripts for anything not included in the frameworks I had laid out. As I worked with the clustered stories, the categories that evolved from the interviews, and my own categories, I found that through considering the evolution of topics over time, themes that linked and gave them meaning could be identified and developed (see I. Seidman, *Interviewing as Qualitative Research*).

Theme is a precarious notion to evoke in a text that draws on poststructural thought. As it is often used in ethnography (see Spradley, *Ethnographic Interview*) and phenomenology (see, for example, Hunnisett, "Developing Phenomenological Method," and van Manen, *Researching Lived Experience*), theme implies coherence and representability. Spradley describes a theme as recurring across domains or linking subsystems in a culture (see 185–189). A certain isomorphism from domain to domain is implicit in his definition. In his description of phenomenological method, van Manen describes themes as "only fasteners, foci, or threads around which the phenomenological description is facilitated" (91). He suggests that theme can enable one to arrive at meaning or express the essence of a notion or experience, and constitutes the sense one is able to make of the phenomenon considered (91–92). Theme may indeed facilitate understanding and the creation of meaning, but theme does not express and cannot impose essence on what are interpretations of interpretations of lived experience. By suggesting an underlying structure or essence, theme may reify what is unstable and transitory (see Willis, "Phenomenological Inquiry"). However, I retain the notion of theme as a starting point for explicitly organizing understanding. I do so with an awareness that theme is a construction in need of deconstruction, mediated by language and discourse just as are the experiences to which it would give meaning.

Although I gave analytical primacy to the women's articulated understandings of their work, other sources of data served to enrich, contradict, or complicate the understandings the interviews engendered. One source of complication was my analysis of classroom observations, which was structured around key topics, events, and patterns, and juxtaposed to the women's words and my reflections in the researcher's journal. In the same way, I juxtaposed my readings of the women's research to their talk of its meanings and purposes. Finally, analysis of my interviews with their colleagues, students, and TAs added another layer of understanding. Throughout the interpretive process, I gave significant attention to the domains in which practices occurred or about which persons spoke.

75. Diane Brunner, *Inquiry and Reflection*, 17.

76. Norman Denzin, *Interpretive Biography*, 23.

77. Marcus and Fischer, *Anthropology as Cultural Critique*; Jean-François Lyotard, *Postmodern Condition*, xxiv.

78. Patti Lather, *Getting Smart*, 1.

79. Jerome Bruner, "Narrative and Paradigmatic Ways of Knowing," 98.

80. Lyotard, *Postmodern Condition*, 20. Lyotard's division of narrative and scientific knowledge could be criticized as a nostalgic longing for (pre)modern eras when narrative was constitutive of communities. Instead, what interests me is his suggestion that scientific knowledge's delegitimation of narrative knowledge may obscure communities' attempts to discuss what is just and unjust as they create prescriptions, norms, and laws.

81. De Certeau, *Practice of Everyday Life*, 118.

82. Rorty, "Method and Morality," 169.

83. Visweswaran, *Fictions of Feminist Ethnography*.

84. De Certeau, *Practice of Everyday Life*, 125.

85. Lincoln and Guba, *Naturalistic Inquiry*, 124.

86. Celia Kitzinger, "Beyond the Boundaries," 174.

CHAPTER 2.
SOCIAL AND INSTITUTIONAL PLACES AND SPACES

1. My study of the university included formal and informal aspects of campus life. I studied the Liberal U Bulletin and course listings, newsletters and brochures of colleges, programs, and centers, the strategic plan and mission statement, and various policies (such as nondiscrimination, promotion and tenure, academic and student handbooks). I followed Hammersley and Atkinson's advice that "official documents and enumerations should be treated as social products" (*Ethnography, Principles in Practice*, 168), reading the documents as justificatory statements produced for specific purposes and audiences. Of interest were definitions of teaching, research, and service, the construction of various "diversities" and their placement in policies, plans, and brochures, and the quality and quantity of attention given to aspects of academic and social life at Liberal U. These documents offered insights into the institution's public presentation of its purposes and means to achieve them, as well as the junctures

and disjunctures between the "official" and the "unofficial" as revealed in newspapers, observations, and interviews across campus. I also gathered census data on the state, county, and town, read histories of the university, consulted registrar's reports on enrollment data, and reviewed reports on faculty composition. At the same time that I observed campus settings, I reviewed three years of campus and local newspapers in order to gain insight into issues of ongoing interest to the university and local communities. I read with an eye not only to what was said but who said it, to whom, for what reasons and in what contexts (see Hodder, "Interpretation of Documents"). I also interviewed staff in diversity offices, activist undergraduate and graduate students, gay and lesbian faculty and staff across campus, an assistant dean, and several women not affiliated with the university. Through these interviews, themes emerged regarding African-American, female and gay and lesbian faculty, diversity initiatives, and the relationships of Oasis, Liberal U, and members of their communities. The perspectives and anecdotes I gleaned offered points of contrast and corroboration to what I uncovered through study of newspapers and university documents.

2. In order to maintain a modicum of anonymity, I do not specify the population any more precisely.

3. Divisions among lesbians are not unique to Oasis. Phelan, for example, has spoken of splits between feminist and non-feminist lesbians, or the "academic" lesbian and the "bar dyke" (*Identity Politics*, 66). While the divisions in Oasis are more nuanced than a twofold grouping suggests, interviews with a number of women confirm the existence of such a divide. Susan Krieger offers a polyvocal description of such splits, as well as occasional connections among disparate groups, in her chapter "Bar Women and Political Women" in *The Mirror Dance*.

4. See Giroux, "Living Dangerously"; Trend, *Crisis of Meaning*; and West, "New Cultural Politics of Difference."

5. Messer-Davidow, "Manufacturing the Attack."

6. On liberalism, see Jaggar, *Feminist Politics and Human Nature*; Torres, "State and Education Revisited."

7. Chandra Mohanty, "On Race and Voice," 146.

8. The administration recently created a high-level administrative position to coordinate minority programs and hired a person with little experience in minority affairs; his background in "operations management" and "performance measurement" suggests concern with efficiency rather than a rethinking of goals and the means to achieve them.

9. See Mohanty, "On Race and Voice," on the depoliticized nature of university diversity programs.

10. Troy Duster, "They're Taking Over," 279.

11. See Farmer, "Place But Not Importance."

12. Scott, "Deconstructing Equality-Versus-Difference," 44.

13. See Moore and Sagaria, "Situation of Women," on the status of women at research universities and the disproportionate number of women in junior rather than senior ranks.

14. Chang Hall, "Compromising Positions"; O'Leary and Mitchell, "Women Connecting with Women."

15. Ruth Farmer, "Place But Not Importance," 202.

16. In addition to published concerns with "economic feasibility" and "proof" of partnership, a faculty member told me, "Faculty voted on it and in fact in the end the faculty was divided because they said, one of the arguments was that, one faculty member told me, 'Well what's going to happen is that all these gay men are going to want to get jobs here and then we're going to be saddled with taking care of their partners who have AIDS.'" The virulence of this comment reveals assumptions that homosexuality, even in its most respectable, coupled form, brings disease and expense to those in officially sanctioned, verifiable relationships.

17. Celia Kitzinger, "Beyond the Boundaries," 169.

18. Eve Kosofsky Sedgwick, *Epistemology of the Closet*, 85, 1.

19. Julie described the writing campaign as one of the "small ways" she has contributed to activist work: "When they had all this flak about the center, they were going to tone it down. I wrote to the President and said I was very disappointed that you were not supporting the gay/lesbian center." Olivia chose not to write: "That's not the tactic, to join them in this argument, because that's what they want. If you make something like this controversial, then how can it ever function? You want to not have this? Well, fine. The result of not having this is it pops up in over fourteen different places. That seems to me the most deeply traumatic and interesting solution to the whole thing." Carol was at another institution for the year and did not participate.

20. The italicized statements constitute part of the flow of words and rhetoric around the creation of the office. Sources include newspaper articles, newspaper editorials and letters, brochures, documents, and leaflets. Speakers include the legislator, administrators, students, faculty, staff, and citizens of Oasis.

21. See Phelan, *Identity Politics*, on the role of liberalism in defining policies concerning gay men and lesbians.

22. Michael Warner, "No Special Rights," 205.

23. S. Seidman, "Identity Politics"; Tierney, *Building Communities of Difference*. In his discussion of campuses as multicultural communities, Carlson makes the point that "multiculturalism and identity politics need to be infused by a politics of the self that disrupts the underlying binary logic that governs identity formation in contemporary culture. For it is this binary construction of identity, and with it the representation of the subaltern Other as deficient and inferior, that provides a common thread that runs throughout histories of class, race, gender, and sexual orientation oppression in the modern era" ("Who Am I," 108).

24. These two groups are constructed as non-intersecting at Liberal U, a fact that elicited little commentary from faculty, staff, and students. One program director, however, did comment, "People sort of have their enclaves, which is one of the ways the system keeps people down, sort of colonizing them." Although the staff in the Gay and Lesbian Office attempt to "build bridges" (a term that reinscribes the boundedness of groups) to the African-American, Asian, and Latino communities at Liberal U, there is resistance. A student activist expressed his dismay: "A very important person in the African-

American community says 'Oh no, we can't bring up GLB issues in a program on blacks.' I'm like, 'Why not?' His why not was the community response might be negative to his office if we deal with GLB issues." He explained: "Students see GLB issues as white issues, and I'm trying to get out there to show that people of color are in this. People of color are afraid to be identified. Coming out will affect their position in the communities they're in already."

25. Robert Rhoads, *Coming out in College*, 23.

26. On funding issues, see Piven, "Academic Freedom and Political Dissent"; and Sabloff, "Another Reason."

27. Joan Scott, "Rhetoric of Crisis in Higher Education."

28. Nelson and Bérubé, "Introduction," 7.

29. Bergquist, *Four Cultures of the Academy*.

30. As Readings describes, "All that the system requires is for activity to take place, and the empty notion of excellence refers to nothing other than the optimal input/output ratio in matters of information" (*University in Ruins*, 39). It is interesting to note that this reliance on accountability reinscribes an "us" that must respond to a "them" that "we" claim to represent and by which "we" are ostensibly constituted. For example, responding to what the chair of the Board of Trustees calls "a crisis of public confidence in higher education," the university recently outlined four issues around which it is developing "strategic plans": assessment of student work, assessment of faculty work, institutional efficiency, and public accountability. Spurred by accrediting agencies and legislators, the first project, "to look at student learning outputs to determine what they learn," proposes finding out "what students are taking away from their education" in order to assess the curriculum. A related plan that reveals a similar logic of education as a measurable commodity to be efficiently delivered and "taken away" is based on studies of "operational efficiency" that have reviewed "high performance" business models for use at Liberal U. One "high performance" suggestion is flexible tuition based on the "services" a student "utilizes." As the President explained, "[Presently], everyone gets the basic package. We are kind of like Henry Ford, everyone gets a car, as long as it's black." Related to the President's Fordism, see Readings' discussion of the bracketing of questions of value and thought in a performative economy in his analysis of a *U.S. News and World Report* article that appropriates the car industry parallel, comparing universities' "sticker prices, "best values," and the like (28).

The plan to monitor faculty productivity is an effort, as one trustee explained, "to satisfy the public that faculty are indeed teaching in classrooms." Its stated goal is to "expose" more first- and second-year students to tenured faculty. In a production-style efficiency model, the administration determines a "unit's" teaching "capacity" based on the number of faculty in a department; the chair then determines teaching responsibilities among the faculty. Departments meeting their teaching capacities are then, presumably, accountable and efficient. In its zeal for quantification and efficiency, this model preempts consideration of the what and how of teaching or of the transformation of teaching practices.

In order to demonstrate its involvement in affairs of the state and to maintain sources of revenue, Liberal U is encouraging partnerships with the public and private sectors in order, as the President explained, "to support and pursue the university's purpose of discovering and disseminating new knowledge." Despite faculty dissent that partnerships regulate intellectual work, the President responded that "private" partnerships are no more regulatory than foundation and government grants. As on the national level, Liberal U's push for partnerships signifies its move from a function as an Althusserian Ideological State Apparatus (a University of Culture) toward a University of Excellence, in which it becomes part of the apparatus for "the production and transfer of globally exchanged information" (Miller, "Literary Study in the Transnational University," 7; see also Readings, *University in Ruins*).

31. David Trend, *Crisis of Meaning*, 103–104.

32. Researchers disagree over the relative influence that disciplines and institutions have in the definition and production of knowledge (see Tierney, "Academic Work"); however, to ignore official policy that is reiterated in faculty and student handbooks, promotion and tenure criteria, and departmental and college initiatives, is to reify disciplines and faculty work as free from the mediations of social and institutional ideologies. The instability of these documents' meanings in practice is exacerbated by the university's diffuse organizational structure, which makes impossible generalizations about how its mission and ongoing initiatives are received or enacted. Comprised of some ten colleges and schools, Liberal U cannot be understood as a single community organizationally, academically, or socially, as underscored by numerous descriptions of it as a decentralized institution comprised of fragmented colleges and departments, in which policy decisions and implementation are often uneven. In fact, in an internal study conducted in the mid-1980s, faculty across colleges and schools complained of the lack of clearly articulated and disseminated university goals. Across domains, changes appear to be enacted unevenly, depending on local initiatives rather than on coordinated institutional efforts. Staff working in diversity efforts and affirmative action even suggested an intentional "disempowerment" of their offices through the decentralized structure.

33. The etymological connections Spanos points to are telling: "It is no accident that the English words 'culture,' 'cultivate,' 'acculturation' (the privileged Latinate names that have figured forth the ideal end of education in the cultural discourses of Arnold, Babbitt, Richards, and more recently Walter Jackson Bate, Allan Bloom, and E. D. Hirsch) are cognates of *colonize* (from the Latin *colonus*, 'tiller,' 'cultivator,' 'planter,' 'settler,') and *colere* ('cultivate,' 'plant': colonies, for example, were called 'plantations' by the English settlers in the New World). All these have their origin, not in ancient Greek words referring to such agents and acts, but in the Roman appropriation of the Greek word . . . 'cycle,' or . . . 'ring,' 'circle,' the spatial image symbolizing beauty and perfection" (*End of Education*, 110).

34. Spanos contends that Enlightenment "'progress' has involved the eventual recognition of the integral relationship between the perennially and increasingly privileged figure of the centered circle as the image of beauty and perfection and the centered circle as the ideal instrument of a totalized sociopolitical domination" (*End of Education*, 29).

35. Carlos Alberto Torres, "State and Education Revisited," 275.

36. I play here with his notion of confession as elaborated in *The History of Sexuality*.

37. In *The Moral Collapse of the University*, a somewhat nostalgic lament for a university that values community, Bruce Wilshire argues that the secularization of the academy and the emergence of the research university have contributed to the contractarian, market-oriented conception of public education and citizenship. Objectivity, in the form of liberation from religious dogma, is implicated in an overemphasis on depersonalized, mechanistic, useful knowledges, the perpetuation of the mind-body split, a cult of disciplinary purity through professionalization, and the fragmentation of knowledge through overspecialization. His mention of secularization points to the historicity of a theological center in higher education, an element missing from Readings' discussion of the centers of culture, reason, and excellence, and relevant to Julie's work in religious studies.

38. Derrida, "Principle of Reason."

39. The role of faculty, students, and members of university communities in redefining knowledge and its organization is not addressed in policy. On these local mediations of conceptions of knowledge, see Gumport, "Curricula as Signposts," "Feminist Scholarship as Vocation"; and Tierney, "Academic Work," "Academic Freedom."

40. Liberal U's Bulletin reveals that the university offers a major in African American Studies; there are nondegree programs in Chicano studies and women's studies; there are no programs in gay and lesbian studies or sexuality studies. As a corollary, it is interesting to note that a two-course "culture studies" requirement in the College of Arts and Sciences can easily be fulfilled with courses such as "Western European Politics," "Classical Mythology," "The Reformation," or "Medieval Philosophy." Through formulating requirements and programs, the university determines and communicates knowledge that is important (see O'Barr, *Feminism in Action*). As Spanos has pointed out, adding a single course is insufficient to activate substantive dialogue beyond a "self-perpetuating representational discourse based on a panoptic ethnocentric perspective" (*End of Education*, 155).

41. These definitions of academic practices alone do not constitute faculty work at Liberal U. In fact, to what extent participants are directly conscious of official universitywide mission is difficult to know. However, the university's policies do affect the work of faculty, as evidenced by the complaints of a faculty member in Women's Studies regarding the manner in which her department must justify itself: "One of the things that's discouraging for me, we've had to constantly say what our majors will go and do. And we have to continually say, 'Oh, they'll get jobs in publishing, they'll get jobs in government organizations, they can get dadadadada.' We have to prove that we can create students who can go out and become employable, and therefore that we can reproduce what the institution understands itself to do." Her frustrations suggest that university policy does call on individual departments to construct themselves along the lines of the university's *economic* mission as dictated by its need to secure funding.

42. See Sandler's "Campus Climate Revisited," a liberal feminist overview of the "chilly professional climate" (175) experienced by female faculty, stu-

dents, and administrators. She mentions the exclusion of women in everyday exchanges and decision-making processes and the trivialization of research and service related to women.

43. *Webster's College Dictionary*, s.v. "specter."

44. See Norris' *Dakota: A Spiritual Geography* for a thoughtful depiction of the Midwestern ethos. She speaks of insularity, an established social order, and what she calls a social inability to render secrets and subtleties easily.

45. Sedgwick, *Epistemology of the Closet*, 3.

46. It is interesting to note that although this woman says she does not know women of color who are lesbian, she sits on a committee with Carol, who complains of the impossibility of her black lesbianism in the eyes of others.

47. Foucault, "Sexual Choice, Sexual Act," 290; italics mine.

48. Michael Warner, "No Special Rights," 289–290.

49. Michel de Certeau, *Practice of Everyday Life*, xi.

CHAPTER 3.
DISPLACING PEDAGOGICAL POSITIONINGS

1. Julie was teaching a lecture class, "Introduction to Christianity," which she teaches every year, and an upper-level undergraduate class, "Mystical Prayer and Western Spirituality," that she had just developed. Olivia was also teaching a lecture class, "Introduction to Writing and the Study of Literature," as well as a graduate class, "American Fiction." Carol was teaching "Race, Gender, and the Media," a mixed undergraduate/graduate class that she has taught every year she has been at Liberal U, and a "skills" class for graduate students, "Public Affairs Reporting." I observed and audiotaped each class between three and five times, with the exception of audiotaping Carol's classes, primarily due to her concern that my doing so would draw attention to her as a subject of study:

> When it would have been useful for you to audiotape, there was some tension in [Race, Gender, and the Media], and I was concerned that it would have been disruptive. . . . I was concerned that it would draw some attention to me that I didn't want to be happening in that class because I'm very concerned about subjectivity in my class and me not becoming the subject, because then they just identify whatever I talk about with me because I'm a black woman, and not because it is a body of knowledge. So this is an instance where I would be made the subject, where this is about me.

As a beginning point for observation, I focused on three aspects of their classrooms: (1) the sorts of pedagogy they employ (for example, how lecture, discussion, or group work are used); (2) interpersonal dynamics (who speaks to whom, how, and when); and, (3) the manner in which knowledge is defined and constructed (is there a canon of knowledge, what content and skills are promoted, what connections between content and students' experiences and interests are made). I was interested in identifying how Julie, Carol, and Olivia positioned themselves in relation to students and the subject matter and encouraged students to grapple with the content and process of their courses. I also looked for evidence that might indicate how sexuality circulated. Would (homo)sexuality be discussed, how, in what contexts, and by whom? Would they highlight or obscure sexuality—their own, or sexuality as topic—in their teaching? If sexuality remained tacit, would there be (identifiable) ways students responded to the women that were related to perceptions of their sexuality? Through fieldwork, specific foci for observation emerged. In Julie's classes, I became interested in the place of personal experience and the potential for hostile responses from students, primarily fundamentalist Christians. Olivia's description of her "improvisational pedagogy" led me to attend closely to the dynamics of student-professor exchanges. Carol's emphasis on encouraging students to think differently about their relations, as producers and consumers, to the media, turned my attention to how the content and approach of the class might embody that goal; her description of problems with authority due to her race and gender alerted me to possibilities of student resistance.

Some six weeks into the semester, I interviewed their Teaching Assistants (TAs) with the exception of Carol, (who did not have TAs) in order to learn about (1) their perspectives on the women's pedagogy and students' responses to classes; (2) their experiences of their departments; and, (3) what they learned from working with each woman, what they found valuable, and what they questioned. I also interviewed between two and five students in each class. The interviews were designed to elicit their perceptions of the content and pedagogical approach of their classes, what they felt they were learning, and how the course related to other classes they had taken. There were standard questions across interviews, with a few questions specific to the content, methods, and events of each class.

2. On the syllabus was a list of "recommended light reading to get you in the mood": Annie Dillard, *Pilgrim at Tinker Creek*; Kathleen Norris, *Dakota: A Spiritual Geography*; J. D. Salinger, *Franny and Zooey*; Patricia Hampl, *Virgin Time*. Required texts were: Reginald M. French, *Way of a Pilgrim*; Thomas Keating, *Intimacy with God*; Rowan Williams, *Wound of Knowledge*; Rowan Williams, *Teresa of Avila*; Teresa of Avila, *Interior Castle*.

3. FN 8/29/95. In referring to classroom scenes, I call both from fieldnotes and audiotapes. In the class sessions I did not audiotape, I rely on fieldnotes only. For those classes, I annotate fieldnotes with FN and the date. For classes in which I audiotaped, I annotate AT and the date. Throughout the transcripts, I include names (pseudonyms) for students whose names I knew at the time or came to know. Others are referred to as "student."

4. The list was as follows: Barnes, *Nightwood*; Acker, *Portrait of an Eye*; Pynchon, *The Crying of Lot 49*; DeLillo, *White Noise*; Nabokov, *Lolita*; Auster, *New York Trilogy*; Dürrenmatt, *The Assignment*; Harris, *Lover*; Burroughs, *Naked Lunch*; Brossard, *Picture Theory*; Duras, *The Malady of Death*; Derrida, *Limited, Inc.*; Baudrillard, *Cool Memories*; various critical texts to be copied from texts available in my office.

5. FN 8/28/95.

6. Pineau, "Teaching is Performance," 6, 13.

7. Gallop, "Im-personation," 9. Consonant with the visual etymology of *theater, to appear* (to come into view or to become visible, derived from the French to show) suggests what is seen, yet what is seen or shown is constituted not only visually but also by what is spoken and enacted. Although Gallop does not acknowledge Goffman's work, her line of argument is strikingly reminiscent of his theatrically inflected *The Presentation of Self in Everyday Life.*

8. Lynch, "Last Onsets," 34.

9. See, for example, Linda Garber, ed., *Tilting the Tower*, and Haggerty and Zimmerman, eds., *Professions of Desire.*

10. Zavarzadeh and Morton, "Theory Pedagogy Politics," 11.

11. Due to the large number of readings, I list the syllabus topics by week: (1) Introduction: Race, gender, and social constructions; (2) Origins of images and stereotypes: Early American media and culture; (3) Technology and the twentieth century: Motion pictures; (4) Race and gender in contemporary cinema; (5) The arrival of television/The shaping of images; (6) Contemporary television/Old Myths in a new package; (7) Music is the message/From blues to hiphop; (8) Sex, gender, and rock 'n roll; (9) Selling the product; (10) The dilemmas of free speech: Pornography, racism, and censorship; (11) Shifting power and social change: The news media; (12) New and recurring issues for the press; (13) The journalistic workforce; (14) Understanding diverse audiences; (15) New demographics/New markets.

12. Weekly topics on the syllabus were listed as follows: (1) Defining public affairs reporting, the beat system, learning about the community; (2) Deciding what's news, developing story ideas, basics of style, observation; (3) Access to information, legal issues, interviewing; (4) Government organization, working with public documents, computer assisted reporting; (5) The criminal justice system, more working with public documents; (6) The judicial system, using multiple sources in stories; (7) Covering a multicultural community, ethical issues for reporters; (8) Reporting on human services and social issues, visualizing the news; (9) Covering politics, the candidates, voters, issues; (10) Covering politics, sources, polling data and statistics, encouraging civic responsibility; (11) Education and the schools beat; (12) Business, economics, and labor; (13) Putting local news in a broader context; (14) Organizing a complex reporting project; (15) Presentation of final stories.

13. FN 9/6/95.

14. Morgan, "Voices in the News," 98.

15. FN 9/6/95.

16. I should note that my experiences of dispassion were not fully corroborated by students' accounts. For example, Ralph emphasized the course's impact on him: "I can hear a lot of different voices in the class, we have a lot of African-Americans, I'm the only Asian, we have two Latinos, and white people, of course, and gays, and that's diverse, and they all come out and tell you, the gay perspective, or another perspective, and that's so interesting. You see issues in different ways." The course, he said, was the most significant he had taken during his Master's program, and would have a "long-lasting effect," unlike his vocational courses. There was little evidence, however, of the exchanges Ralph described on the days I was present.

17. Karamcheti, "Caliban in the Classroom," 138.

18. Patricia Williams, *Alchemy of Race and Rights*, 95; italics mine; 96. See also Joy James' discussion of being "continuously challenged to 'prove' that I am qualified": "[D]espite our [African-American female academics] having been hired through a highly competitive process, we seem to be asked more routinely, almost reflexively, if we have Ph.D.s" ("Teaching Theory, Talking Community," 124).

19. Karamcheti, "Caliban in the Classroom," 142.

20. Fuss, *Essentially Speaking*, 116. On the dangers of placing experience as an authorizing ground of knowledge and psychologizing difference through the validation of voices, see Mohanty, "On Race and Voice."

21. See Johnson on her desire to maintain her "mysterious, impenetrable, black essence" ("Disinfecting Dialogues," 135) in light of commodifying pressures to reveal herself and offer others knowledge of multicultural subjects.

22. Litvak, "Pedagogy and Sexuality," 28.

23. Spivak, "The Post-Colonial Critic," 59.

24. Hoodfar, "Feminist Anthropology and Critical Pedagogy," 314, 315.

25. Britzman, *Lost Subjects, Contested Objects*, 2, 88.

26. Penley, "Teaching in Your Sleep," 136. In "Pedagogy as Transference," Deborah Britzman and Alice Pitt argue that the pedagogical is defined by "the possibility of learners implicating themselves in their learning" (117). They examine the role of transference, "the idea that one's past unresolved conflicts with others and within the self are projected onto the meanings of new interactions" (117), as a destabilizing force whose temporality disrupts the linear continuity of rational models of learning.

27. Ellsworth, *Teaching Positions*, 46.

28. Although I do not dwell on Julie's interactive pedagogy, I should note that I experienced a tension between reading it as a panoptic control with its system of points, and the location, division, and monitoring of students, and reading it as a humanizing space in which students were not anonymous faces but individuals with names who were to know each other and their TAs in dialogic engagement with problems. The exigencies of teaching a large lecture create a situation in which, in order to assert students' responsibility for and to the class, a disciplinary monitoring of names and points becomes one logistical means to encourage engagement. A challenge, one to which Julie adjusted by later dropping the monitoring of points for in-class participation, becomes one of shifting students' focus from the extrinsic enforcement of points to the intrinsic worth of the material and process. See Canaan's "Examining the Examination" on lecture halls as ideal sites for hierarchical observation and normalizing judgment.

29. Michel de Certeau, *Heterologies*, 81.

30. Britzman, "Is There a Queer Pedagogy," 154.

31. Frank has emphasized that the presence of a speaker offers a text beneath the text: "Even if the lecture is thoroughly scripted, auditors retain the belief that they can glean more about the speaker through personal delivery than they could learn from reading a written text" ("Lecturing and Transference," 29).

32. Students' readings of Julie's humor were neither uniform nor predictable. Tim remarked, "When she says things like that you feel like she's on

your level, she can relate to you." Kate said her humor put her "right there with us." Stephanie explained, "I like the fact that she's not afraid of offending people, she's going to say what she thinks."

33. See Lorde, *Cancer Journals*, on the pressures for concealment of breast cancer; see Urla and Swedlund, "Anthropometry of Barbie," on the gendered nature of these pressures.

34. Urla and Terry, "Introduction," 2.

35. Foucault, *History of Sexuality*, 43.

36. D. A. Miller, *Novel and the Police*; Sedgwick, *Epistemology of the Closet*.

37. D. A. Miller, *Novel and the Police*, 205.

38. Frank, "Lecturing and Transference," 31.

39. Simon, "Face to Face with Alterity," 93, 100.

40. Lynch, "Last Onsets."

41. Margaret Thompson, a faculty member known on her campus as feminist and Catholic, says of students' coming to her to speak with her about matters of faith, "Consequently, I think I've seen some aspects of my students that probably few of my colleagues have seen, and my understanding of my role and responsibilities has been significantly deepened and altered. As a teacher, as a feminist, as a person of faith, I now believe that my responsibilities to my students go well beyond the merely academic" ("A View from the Pews," 150).

42. Burbules points out that one must first have authority in order to open it to challenge: "even such choices as encouraging the questioning of one's authority, or provisionally setting it aside are decisions that only a person in authority has the latitude to make; indeed, such decisions have the effect they do, in many cases, precisely because it is clear in all parties' minds that they occur within a broader framework in which authority is agreed to" ("Authority and the Tragic Dimension of Teaching," 38).

43. AT 11/22/95.

44. Lyotard, *Postmodern Condition*, 4.

45. Murray, "Charisma and Authority," 196.

46. Barthes, "Writers, Intellectuals, Teachers," 206.

47. Spanos, *End of Education*, 207.

48. See Burbules, "Authority and the Tragic Dimension of Teaching," 33.

49. Briton, "Decentered Subject," 69.

50. See Foucault, "What Is an Author?"

51. Pedagogy in which teachers overtly position themselves and invite students to do the same has a particular history in feminist classrooms. For a key, early work on feminist pedagogy, see Culley and Portuges, *Gendered Subjects*; for a contemporary study focused on positionality in university classrooms, see Maher and Tetreault, *Feminist Classroom*; for a historicization of feminist pedagogy, see Weiler, "Freire and a Feminist Pedagogy"; on the personal as "mantra" of feminist pedagogy, see Gallop, "Im-person-ation"; for a critique of critical pedagogy's reiteration of the very norms it would challenge, see Ellsworth, "Why Doesn't This Feel Empowering?" At stake in the use of the "personal" in pedagogy has been a challenge to ide-

ologies of neutrality and objectivity in teaching and learning by bringing instructors' and students' lived experiences to bear on subjects of study. For example, as Paula Salvio has pointed out, personal and emotional responses to readings form part of readers' experiences of and implications in texts. Although empathy and feelings can become a problematic substitute for critical engagement with texts, they should not be dismissed as part of pedagogical practice (see her "On the Forbidden Pleasures and Hidden Dangers of Covert Reading"). Rather, reading should be cast as a social practice in which private experiences and processes of becoming are in dialogue with the curriculum (Salvio, "Transgressive Daughters"). David Bleich argues for such thoughtful disclosure, in which individual experience is connected to the collective as part of the class' subject matter: "Teaching through disclosure, which has grown out of self-consciously practiced subjectivist styles of teaching by some faculty members, reminds us that 'truth' includes the personal, the emotional, the ideological, and sometimes the irrational in each subject matter" (*Know and Tell*, 12). As efficacious as moves to incorporating the personal have been in enabling multiple pedagogical forms, there is a risk of reifying teacher and student identities as "authentic" or as transcendental egos abstracted from the social, cultural, and political contexts that construct the self (see Benstock, ed., *The Private Self*, and Graham, *Reading and Writing the Self*). Moreover, the salience of certain "identities" in social discourses can set instructors and students up as "representatives" of differences and positions. Olivia attends more to the dangers than the possibilities of drawing on the "personal" in her teaching.

52. Brecht, *Brecht on Theater*, 125.

53. Olivia's juxtaposition of Harris's experimental, postmodern lesbian novel to Butler's text is no accident. As Victoria Smith has argued, *Lover* is a performative narrative that represents duplicitously and fragmentarily the identity of "lesbian lover" and "stands as a 'fictional' version of work by contemporary theorists such as Luce Irigaray, Teresa de Lauretis, Judith Butler, Sue-Ellen Case, and Mary Ann Doane" (69). In fact, Smith suggests that Harris's examination of lesbian self-representation enacts Butler's argument that gender is performance, an imitation that lacks an original, "an act and not an act, real and artifice, in part because the process of its coming into being has been disguised" ("Starting from Snatch," 79). I should note that, unfortunately, pertaining to the scene that follows, I was unable to secure a copy of the questions Olivia handed to her students to set the stage for the ensuing dialogue.

54. AT 10/2/95.

55. Felman, "Psychoanalysis and Education," 31, 31–32.

56. AT 10/2/95.

57. Barthes, "From Work to Text," 162.

58. The syllabus contained the following readings in the order listed (those without titles are essays or short stories): Slater; O'Connor; Updike; O'Neill, *Long Day's Journey into Night*; Miller, *Death of a Salesman*; Shepard, *Buried Child*; Albee, *The American Dream*; Paley; Olsen; Morrison, *The Bluest Eye*; Cosby; *Father Knows Best*; *Leave It to Beaver*; *Brady Bunch*; *Full House*; *Roseanne*; *The Simpsons*; *White Noise*; *Star Trek*; talk shows.

59. FN 8/28/95.

60. Brecht, *Brecht on Theater*.

61. AT 9/20/95.

62. Teloh, "Educational Theory in the *Meno*," 153.

63. Reich, "Confusion about the Socratic Method," 70, 73.

64. Finke, "Knowledge as Bait," 16.

65. Canaan, "Examining the Examination," 163.

66. Epstein, "Voice of Authority," 182.

67. Wright, *Postmodern Brecht*, 24.

68. Zavarzadeh and Morton argue that the construct "teacher as midwife of truth" is predicated on assumptions that "the student already contains knowledge, and that the function of the teacher is to help bring that knowledge to life" ("Theory Pedagogy Politics," 11). They contend that "[t]he ideological function of this theory of teaching and this view of the teacher is, of course, to represent the values actively advocated by the dominant curriculum" (11). However, as Olivia's pedagogy dramatizes, the maieutic process can be appropriated to counter dominant values.

69. AT 10/3/95.

70. hooks, *Teaching to Transgress*, 136–37.

71. Haggerty, "Promoting Homosexuality in the Classroom," 12. Adams and Emery, for example, argue, "You say it so that you can say something else. You say it because doing so allows you to say so many other things" ("Classroom Coming Out Stories," 30–31). But what if one doesn't care to say those "other things"? And what other "other things" might one not be able to say? How might what one says be received and transformed by one's interlocutors? How can one's speech affect what others may say?

72. Toni McNaron, *Poisoned Ivy*, 112.

73. Litvak, "Pedagogy and Sexuality," 25.

74. Khayatt, "Sex and the Teacher," 140.

75. Agamben, *Coming Community*, 43.

76. Goffman, *Forms of Talk*, 193.

77. Britzman, "Is There a Queer Pedagogy," 159.

78. Grossberg, "Introduction," 19.

79. Radhakrishnan, "Canonicity and Theory," 129.

80. Lyotard, *Political Writings*, 45. See also Readings' argument in *University in Ruins* that "the transgressive force of teaching does not lie so much in matters of content as in the way pedagogy can hold open the temporality of questioning so as to resist being characterized as a transaction that can be concluded" (19).

81. Barthes, "Writers, Intellectuals, Teachers," 205.

82. De Certeau, *Practice of Everyday Life*, 31.

83. Bill Readings, *The University in Ruins*, 19.

84. De Certeau, *Culture in the Plural*, 64.

85. Ibid., *Culture in the Plural*, 92, 49.

86. De Certeau, *Heterologies*, 187.

87. Butler, *Excitable Speech*, 145.

CHAPTER 4.
DEPARTMENTAL ACADEMIC AND SOCIAL KNOWLEDGES

1. Foucault, *Discipline and Punish*, 146, 149.
2. Messer-Davidow, "Know-How," 285.
3. De Certeau, *Heterologies*, 189.
4. See, for example, Hartman & Messer-Davidow, "Introduction," or Giddens, *Modernity and Self-Identity*.
5. I was interested in learning not only about the women's experiences of their research, their goals, what they valued, and its relationship to other facets of their lives, but also how their ongoing intellectual projects have positioned them in their disciplines and departments. I spoke with the women, their colleagues and graduate students to gain insights into the ways in which scholarship is understood, valued, and marginalized. I interviewed two colleagues in each woman's department (three in the case of Olivia), one of whom was senior and the other a gay man or lesbian. The interviews included questions about what scholarship is departmentally valued, what "groups" exist within the department, how faculty are evaluated, and what the women's contributions are to their departments. In my interviews with gay and lesbian colleagues, I included questions specific to their experiences as gay or lesbian. I also read several articles or book chapters pertaining to shifting norms of scholarship in each woman's field.
6. Trinh Minh-ha, *When the Moon Waxes Red*, 74; italics mine.
7. Peter Stayllybras and Allan White, *Politics and Poetics of Transgression*, 2.
8. Babcock, cited in Stallybras and White, 17.
9. The increasing institutionalization of Religious Studies in academia since the late 1960s has been legitimated to skeptics largely by "professionalizing," or "scientizing," it so that it might appear objective (see Marsden, *Soul of the American University*). As Dawes points out in his discussion of the uneasy position of religious sudies in secular universities, religious studies includes all religions rather than taking as a starting point the claims of a particular faith; thus, "more clearly than theology, religious studies appears to be scientific in its method and 'neutral' in its religious stance" ("Theology and Religious Studies," 52). At the time religious studies was beginning to be institutionalized, Arthur McGill wrote: "The faculties of arts and sciences have made it clear that their departments are to be agents of rationality and not of religion. These departments are expected to exclude all confessionalism, all advocacy, and all indoctrination. They are not to represent any particular religion or even religion in general. They are not to let reason become the instrument of some faith, nor allow the religious posture to hold sway. They are to show how the power of descriptive reasoning can penetrate and understand the phenomena of religion. In short, they are to proceed by the same canons of competent thought as every other department in the faculty of arts and sciences" ("Ambiguous Position of Christian Theology," 131).
10. Giorgio Agamben, *Coming Community*, 68.

11. Kal Alston, "Unicorn's Memoirs," 103.

12. I asked Michael how he came to choose Julie as his mentor: "I decided if I was going to have such a formal relationship with a person, I wanted it to be someone who I could indeed ask for advice about the whole range of issues that could arise for a junior faculty member, which are not just issues of where should I publish this, or what should my next project be, or do you think I should teach this kind of course. But also issues of how to arrange one's personal life and things like this that often come up. And I just felt more comfortable talking to her about these things, and we had already developed an informal, a real such relationship, and it just seemed to me absurd to create one artificially when I already had such a thing. I think she plays a good role, she's made herself available to other junior faculty members in this way at appropriate times. But I think we just ended up having this relationship for a variety of reasons, queerness being an important one."

13. Patricia Williams, *Alchemy of Race and Rights*, 92.

14. On this trend nationally, see Astin, *Achieving Educational Excellence*.

15. Michael confirmed this departmental bias: "I can see it manifesting itself in the way graduate education is worked out, who's thought appropriate to teach certain courses and who is not. People are very suspicious of any of us who work on the Christian tradition who are Christian, but there's almost an embracing of people who study Eastern religions and might actually practice them or consider them valid."

16. In "Sin Big," a short autobiographical essay, Mary Daly described the difficulties she faced in the 1950s in attempting to enter graduate school, as women could not teach or study Catholic theology. She also recounts her treatment as a faculty member at the purportedly liberal Boston College in the late 1960s (her contract was not renewed) through the 1970s and 1980s (she was denied promotion to full professor twice, despite—or perhaps because of—her numerous publications and international notoriety). Daly's account offers a helpful context for understanding the reception of women and feminist work in Catholic and religious studies over the last three decades. Although demands for feminist work in religious studies have enabled Julie's work, I should note another layer of scholarly liminality even in the space that brings together religious studies and feminism: "There are certain things, like women and religion, you couldn't get a paper accepted in the American Academy of Religion in the women's caucus section years ago unless you were doing something on the Goddess or Alice Walker and Shug's great religion in *The Color Purple*. . . . I don't know that we've said everything that can be said intellectually, and I think there's a lot of new stuff happening that's worth paying attention to, but what gets the attention are the active movements, the Women's Ordination Conference, or take back the night."

17. Plaskow, "What's in a Name," 136. Keller has written of the development of feminist scholarship on religion and problems of institutional location: "My academic advocacy stance regarding the institutional church is fitting to seminary teaching and administration, which would not be the case were I related to a religion or history department in a secular college or university" ("Female Experience in American Religion," 4). See Chopp, *Saving Work*, on

the increasing legitimacy of feminism in religious and theological studies.

18. In an interesting coincidence, in a 1970 essay about religious studies' defensive posture in secular institutions, Gustafson attributed its increasing legitimacy to "the development of a posture of analytical rigor, of disinterested objectivity, and sometimes of disinterested irreverence" ("Study of Religion in Colleges and Universities," 335).

19. Urla and Terry, "Introduction," 2.

20. Kath Weston, *Render Me, Gender Me*, 7.

21. Abena Busia, "Performance, Transcription, and Languages of the Self," 207.

22. Elizabeth Wilson, "Deviant Dress," 68. See her discussion of the influence of fashion changes on "the ways in which lesbians and male homosexuals can and will represent themselves and inscribe their deviant sexuality on their bodies" (69).

23. Susan Gal, "Between Speech and Silence," 176.

24. Lorde, *Cancer Journals*; Urla and Swedlund, "Anthropometry of Barbie."

25. Carol's age (she is in her early forties) is uncommonly young for the profession, as many people do not begin their doctorates until their late thirties or early forties, after they have worked as professionals for a number of years.

26. Ben made an interesting slip when describing the department, saying, "We went to the opening family—I mean faculty—picnic" In fact, he spoke of himself as outside collegial networks as a gay man: "It's my perception that there are groups and clumps of people who tend to do things with each other, they go out to lunch, or they have children in the same high school and so their lives seem to overlap more than my life seems overlap with others."

27. Patricia Williams, *Alchemy of Race and Rights*, 65.

28. Eve Kosofsky Sedgwick, *Tendencies*, 23.

29. The privilege of unknowing structures social difference in general. For example, in *Seeing a Color-Blind Future*, Patricia Williams writes of the desire to ignore the significance of race: "[I]t is imperative to think about this phenomenon of closeting race. . . . In a sense, race matters are resented and repressed in much the same way as matters of sex and scandal: the subject is considered a rude and transgressive one in mixed company, a matter whose observation is sometimes inevitable, but about which, once seen, little should be heard nonetheless. Race thus tends to be treated as though it were an especially delicate category of social infirmity" (8).

30. These issues have been discussed frequently for white women (e.g., O'Leary and Mitchell, "Women Connecting with Women") and African-American women (Moses, *Black Women in Academe*; see Gordon, "Speaking in Tongues," for a first-person account), but rarely for lesbian faculty (see Kitzinger, "Beyond the Boundaries," and Garber, ed., *Tilting the Tower*, for brief references), and, to my knowledge, not at all for African-American lesbians.

31. For discussion of this contradiction, see Moses, *Black Women in Academe*; and Milem and Astin, "Changing Composition of the Faculty."

32. Williams, *Alchemy of Race and Rights*, 103.

33. Reyes and Halcón, "Racism in Academia," 304.

34. Evelynn Hammonds, "Black (W)holes and the Geometry of Black Female Sexuality," 135.

35. Homi Bhabha, "Third Space," 208.

36. Cornel West, "New Cultural Politics of Difference," 21–22.

37. Carol's refusal of representational status occurs across domains: "I don't like the token stuff, and I refuse to do most of it. The Dean sends these memos around, 'we're having a red carpet day for these people who are visiting the campus, and we'd like for faculty to show up,' and I know they want me to go. I won't go. Sorry. I'm not doing it, I'm not going to be your black person this week. And I say that pretty routinely. So I pick and choose which of those I'm willing to do, . . . whether or not I'm simply on display or whether or not I can really do something."

38. Sagri Dhairyan, "Racing the Lesbian," 32.

39. On trends in literary studies, see Christopher Newfield, who suggests that "[l]iterary study, particularly at larger universities, has been shifting from literary history to cultural problems, from a field defined by its object of study (the expanded literary canon) to one defined by its questions and methods" ("What Was 'Political Correctness,'" 113). Zavarzadeh and Morton discuss the implications of moving from textual to cultural studies, in which "the politics of the production and maintenance of subjectivities" ("Theory Pedagogy Politics," 23) becomes central to inquiry.

40. For a report of Ph.D. job placement in the field of English that reveals what many have called the "job crisis" in the humanities, see Modern Language Association, "MLA's 1993–94 Survey of PhD Placement." Closely linked to the commodification of theory and multicultural subjects is the academic star system, which has become entrenched in literary studies with the advent of the importance of literary theory in the 1970s. Literary theory, which began as a specialization in literary studies, has become "the broadest discourse in the discipline" (Shumway, "Star System in Literary Studies," 95) and thus has an audience that spans specializations. Gayle Greene has critiqued the attachment of theory to "legitimation, validation—personal, intellectual, institutional power" in an increasingly hierarchical structure in which stars are "those who do theory [and] are invited to speak in prominent places, get offered glitzy jobs, high salaries and other perks" ("Looking at History," 18). This disciplinary creation of stars plays into universities' searches for prestige and visibility, part of which is gained through faculty they hire.

41. See Sayre, "Performance."

42. Dwight Conquergood, "Between Experience and Meaning," 38.

43. If Karen's claim that the success of queer theory and the gay and lesbian constituency at Liberal U have prompted the English department's choice of faculty is correct, it is important to note that in very few locations besides English could Olivia's categorization as lesbian theorist be considered a commodity. Lisa Duggan, for example, points to the way, "[i]n the arena of academic cultural theory, queer theory is breaking into the mainstream, making a difference and providing (some, limited) material support in the form of careers" ("Making It Perfectly Queer," 170). However, she acknowledges the hegemony

of English studies in its rise: "Academic institutions—well, English departments, to be specific, are offering jobs" ("Scholars and Sense," 173). Whether Olivia's commodity status is due to "lesbian" or "theorist" or a combination of the two is difficult to know.

44. Roland Barthes, *S/Z*, 4.

45. The constitution of a "field" of gay and lesbian studies, suggested by the canonization of *The Lesbian and Gay Studies Reader*, edited by Henry Abelove, Michèle Barale, and David Halperin, includes suggestions for the creation of an interdisciplinary field that includes scholarship that focuses on gay and lesbian issues in courses and disciplines (see Román, "Teaching Differences"). Much of the talk has followed thinking implicit in identity politics. Yarbro-Bejarano, for example, has argued that "the establishment of lesbian and gay studies within the university is important because of the enforced visibility and silence of lesbians and gays in our society. . . . The challenge remains to foreground the specificity of the oppression, subjectivity, and experience of lesbians and gays without reinscribing exclusionary gestures" ("Expanding the Categories," 131). It is precisely such talk that Olivia rejects.

46. David Román, "Speaking with the Dead," 171, 173.

47. Elizabeth Grosz, "Bodies and Pleasures in Queer Theory," 226.

48. Hartman and Messer-Davidow, "Introduction," 3.

49. See William Tierney, "Organizational Socialization in Higher Education."

50. Patricia Williams, *Seeing a Color-Blind Future*, 74.

51. Martin Jay, *Downcast Eyes*, 24.

52. Biddy Martin, "Sexualities without Genders," 105–106.

53. Roof and Wiegman, *Who Can Speak?*, x.

54. David Palumbo-Liu, "Historical Permutations of the Place of Race," 1078.

55. Judith Roof, "Buckling Down or Knuckling Under," 182. Indeed, the creation of a disciplinary location in many ways reiterates capitalism's appropriation of multiculturalism in its creation of new markets niches. In a late capitalist political economy that constructs freedom as individual choice—consumptive choice—differences become self-fashioned consumer lifestyles, as Clark argues in "Commodity Lesbianism," that are depoliticized as the marketplace appropriates (colonizes) subcultural practices of resistance under the guise of tolerance. See Hennessy, "Queer Visibility in Commodity Culture," for a discussion of the normalization of gays and lesbian through the commodification of the visible, which also controls what becomes visible.

56. Lauren Berlant, "National Brands/National Body," 175.

57. Michel de Certeau, *Culture in the Plural*, 145.

58. Giorgio Agamben, *Coming Community*, 43.

CHAPTER 5.
LESBIAN/INTELLECTUAL

1. I do not mean to leave the term "the self" as an unquestioned or stable category, for, as Anthony Giddens has argued, "[s]elf-identity . . . is *the self as*

reflexively understood by the person in terms of her or his biography" (*Modernity and Self-Identity*, 53). By his formulation, actors construct identities for the "self" that they understand themselves to have or to be; these selves have a degree of continuity across time and space but are continually reinterpreted reflexively. Thus, the understandings of self that Julie, Olivia, and Carol express are socially and historically constituted narrative understandings (re)constructed according to their lived experiences.

2. David Román, "Performing All Our Lives," 212.

3. For a cogent argument against subsuming lesbian under the queer mantle, see Jeffreys' "The Queer Disappearance of Lesbians: Sexuality in the Academy," in which she critiques the hegemony of male sexuality and cultural codes and the "feminism-free" (459) nature of much queer theorizing.

4. Foucault, *Discipline and Punish*, 200.

5. On identity politics' implication in lesbian-feminist literary practices in the 1970s and 1980s, see P. Bennett, "Lesbian Poetry in the United States"; and Faderman, "What is Lesbian Literature?" On the formation and practices of bar dyke and lesbian feminist communities, see Faderman, *Odd Girls and Twilight Lovers*; Franzen, "Differences and Identities"; Krieger, *Mirror Dance*; and Phelan, *Identity Politics*.

6. June Jordan, "Report from the Bahamas," 124.

7. See Ekua Omosupe, "Black/Lesbian/Bulldagger," for a critique of the universalization of lesbian culture, experience, and identity as white.

8. June Jordan, "Report from the Bahamas," 124. For accounts and discussion of the problems of privileging one category of difference over others, see Anzaldúa, ed., *Making Face, Making Soul*; Moraga, *Loving in the War Years*; Moraga and Anzaldúa, eds., *Bridge Called My Back*; and Hull, Scott, and Smith, eds., *All the Women Are White*.

9. Moraga, "La Güera," and Barbara and Beverly Smith, "Across the Kitchen Table," describe the isolation resulting from claiming lesbianism in African-American and communities of color. In "Lesbianism: An Act of Resistance," Clarke historicizes taboos against white-black lesbian relationships, both in lesbian and nonlesbian communities.

10. Hammonds, "Black (W)holes and the Geometry of Black Female Sexuality," 137.

11. Michele Wallace, *Invisibility Blues*, 135.

12. Laura Harris, "Queer Black Feminism," 4, 7. See also Phelan's discussion of Gloria Anzaldúa's "new mestiza," whose dislocation, or never fully belonging, functions as a source of strength and a resource for change. Phelan likens mestizaje to "the very transgression of essence," a formulation that recalls Trinh's "Inappropriate Other/Same" in its rejection of "the ideal of the unitary, harmonious self" ("Lesbians and Mestizas," 83, 84). Similarly, Leslie Bloom argues that recognizing non-unitary subjectivity "allows respect for the complexity of subjectivity and the validation of conflict as a source through which women become strong and learn to speak their own experiences" (*Under the Sign of Hope*, 93).

13. María Lugones, "Playfulness, 'World'-Traveling, and Loving Perception," 636.

14. Hazel Carby, "Politics of Difference," 84.

15. In coming to know Carol, I did not find myself as mired in the "why not (gay and) lesbian issues in your work?" question as I had with Julie (which I discuss below), although it is a logical question to ask of a person whose commitments are largely political and personal. The professional salience of her race and gender as she "came of age against the backdrop of affirmative action," as she puts it, made her foci on those dimensions of her experience seem logical. She is, however, moving to integrate some queer theory into an upcoming manuscript.

16. Toni Morrison, *Playing in the Dark*, xii.

17. Relatedly, Franzen identified disjunctures in lesbian subcultures in Albuquerque that made social or political solidarity difficult between "public" lesbian feminists, who were theoretical and political, and "closeted" lesbians, who had "little articulated analysis of their lives and their oppression" ("Differences and Identities," 904).

18. In "Passing," Carole-Anne Tyler has pointed to a countercultural propensity to privilege coming out or making difference visible as a representation of self that is authentic *and* a form of authentic resistance. However, "coming out" through visibility is no more authentic than remaining "in," for realist representations of the subject are impossible; there are always disjunctures between what is shown and what is seen.

19. In turning to writings on homosexuality and the Church, I have learned that Julie's response is not "atypical." While activist groups such as Dignity have been formed among practicing gay and lesbian Catholics and theological solutions have been sought by scholars, gay and lesbian Catholics appear to be faced with three choices: (1) to remain active in the Church but not in their homosexual lives; (2) to remain actively homosexual and to leave the Church; and, (3) to maintain active homosexual and Catholic lives (see Francoeur, "Two Different Worlds"; Milhaven, "How the Church Can Learn"; Nugent and Gramick, *Building Bridges*). Writers who speak of the viability of practicing both homosexuality and Catholicism speak in terms similar to Julie's, arguing that many practicing Catholics who agree with the church on one issue are likely to disagree on another (Gramick, "Rome Speaks"; Milhaven, "How the Church Can Learn"; Thompson, "View from the Pews"); morality does not reside in sexual acts per se, but in their meanings in specific relationships (Nugent and Gramick, *Building Bridges*); and Catholics can separate the doctrines of Church officials from faith experiences (Gramick, "Rome Speaks"). Gramick points out that several polls reveal that some fifty percent of U.S. Catholics accept homosexuality as a *private, individual* decision ("Rome Speaks," 99). However, Harris emphasizes, "the task of trying to put together the two things . . . [is] a lifetime's work. . . . [T]here may not be answers, only a new shaping of thoughts" ("Speaking," 115).

20. Audre Lorde, *Cancer Journals*, 47. Sandra Steingraber has said that the experience of breast cancer is a "profoundly gendered experience in that it requires a rethinking of the relationship between the body and the self and between the self and other people" ("We All Live Downwind," 45). It is not only a profoundly gendered experience but a profoundly individual, yet social, expe-

rience. As Susan Sontag has pointed out in *Illness as Metaphor*, cancer is laden with multiple personal, social, and moral meanings. Breasts as well carry meanings that are lived in personal and material ways. Thames and Gazzaniga's description of responses they received to a call for papers for *The Breast: An Anthology* reveals their complexity: "The scope of meaning people found in this gland amazed us: food, secrets, desire, power, a weapon, an accessory, loss, abundance, disinterest, life, death, joy, the heart" (ix).

21. See Butler and Rosenblum's *Cancer in Two Voices*, in which Sandra Butler described an "identity change" (54) in choosing to write about her cancer.

22. Foucault, *Use of Pleasure*, 11.

23. Lillian Faderman, *Odd Girls and Twilight Lovers*, 35. While Faderman has been criticized for overemphasizing medicoscientific texts and characterizing working-class lesbian subcultures as oppressive (see Martindale, *Un/Popular Culture*, 42), I find useful her understanding of the formation of communities as practices, responses to social and historical circumstances.

24. See the discussions in O'Brien, "Thing Not Named"; Vicinus, "Distance and Desire."

25. D'Emilio, *Sexual Politics*, 32.

26. Bonnie Zimmerman, "Politics of Transliteration," 268. "Lesbian community," Zimmerman has written, developed around "woman identification, cultural feminism, and separatism" ("Politics of Transliteration," 257).

27. As Faderman describes it, "As radicals, lesbian-feminists generally shared the intellectual Left's romance with the working class. Women who had the skills to make a living at nontraditional jobs—carpenters, house painters, welders—were far more politically correct than professionals, who were seen as having to compromise themselves in the system in order to advance" (*Odd Girls and Twilight Lovers*, 236). In addition, Kathleen Martindale has pointed out that lesbian feminism "reject[ed] high culture as elitist, popular or mass culture as mindless, and both as sexist and misogynist" (*Un/Popular Culture*, 13). The exclusion of professionals, intellectuals, and academics from what was constituted as the lesbian community continues to be reiterated in debates over privilege, authentic commitment to community and political organizing, and the type and location of work that is relevant to projects for change. See, for example, Kitzinger, "Beyond the Boundaries"; Krieger, *Mirror Dance*; and Phelan, *Identity Politics*.

28. As I discussed in chapter 1, the exclusions were eloquently critiqued by lesbians of color who did not fit assumed norms of race and class, later joined by "sex radicals" who critiqued cultural lesbian feminist ideals for identity and sexual practice. Even with the exclusions of lesbian feminist communities, writers such as Taylor and Rupp argue for their importance in promoting feminist practices, particularly during "periods of waning activity." They contend that within the "essentialism, separatism, and 'life-style politics'" for which cultural feminism is often critiqued, "the ideas, separatist strategies, primary relationships, and symbolic practices of community members reveal that these elements of lesbian feminist culture are what nourish and sustain feminist activism" ("Women's Culture and Feminist Activism," 34, 41). But, one must ask, what kind of activism does it sustain?

29. De Certeau's distinction between subculture and counterculture is revealing in this regard: "The former designates the culture of a subgroup, of a minority, and so on. The latter refers to the judgment that a majority makes of subcultures or subgroups and whose social implications the subgroups often confirm when they take them up in order to define themselves" (*Culture in the Plural*, 104).

30. Raymond Willliams, *Keywords*, 66.

31. Rinaldo Walcott, "Queer Texts and Performativity," 162.

32. Laura Harris, "Queer Black Feminism," 25.

33. Rinaldo Walcott, "Queer Texts and Performativity," 165.

34. Foucault, "Sex, Power and the Politics of Identity," 385.

35. Maurice Blanchot, *Unavowable Community*, 6, 43.

36. See Jacques Derrida, "Principle of Reason."

37. Gayle Rubin, "Interview," 92.

38. William Haver, "Queer Research," 284.

39. Victor Turner, *Anthropology of Performance*, 22, 76.

40. Renato Rosaldo, *Culture and Truth*, 107.

41. De Certeau, *Practice of Everyday Life*, xviii.

42. On nonunitary subjectivity in research relations, see Bloom, *Under the Sign of Hope*.

43. De Certeau, *Culture in the Plural*, 3, 8.

BIBLIOGRAPHY

Abelove, Henry, Michèle A. Barale, and David M. Halperin, eds. *The Lesbian and Gay Studies Reader*. New York: Routledge, 1993.

Adams, Kate, and Kim Emery. "Classroom Coming Out Stories: Practical Strategies for Productive Self-Disclosure." In *Tilting the Tower: Lesbians Teaching Queer Subjects*, edited by Linda Garber, 25–34. New York: Routledge, 1994.

Agamben, Giorgio. *The Coming Community*. Trans. Michael Hardt. Minneapolis: University of Minnesota Press, 1993.

Alcoff, Linda. "Cultural Feminism Versus Post-Structuralism: The Identity Crisis in Feminist Theory." *Signs: Journal of Women in Culture and Society* 13, no. 3 (1988): 405–436.

Alston, Kal. "A Unicorn's Memoirs: Solitude and the Life of Teaching and Learning." In *The Center of the Web: Women and Solitude*, edited by Delese Wear, 95–107. Albany: SUNY Press, 1993.

Anzaldúa, Gloria, ed. *Making Face, Making Soul = Haciendo Caras: Creative and Critical Perspectives by Feminists of Color*. San Francisco: Aunt Lute, 1990.

Association of American Colleges. *Integrity in the College Curriculum: A Report to the Academic Community*. Washington, D.C.: Association of American Colleges, 1985.

Astin, Alexander W. *Achieving Educational Excellence: A Critical Assessment of Priorities and Practices in Higher Education*. San Francisco: Jossey-Bass, 1988.

Barale, Michèle A. "The Romance of Class and Queers: Academic Erotic Zones." In *Tilting the Tower: Lesbians Teaching Queer Subjects*, edited by Linda Garber, 16–24. New York: Routledge, 1994.

Barthes, Roland. *S/Z*. New York: Hill & Wang, 1974.

———. "From Work to Text." In *Image/Music/Text*, 154–164. New York: Hill & Wang, 1977.

———. "Writers, Intellectuals, Teachers." In *Image/Music/Text*, 190–215. New York: Hill & Wang, 1977.

Bennett, Paula. "Lesbian Poetry in the United States, 1890–1990: A Brief Overview." In *Professions of Desire: Lesbian and Gay Studies in Literature*, edited by George E. Haggerty and Bonnie Zimmerman, 98–110. New York: Modern Language Association, 1995.

Bennett, William J. *To Reclaim a Legacy: Report on the Humanities in Higher Education*. Washington, D.C.: National Endowment for the Humanities, 1984.

Bensimon, Estella M. "Lesbian Existence and the Challenge to Normative Constructions of the Academy." *Journal of Education* 174, no. 3 (1992): 98–113.

Benstock, Shari, ed. *The Private Self: Theory and Practice of Women's Autobiographical Writings*. Chapel Hill: University of North Carolina Press, 1988.

Bergquist, William H. *The Four Cultures of the Academy: Insights and Strategies for Improving Leadership in Collegiate Organizations*. San Francisco: Jossey-Bass, 1992.

Berlant, Lauren. "National Brands/National Body: *Imitation of Life*." In *The Phantom Public Sphere*, edited by Bruce Robbins, 173–208. Minneapolis: University of Minnesota Press, 1993.

Bhabha, Homi. "The Third Space: Interview with Homi Bhabha." By Jonathan Rutherford. In *Identity: Community, Culture, Difference*, edited by Jonathan Rutherford, 207–221. London: Lawrence & Wishart, 1990.

Blanchot, Maurice. *The Unavowable Community*. Trans. Pierre Joris. Barrytown, N.Y.: Station Hill Press, 1988.

Bleich, David. *Know and Tell: A Writing Pedagogy of Disclosure, Genre, and Membership*. Portsmouth, N.H.: Boynton/Cook, 1998.

Bloom, Allan. *The Closing of the American Mind: How Higher Education Has Failed Democracy and Impoverished the Souls of Today's Students*. New York: Simon & Schuster, 1987.

Bloom, Leslie Rebecca. *Under the Sign of Hope: Feminist Methodology and Narrative Interpretation*. Albany: SUNY Press, 1998.

Bourdieu, Pierre. *Outline of a Theory of Practice*. Trans. Richard Nice. Cambridge: Cambridge University Press, 1977.

Brecht, Bertolt. *Brecht on Theatre: The Development of an Aesthetic*. Edited and translated by John Willett. New York: Hill & Wang, 1964.

Briton, Derek. "The Decentered Subject: Pedagogical Implications." *JCT: An Interdisciplinary Journal of Curriculum Studies* 11, no. 4 (1995): 57–73.

Britzman, Deborah P. "Could This Be Your Story? Guilty Readings and Other Ethnographic Dramas." Paper presented at the Bergamo Conference on Curriculum Theorizing, Dayton, Ohio, October, 1990.

———. "Is There a Queer Pedagogy; Or, Stop Reading Straight." *Educational Theory* 45, no. 2 (1995): 151–165.

———. *Lost Subjects, Contested Objects: Toward a Psychoanalytic Inquiry of Learning*. Albany: SUNY Press, 1998.

Britzman, Deborah P., and Alice J. Pitt. "Pedagogy and Transference: Casting the Past of Learning into the Presence of Teaching." *Theory into Practice* 35, no. 2 (1996): 117–123.

Brossard, Nicole. "Kind Skin My Mind." *Trivia* 12 (1988): 43–44.

Bruner, Jerome. "Narrative and Paradigmatic Ways of Knowing." In *Learning and Teaching the Ways of Knowing*, edited by Elliot W. Eisner, 97–115. Chicago: University of Chicago Press, 1985.

Brunner, Diane D. *Inquiry and Reflection: Framing Narrative Practice in Education*. Albany: SUNY Press, 1994.

Burbules, Nicholas. "Authority and the Tragic Dimension of Teaching. In *The Educational Conversation: Closing the Gap*, edited by James W. Garrison and Anthony J. Rud Jr., 29–40. Albany: SUNY Press, 1995.

Busia, Abena P. A. "Performance, Transcription and the Languages of the Self: Interrogating Identity as a 'Post-Colonial' Poet." In *Theorizing Black Femi-*

nisms: The Visionary Pragmatism of Black Women, edited by Stanlie M. James and Abena P. A. Busia, 203–213. New York: Routledge, 1993.

Butler, Judith. *Gender Trouble: Feminism and the Subversion of Identity*. New York: Routledge, 1990.

———. "Imitation and Gender Insubordination." In *The Lesbian and Gay Studies Reader*, edited by Henry Abelove, Michèle A. Barale, and David M. Halperin, 307–320. New York: Routledge, 1993.

———. *Bodies that Matter: On the Discursive Limits of "Sex."* New York: Routledge, 1993.

———. "For a Careful Reading." In *Feminist Contentions: A Philosophical Exchange*, edited by Seyla Benhabib, Judith Butler, Drucilla Cornell, and Nancy Fraser, 127–144. New York: Routledge, 1995.

———. *Excitable Speech: A Politics of the Performative*. New York: Routledge, 1997.

Butler, Sandra, and Barbara Rosenblum. *Cancer in Two Voices*. San Francisco: Spinsters, 1991.

Canaan, Joyce E. "Examining the Examination: Tracing the Effects of Pedagogic Authority on Cultural Studies Lecturers and Students." In *A Question of Discipline: Pedagogy, Power, and the Teaching of Cultural Studies*, edited by Joyce E. Canaan and Debbie Epstein, 157–177. Boulder: Westview, 1997.

Carby, Hazel. "The Politics of Difference." *Ms.*, July/August 1990, 84–85.

Carlson, Dennis. "Who Am I? Gay Identity and a Democratic Politics of the Self." In *Queer Theory in Education*, edited by Willliam F. Pinar, 107–119. Mahwah, N.J.: Lawrence Erlbaum, 1998.

Carnochan, W. B. *The Battleground of the Curriculum: Liberal Education and the American Experience*. Stanford, Calif.: Stanford University Press, 1993.

Certeau, Michel de. *The Practice of Everyday Life*. Trans. Steven F. Rendall. Berkeley: University of California Press, 1984.

———. *Heterologies: Discourse on the Other*. Trans. Brian Massumi. Minneapolis: University of Minnesota Press, 1986.

———. *The Writing of History*. Trans. Tom Conley. New York: Columbia University Press, 1988.

———. *Culture in the Plural*. Edited by Luce Giard. Trans. Tom Conley. Minneapolis: University of Minnesota Press, 1997.

Chang Hall, Lisa Kahaleole. "Compromising Positions." In *Beyond a Dream Deferred: Multicultural Education and the Politics of Excellence*, edited by Becky W. Thompson and Sangeeta Tyagi, 162–173. Minneapolis: University of Minnesota Press, 1993.

Chapkis, Wendy. "Explicit Instruction: Talking Sex in the Classroom." In *Tilting the Tower: Lesbians Teaching Queer Subjects*, edited by Linda Garber, 11–15. New York: Routledge, 1994.

Chauncey, George, Jr., Martin B. Duberman, and Martha Vicinus. Introduction to *Hidden from History: Reclaiming the Gay and Lesbian Past*, edited by Martin B. Duberman, Martha Vicinus, and George Chauncey Jr., 1–13. New York: New American Library, 1989.

Cheney, Lynne V. *50 Hours: A Core Curriculum for College Students*. Washington, D.C.: National Endowment for the Humanities, 1989.

Chopp, Rebecca S. *Saving Work: Feminist Practices of Theological Education.* Louisville, Ky.: Westminster John Knox Press, 1995.

Clandinin, D. Jean, and F. Michael Connelly. "Personal Experience Methods." In *Handbook of Qualitative Research*, edited by Norman K. Denzin and Yvonna S. Lincoln, 413–427. Thousand Oaks, Calif.: Sage, 1994.

Clark, Danae. "Commodity Lesbianism." In *The Lesbian and Gay Studies Reader*, edited by Henry Abelove, Michèle A. Barale, and David M. Halperin, 186–201. New York: Routledge, 1993.

Clarke, Cheryl. "Lesbianism: An Act of Resistance." In *This Bridge Called My Back: Writings by Radical Women of Color*, edited by Cherríe Moraga and Gloria Anzaldúa, 128–137. New York: Kitchen Table Women of Color Press, 1981.

Conquergood, Dwight. "Between Experience and Meaning: Performance as a Paradigm for Meaningful Action." In *Renewal and Revision: The Future of Interpretation*, edited by Ted Colson, 26–59. Denton, Tex.: Omega, 1986.

Crosby, Christina. "Dealing with Differences." In *Feminists Theorize the Political*, edited by Judith Butler and Joan W. Scott, 130–143. New York: Routledge, 1992.

Culler, Johnathan. *Framing the Sign: Criticism and Its Institutions.* Norman: University of Oklahoma Press, 1988.

Culley, Margo, and Catherine Portuges. *Gendered Subjects: The Dynamics of Feminist Teaching.* Boston: Routledge & Kegan Paul, 1985.

Daly, Mary. "Sin Big." *The New Yorker*, 26 February and 4 March 1996, 76–84.

D'Augelli, Anthony R. "Lesbians and Gay Men on Campus: Visibility, Empowerment, and Educational Leadership." *Peabody Journal of Education* 66, no. 3 (1991): 121–141.

Dawes, G. W. "Theology and Religious Studies in the University: 'Some Ambiguities' Revisited." *Religion* 26 (1996): 49–68.

D'Emilio, John. *Sexual Politics, Sexual Communities: The Making of a Homosexual Minority in the United States 1940–1970.* Chicago: The University of Chicago Press, 1983.

———. *Making Trouble: Essays on Gay History, Politics, and the University.* New York: Routledge, 1992.

Denzin, Norman. *Interpretive Biography.* Newbury Park, Calif.: Sage, 1989.

Derrida, Jacques. "The Principle of Reason: The University in the Eyes of Its Pupils." *diacritics* 13 (1983): 3–20.

Dhairyan, Sagri. "Racing the Lesbian, Dodging White Critics." In *The Lesbian Postmodern*, edited by Laura Doan, 25–46. New York: Columbia University Press, 1994.

D'Souza, Dinesh. *Illiberal Education: The Politics of Race and Sex on Campus.* New York: The Free Press, 1991.

Duberman, Martin. *About Time: Exploring the Gay Past.* New York: Meridian, 1991.

Duggan, Lisa. "Making It Perfectly Queer." In *Sex Wars: Sexual Dissent and Political Culture*, edited by Lisa Duggan and Nan Hunter, 155–172. New York: Routledge, 1995.

———. "Scholars and Sense." In *Sex Wars: Sexual Dissent and Political Culture*, edited by Lisa Duggan and Nan Hunter, 173–178. New York: Routledge, 1995.

Duster, Troy. "They're Taking Over! And Other Myths about Race on Campus." In *Higher Education under Fire: Politics, Economics, and the Crisis of the Humanities*, edited by Michael Bérubé and Cary Nelson, 276–283. New York: Routledge, 1995.

Ellsworth, Elizabeth. "Why Doesn't This Feel Empowering? Working through the Repressive Myths of Critical Pedagogy." *Harvard Educational Review* 59, no. 3 (1989): 297–324.

———. *Teaching Positions: Difference, Pedagogy, and the Power of Address.* New York: Teachers College Press, 1997.

Epstein, Debbie. "The Voice of Authority: On Lecturing in Cultural Studies." In *A Question of Discipline: Pedagogy, Power, and the Teaching of Cultural Studies*, edited by Joyce E. Canaan and Debbie Epstein, 178–191. Boulder: Westview, 1997.

Escoffier, Jeffrey. "Inside the Ivory Closet: The Challenges Facing Lesbian and Gay Studies." *Outlook* 10 (1990): 40–48.

———. "Generations and Paradigms: Mainstreams in Lesbian and Gay Studies." In *Gay and Lesbian Studies*, edited by Henry L. Minton, 7–26. Binghamton, N.Y.: Haworth Press, 1992.

Faderman, Lillian. *Surpassing the Love of Men: Romantic Friendship and Love between Women from the Renaissance to the Present.* New York: William Morrow, 1981.

———. *Odd Girls and Twilight Lovers: A History of Lesbian Life in Twentieth-Century America.* New York: Columbia University Press, 1991.

———. "What Is Lesbian Literature? Forming a Historical Canon." In *Professions of Desire: Lesbian and Gay Studies in Literature*, edited by George E. Haggerty and Bonnie Zimmerman, 49–59. New York: Modern Language Association, 1995.

Farmer, Ruth. "Place but Not Importance: The Race for Inclusion in Academe." In *Spirit, Space and Survival: African American Women in (White) Academe*, edited by Joy James and Ruth Farmer, 196–217. New York: Routledge, 1993.

Felman, Shoshana. "Psychoanalysis and Education: Teaching Terminable and Interminable." *Yale French Studies* 63 (1982): 21–44.

Finke, Laurie. "Knowledge as Bait: Feminism, Voice, and the Pedagogical Unconscious." *College English* 55, no. 1 (1993): 7–27.

Foucault, Michel. *Discipline and Punish: The Birth of the Prison.* Trans. Alan Sheridan. New York: Pantheon, 1977.

———. *The History of Sexuality: An Introduction.* Vol. 1. Trans. Robert Hurley. New York: Vintage, 1978.

———. *The Use of Pleasure: The History of Sexuality.* Vol. 2. Trans. Robert Hurley. New York: Vintage, 1984.

———. "What Is an Author?" In *Critical Theory since 1965*, edited by Hazard Adams and Leroy Searle, 138–148. Tallahassee: Florida State University Press, 1986.

———. "The Concern for Truth." Interview by François Ewald. Trans. Alan Sheridan. In *Michel Foucault: Politics, Philosophy, Culture: Interviews and Other Writings 1977–1984*, edited by Lawrence D. Kritzman, 255–267. New York: Routledge, 1988.

———. "Sexual Choice, Sexual Act: Foucault and Homosexuality." Interview and Translation by James O'Higgins. In *Michel Foucault: Politics, Philosophy, Culture: Interviews and Other Writings 1977–1984*, edited by Lawrence D. Kritzman, 286–303. New York: Routledge, 1988.

———. "The Masked Philosopher." Trans. John Johnston. In *Foucault Live: Interviews, 1966–1984*, edited by Sylvere Lotringer, 302–307. New York: Semiotext(e), 1989.

———. "Sex, Power and the Politics of Identity." Trans. Lysa Hochroth and John Johnston. In *Foucault Live: Interviews, 1966–1984*, edited by Sylvere Lotringer, 382–390. New York: Semiotext(e), 1989.

Francoeur, Robert. "Two Different Worlds, Two Different Moralities." In *The Vatican and Homosexuality: Reactions to the "Letter to the Bishops of the Catholic Church on the Pastoral Care of Homosexual Persons,"* edited by Jeannine Gramick and Pat Furey, 189–200. New York: Cross Road, 1988.

Frank, Arthur W. "Lecturing and Transference: The Undercover Work of Pedagogy." In *Pedagogy: The Question of Impersonation*, edited by Jane Gallop, 28–35. Bloomington: Indiana University Press, 1995.

Franzen, Trisha. "Differences and Identities: Feminism and the Albuquerque Lesbian Community." *Signs* 18, no. 4 (1993): 891–906.

Fuss, Diana. *Essentially Speaking: Feminism, Nature, and Difference.* New York: Routledge, 1989.

Gadamer, Hans-Georg. *Truth and Method.* Rev. ed. Trans. Joel Weinsheimer and Donald. G. Marshall. New York: Continuum, 1989.

Gal, Susan. "Between Speech and Silence: The Problematics of Research on Language and Gender." In *Gender at the Crossroads of Knowledge: Feminist Anthropology in the Postmodern Era*, edited by Micaela di Leonardo, 175–203. Berkeley: University of California Press, 1991.

Gallop, Jane. *Around 1981: Academic Feminist Literary Theory.* New York: Routledge, 1992.

———. "Im-personation: A Reading in the Guise of an Introduction." In *Pedagogy: The Question of Impersonation*, edited by Jane Gallop, 1–18. Bloomington: Indiana University Press, 1995.

Garber, Linda, ed. *Tilting the Tower: Lesbians Teaching Queer Subjects.* New York: Routledge, 1994.

Gay Academic Union. *The Universities and the Gay Experience: Proceedings of the Conference Sponsored by the Women and Men of the Gay Academic Union, November 23 and 24, 1973.* New York: Gay Academic Union, 1974.

Giddens, Anthony. *The Constitution of Society.* Berkeley: University of California, 1984.

———. *Modernity and Self-Identity: Self and Society in the Late Modern Age.* Stanford, Calif.: Stanford University Press, 1991.

Gillan, Garth. "Foucault's Philosophy." In *The Final Foucault*, edited by James Bernauer and David Rasmussen, 34–44. Cambridge, Mass.: MIT Press, 1988.

Giroux, Henry A. *Teachers as Intellectuals: Toward a Critical Pedagogy of Learning.* Granby, Mass.: Bergin & Garvey, 1988.

———. "Living Dangerously: Identity Politics and the New Cultural Racism." In *Between Borders: Pedagogy and the Politics of Cultural Studies,* edited by Henry A. Giroux and Peter McLaren, 29–55. New York: Routledge, 1994.

———. "Academics as Public Intellectuals: Rethinking Classroom Politics. In *PC Wars: Politics and Theory in the Academy,* edited by Jeffrey Williams, 294–307. New York: Routledge, 1995.

Gitlin, Andrew, ed. *Power and Method: Political Activism and Educational Research.* New York: Routledge, 1994.

Goffman, Erving. *The Presentation of Self in Everyday Life.* New York: Doubleday, 1959.

———. *Stigma: Notes on the Management of Spoiled Identity.* Englewood Cliffs, N.J.: Prentice Hall, 1963.

———. *Forms of Talk.* Philadelphia: University of Pennsylvania Press, 1981.

Gordon, Beverly M. "Speaking in Tongues: An African-American Woman in the World and the Academy." In *The Center of the Web: Women and Solitude,* edited by Delese Wear, 153–169. Albany: SUNY Press, 1993.

Graham, Robert J. *Reading and Writing the Self: Autobiography in Education and the Curriculum.* New York: Teachers College Press, 1991.

Gramick, Jeannine. "Rome Speaks, the Church Responds." In *The Vatican and Homosexuality: Reactions to the "Letter to the Bishops of the Catholic Church on the Pastoral Care of Homosexual Persons,"* edited by Jeannine Gramick and Pat Furey, 93–104. New York: Cross Road, 1988.

Greene, Gayle. "Looking at History." In *Changing Subjects: The Making of Feminist Literary Criticism,* edited by Gayle Greene and Coppélia Kakn, 4–27. New York: Routledge, 1993.

Griffin, Pat. "Identity Management Strategies among Lesbian and Gay Educators." *Qualitative Studies in Education* 4, no. 3 (1991): 189–202.

Grossberg, Lawrence. "Introduction: Bringin' It All Back Home: Pedagogy and Cultural Studies." In *Between Borders: Pedagogy and the Politics of Cultural Studies,* edited by Henry A. Giroux and Peter McLaren, 1–25. New York: Routledge, 1994.

Grosz, Elizabeth. "Bodies and Pleasures in Queer Theory." In *Who Can Speak? Authority and Critical Identity,* edited by Judith Roof and Robyn Wiegman, 221–230. Urbana: University of Illinois Press, 1995.

Gumport, Patricia J. "Curricula as Signposts of Cultural Change." *The Review of Higher Education* 12, no. 1 (1988): 49–61.

———. "Feminist Scholarship as Vocation." *Higher Education* 20 (1990): 231–243.

Gustafson, James M. "The Study of Religion in Colleges and Universities: A Practical Commentary." In *The Study of Religion in Colleges and Universities,* edited by Paul Ramsey and John F. Wilson, 330–346. Princeton: Princeton University Press.

Haggerty, George E. "'Promoting Homosexuality' in the Classroom." In *Professions of Desire: Lesbian and Gay Studies in Literature,* edited by George

E. Haggerty and Bonnie Zimmerman, 1–18. New York: Modern Language Association, 1995.

Haggerty, George E., and Bonnie Zimmerman, eds. *Professions of Desire: Lesbian and Gay Studies in Literature.* New York: Modern Language Association, 1995.

Hammersley, Martyn, and Paul Atkinson. *Ethnography: Principles in Practice.* 2nd ed. New York: Routledge, 1995.

Hammonds, Evelynn. "Black (W)holes and the Geometry of Black Female Sexuality." *differences: A Journal of Feminist Cultural Studies* 6, nos. 2–3 (1994): 125–145.

Harris, Laura Alexandra. "Queer Black Feminism: The Pleasure Principle." *Feminist Review* 54 (1996): 3–30.

Harris, Peter E. B. "Speaking the Truth in Love." In *The Vatican and Homosexuality: Reactions to the "Letter to the Bishops of the Catholic Church on the Pastoral Care of Homosexual Persons,"* edited by Jeannine Gramick and Pat Furey, 112–118. New York: Cross Road, 1988.

Hartman, Joan E., and Ellen Messer-Davidow. "Introduction: A Position Statement." In *(En)gendering Knowledge: Feminists in Academe,* edited by Joan E. Hartman and Ellen Messer-Davidow, 1–7. Knoxville: University of Tennessee Press, 1991.

Harvey, Elizabeth. "Trope." In *Encyclopedia of Contemporary Literary Theory: Approaches, Scholars, Terms,* edited by Irene R. Makaryk, 647–649. Toronto: University of Toronto Press, 1993.

Haver, William. "Queer Research; Or, How to Practise Invention to the Brink of Intelligibility." In *The Eight Technologies of Otherness,* edited by Sue Golding, 277–292. New York: Routledge, 1997.

Hennessy, Rosemary. "Queer Visibility in Commodity Culture." In *Social Postmodernism: Beyond Identity Politics,* edited by Linda Nicholson and Steven Seidman, 142–183. Cambridge: Cambridge University Press, 1995.

Hodder, Ian. "The Interpretation of Documents and Material Culture." In *Handbook of Qualitative Research,* edited by Norman K. Denzin and Yvonna S. Lincoln, 393–402. Thousand Oaks, Calif.: Sage, 1994.

Hoodfar, Homa. "Feminist Anthropology and Critical Pedagogy: The Anthropology of Classrooms' Excluded Voices." *Canadian Journal of Education* 17, no. 3 (1992): 303–320.

hooks, bell. *Teaching to Transgress: Education as the Practice of Freedom.* New York: Routledge, 1994.

hooks, bell, and Cornel West. *Breaking Bread: Insurgent Black Intellectual Life.* Boston: South End Press, 1991.

Hull, Gloria T., Patricia Bell Scott, and Barbara Smith, eds. *All the Women Are White, All the Blacks Are Men, but Some of Us Are Brave: Black Women's Studies.* Old Westbury, N.Y.: The Feminist Press, 1982.

Hunnisett, Rowena J. "Developing Phenomenological Method for Researching Lesbian Existence." *Canadian Journal of Counseling* 20, no. 4 (1986): 255–268.

Jaggar, Alison M. *Feminist Politics and Human Nature.* Totowa, N.J.: Rowman and Allanheld, 1983.

James, Joy. "Teaching Theory, Talking Community." In *Spirit, Space, and Survival: African American Women in (White) Academe*, edited by Joy James and Ruth Farmer, 118–135. New York: Routledge, 1993.

Jay, Martin. *Downcast Eyes: The Denigration of Vision in Twentieth-Century French Thought*. Berkeley: University of California Press, 1993.

Jeffreys, Sheila. "The Queer Disappearance of Lesbians: Sexuality in the Academy." *Women's Studies International Forum* 17, no. 5 (1994): 459–472.

Johnson, Cheryl. "Disinfecting Dialogues." In *Pedagogy: The Question of Impersonation*, edited by Jane Gallop, 129–137. Bloomington: Indiana University Press, 1995.

Jordan, June. "Report from the Bahamas." In *Women's Voices: Visions and Perspectives*, edited by Pat Hoy II, Esther Schor, and Robert Di Yonni, 119–126. New York: McGraw-Hill, 1990.

Karamcheti, Indira. "Caliban in the Classroom." In *Pedagogy: The Question of Impersonation*, edited by Jane Gallop, 138–146. Bloomington: Indiana University Press, 1995.

Keller, Rosemary Skinner. "Forum: Female Experience in American Religion." *Religion and American Culture: A Journal of Interpretation* 5, no. 1 (1995): 1–21.

Khayatt, Didi. "Sex and the Teacher: Should We Come Out in Class?" *Harvard Educational Review* 67, no. 1 (1997): 126–143.

Kimball, Roger. *Tenured Radicals: How Politics Has Corrupted Our Higher Education*. New York: Harper & Row, 1990.

Kitzinger, Celia. "Beyond the Boundaries: Lesbians in Academe." In *Storming the Tower: Women in the Academic World*, edited by Suzanne S. Lie and Virgina E. O'Leary, 163–177. New York: Kogan Page, 1990.

Kleinman, Sherryl, and Martha A. Copp. *Emotions and Fieldwork*. Newbury Park, Calif.: Sage, 1993.

Krieger, Susan. *The Mirror Dance: Identity in a Women's Community*. Philadelphia: Temple University Press, 1983.

Kritzman, Lawrence D. "Introduction: Foucault and the Politics of Experience." In *Michel Foucault: Politics, Philosophy, Culture: Interviews and Other Writings 1977–1984*, edited by Lawrence D. Kritzman, ix–xxvi. New York: Routledge, 1988.

Lanove, Nancy. "Fighting Spirit." In *Cancer as a Women's Issue: Scratching the Surface*, edited by Midge Stocker, 59–68. Chicago: Third Side Press, 1991.

Lather, Patti. *Getting Smart: Feminist Research and Pedagogy with/in the Postmodern*. New York: Routledge, 1991.

Lauretis, Teresa de. "Feminist Studies/Critical Studies: Issues, Terms, and Contexts." In *Feminist Studies: Critical Studies*, edited by Teresa de Lauretis, 1–19. Bloomington: Indiana University Press, 1986.

Lincoln, Yvonna S., and Egon G. Guba. *Naturalistic Inquiry*. Beverly Hills, Calif.: Sage, 1985.

Litvak, Joseph. "Pedagogy and Sexuality." In *Professions of Desire: Lesbian and Gay Studies in Literature*, edited by George E. Haggerty and Bonnie Zimmerman, 19–30. New York: Modern Language Association, 1995.

Lorde, Audre. *The Cancer Journals*. San Francisco: Spinsters/Aunt Lute, 1980.

Lugones, María. "Playfulness, 'World'-Travelling, and Loving Perception." In *The Woman that I Am: The Literature and Culture of Women of Color*, edited by D. Soyini Madison, 626–638. New York: St. Martin's Press, 1994.

Lynch, Michael. "Last Onsets: Teaching with AIDS." *Profession 1990* (1990), 32–36.

Lyotard, Jean-François. *The Postmodern Condition: A Report on Knowledge*. Trans. Geoff Bennington and Brian Massumi. Minneapolis: University of Minnesota Press, 1979.

———. *Political Writings*. Trans. Bill Readings and Kevin Paul. Minneapolis: University of Minnesota Press, 1993.

Maher, Frances A., and Mary Kay Thompson Tetreault. *The Feminist Classroom*. New York: Basic Books, 1994.

Marcus, George E., and Michael J. Fischer. *Anthropology as Cultural Critique: An Experimental Moment in the Human Sciences*. Chicago: University of Chicago Press, 1986.

Marotta, Toby. *The Politics of Homosexuality*. Boston: Houghton Mifflin, 1981.

Marsden, George M. *The Soul of the American University: From Protestant Establishment to Established Nonbelief*. New York: Oxford University Press, 1994.

Martin, Biddy. "Sexualities without Genders and Other Queer Utopias." *diacritics* 24, nos. 2–3 (1994): 104–121.

Martindale, Kathleen. *Un/Popular Culture: Lesbian Writing after the Sex Wars*. Albany: SUNY Press, 1997.

McGill, Arthur C. "The Ambiguous Position of Christian Theology." In *The Study of Religion in Colleges and Universities*, edited by Paul Ramsey and John F. Wilson, 105–138. Princeton: Princeton University Press.

McLaughlin, Thomas. "Figurative Language." In *Critical Terms for Literary Study*. 2nd ed., edited by Frank Lentricchia and Thomas McLaughlin, 80–90. Chicago: University of Chicago Press, 1995.

McNaron, Toni A. H. *Poisoned Ivy: Lesbian and Gay Academics Confronting Homophobia*. Philadelphia: Temple University Press, 1997.

Messer-Davidow, Ellen. "Know-How." In *(En)gendering Knowledge: Feminists in Academe*, edited by Joan E. Hartman and Ellen Messer-Davidow, 281–309. Knoxville: University of Tennessee Press, 1991.

———. "Manufacturing the Attack on Liberalized Higher Education." *Social Text* 11 (1993): 40–80.

Milem, Jeffrey F., and Helen S. Astin. "The Changing Composition of the Faculty: What Does It Really Mean for Diversity?" *Change*, March/April 1993, 21–27.

Milhaven, J. Giles. "How the Church Can Learn from Gay and Lesbian Experience." In *The Vatican and Homosexuality: Reactions to the "Letter to the Bishops of the Catholic Church on the Pastoral Care of Homosexual Persons,"* edited by Jeannine Gramick and Pat Furey, 216–223. New York: Cross Road, 1988.

Miller, D. A. *The Novel and the Police*. Berkeley: University of California Press, 1988.

Miller, J. Hillis. "Literary Study in the Transnational University." *Profession 1996* (1996), 6–14.

Mintz, Beth and Esther Rothblum, eds. *Lesbians in Academia: Degrees of Freedom.* New York: Routledge, 1997.

Modern Language Association. "The MLA's 1993–94 Survey of PhD Placement: Major Findings." *MLA Newsletter* 27, no. 4 (1995): 1–3.

Mohanty, Chandra Talpade. "On Race and Voice: Challenges for Liberal Education in the 1990s." In *Between Borders: Pedagogy and the Politics of Cultural Studies,* edited by Henry A. Giroux and Peter McLaren, 145–166. New York: Routledge, 1994.

Moore, Kathryn M. and Mary Ann D. Sagaria. "The Situation of Women in Research Universities in the United States: Within the Inner Circles of Academic Power." In *Women in Higher Education: A Feminist Perspective,* edited by Judith S. Glazer, Estela M. Bensimon, and Barbara K. Townsend, 227–240. Needham Heights, Mass.: Association for the Study of Higher Education, 1993.

Moraga, Cherríe. "La Güera." In *This Bridge Called My Back: Writings by Radical Women of Color,* edited by Cherríe Moraga and Gloria Anzaldúa, 27–34. New York: Kitchen Table Women of Color Press, 1981.

———. *Loving in the War Years: Lo Que Nunca Pasó por sus Labios.* Boston: South End Press, 1983.

Moraga, Cherríe, and Gloria Anzaldúa, eds. *This Bridge Called My Back: Writings by Radical Women of Color.* New York: Kitchen Table Women of Color Press, 1981.

Morgan, Meg. "Voices in the News." In *Voices on Voice: Perspectives, Definitions, Inquiry,* edited by Kathleen Blake Yancey, 97–110. Urbana, Ill.: NCTE, 1994.

Morrison, Toni. *Playing in the Dark: Whiteness and the Literary Imagination.* Cambridge, Mass.: Harvard University Press, 1992.

Moses, Yolanda T. *Black Women in Academe: Issues and Strategies.* Washington, D.C.: Association of American Colleges, 1989.

Murray, Heather. "Charisma and Authority in Literary Study and Theory Study." In *Theory/Pedagogy/Politics: Texts for Change,* edited by Donald Morton and Mas'ud Zavarzadeh, 187–200. Urbana: University of Illinois Press, 1991.

Nelson, Cary, and Michael Bérubé. "Introduction: A Report from the Front." In *Higher Education under Fire: Politics, Economics, and the Crisis of the Humanities,* edited by Michael Bérubé and Cary Nelson, 1–32. New York: Routledge, 1995.

Newfield, Christopher. "What Was 'Political Correctness'? Race, the Right, and Managerial Democracy in the Humanities." In *PC Wars: Politics and Theory in the Academy,* edited by Jeffrey Williams, 109–145. New York: Routledge, 1995.

Norris, Kathleen. *Dakota: A Spiritual Geography.* New York: Ticknor & Fields, 1993.

Nugent, Robert, and Jeannine Gramick. *Building Bridges: Gay and Lesbian Reality and the Catholic Church.* Mystic, Conn.: Twenty-third Publications, 1992.

O'Barr, Jean F. *Feminism in Action: Building Institutions and Community through Women's Studies.* Chapel Hill: University of North Carolina Press, 1994.

O'Brien, Sharon. "'The Thing Not Named': Willa Cather as Lesbian Writer." In *The Lesbian Issue: Essays from Signs,* edited by Estelle B. Freedman, Barbara C. Gelpi, Susan L. Johnson, and Kathleen M. Weston, 67–90. Chicago: University of Chicago Press, 1985.

O'Leary, Virigina E., and Judith M. Mitchell. "Women Connecting with Women: Networks and Mentors in the United States." In *Storming the Tower: Women in the Academic World,* edited by Suzanne S. Lie and Virginia E. O'Leary, 58–74. New York: Kogan Page, 1990.

Omosupe, Ekua. "Black/Lesbian/Bulldagger." *differences: A Journal of Feminist Cultural Studies* 3, no. 2 (1991): 101–111.

Palumbo-Liu, David. "Historical Permutations of the Place of Race." *PMLA* 111, no. 5 (1996): 1075–1078.

Patton, Cindy. "Performativity and Spatial Distinction: The End of AIDS Epidemiology." In *Performativity and Performance,* edited by Andrew Parker and Eve Sedgwick, 173–196. New York: Routledge, 1995.

Penley, Constance. "Teaching in Your Sleep: Feminism and Psychoanalysis." In *Theory in the Classroom,* edited by Cary Nelson, 129–148. Urbana: University of Illinois Press, 1986.

Phelan, Shane. *Identity Politics: Lesbian Feminism and the Limits of Community.* Philadelphia: Temple University Press, 1989.

———. "Lesbians and Mestizas: Appropriation and Equivalence." In *Playing with Fire: Queer Politics, Queer Theories,* edited by Shane Phelan, 75–95. New York: Routledge, 1997.

Pineau, Elyse Lamm. "Teaching is Performance: Reconceptualizing a Problematic Metaphor." *American Educational Research Journal* 31, no. 1 (1994): 3–25.

Piven, Frances Fox. "Academic Freedom and Political Dissent." In *Regulating the Intellectuals: Perspectives on Academic Freedom in the 1980s,* edited by Craig Kaplan and Ellen Schrecker, 17–23. New York: Praeger, 1983.

Plaskow, Judith. "Roundtable Discussion: What's in a Name? Exploring the Dimension of What 'Feminist Studies in Religion' Means." *Journal of Feminist Studies in Religion* 11, no. 1 (1995): 111–136.

Pratt, Mary Louise. "Humanities for the Future: Reflections on the Western Culture Debate at Stanford." In *The Politics of Liberal Education,* edited by Daryl J. Gless and Barbara Herrnstein Smith, 13–31. Durham: Duke University Press, 1992.

Radhakrishnan, R. "Toward an Effective Intellectual: Foucault or Gramsci?" In *Intellectuals: Aesthetics, Politics, Academics,* edited by Bruce Robbins, 57–99. Minneapolis: University of Minnesota Press, 1990.

———. "Canonicity and Theory: Toward a Post-Structuralist Pedagogy." In *Theory/Pedagogy/Politics: Texts for Change,* edited by Donald Morton and Mas'ud Zavarzadeh, 112–135. Urbana: University of Illinois Press, 1991.

Readings, Bill. *The University in Ruins.* Cambridge, Mass.: Harvard University Press, 1996.

Reich, Rob. "Confusion about the Socratic Method: Socratic Paradoxes and Contemporary Invocations of Socrates." In *Philosophy of Education, 1998,* edited by Steven Tozer, 68–78. Urbana, Ill.: Philosophy of Education Society, 1999.

Reyes, María, and John J. Halcón. "Racism in Academia: The Old Wolf Revisited." *Harvard Educational Review* 58, no. 3 (1988): 299–313.

Rhoads, Robert. *Coming Out in College: The Struggle for a Queer Identity.* Westport, Conn.: Bergin & Garvey, 1994.

Rich, Adrienne. "Compulsory Heterosexuality and Lesbian Existence." In *The Lesbian and Gay Studies Reader,* edited by Henry Abelove, Michèle A. Barale, and David M. Halperin, 227–254. New York: Routledge, 1993.

———. "Resisting Amnesia: History and Personal Life." In *Blood, Bread, and Poetry: Selected Prose 1979–1985,* 136–155. New York: W. W. Norton, 1986.

———. "Invisibility in Academe." In *Blood, Bread, and Poetry: Selected Prose 1979–1985,* 198–201. New York: W. W. Norton, 1986.

———. *What Is Found There: Notebooks on Poetry and Politics.* New York: W. W. Norton, 1993.

Roach, Joseph. "Culture and Performance in the Circum-Atlantic World." In *Performativity and Performance,* edited by Andrew Parker and Eve Sedgwick, 45–63. New York: Routledge, 1995.

Robbins, Bruce. Introduction to *Intellectuals: Aesthetics, Politics, Academics,* ix–xxvii. Minneapolis: University of Minnesota Press, 1990.

Román, David. "Performing All Our Lives: AIDS, Performance, Community." In *Critical Theory and Performance,* edited by Janelle G. Reinelt and Joseph R. Roach, 208–221. Ann Arbor: The University of Michigan Press, 1992.

———. "Speaking with the Dead." In *Who Can Speak? Authority and Critical Identity,* edited by Judith Roof and Robyn Wiegman, 165–179. Urbana: University of Illinois Press, 1995.

———. "Teaching Differences: Theory and Practice in a Lesbian and Gay Studies Seminar." In *Professions of Desire: Lesbian and Gay Studies in Literature,* edited by George E. Haggerty and Bonnie Zimmerman, 113–123. New York: Modern Language Association, 1995.

Roof, Judith. "Lesbians and Lyotard: Legitimation and the Politics of the Name." In *The Lesbian Postmodern,* edited by Laura Doan, 47–66. New York: Columbia University Press, 1994.

———. "Buckling Down or Knuckling Under: Discipline or Punish in Gay and Lesbian Studies." In *Who Can Speak? Authority and Critical Identity,* edited by Judith Roof and Robyn Wiegman, 180–192. Urbana: University of Illinois Press, 1995.

Roof, Judith, and Robyn Wiegman, eds. *Who Can Speak? Authority and Critical Identity.* Urbana: University of Illinois Press, 1995.

Rorty, Richard. "Method and Morality." In *Social Science as Moral Inquiry,* edited by Norma Haan, Robert N. Bellah, Paul Rabinow, and William H. Sullivan, 155–176. New York: Columbia University Press, 1983.

Rosaldo, Renato. *Culture and Truth: The Remaking of Social Analysis.* Boston: Beacon Press, 1989.

Ross, Andrew. *No Respect: Intellectuals and Popular Culture.* New York: Routledge, 1989.

Rothblum, Esther D. "Lesbians in Academia." *National Women's Studies Association Journal* 7, no. 1 (1995): 123–130.

Rubin, Gayle. "Interview: Sexual Traffic." By Judith Butler. *differences: A Journal of Feminist Cultural Studies* 6, nos. 2–3 (1994): 62–99.

Sabloff, Paula W. "Another Reason Why State Legislators Will Continue to Restrict Public University Autonomy." *The Review of Higher Education* 20, no. 2 (1997): 141–162.

Said, Edward. "Intellectuals in the Post-Colonial World." *Salmagundi* 70–71 (1986): 44–64.

———. "American Intellectuals and Middle East Politics." In *Intellectuals: Aesthetics, Politics, Academics,* edited by Bruce Robbins, 135–151. Minneapolis: University of Minnesota Press, 1990.

Salvio, Paula M. "Transgressive Daughters: Student Autobiography and the Project of Self-Creation." *Cambridge Journal of Education* 20, no. 3 (1990): 283–289.

———. "On the Forbidden Pleasures and Dangers of Covert Reading." *English Quarterly* 27, no. 3 (1995): 8–15.

Sandler, Bernice. "The Campus Climate Revisited: Chilly for Women Faculty, Administrators, and Graduate Students." In *Women in Higher Education: A Feminist Perspective,* edited by Judith S. Glazer, Estela M. Bensimon, and Barbara K. Townsend, 175–203. Needham Heights, Mass.: Association for the Study of Higher Education, 1993.

Sandoval, Chela. "Feminism and Racism: A Report on the 1981 National Women's Studies Association Conference." In *Making Face, Making Soul = Haciendo Caras: Creative and Critical Perspectives by Feminists of Color,* edited by Gloria Anzaldúa, 55–71. San Francisco: Aunt Lute, 1990.

Saslow, James W. "Lavendar Academia Debates Its Role: Gay and Lesbian Studies Programs Experience Growing Pains." *Advocate,* 24 September 1991, 66–69.

Sayre, Henry. "Performance." In *Critical Terms for Literary Study,* edited by Frank Lentricchia and Thomas McLaughlin, 91–104. Chicago: University of Chicago Press, 1990.

Schor, Naomi, and Elizabeth Weed, eds. Special Issue: "More Gender Trouble: Feminism Meets Queer Theory." *differences: A Journal of Feminist Cultural Studies* 6, nos. 2–3 (1994).

Scott, Joan W. "Deconstructing Equality-Versus-Difference: Or, the Uses of Poststructuralist Theory for Feminism." *Feminist Studies* 14, no. 1 (1988): 33–50.

———. "Experience." In *Feminists Theorize the Political,* edited by Judith Butler and Joan W. Scott, 22–40. New York: Routledge, 1992.

———. "The Rhetoric of Crisis in Higher Education." In *Higher Education under Fire: Politics, Economics, and the Crisis of the Humanities,* edited by Michael Bérubé and Cary Nelson, 293–304. New York: Routledge, 1995.

Sears, James T. "Researching the Other/Searching for Self: Qualitative Research on [Homo]sexuality in Education." *Theory into Practice* 31, no. 2 (1992): 147–156.

Sedgwick, Eve Kosofsky. *Epistemology of the Closet*. Berkeley: University of California Press, 1990.

———. *Tendencies*. Durham: Duke University Press, 1993.

Seidman, Irving E. *Interviewing as Qualitative Research: A Guide for Researchers in Education and the Social Sciences*. New York: Teachers College Press, 1991.

Seidman, Steven. "Identity Politics in a 'Postmodern' Gay Culture: Some Historical and Conceptual Notes." In *Fear of a Queer Planet: Politics and Social Theory*, edited by Michael Warner, 105–142. Minneapolis: University of Minnesota Press, 1993.

———. "Deconstructing Queer Theory or the Under-Theorization of the Social and the Ethical." In *Social Postmodernism: Beyond Identity Politics*, edited by Linda Nicholson and Steven Seidman, 116–141. Cambridge: Cambridge University Press, 1995.

Sewell, William H. "A Theory of Structure: Duality, Agency, and Transformation." *American Journal of Sociology* 98, no. 1 (1992): 1–29.

Showalter, Elaine, ed. *The New Feminist Criticism: Essays on Women, Literature, and Theory*. New York: Pantheon Books, 1985.

Showalter, Elaine. "A Criticism of Our Own: Autonomy and Assimilation in Afro-American and Feminist Literary Theory." In *Feminisms: An Anthology of Literary Theory and Criticism*, edited by Robyn R. Warhol and Diane Price Herndl, 168–188. New Brunswick, N.J.: Rutgers University Press, 1991.

Shumway, David R. "The Star System in Literary Studies." *PMLA* 112, no. 1 (1997): 85–100.

Simon, Roger I. "Face to Face with Alterity: Postmodern Jewish Identity and the Eros of Pedagogy." In *Pedagogy: The Question of Impersonation*, edited by Jane Gallop, 90–105. Bloomington: Indiana University Press, 1995.

Smith, Barbara. "Toward a Black Feminist Criticism." In *The New Feminist Criticism: Essays on Women, Literature, and Theory*, edited by Elaine Showalter, 168–185. New York: Pantheon, 1985.

Smith, Barbara, and Beverly Smith. "Across the Kitchen Table: A Sister-to-Sister Dialogue." In *This Bridge Called My Back: Writings by Radical Women of Color*, edited by Cherríe Moraga and Gloria Anzaldúa, 113–127. New York: Kitchen Table Women of Color Press, 1981.

Smith, David. "Hermeneutic Inquiry: The Hermeneutic Imagination and the Pedagogic Text." In *Forms of Curriculum Inquiry*, edited by Edmund C. Short, 187–210. Albany: SUNY Press, 1991.

Smith, Victoria L. "Starting from Snatch: The Seduction of Performance in Bertha Harris's *Lover*." In *Sex Positives? The Cultural Politics of Dissident Sexualities*, edited by Thomas Foster, Carol Siegel, and Ellen E. Perry, 68–94. New York: New York University Press.

Smith-Rosenberg, Caroll. "The Female World of Love and Ritual: Relations between Women in Nineteenth-Century America." *Signs: Journal of Women in Culture and Society* 1, no. 1 (1975): 1–29.

Sontag, Susan. *Illness as Metaphor*. New York: Farrar, Straus, & Giroux, 1977.

Spanos, William. *The End of Education: Toward Posthumanism*. Minneapolis: University of Minnesota Press, 1993.

Spelman, Elizabeth. *Inessential Woman: Problems of Exclusion in Feminist Thought*. Boston: Beacon, 1988.

Spivak, Gayatri Chakravorty. *The Post-Colonial Critic: Interviews, Strategies, Dialogues*. Edited by Sarah Harasym. New York: Routledge, 1990.

Spradley, James P. *The Ethnographic Interview*. Fort Worth: Holt, Rinehart & Winston, 1979.

Stallybras, Peter, and Allan White. *The Politics and Poetics of Transgression*. London: Methuen, 1986.

Steingraber, Sandra. "We All Live Downwind." In *1 in 3: Women with Cancer Confront an Epidemic*, edited by Judith Brady, 36–48. Pittsburgh and San Francisco: Cleis Press, 1991.

Stimpson, Catharine. "Zero Degree Deviancy: The Lesbian Novel in English." In *Feminisms: An Anthology of Literary Theory and Criticism*, edited by Robyn. R. Warhol and Diane P. Herndl, 301–315. New Brunswick, N.J.: Rutgers University Press, 1991.

Swidler, Ann. "Culture in Action: Symbols and Strategies." *American Sociological Review* 51 (1986): 273–286.

Taylor, Verta, and Leila J. Rupp. "Women's Culture and Lesbian Feminist Activism: A Reconsideration of Cultural Feminism." *Signs* 19, no. 1 (1993): 32–61.

Teloh, Henry. "Educational Theory in the *Meno*." In *Socratic Education in Plato's Early Dialogues*, 151–163. Notre Dame, Ind.: University of Notre Dame Press, 1986.

Terdiman, Richard. "The Response of the Other." *diacritics* 22, no. 2 (1992): 2–10.

Thames, Susan, and Marin Gazzaniga, eds. Introduction to *The Breast: An Anthology*, ix–x. Global City Press, 1995.

Thompson, Margaret Susan. "A View from the Pews." In *The Vatican and Homosexuality: Reactions to the "Letter to the Bishops of the Catholic Church on the Pastoral Care of Homosexual Persons,"* edited by Jeannine Gramick and Pat Furey, 149–156. New York: Cross Road, 1988.

Tierney, William G. "Academic Work and Institutional Culture: Constructing Knowledge." *The Review of Higher Education* 14, no. 2 (1991): 199–216.

———. "Academic Freedom and the Parameters of Knowledge." *Harvard Educational Review* 63, no. 2 (1993): 143–160.

———. *Building Communities of Difference: Higher Education in the Twenty-first Century*. Westport, Conn.: Bergin & Garvey, 1993.

———. "Organizational Socialization in Higher Education." *Journal of Higher Education* 68, no. 1 (1997): 1–16.

Torres, Carlos Alberto. "State and Education Revisited: Why Educational Researchers Should Think Politically about Education." *Review of Research in Education* 21 (1995–1996): 255–331.

Traub, Valerie. "The Ambiguities of 'Lesbian' Viewing Pleasure: The (Dis)articulations of *Black Widow*." In *Body Guards: The Cultural Politics of Gender Ambiguity*, edited by Julia Epstein and Kristina Straub, 305–328. New York: Routledge, 1991.

Trend, David. *The Crisis of Meaning in Culture and Education.* Minneapolis: University of Minnesota Press, 1995.

Trinh, T. Minh-ha. *When the Moon Waxes Red: Representation, Gender and Cultural Politics.* New York: Routledge, 1991.

Turner, Victor. *The Anthropology of Performance.* New York: PAJ Publications, 1987/1988.

Tyler, Carole-Anne. "Passing: Narcissism, Identity, and Difference." *differences: A Journal of Feminist Cultural Studies* 6, nos. 2–3 (1994): 212–248.

Urla, Jacqueline, and Alan C. Swedlund. "The Anthropometry of Barbie: Unsettling Ideals of the Feminine Body in Popular Culture." In *Deviant Bodies: Critical Perspectives on Differences in Science and Popular Culture*, edited by Jennifer Terry and Jacqueline Urla, 277–313. Bloomington: Indiana University Press, 1995.

Urla, Jacqueline, and Jennifer Terry. "Introduction: Mapping Embodied Deviance." In *Deviant Bodies: Critical Perspectives on Differences in Science and Popular Culture*, edited by Jennifer Terry and Jacqueline Urla, 1–18. Bloomington: Indiana University Press, 1995.

van Manen, Max. *Researching Lived Experience: Human Science for an Action Sensitive Pedagogy.* Albany: SUNY Press, 1990.

Vance, Carol, ed. *Pleasure and Danger: Exploring Female Sexuality.* New York: Routledge, 1984.

Vicinus, Martha. "Distance and Desire: English Boarding-School Friendships." In *The Lesbian Issue: Essays from Signs*, edited by Estelle B. Freedman, Barbara C. Gelpi, Susan L. Johnson, and Kathleen M. Weston, 43–65. Chicago: University of Chicago Press, 1985.

Visweswaran, Kamala. *Fictions of Feminist Ethnography.* Minneapolis: University of Minnesota Press, 1994.

Walcott, Rinaldo. "Queer Texts and Performativity: Zora, Rap, and Community." In *Queer Theory in Education*, edited by William F. Pinar, 157–171. Mahwah, N.J.: Lawrence Erlbaum, 1998.

Wallace, Michele. *Invisibility Blues.* New York: Routledge, 1990.

Warner, Michael. "No Special Rights." In *Higher Education under Fire: Politics, Economics, and the Crisis of the Humanities*, edited by Michael Bérubé and Cary Nelson, 284–292. New York: Routledge, 1995.

Weiler, Kathleen. "Freire and a Feminist Pedagogy of Difference." *Harvard Educational Review* 61, no. 4 (1991): 449–474.

West, Cornel. "The New Cultural Politics of Difference." In *Race, Identity, and Representation in Education*, edited by Cameron McCarthy and Warren Crichlow, 11–23. New York: Routledge, 1993.

Weston, Kath. *Render Me, Gender Me: Lesbians Talk Sex, Class, Color, Nation, Studmuffins . . .* New York: Columbia University Press, 1996.

Williams, Patricia J. *The Alchemy of Race and Rights.* Cambridge, Mass.: Harvard University Press, 1991.

———. *Seeing a Color-Blind Future: The Paradox of Race.* New York: Noonday Press, 1997.

Williams, Raymond. *Keywords: A Vocabulary of Culture and Society.* New York: Oxford University Press, 1976.

Willis, George. "Phenomenological Inquiry: Life-World Perceptions." In *Forms of Curriculum Inquiry*, edited by Edmund C. Short, 173–186. Albany: SUNY Press, 1991.

Wilshire, Bruce. *The Moral Collapse of the University: Professionalism, Purity, and Alienation*. Albany: SUNY Press, 1990.

Wilson, Elizabeth. "Deviant Dress." *Feminist Review* 35 (1990): 69–74.

Wright, Elizabeth. *Postmodern Brecht: A Re-Presentation*. New York: Routledge, 1989.

"Yale Report of 1828." In *Handbook on Undergraduate Curriculum*, edited by Arthur Levine, 544–556. San Francisco: Jossey-Bass, 1978.

Yarbro-Bejarano, Yvonne. "Expanding the Categories of Race and Sexuality in Lesbian and Gay Studies." In *Professions of Desire: Lesbian and Gay Studies in Literature*, edited by George E. Haggerty and Bonnie Zimmerman, 124–135. New York: Modern Language Association, 1995.

Zavarzadeh, Mas'ud, and Donald Morton. "Theory Pedagogy Politics: The Crisis of 'the Subject' in the Humanities." In *Theory/Pedagogy/Politics: Texts for Change*, edited by Donald Morton and Mas'ud Zavarzadeh, 1–32. Urbana: University of Illinois Press, 1991.

Zimmerman, Bonnie. "What Has Never Been: An Overview of Lesbian Feminist Criticism." In *Feminisms: An Anthology of Literary Theory and Criticism*, edited by Robyn R. Warhol and Diane Price Herndl, 117–137. New Brunswick, N.J.: Rutgers University Press, 1991.

———. "The Politics of Transliteration: Lesbian Personal Narratives." In *The Lesbian Issue: Essays from Signs*, edited by Estelle B. Freedman, Barbara C. Gelpi, Susan L. Johnson, and Kathleen M. Weston, 251–270. Chicago: University of Chicago Press, 1985.

INDEX

academic v. intellectual, 17
  See also intellectual practice;
    lesbian academic;
    lesbian/intellectual
academic and social knowledges. *See*
    departmental academic and social
    knowledges; knowledge
accountability, 132, 134
  See also Liberal U, and
    accountability
activism and academia, 4, 5–8,
    21–22, 196, 197–98
  See also Gay Academic Union; gay
    and lesbian scholarship
affiliations
  and Carol, 199–203
  and Julie, 208
  See also identification; identity, v.
    identification
affirmative action, 45, 46
  See also departmental academic
    and social knowledges, and
    race; Liberal U, and affirmative
    action
African-American community, 201–3,
    252n. 9
  See also Liberal U, and race; Oasis,
    and African-Americans; race
Agamben, Giorgio, 131, 145, 190
agency, 13–15, 17, 132, 138, 186,
    215, 220
  See also appropriation;
    performance; practice
Anzaldúa, Gloria, 252nn. 8, 12
appropriation, 15, 16, 17, 184, 186,
    188–89
  See also agency;
    (in)appropriateness; movement

authenticity, 23, 95, 114, 165, 171,
    189, 253n. 18
authority
  and Carol's department, 157–58,
    164, 165–66, 168
  and classroom authorship, 79,
    114, 116–17, 121
  and experience in Julie's
    classroom, 83
  and gender and race in Carol's
    classrooms, 91–93, 94–95,
    96–97
  institutional and epistemic, 114,
    121, 244n. 42
  and Olivia's department, 179
  and questioning of in Olivia's
    classrooms, 112, 114–17, 121,
    122
  See also intentionality; pedagogy

Barthes, Roland, 121, 134, 180
Berlant, Lauren, 189
Bhabha, Homi, 164
Blanchot, Maurice, 217–18
Bleich, David, 244–45n. 51
Bloom, Leslie R., 252n. 12, 255n. 42
Bourdieu, Pierre, 15, 17
breast cancer
  and Julie's classrooms, 83, 107,
    109–10
  and Julie's department, 150, 151,
    155–56
  and lesbian/intellectual, 212–14,
    254n. 21
  and liminality, 155
  and meanings of, 253–54n. 20
  and (un)concealment, 25, 26,
    31–32, 212–14, 243n. 33

of Reason, 17–18
See also excellence; Liberal U;
posthistorical university
Urla, Jacqueline, and Jennifer Terry,
107, 152

visibility
and authenticity, 253n. 18
and Carol, 91–95, 162, 168,
187–88
and classroom social knowledges,
84, 91–95, 96, 108, 111, 183,
as concealment, 151–53
and departmental academic and
social knowledges, 151–56,
162, 187–88
and identity politics, 8–13
and Julie, 108, 111, 143, 151–56,
186–87, 208
and knowledge, 10–13, 24
as mediated, 143, 208
as nonrepresentational, 154–56
and Olivia, 183, 187–88
and performance, 187
and placement, 162
and race and sexuality, 168
and voice, 8–13, 72, 108, 111,
143, 152–56, 187–88, 220
See also hypervisibility; identity
politics; voice
Visweswaran, Kamala, 36
voice
and Carol, 94–97, 169–70,
187–88
and classroom social knowledges,
84, 94–97, 108, 111

and departmental academic and
social knowledges, 154–56,
169–70, 183, 186–88
and identity politics, 8–13
and Julie, 108, 111, 143, 154–56,
186–88
as nonrepresentational, 154–56
and Olivia, 183, 187–188
and performance, 187
as performative, 222
and practice, 220
and recognition, 22
and visibility, 8–13, 72, 108, 111,
143, 152–56, 187–88, 220
See also gaze of students; identity
politics; knowledge; visibility

Walcott, Rinaldo, 217
Wallace, Michele, 202–3
Warner, Michael, 58, 73
Weiler, Kathleen, 244n. 51
West, Cornel, 164, 171
Weston, Kath, 152
Williams, Patricia J., 92, 148, 158,
187, 249n. 29
Williams, Raymond, 216
willful ignorance, 55, 70–71
See also "don't ask-don't tell";
privilege, of unknowing
Wilshire, Bruce, 239n. 37
women's studies, 6
See also feminist scholarship

Zavarzadeh, Mas'ud, and Donald
Morton, 246n. 68, 250n. 39
Zimmerman, Bonnie, 10, 254n. 26